P9-DWP-434

1930/1939

Here are five plays from the critical decade of the Thirties—the decade of the Group Theatre and the Federal Theatre—when American drama challenged the depression years with a stirring force of protest and hope.

HAROLD CLURMAN, distinguished director, critic and lecturer, is one of the most vigorous figures in the American theatre. A founder of the Group Theatre (1931-41), Mr. Clurman directed the Group Theatre Acting Company's production of *Awake and Sing*. Since that time he has directed a notable succession of Broadway plays: McCullers' *The Member of the Wedding*, Inge's *Bus Stop*, Giraudoux's *Tiger at the Gates*, Anouilh's *The Waltz of the Toreadors*, O'Neill's *A Touch of the Poet*. Mr. Clurman has served as drama critic for *The Nation* since 1953. He is the author of three engrossing books on the theatre, *The Fervent Years*, *Lies, Like Truth* and *The Naked Image*.

OTHER LAUREL AMERICAN DRAMA SERIES EDITIONS:

Famous American Plays of the 1920s
Selected and introduced by Kenneth Macgowan

Famous American Plays of the 1940s
Selected and introduced by Henry Hewes

Famous American Plays of the 1950s
Selected and introduced by Lee Strasberg

Famous American Plays of the 1960s
Selected and introduced by Harold Clurman

Selected and introduced by

HAROLD CLURMAN

FAMOUS
AMERICAN PLAYS
OF THE

1930s

THE LAUREL DRAMA SERIES

PS
634
.C57

Published by Dell Publishing Co., Inc.
1 Dag Hammarskjold Plaza
New York, N.Y. 10017
Copyright © 1959 by Harold Clurman
Laurel ® TM 674623, Dell Publishing Co., Inc.
All rights reserved
Printed in U.S.A.
Previous Dell Edition #2478
New Dell Edition

First printing—January, 1968
Second printing—February, 1970
Third printing—August, 1970
Fourth printing—November, 1971
Fifth printing—August, 1972
Sixth printing—May, 1973
Seventh printing—October, 1974
Eighth printing—October, 1975

Contents

Introduction

There is a tendency nowadays to downgrade the thirties. The reason for this is that the prevailing mood of the thirties was what used to be called "left of center." Beginning with the late forties—from the time the phrase about the "iron curtain" became part of the common vocabulary—our "intelligentsia" sounded the retreat. The Roosevelt administration, subjected to sharp criticism not infrequently close to slander, seemed to be in bad odor. "Left of center" might be construed as something worse than liberalism. To be "radical" implied that one might be tainted with some degree of "pink."

A good many of the writers, artists and theatre folk in the thirties were inclined to radicalism. (Had not the Roosevelt administration sponsored the Projects for writers, artists and theatre?) In the early forties the fervor of the thirties was gradually absorbed by the pressures of the war. Since Russia was one of our allies there was less strictly political feeling: everyone was chiefly concerned with victory and the return to peaceful prosperity.

Shortly after the peace conference suspicion of the Soviet Union increased. Radicalism of any sort might be interpreted as "softness" toward the potential enemy. Our artists and writers, including theatre people, had not only shown too much sympathy for social experiment but had also been too emphatic about the real or supposed shortcomings of their own country. At best the enthusiasm of the thirties was now considered a sign of juvenile simple-mindedness, at worst something close to treason.

Around the year 1953 this reaction to the thirties had come close to hysteria. Today there is certainly more calm but the notion that the thirties was a foolish period persists.

Presumably we are now far sounder in our thinking and work than we were then.

There is another aspect to the rather low esteem in which much of the dramatic work of the thirties is now held. The immediate past in the theatre always makes a poor impression. Writing about the twenties, which every student of our theatre history regards as a high point of the American theatre both in volume of activity and in achievement, Joseph Wood Krutch in the early thirties said that the record no longer seemed as bright as it once appeared. Very few of the best plays of that time would endure.

What most of us fail to note in this connection is that very few plays measured in the light of decades or generations have ever "endured." Shakespeare as we know Shakespeare is a nineteenth-century discovery! (He was neglected or disgracefully altered during the seventeenth and eighteenth centuries.) The number of plays which have come down to us from the Greeks of the fifth century B.C. and from the Elizabethan era are a paltry few compared to the number produced. How cavalier was the attitude of our drama critics toward Marlowe's *Tamburlaine* because he was not equal to Shakespeare!

We may explain this paradox through our own theatre-going experience. A play may be both enjoyable and important to us at the moment we see it, but when the circumstances of our lives have changed, it may well have lost its appeal. One of the most popular plays the American theatre has ever produced is the dramatization of *Uncle Tom's Cabin*. No one can deny its importance for its day even if we no longer have much regard for it as literature.

It is downright stupid to sneer at our erstwhile excitement over *Waiting for Lefty* because today a good many people (in Europe at any rate) are waiting for Godot. As theatre-goers we are very rarely able to estimate a play in the present as we shall view it twenty-five years hence. What appeared a very inconsiderable play to England's finest dramatic critic, Bernard Shaw, Oscar Wilde's *The Importance of Being Earnest*, has proved durable beyond anyone's belief when it was first presented.

I recall having seen Robert Sherwood's *The Petrified Forest* (1935) in the company of one of our country's most astute men of letters. He enjoyed it thoroughly. A few days later we spoke on the phone. He remarked that the theatre was a hoax: he had been "taken in" by the play as he watched it, he said, but on further reflection he realized the play's flaws in thought and plot. Most readers who are also playgoers are like that.

We enjoy the "show," but we *think* about the play. There is often a disparity of judgment between the two activities. For though we are intellectually aware that literature and theatre are not identical, we are prone to assume that the text of a play is equivalent to the texture of its production. But a play in the theatre communicates qualities beyond—sometimes, in a bad performance, less than—what we find on the printed page. Thus to evaluate the theatre of any period only with regard to its texts is a falsification.

The plays of the thirties sharpen certain tendencies that were already evident, and comparatively new, in the plays of the twenties. For the twenties, which may be said to represent America's second coming of age in literature (the first might be dated around 1850) and its true coming of age in the theatre, were marked by a rather harsh critical realism. What such men as Frank Norris and Theodore Dreiser had been saying about us in their novels began to be said somewhat more lyrically (though no less vehemently) in the plays of Eugene O'Neill. The theatre is ideologically almost always behind the times because it is a mass medium. It takes a while for people to acknowledge publicly what a few individuals may think and say privately.

It was the artistic pleasure of the twenties to deride, curse, bemoan the havoc, spiritual blindness and absurdity of America's materialistic functionalism with its concomitant acquisitiveness and worship of success.

Another marked feature of the theatrical twenties was the fact that plays which had previously satisfied audiences with the mere tracing of types (or stereotypes) began to strike them as increasingly hollow. Characters began to show their faces on the stage. Psychology was "introduced."

Men and women were no longer heroes or villains but "human," a mixture of contradictory traits. The standardized Puritanism typified by the old anti-vice societies became an object of scorn and ridicule.

The sentiment against war in *What Price Glory?* of the twenties was converted into the poignant and pointed satire of Paul Green's *Johnny Johnson* in the thirties. The sense c: loneliness which informs O'Neill's pieces is rendered more acute and more general in Steinbeck's *Of Mice and Men* some ten years later. The plight of the colored people in the Heywards' *Porgy* or in Green's *In Abraham's Bosom* is intensified in John Wexley's *They Shall Not Die* in the thirties. The playful probing of Behrman's *The Second Man* in 1927 is given a social connotation in the same author's *Biography* and other of his later plays in the thirties. The laborer as a symbol of inner disharmony within the apparent health of the American commonwealth which we observe in O'Neill's *The Hairy Ape* (1922) becomes a leading theme on a more concrete basis in the thirties.

The most significant difference between the theatre of the twenties and that of the thirties is the emphasis in the later period on the social, economic and political background of the individual psychological case. The Wall Street crash of 1929, the Great Depression of the early thirties with its attendant scar of widespread unemployment, the hopeful attempt to remedy this bitter condition which ensued are the effective causes for the abrupt and drastic change.

The plays included in this volume are not all necessarily the "best" of the thirties, but all are representative. Space and other factors of publication permitting, I should certainly have included O'Neill's *Mourning Becomes Electra* (1931), an Irish play of Denis Johnston's, *The Moon in the Yellow River* (1932), Maxwell Anderson's *Winterset* (1935), Sidney Kingsley's *Dead End* (1935), Thornton Wilder's *Our Town* (1938), Robert Sherwood's *Abe Lincoln in Illinois* (1938), Lillian Hellman's *The Little Foxes* (1939).

Of the plays included one had to be the work of Clifford

Odets. Historically speaking he is the dramatist of the thirties *par excellence*. His immediate sources of inspiration, his point of view, his language, his import and perhaps some of his weaknesses are typical of the thirties.

I am not at all sure that *Awake and Sing!*, first presented by the Group Theatre on February 19, 1935, is the best of Odets' plays. The 1937 *Golden Boy* has a more striking story line and is more varied and personal in its meaning. But *Awake and Sing!* contains the "seed" themes of the Odets plays and indicates most unaffectedly the milieu and the quality of feeling in which his work is rooted. One might even go so far as to say that there is hardly another play of the thirties—except perhaps John Howard Lawson's *Success Story* (1932)— which so directly communicates the very "smell" of New York in the first years of the depression.

The keynotes of the period are struck in *Awake and Sing!* as never again with such warm intimacy. There is first of all the bafflement and all-pervading worry of lower middle-class poverty. This is conveyed in language based on common speech and local New York (including Jewish) idiom, but it is not precisely naturalistic speech, for Odets' writing is a personal creation, essentially lyric, in which vulgarity, tenderness, energy, humor and a headlong idealism are commingled.

What is Odets' basic impulse; what is his "program"? They are contained in Jacob's exhortation to his grandson, "Go out and fight so life shouldn't be printed on dollar bills," and in another reflection, "Life should have some dignity." It seems to me that not only is most of Odets expressed in these bare words but the greater part of the whole cry of the American "progressive" movement—its radicalism if you will—as the artists of the thirties sensed it, is summed up in these innocent mottoes.

The "biblical" fervor in *Awake and Sing!* impels a "revolutionary" conviction expressed in Jacob's comment, "It needs a new world," which leads his grandson to take heart and proclaim, "Fresh blood, arms. We've got 'em. We're glad we're living." This was the "wave" of the thirties. If that wave did not carry us on to the millennium, it is surely the height of folly to believe that it had no vital force and accomplished nothing of value in the arts as well as in our community life.

S. N. Behrman's *End of Summer,* produced by the Theatre Guild on February 17, 1936, gives us the depression period seen from another angle: that of the "privileged" classes. It is a comedy of manners which besides its merits in the way of urbane dialogue, etc., presents a central character who (apart from having a decided semblance to the play's author) is kin to most of the folk who buy the best seats in our metropolitan theatres. Leonie, says Behrman, "is repelled by the gross and the voluptuary: this is not hypocrisy. . . . In the world in which she moves hypocrisy is merely a social lubricant, but this very often springs from a congenital and temperamental inability to face anything but the pleasantest and most immediately appealing and the most flattering aspect of things, in life and in her own nature."

What *End of Summer* presents is the spectacle of such a person confronted by the unhappy phenomenon of mass unemployment, nascent radicalism, spectres of fascism and the ambiguities of the psychoanalysts. The treatment is characteristic of Behrman—joshing, debonair, slightly more lighthearted than the author actually feels.

The lady of the play for the first time meets "the young radicals our colleges are said to be full of nowadays." One such radical, a somewhat fictitious Irish Catholic young fellow, tells the lady, "The world is middle-aged and tired," at which the lady queries, "Can you refresh us?" The young man rejoins, "Refresh you! Leonie, we can rejuvenate you." That was another hope of the youth which during the thirties had reached the ages of twenty-five to thirty-five. It was not altogether a vain hope for, as I have already indicated and shall continue to indicate, there was a young and invigorating spirit that relieved the thirties of its blues and led to concrete benefits.

One of the faults easily spotted in *End of Summer* is also evident in Robert Sherwood's *Idiot's Delight,* produced by the Theatre Guild in the spring of 1936. Just as the young radicals of Behrman's play seem to be known by hearsay rather than by intimate acquaintance, so in *Idiot's Delight*

Sherwood's grasp of the European political situation is informed as it were by headlines rather than truly experienced. Thus he makes his French pacifist a Radical-Socialist who speaks of the workers' uprising and alludes to Lenin with reverence, whereas any knowledgeable foreign correspondent could have told Sherwood that the Radical-Socialists of France are the party of small business, abhor Lenin's doctrines and are neither radical nor socialist.

This slight error is worth mentioning because it is symptomatic of a not uncommon failing in American playwrights when they generalize or "intellectualize" on social or ethical themes. It is a species of dilettantism which consists of dealing with subjects in which one is certainly interested but not truly familiar.

More cogent than this flaw is the sentiment which inspired Sherwood to write *Idiot's Delight*. It echoes the American fear of and profound estrangement from the facts of European intrigue which led to war. One merit of Sherwood's play is that it gives us an inkling of the moral climate in our country shortly after the Italian-Ethiopian conflagration and at the outset of the Spanish civil conflict—two omens of the future scarcely understood by an average citizen. Sherwood's "solution" to the problem in his play is the idealistic injunction "You can refuse to fight."

This is significant because it shows that the attitude of our dramatists, generally speaking, was fundamentally moral rather than, as some are now inclined to believe, political. This explains why Sherwood, whose *Idiot's Delight* might indicate the opposition to war of the "conscientious objector," took a very different stand when Nazism threatened to engulf Europe and the world. The play also marks the transition from skepticism and pessimism in regard to modern life, suggested by several of Sherwood's earlier plays, to the willingness to be engaged in political struggle and an acceptance of war, exemplified by his *Abe Lincoln in Illinois*.

Sherwood was a shrewd showman: *Idiot's Delight* gives striking evidence of this. He himself is supposed to have said, "The trouble with me is that I start off with a big message and end with nothing but good entertainment." *Idiot's Delight* was good entertainment, particularly in the acting opportunities it afforded Alfred Lunt and Lynn Fontanne, just as Leonie in *End of Summer,* in itself a charming characterization, was given special fragrance by Ina Claire's delightful talent.

John Steinbeck's *Of Mice and Men,* produced by Sam H. Harris on November 23, 1937, is a parable of American loneliness and of our hunger for "brotherhood"—two feelings the depression greatly enhanced. This play, unlike most of the others we have cited, concentrates on the unemployed of the farm lands, the itinerants and ranch workers, while it alludes to the bus and truck drivers whose travels through the country permitted them to observe the state of the nation in its broad horizon.

The American theatre, centered in New York, is on the whole cut off from the rest of the country. The thirties was the time when the theatre, along with the other arts, rediscovered America. *Green Grow the Lilacs* (1931) is one of the several Lynn Riggs Oklahoma plays, Erskine Caldwell's *Tobacco Road* (1933), Osborn's *Morning's at Seven* (1939)—to mention only a few—are among the many which in one way or another perform a similar function. One of the reasons why Steinbeck's parable carries conviction on naturalistic grounds is that the author shares the background and the earthiness of his characters.

Steinbeck knows our longing for a home, not a mere feeding place. He has the same true sympathy for the lonesome devil whose sole companion is a mangy old dog as for the Negro cut off by his fellow workers because of his color. He suggests with something like an austere sorrow that America's "underprivileged" will never reach the home they crave till they arrive at greater consciousness.

Speaking of "austerity" I should point out that one of the ground tones of American art and theatre (particularly the latter) is sentimentality. This is also true of Steinbeck's play, though he tries to control his sentimentality. Now sentimentality is usually accounted a vice, because it bespeaks a propensity to express a greater degree of feeling than a specific situation warrants. But sentimentality need not be a vital flaw; it isn't in *Of Mice and Men.* It is often the characteristic of a young and vigorous people whose experience of life is, so to speak, still new and uncontaminated by too frequent disillusionment. In this sense our history makes us a sentimental people and it is only natural that our arts, particularly our folk arts, should reveal this quality.

This brings us to the last play of this volume: William Saroyan's *The Time of Your Life,* presented by the Theatre Guild in association with Eddie Dowling on October 25, 1939. This sentimental comedy is by way of being a little classic. It marks the deliquescence of the aggressive mood of the thirties. For though the moralistic and critical rationale of the thirties is still present in *The Time of Your Life,* it is there in a lyrically anarchistic manner, a sort of sweet (here and there mawkish) dream.

Another way, distinctly 1959, of describing this play is to call it pre-beatnik! "I believe dreams more than statistics," one character says. "Everybody is behind the eight ball," says another. Money appears as the root of most evil—anyway it is the filthiest thing that goes and "there's no foundation all the way down the line," as the old man from the Orient mutters throughout the play.

In a way *The Time of Your Life* is a social fable: it turns its head away from and thumbs its nose at our monstrously efficient society which produces arrogance, cruelty, fear, headaches, constipation and the yammering of millions of humble folk, only to conclude that "all people are wonderful." Though this evinces more bewilderment than insight, it is nevertheless honestly American in its fundamental benevolence.

What saves this play, or rather what "makes" it, is its infectious humor, its anti-heroism (an oblique form of rebelliousness), its San Francisco colorfulness, its succulent dialogue, its wry hoboism and nonconformity. Though it is of another time, one still reads it with a sense of relief.

No account of the theatre of the thirties can convey any sense of its true nature and its contribution to our culture without emphasizing certain purely theatrical factors which played as decisive a role as the plays themselves.

The importance of the Group Theatre (1931–1941), whose origins may be traced back to the late twenties, can hardly be overestimated. (The first unofficial "group" meetings were held in 1928.) The Group Theatre was important not alone because it developed Odets from among its acting members, or even because it presented Sidney Kingsley's first play, *Men in White* (1933), Saroyan's first play, *My Heart's in the Highlands* (1939) as well as various plays by Paul Green, John Howard Lawson, Irwin Shaw and Robert Ardrey, but also because it organized its actors as a permanent company and trained them in a common craftsmanship which not only became emblematic for the era but which in many ways influenced the course of our theatre practice in the ensuing years.

Among the actors, directors, producers, designers, teachers trained or brought into prominence by the Group Theatre were: Stella Adler, Luther Adler, Boris Aronson, Harold Clurman, Lee Cobb, Cheryl Crawford, Morris Carnovsky, John Garfield, Elia Kazan, Mordecai Gorelik, Robert Lewis, Lee Strasberg, Franchot Tone.

The Group Theatre in certain respects continued a tradition established by such pioneer organizations as the Provincetown Players, the Theatre Guild, the Neighborhood Playhouse. In another way the Group served as a model for such organizations as the Theatre Union, the Theatre Collective, the Theatre of Action, which were "workers' theatres" with a more specifically political orientation. These were valuable organizations, particularly the Theatre Union, offering vivid productions of social plays. Our theatre needs more such organizations (there are none at present) which commit themselves to definite ideals or policies rather than wallowing in hit-or-miss show-shop opportunism.

Far more important than these special organizations was the Federal Theatre Project (1935–1939). Its rudest critics will not deny the interest of such productions as the "Living Newspaper," *One Third of a Nation*, the Negro *Macbeth*, Marlowe's *Dr. Faustus*, T. S. Eliot's *Murder in the Cathedral*, and the attempted production of Marc Blitzstein's momentous musical play, *The Cradle Will Rock*—ultimately presented under different auspices.

The Federal Theatre Project brought much excellent theatre fare to a national public at nominal prices, a public the greater part of which was barely acquainted with any form of "live" theatre. This was the first government-sponsored theatre in our history and it indicated how beneficial such an effort could be, even when circumstances were far from favorable.

Orson Welles was given his first opportunity as a director under the Federal Theatre Project. Because of his success there he was enabled to establish (with John Houseman) the short-lived but animated Mercury Theatre which produced a remarkably provocative *Julius Caesar* in the spirit of the times (1937).

Looking back from the vantage point of 1959 we may say that although admirable work still continues to be done on our constantly harassed and considerably shrunken stage, there are two virtues which may be claimed for the theatre of the thirties conspicuously lacking today. The theatre of the thirties attempted to make the stage an instrument of public enlightenment through a passionate involvement with the national scene. It made valiant and, to a remarkable degree, effective efforts to bring order and discipline into the helter-skelter of our theatre's artistic and financial organization.

An intelligent and successful Broadway producer of today recently said to me, "The theatre at present is twenty times more 'commercial' than it was in the thirties. For one thing, you could reach the hearts and souls of actors, playwrights, designers, etc., with good sense and considerations of sound craftsmanship. Today these people, whatever their personal dispositions, appear encircled by an iron ring forged by agents who protect their clients from all thought beyond income, percentages and publicity."

The lean days and hungry nights of the thirties were a brave time. Aren't we a little torpid now?

HAROLD CLURMAN

AWAKE AND SING!

by Clifford Odets

For my Father and Mother

From *Six Plays of Clifford Odets.*
Copyright 1935 by Clifford Odets.
Reprinted by permission of Random House, Inc.

CAUTION: *Professionals and amateurs are hereby warned that Awake and Sing, being fully protected under the copyright laws of the United States of America, the British Empire, including the Dominion of Canada, and all other countries of the copyright union, is subject to royalty. All rights, including professional, amateur, motion picture, recitation, lecturing, public reading, radio broadcasting, and the rights of translation into foreign languages are strictly reserved. Particular emphasis is laid on the question of readings, permission for which must be secured from the author's agent in writing. All inquiries should be addressed to the author's agent, Harold Freedman, 101 Park Avenue, New York City.*

First production, February 19th, 1935,
at the Belasco Theatre, New York,
with the following cast from the
Group Theatre Acting Company:

MYRON BERGER, *Art Smith*
BESSIE BERGER, *Stella Adler*
JACOB, *Morris Carnovsky*
HENNIE BERGER, *Phoebe Brand*
RALPH BERGER, *Jules Garfield*
SCHLOSSER, *Roman Bohnen*
MOE AXELROD, *Luther Adler*
UNCLE MORTY, *J. E. Bromberg*
SAM FEINSCHREIBER, *Sanford Meisner*

The entire action takes place in an apartment
in the Bronx, New York City.

The Characters of the Play

All of the characters in Awake and Sing!
share a fundamental activity:
a struggle for life amidst petty conditions.

BESSIE BERGER, *as she herself states, is not only the
mother in this home but also the father. She is constantly arranging and taking care of her family. She
loves life, likes to laugh, has great resourcefulness and
enjoys living from day to day. A high degree of energy
accounts for her quick exasperation at ineptitude. She
is a shrewd judge of realistic qualities in people in the
sense of being able to gauge quickly their effectiveness.
In her eyes all of the people in the house are equal.
She is naïve and quick in emotional response. She is
afraid of utter poverty. She is proper according to her
own standards, which are fairly close to those of most
middle-class families. She knows that when one lives in
the jungle one must look out for the wild life.*

MYRON, *her husband, is a born follower. He would like
to be a leader. He would like to make a million dollars. He is not sad or ever depressed. Life is an even
sweet event to him, but the "old days" were sweeter
yet. He has a dignified sense of himself. He likes people. He likes everything. But he is heartbroken without being aware of it.*

HENNIE *is a girl who has had few friends, male or female. She is proud of her body. She won't ask favors.
She travels alone. She is fatalistic about being trapped,
but will escape if possible. She is self-reliant in the best*

sense. Till the day she dies she will be faithful to a loved man. She inherits her mother's sense of humor and energy.

RALPH *is a boy with a clean spirit. He wants to know, wants to learn. He is ardent, he is romantic, he is sensitive. He is naïve too. He is trying to find why so much dirt must be cleared away before it is possible to "get to first base."*

JACOB, *too, is trying to find a right path for himself and the others. He is aware of justice, of dignity. He is an observer of the others, compares their activities with his real and ideal sense of life. This produces a reflective nature. In this home he is a constant boarder. He is a sentimental idealist with no power to turn ideal to action.*

With physical facts—such as housework—he putters. But as a barber he demonstrates the flair of an artist. He is an old Jew with living eyes in his tired face.

UNCLE MORTY *is a successful American business man with five good senses. Something sinister comes out of the fact that the lives of others seldom touch him deeply. He holds to his own line of life. When he is generous he wants others to be aware of it. He is pleased by attention—a rich relative to the* BERGER *family. He is a shrewd judge of material values. He will die unmarried. Two and two make four, never five with him. He can blink in the sun for hours, a fat tomcat. Tickle him, he laughs. He lives in a penthouse with a real Japanese butler to serve him. He sleeps with dress models, but not from his own showrooms. He plays cards for hours on end. He smokes expensive cigars. He sees every Mickey Mouse cartoon that appears. He is a 32-degree Mason. He is really deeply intolerant finally.*

MOE AXELROD *lost a leg in the war. He seldom forgets that fact. He has killed two men in extra-martial activity. He is mordant, bitter. Life has taught him a disbelief in everything, but he will fight his way through. He seldom shows his feelings: fights against his own sensitivity. He has been everywhere and seen everything. All he wants is* HENNIE. *He is very proud. He scorns the inability of others to make their way in life, but he likes people for whatever good qualities they possess. His passionate outbursts come from a strong but contained emotional mechanism.*

SAM FEINSCHREIBER *wants to find a home. He is a lonely man, a foreigner in a strange land, hypersensitive about this fact, conditioned by the humiliation of not making his way alone. He has a sense of others laughing at him. At night he gets up and sits alone in the dark. He hears acutely all the small sounds of life. He might have been a poet in another time and place. He approaches his wife as if he were always offering her a delicate flower. Life is a high chill wind weaving itself around his head.*

SCHLOSSER, *the janitor, is an overworked German whose wife ran away with another man and left him with a young daughter who in turn ran away and joined a burlesque show as chorus girl. The man suffers rheumatic pains. He has lost his identity twenty years before.*

SCENE—*Exposed on the stage are the dining room and adjoining front room of the* BERGER *apartment. These two rooms are typically furnished. There is a curtain between them. A small door off the front room leads to* JACOB'S *room. When his door is open one sees a picture of Sacco and Vanzetti on the wall and several shelves of books. Stage left of this door presents the entrance to the foyer hall of the apartment. The two other bedrooms of the apartment are off this hall, but not necessarily shown.*

Stage left of the dining room presents a swinging door which opens on the kitchen.

Awake and sing, ye that dwell in dust:
ISAIAH—26:19

Act one

TIME. *The present; the family finishing supper.*
PLACE. *An apartment in the Bronx, New York City.*

RALPH. Where's advancement down the place? Work
like crazy! Think they see it? You'd drop dead first.

MYRON. Never mind, son, merit never goes unrewarded.
Teddy Roosevelt used to say—

HENNIE. It rewarded you—thirty years a haberdashery
clerk!

[*Jacob laughs.*]

RALPH. All I want's a chance to get to first base!

HENNIE. That's all?

RALPH. Stuck down in that joint on Fourth Avenue—
a stock clerk in a silk house! Just look at Eddie.
I'm as good as he is—pulling in two-fifty a week for
forty-eight minutes a day. A headliner, his name in
all the papers.

JACOB. That's what you want, Ralphie? Your name in
the paper?

RALPH. I wanna make up my own mind about things
. . . be something! Didn't I want to take up tap
dancing, too?

BESSIE. So take lessons. Who stopped you?

RALPH. On what?

BESSIE. On what? Save money.

RALPH. Sure, five dollars a week for expenses and the rest in the house. I can't save even for shoe laces.

BESSIE. You mean we shouldn't have food in the house, but you'll make a jig on the street corner?

RALPH. I mean something.

BESSIE. You also mean something when you studied on the drum, Mr. Smartie!

RALPH. I don't know. . . . Every other day to sit around with the blues and mud in your mouth.

MYRON. That's how it is—life is like that—a cake-walk.

RALPH. What's it get you?

HENNIE. A four-car funeral.

RALPH. What's it for?

JACOB. What's it for? If this life leads to a revolution it's a good life. Otherwise it's for nothing.

BESSIE. Never mind, Pop! Pass me the salt.

RALPH. It's crazy—all my life I want a pair of black and white shoes and can't get them. It's crazy!

BESSIE. In a minute I'll get up from the table. I can't take a bite in my mouth no more.

MYRON [*restraining her*]. Now, Mamma, just don't excite yourself—

BESSIE. I'm so nervous I can't hold a knife in my hand.

MYRON. Is that a way to talk, Ralphie? Don't Momma work hard enough all day?

[BESSIE *allows herself to be reseated.*]

BESSIE. On my feet twenty-four hours?

MYRON. On her feet—

RALPH [*jumps up*]. What do I do—go to night-clubs with Greta Garbo? Then when I come home can't even have my own room? Sleep on a day-bed in the front room! [*Choked, he exits to front room.*]

BESSIE. He's starting up that stuff again. [*Shouts to him.*] When Hennie here marries you'll have her room—I should only live to see the day.

HENNIE. Me, too. [*They settle down to serious eating.*]

MYRON. This morning the sink was full of ants. Where they come from I just don't know. I thought it was coffee grounds . . . and then they began moving.

BESSIE. You gave the dog eat?

JACOB. I gave the dog eat.

[HENNIE *drops a knife and picks it up again.*]

BESSIE. You got dropsy tonight.

HENNIE. Company's coming.

MYRON. You can buy a ticket for fifty cents and win fortunes. A man came in the store—it's the Irish Sweepstakes.

BESSIE. What?

MYRON. Like a raffle, only different. A man came in—

BESSIE. Who spends fifty-cent pieces for Irish raffles? They threw out a family on Dawson Street today. All the furniture on the sidewalk. A fine old woman with gray hair.

JACOB. Come eat, Ralph.

MYRON. A butcher on Beck Street won eighty thousand dollars.

BESSIE. Eighty thousand dollars! You'll excuse my expression, you're bughouse!

MYRON. I seen it in the paper—on one ticket—765 Beck Street.

BESSIE. Impossible!

MYRON. He did . . . yes he did. He says he'll take his old mother to Europe . . . an Austrian—

HENNIE. Europe . . .

MYRON. Six per cent on eighty thousand—forty-eight hundred a year.

BESSIE. I'll give you money. Buy a ticket in Hennie's name. Say, you can't tell—lightning never struck us yet. If they win on Beck Street we could win on Longwood Avenue.

JACOB [*ironically*]. If it rained pearls—who would work?

BESSIE. Another county heard from.

[RALPH *enters and silently seats himself.*]

MYRON. I forgot, Beauty—Sam Feinschreiber sent you a present. Since I brought him for supper he just can't stop talking about you.

HENNIE. What's that "mockie" bothering about? Who needs him?

MYRON. He's a very lonely boy.

HENNIE. So I'll sit down and bust out crying " 'cause he's lonely."

BESSIE [*opening candy*]. He'd marry you one two three.

HENNIE. Too bad about him.

BESSIE [*naïvely delighted*]. Chocolate peanuts.

HENNIE. Loft's week-end special, two for thirty-nine.

BESSIE. You could think about it. It wouldn't hurt.

HENNIE [*laughing*]. To quote Moe Axelrod, "Don't make me laugh."

BESSIE. Never mind laughing. It's time you already had in your head a serious thought. A girl twenty-six don't grow younger. When I was your age it was already a big family with responsibilities.

HENNIE [*laughing*]. Maybe that's what ails you, Mom.

BESSIE. Don't you feel well?

HENNIE. 'Cause I'm laughing? I feel fine. It's just funny —that poor guy sending me presents 'cause he loves me.

BESSIE. I think it's very, very nice.

HENNIE. Sure . . . swell!

BESSIE. Mrs. Marcus' Rose is engaged to a Brooklyn boy, a dentist. He came in his car today. A little dope should get such a boy.

[*Finished with the meal,* BESSIE, MYRON *and* JACOB *rise. Both* HENNIE *and* RALPH *sit silently at the table, he eating. Suddenly she rises.*]

HENNIE. Tell you what, Mom. I saved for a new dress, but I'll take you and Pop to the Franklin. Don't need a dress. From now on I'm planning to stay in nights. Hold everything!

BESSIE. What's the matter—a bedbug bit you suddenly?

HENNIE. It's a good bill—Belle Baker. Maybe she'll sing "Eli, Eli."

BESSIE. We was going to a movie.

HENNIE. Forget it. Let's go.

MYRON. I see in the papers [*as he picks his teeth*] Sophie Tucker took off twenty-six pounds. Fearful business with Japan.

HENNIE. Write a book, Pop! Come on, we'll go early for good seats.

MYRON. Moe said you had a date with him for tonight.

BESSIE. Axelrod?

HENNIE. I told him no, but he don't believe it. I'll tell him no for the next hundred years, too.

MYRON. Don't break appointments, Beauty, and hurt people's feelings.

[*Bessie exits.*]

HENNIE. His hands got free wheeling. [*She exits.*]

MYRON. I don't know . . . people ain't the same. N-O. The whole world's changing right under our eyes. Presto! No manners. Like the great Italian lover in the movies. What was his name? The Shiek. . . . No one remembers? [*Exits, shaking his head.*]

RALPH [*unmoving at the table*]. Jake . . .

JACOB. Noo?

RALPH. I can't stand it.

JACOB. There's an expression—"strong as iron you must be."

RALPH. It's a cock-eyed world.

JACOB. Boys like you could fix it some day. Look on the world, not on yourself so much. Every country with starving millions, no? In Germany and Poland a Jew couldn't walk in the street. Everybody hates, nobody loves.

RALPH. I don't get all that.

JACOB. For years, I watched you grow up. Wait! You'll graduate from my university.

[*The others enter, dressed.*]

MYRON [*lighting*]. Good cigars now for a nickel.

BESSIE [*to* JACOB]. After take Tootsie on the roof. [*To* RALPH.] What'll you do?

RALPH. Don't know.

BESSIE. You'll see the boys around the block?

RALPH. I'll stay home every night!

MYRON. Momma don't mean for you—

RALPH. I'm flying to Hollywood by plane, that's what I'm doing.

[*Doorbell rings.* MYRON *answers it.*]

BESSIE. I don't like my boy to be seen with those tramps on the corner.

MYRON [*without*]. Schlosser's here, Momma, with the garbage can.

BESSIE. Come in here, Schlosser. [*Sotto voce.*] Wait, I'll give him a piece of my mind. [MYRON *ushers in* SCHLOSSER *who carries a garbage can in each hand.*] What's the matter, the dumbwaiter's broken again?

SCHLOSSER. Mr. Wimmer sends new ropes next week. I got a sore arm.

BESSIE. He should live so long your Mr. Wimmer. For seven years already he's sending new ropes. No dumbwaiter, no hot water, no steam— In a respectable house, they don't allow such conditions.

SCHLOSSER. In a decent house dogs are not running to make dirty the hallway.

BESSIE. Tootsie's making dirty? Our Tootsie's making dirty in the hall?

SCHLOSSER [*to* JACOB]. I tell you yesterday again. You must not leave her—

BESSIE [*indignantly*]. Excuse me! Please don't yell on an old man. He's got more brains in his finger than you got—I don't know where. Did you ever see—he should talk to you an old man?

MYRON. Awful.

BESSIE. From now on we don't walk up the stairs no more. You keep it so clean we'll fly in the windows.

SCHLOSSER. I speak to Mr. Wimmer.

BESSIE. Speak! Speak. Tootsie walks behind me like a lady any time, any place. So good-bye . . . good-bye, Mr. Schlosser.

SCHLOSSER. I tell you dot—I verk verry hard here. My arms is . . . [*Exits in confusion.*]

BESSIE. Tootsie should lay all day in the kitchen maybe. Give him back if he yells on you. What's funny?

JACOB [*laughing*]. Nothing.

BESSIE. Come. [*Exits.*]

JACOB. Hennie, take care. . . .

HENNIE. Sure.

JACOB. Bye-bye.

[HENNIE *exits.* MYRON *pops head back in door.*]

MYRON. Valentino! That's the one! [*He exits.*]

RALPH. I never in my life even had a birthday party. Every time I went and cried in the toilet when my birthday came.

JACOB [*seeing* RALPH *remove his tie*]. You're going to bed?

RALPH. No, I'm putting on a clean shirt.

JACOB. Why?

RALPH. I got a girl. . . . Don't laugh!

JACOB. Who laughs? Since when?

RALPH. Three weeks. She lives in Yorkville with an aunt and uncle. A bunch of relatives, but no parents.

JACOB. An orphan girl—tch, tch.

RALPH. But she's got me! Boy, I'm telling you I could sing! Jake, she's like stars. She's so beautiful you look at her and cry! She's like French words! We went to the park the other night. Heard the last band concert.

JACOB. Music . . .

RALPH [*stuffing shirt in trousers*]. It got cold and I gave her my coat to wear. We just walked along like that, see, without a word, see. I never was so happy in all my life. It got late . . . we just sat there. She looked at me—you know what I mean, how a girl looks at you—right in the eyes? "I love you," she says, "Ralph." I took her home. . . . I wanted to cry. That's how I felt!

JACOB. It's a beautiful feeling.

RALPH. You said a mouthful!

JACOB. Her name is—

RALPH. Blanche.

JACOB. A fine name. Bring her sometimes here.

RALPH. She's scared to meet Mom.

JACOB. Why?

RALPH. You know Mom's not letting my sixteen bucks out of the house if she can help it. She'd take one look at Blanche and insult her in a minute—a kid who's got nothing.

JACOB. Boychick!

RALPH. What's the diff?

JACOB. It's no difference—a plain bourgeois prejudice— but when they find out a poor girl—it ain't so kosher.

RALPH. They don't have to know I've got a girl.

JACOB. What's in the end?

RALPH. Out I go! I don't mean maybe!

JACOB. And then what?

RALPH. Life begins.

JACOB. What life?

RALPH. Life with my girl. Boy, I could sing when I think about it! Her and me together—that's a new life!

JACOB. Don't make a mistake! A new death!

RALPH. What's the idea?

JACOB. Me, I'm the idea! Once I had in *my* heart a dream, a vision, but came marriage and then you forget. Children come and you forget because—

RALPH. Don't worry, Jake.

JACOB. Remember, a woman insults a man's soul like no other thing in the whole world!

RALPH. Why get so excited? No one—

JACOB. Boychick, wake up! Be something! Make your life something good. For the love of an old man who sees in your young days his new life, for such love take the world in your two hands and make it like new. Go out and fight so life shouldn't be printed on dollar bills. A woman waits.

RALPH. Say, I'm no fool!

JACOB. From my heart I hope not. In the meantime— [*Bell rings.*]

RALPH. See who it is, will you? [*Stands off.*] Don't want Mom to catch me with a clean shirt.

JACOB [*calls*]. Come in. [*Sotto voce.*] Moe Axelrod. [MOE *enters.*]

MOE. Hello girls, how's your whiskers? [*To* RALPH.] All dolled up. What's it, the weekly visit to the cat house?

RALPH. Please mind your business.

MOE. Okay, sweetheart.

RALPH [*taking a hidden dollar from a book*]. If Mom asks where I went—

JACOB. I know. Enjoy yourself.

RALPH. Bye-bye. [*He exits.*]

JACOB. Bye-bye.

MOE. Who's home?

JACOB. Me.

MOE. Good. I'll stick around a few minutes. Where's Hennie?

JACOB. She went with Bessie and Myron to a show.

MOE. She what?!

JACOB. You had a date?

MOE [*hiding his feelings*]. Here—I brought you some halavah.

JACOB. Halavah? Thanks. I'll eat a piece after.

MOE. So Ralph's got a dame? Hot stuff—a kid can't even play a card game.

JACOB. Moe, you're a no-good, a bum of the first water. To your dying day you won't change.

MOE. Where'd you get that stuff, a no-good?

JACOB. But I like you.

MOE. Didn't I go fight in France for democracy? Didn't I get my goddam leg shot off in that war the day before the armistice? Uncle Sam give me the Order of the Purple Heart, didn't he? What'd you mean, a no-good?

JACOB. Excuse me.

MOE. If you got an orange I'll eat an orange.

JACOB. No orange. An apple.

MOE. No oranges, huh?—what a dump!

JACOB. Bessie hears you once talking like this she'll knock your head off.

MOE. Hennie went with, huh? She wantsa see me squirm, only I don't squirm for dames.

JACOB. You came to see her?

MOE. What for? I got a present for our boy friend, Myron. He'll drop dead when I tell him his gentle horse galloped in fifteen to one. He'll die.

JACOB. It really won? The first time I remember.

MOE. Where'd they go?

JACOB. A vaudeville by the Franklin.

MOE. What's special tonight?

JACOB. Someone tells a few jokes . . . and they forget the street is filled with starving beggars.

MOE. What'll they do—start a war?

JACOB. I don't know.

MOE. You oughta know. What the hell you got all the books for?

JACOB. It needs a new world.

MOE. That's why they had the big war—to make a new world, they said—safe for democracy. Sure every big general laying up in a Paris hotel with a half dozen broads pinned on his mustache. Democracy! I learned a lesson.

JACOB. An imperial war. You know what this means?

MOE. Sure, I know everything!

JACOB. By money men the interests must be protected. Who gave you such a rotten haircut? Please [*fishing in his vest pocket*], give me for a cent a cigarette. I didn't have since yesterday—

MOE [*giving one*]. Don't make me laugh. [*A cent passes back and forth between them,* MOE *finally throwing it over his shoulder.*] Don't look so tired all the time. You're a wow—always sore about something.

JACOB. And you?

MOE. You got one thing—you can play pinochle. I'll take you over in a game. Then you'll have something to be sore on.

JACOB. Who'll wash dishes?

[*Moe takes deck from buffet drawer.*]

MOE. Do 'em after. Ten cents a deal.

JACOB. Who's got ten cents?

MOE. I got ten cents. I'll lend it to you.

JACOB. Commence.

MOE [*shaking cards*]. The first time I had my hands on a pack in two days. Lemme shake up these cards. I'l! make 'em talk.

[JACOB *goes to his room where he puts on a Caruso record.*]

JACOB. You should live so long.

MOE. Ever see oranges grow? I know a certain place—

One summer I laid under a tree and let them fall right in my mouth.

JACOB [*off, the music is playing; the card game begins*]. From "L'Africana" . . . a big explorer comes on a new land—"O Paradiso." From act four this piece. Caruso stands on the ship and looks on a Utopia. You hear? "Oh paradise! Oh paradise on earth! Oh blue sky, oh fragrant air—"

MOE. Ask him does he see any oranges?

[BESSIE, MYRON *and* HENNIE *enter*.]

JACOB. You came back so soon?

BESSIE. Hennie got sick on the way.

MYRON. Hello, Moe . . .

[MOE *puts cards back in pocket*.]

BESSIE. Take off the phonograph, Pop. [*To* HENNIE.] Lay down . . . I'll call the doctor. You should see how she got sick on Prospect Avenue. Two weeks already she don't feel right.

MYRON. Moe . . . ?

BESSIE. Go to bed, Hennie.

HENNIE. I'll sit here.

BESSIE. Such a girl I never saw! Now you'll be stubborn?

MYRON. It's for your own good, Beauty. Influenza—

HENNIE. I'll sit here.

BESSIE. You ever seen a girl should say no to everything. She can't stand on her feet, so—

HENNIE. Don't yell in my ears. I hear. Nothing's wrong. I ate tuna fish for lunch.

MYRON. Canned goods . . .

BESSIE. Last week you also ate tuna fish?

HENNIE. Yeah, I'm funny for tuna fish. Go to the show —have a good time.

BESSIE. I don't understand what I did to God He blessed me with such children. From the whole world—

MOE [*coming to aid of* HENNIE]. For Chris' sake, don't kibitz so much!

BESSIE. You don't like it?

MOE [*aping*]. No, I don't like it.

BESSIE. That's too bad, Axelrod. Maybe it's better by your cigar store friends. Here we're different people.

MOE. Don't gimme that cigar store line, Bessie. I walked up five flights—

BESSIE. To take out Hennie. But my daughter ain't in your class, Axelrod.

MOE. To see Myron.

MYRON. Did he, did he, Moe?

MOE. Did he what?

MYRON. "Sky Rocket"?

BESSIE. You bet on a horse!

MOE. Paid twelve and a half to one.

MYRON. There! You hear that, Momma? Our horse came in. You see, it happens, and twelve and a half to one. Just look at that!

MOE. What the hell, a sure thing. I told you.

BESSIE. If Moe said a sure thing, you couldn't bet a few dollars instead of fifty cents?

JACOB [*laughs*]. "Aie, aie, aie."

MOE [*at his wallet*]. I'm carrying six hundred "plunks" in big denominations.

BESSIE. A banker!

MOE. Uncle Sam sends me ninety a month.

BESSIE. So you save it?

MOE. Run it up. Run-it-up-Axelrod, that's me.

BESSIE. The police should know how.

MOE [*shutting her up*]. All right, all right— Change twenty, sweetheart.

MYRON. Can you make change?

BESSIE. Don't be crazy.

MOE. I'll meet a guy in Goldman's restaurant. I'll meet 'im and come back with change.

MYRON [*figuring on paper*]. You can give it to me to-morrow in the store.

BESSIE [*acquisitive*]. He'll come back, he'll come back!

MOE. Lucky I bet some bucks myself. [*In derision to* HENNIE.] Let's step out tomorrow night, Par-a-dise. [*Thumbs his nose at her, laughs mordantly and exits.*]

MYRON. Oh, that's big percentage. If I picked a winner every day . . .

BESSIE. Poppa, did you take Tootsie on the roof?

JACOB. All right.

MYRON. Just look at that—a cake-walk. We can make—

BESSIE. It's enough talk. I got a splitting headache. Hennie, go in bed. I'll call Dr. Cantor.

HENNIE. I'll sit here . . . and don't call that old Ignatz 'cause I won't see him.

MYRON. If you get sick Momma can't nurse you. You don't want to go to a hospital.

JACOB. She don't look sick, Bessie, it's a fact.

BESSIE. She's got fever. I see in her eyes, so he tells me no. Myron, call Dr. Cantor.

[MYRON *picks up phone, but* HENNIE *grabs it from him.*]

HENNIE. I don't want any doctor. I ain't sick. Leave me alone.

MYRON. Beauty, it's for your own sake.

HENNIE. Day in and day out pestering. Why are you always right and no one else can say a word?

BESSIE. When you have your own children—

HENNIE. I'm not sick! Hear what I say? I'm not sick! Nothing's the matter with me! I don't want a doctor.

[BESSIE *is watching her with slow progressive under-standing.*]

BESSIE. What's the matter?

HENNIE. Nothing, I told you!

BESSIE. You told me, but— [*A long pause of examination follows.*]

HENNIE. See much?

BESSIE. Myron, put down the . . . the . . . [*He slowly puts the phone down.*] Tell me what happened. . . .

HENNIE. Brooklyn Bridge fell down.

BESSIE [*approaching*]. I'm asking a question. . . .

MYRON. What's happened, Momma?

BESSIE. Listen to me!

HENNIE. What the hell are you talking?

BESSIE. Poppa—take Tootsie on the roof.

HENNIE [*holding* JACOB *back*]. If he wants he can stay here.

MYRON. What's wrong, Momma?

BESSIE [*her voice quivering slightly*]. Myron, your fine Beauty's in trouble. Our society lady . . .

MYRON. Trouble? I don't under—is it—?

BESSIE. Look in her face. [*He looks, understands and slowly sits in a chair, utterly crushed.*] Who's the man?

HENNIE. The Prince of Wales.

BESSIE. My gall is busting in me. In two seconds—

HENNIE [*in a violent outburst*]. Shut up! Shut up! I'll jump out the window in a minute! Shut up! [*Finally she gains control of herself, says in a low, hard voice:*] You don't know him.

JACOB. Bessie . . .

BESSIE. He's a Bronx boy?

HENNIE. From out of town.

BESSIE. What do you mean?

HENNIE. From out of town!!

BESSIE. A long time you know him? You were sleeping by a girl from the office Saturday nights? You slept good, my lovely lady. You'll go to him . . . he'll marry you.

HENNIE. That's what you say.

BESSIE. That's what I say! He'll do it, take *my* word he'll do it!

HENNIE. Where? [*To* JACOB.] Give her the letter.

[JACOB *does so*.]

BESSIE. What? [*Reads*.] "Dear sir: In reply to your request of the 14th inst., we can state that no Mr. Ben Grossman has ever been connected with our organization . . ." You don't know where he is?

HENNIE. No.

BESSIE [*walks back and forth*]. Stop crying like a baby, Myron.

MYRON. It's like a play on the stage. . . .

BESSIE. To a mother you couldn't say something before. I'm old-fashioned—like your friends I'm no' smart—I don't eat chop suey and run around Coney Island with tramps. [*She walks reflectively to buffet, picks up a box of candy, puts it down, says to* MYRON:] Tomorrow night bring Sam Feinschreiber for supper.

HENNIE. I won't do it.

BESSIE. You'll do it, my fine beauty, you'll do it!

HENNIE. I'm not marrying a poor foreigner like him. Can't even speak an English word. Not me! I'll go to my grave without a husband.

BESSIE. You don't say! We'll find for you somewhere a millionaire with a pleasure boat. He's going to night school, Sam. For a boy only three years in the country he speaks very nice. In three years he put enough in the bank, a good living.

JACOB. This is serious?

BESSIE. What then? I'm talking for my health? He'll come tomorrow night for supper. By Saturday they're engaged.

JACOB. Such a thing you can't do.

BESSIE. Who asked your advice?

JACOB. Such a thing—

BESSIE. Never mind!

JACOB. The lowest from the low!

BESSIE. Don't talk! I'm warning you! A man who don't believe in God—with crazy ideas—

JACOB. So bad I never imagined you could be.

BESSIE. Maybe if you didn't talk so much it wouldn't happen like this. You with your ideas—I'm a mother. I raise a family, they should have respect.

JACOB. Respect? [*Spits.*] Respect! For the neighbors' opinion! You insult me, Bessie!

BESSIE. Go in your room, Papa. Every job he ever had he lost because he's got a big mouth. He opens his mouth and the whole Bronx could fall in. Everybody said it—

MYRON. Momma, they'll hear you down the dumbwaiter.

BESSIE. A good barber not to hold a job a week. Maybe you never heard charity starts at home. You never heard it, Pop?

JACOB. All you know, I heard, and more yet. But Ralph you don't make like you. Before you do it I'll die first. He'll find a girl. He'll go in a fresh world with her. This is a house? Marx said it— abolish such families.

BESSIE. Go in your room, Papa.

JACOB. Ralph you don't make like you!

BESSIE. Go lay in your room with Caruso and the books together.

JACOB. All right!

BESSIE. Go in the room!

JACOB. Some day I'll come out, I'll— [*Unable to continue, he turns, looks at* HENNIE, *goes to his door and there says with an attempt at humor:*] Bessie, some day you'll talk to me so fresh . . . I'll leave th house for good! [*He exits.*]

BESSIE [*crying*]. You ever in your life seen it? He should dare! He should just dare say in the house another word. Your gall could bust from such a man. [*Bell rings*, MYRON *goes.*] Go to sleep now. It won't hurt.

HENNIE. Yeah?

[MOE *enters, a box in his hand.* MYRON *follows and sits down.*]

MOE [*looks around first—putting box on table*]. Cake. [*About to give* MYRON *the money, he turns instead to* BESSIE.] Six fifty, four bits change . . . come on, hand over half a buck. [*She does so. Of* MYRON.] Who bit him?

BESSIE. We're soon losing our Hennie, Moe.

MOE. Why? What's the matter?

BESSIE. She made her engagement.

MOE. Zat so?

BESSIE. Today it happened . . . he asked her.

MOE. Did he? Who? Who's the corpse?

BESSIE. It's a secret.

MOE. In the bag, huh?

HENNIE. Yeah . . .

BESSIE. When a mother gives away an only daughter it's no joke. Wait, when you'll get married you'll know. . . .

MOE [*bitterly*]. Don't make me laugh—when I get married! What I think a women? Take 'em all, cut 'em in little pieces like a herring in Greek salad. A guy in France had the right idea—dropped his wife in bathtub fulla acid. [*Whistles.*] Sss, down the pipe! Pfft—not even a corset button left!

MYRON. Corsets don't have buttons.

MOE [*to* HENNIE]. What's the great idea? Gone big time, Paradise? Christ, it's suicide! Sure, kids you'll have, gold teeth, get fat, big in the tangerines—

HENNIE. Shut your face!

MOE. Who's it—some dope pullin' down twenty bucks a week? Cut your throat, sweetheart. Save time.

BESSIE. Never mind your two cents, Axelrod.

MOE. I say what I think—that's me!

HENNIE. That's you—a lousy fourflusher who'd steal the glasses off a blind man.

MOE. Get hot!

HENNIE. My God, do I need it—to listen to this mutt shoot his mouth off?

MYRON. Please. . . .

MOE. Now wait a minute, sweetheart, wait a minute. I don't have to take that from you.

BESSIE. Don't yell at her!

HENNIE. For two cents I'd spit in your eye.

MOE [*throwing coin to table*]. Here's two bits.

[HENNIE *looks at him and then starts across the room.*]

BESSIE. Where are you going?

HENNIE [*crying*]. For my beauty nap, Mussolini. Wake me up when it's apple blossom time in Normandy. [*Exits.*]

MOE. Pretty, pretty—a sweet gal, your Hennie. See the look in her eyes?

BESSIE. She don't feel well. . . .

MYRON. Canned goods . . .

BESSIE. So don't start with her.

MOE. Like a battleship she's got it. Not like other dames—shove 'em and they lay. Not her. I got a yen for her and I don't mean a Chinee coin.

BESSIE. Listen, Axelrod, in my house you don't talk this way. Either have respect or get out.

MOE. When I think about it . . . maybe I'd marry her myself.

BESSIE [*suddenly aware of* MOE]. You could— What do you mean, Moe?

MOE. You ain't sunburnt—you heard me.

BESSIE. Why don't you, Moe? An old friend of the

family like you. It would be a blessing on all of us.

MOE. You said she's engaged.

BESSIE. But maybe she don't know her own mind. Say, it's—

MOE. I need a wife like a hole in the head. . . . What's to know about women, I know. Even if I asked her. She won't do it! A guy with one leg—it gives her the heebie-jeebies. I know what she's looking for. An arrow-collar guy, a hero, but with a wad of jack. Only the two don't go together. But I got what it takes . . . plenty, and more where it comes from. . . . [*Breaks off, snorts and rubs his knee.*]

[*A pause. In his room* JACOB *puts on Caruso singing the lament from "The Pearl Fishers."*]

BESSIE. It's right—she wants a millionaire with a mansion on Riverside Drive. So go fight City Hall. Cake?

MOE. Cake.

BESSIE. I'll make tea. But one thing—she's got a fine boy with a business brain. Caruso! [*Exits into the front room and stands in the dark, at the window.*]

MOE. No wet smack . . . a fine girl. . . . She'll burn that guy out in a month. [MOE *retrieves the quarter and spins it on the table.*]

MYRON. I remember that song . . . beautiful. Nora Bayes sang it at the old Proctor's Twenty-third Street—"When It's Apple Blossom Time in Normandy." . . .

MOE. She wantsa see me crawl—my head on a plate she wants! A snowball in hell's got a better chance. [*Out of sheer fury he spins the quarter in his fingers.*]

MYRON [*as his eyes slowly fill with tears*]. Beautiful . . .

MOE. Match you for a quarter. Match you for any goddam thing you got. [*Spins the coin viciously.*] What the hell kind of house is this it ain't got an orange!!

SLOW—CURTAIN

Act two

One year later, a Sunday afternoon. The front room.
JACOB *is giving his son* MORDECAI (UNCLE MORTY) *a
haircut, newspapers spread around the base of the
chair.* MOE *is reading a newspaper, leg propped on a
chair.* RALPH, *in another chair, is spasmodically reading a paper.* UNCLE MORTY *reads colored jokes. Silence,
then* BESSIE *enters.*

BESSIE. Dinner's in half an hour, Morty.
MORTY [*still reading jokes*]. I got time.
BESSIE. A duck. Don't get hair on the rug, Pop. [*Goes
   to window and pulls down shade.*] What's the mat-
   ter the shade's up to the ceiling?
JACOB [*pulling it up again*]. Since when do I give a
   haircut in the dark? [*He mimics her tone.*]
BESSIE. When you're finished, pull it down. I like my
   house to look respectable. Ralphie, bring up two
   bottles seltzer from Weiss.
RALPH. I'm reading the paper.
BESSIE. Uncle Morty takes a little seltzer.
RALPH. I'm expecting a phone call.
BESSIE. Noo, if it comes you'll be back. What's the mat-
   ter? [*Gives him money from apron pocket.*] Take
   down the old bottles.
RALPH [*to* JACOB]. Get that call if it comes. Say I'll
   be right back.
[JACOB *nods assent.*]
MORTY [*giving change from vest*]. Get grandpa some
   cigarettes.
RALPH. Okay. [*Exits.*]

JACOB. What's new in the paper, Moe?

MOE. Still jumping off the high buildings like flies— the big shots who lost all their cocoanuts. Pfft!

JACOB. Suicides?

MOE. Plenty can't take it—good in the break, but can't take the whip in the stretch.

MORTY [*without looking up*]. I saw it happen Monday in my building. My hair stood up how they shoveled him together—like a pancake—a bankrupt manufacturer.

MOE. No brains.

MORTY. Enough . . . all over the sidewalk.

JACOB. If someone said five-ten years ago I couldn't make for myself a living, I wouldn't believe—

MORTY. Duck for dinner?

BESSIE. The best Long Island duck.

MORTY. I like goose.

BESSIE. A duck is just like a goose, only better.

MORTY. I like a goose.

BESSIE. The next time you'll be for Sunday dinner I'll make a goose.

MORTY [*sniffs deeply*]. Smells good. I'm a great boy for smells.

BESSIE. Ain't you ashamed? Once in a blue moon he should come to an only sister's house.

MORTY. Bessie, leave me live.

BESSIE. You should be ashamed!

MORTY. Quack quack!

BESSIE. No, better to lay around Mecca Temple playing cards with the Masons.

MORTY [*with good nature*]. Bessie, don't you see Pop's giving me a haircut?

BESSIE. You don't need no haircut. Look, two hairs h' took off.

MORTY. Pop likes to give me a haircut. If I said no he

don't forget for a year, do you, Pop? An old man's like that.

JACOB. I still do an A-1 job.

MORTY [*winking*]. Pop cuts hair to fit the face, don't you, Pop?

JACOB. For sure, Morty. To each face a different haircut. Custom built, no ready made. A round face needs special—

BESSIE [*cutting him short*]. A graduate from the B.M.T. [*Going.*] Don't forget the shade. [*The phone rings. She beats* JACOB *to it.*] Hello? Who is it, please? . . . Who is it, please? . . . Miss Hirsch? No, he ain't here. . . . No, I couldn't say when. [*Hangs up sharply.*]

JACOB. For Ralph?

BESSIE. A wrong number.

[JACOB *looks at her and goes back to his job.*]

JACOB. Excuse me!

BESSIE [*to* MORTY]. Ralphie took another cut down the place yesterday.

MORTY. Business is bad. I saw his boss Harry Glicksman Thursday. I bought some velvets . . . they're coming in again.

BESSIE. Do something for Ralphie down there.

MORTY. What can I do? I mentioned it to Glicksman. He told me they squeezed out half the people. . . .

[MYRON *enters dressed in apron.*]

BESSIE. What's gonna be the end? Myron's working only three days a week now.

MYRON. It's conditions.

BESSIE. Hennie's married with a baby . . . money just don't come in. I never saw conditions should be so bad.

MORTY. Times'll change.

MOE. The only thing'll change is my underwear.

MORTY. These last few years I got my share of gray hairs. [*Still reading jokes without having looked up once.*] Ha, ha, ha— Popeye the sailor ate spinach and knocked out four bums.

MYRON. I'll tell you the way I see it. The country needs a great man now—a regular Teddy Roosevelt.

MOE. What this country needs is a good five-cent earthquake.

JACOB. So long labor lives it should increase private gain—

BESSIE [*to* JACOB]. Listen, Poppa, go talk on the street corner. The government'll give you free board the rest of your life.

MORTY. I'm surprised. Don't I send a five-dollar check for Pop every week?

BESSIE. You could afford a couple more and not miss it.

MORTY. Tell me jokes. Business is so rotten I could just as soon lay all day in the Turkish bath.

MYRON. Why'd I come in here? [*Puzzled, he exits.*]

MORTY [*to* MOE]. I hear the bootleggers still do business, Moe.

MOE. Wake up! I kissed bootlegging bye-bye two years back.

MORTY. For a fact? What kind of racket is it now?

MOE. If I told you, you'd know something.

[HENNIE *comes from bedroom.*]

HENNIE. Where's Sam?

BESSIE. Sam? In the kitchen.

HENNIE [*calls*]. Sam. Come take the diaper.

MORTY. How's the Mickey Louse? Ha, ha, ha . . .

HENNIE. Sleeping.

MORTY. Ah, that's life to a baby. He sleeps—gets it in the mouth—sleeps some more. To raise a family nowadays you must be a damn fool.

BESSIE. Never mind, never mind, a woman who don't

raise a family—a girl—should jump overboard. What's she good for? [*To* MOE—*to change the subject.*] Your leg bothers you bad?

MOE. It's okay, sweetheart.

BESSIE [*to* MORTY]. It hurts him every time it's cold out. He's got four legs in the closet.

MORTY. Four wooden legs?

MOE. Three.

MORTY. What's the big idea?

MOE. Why not? Uncle Sam gives them out free.

MORTY. Say, maybe if Uncle Sam gave out less legs we could balance the budget.

JACOB. Or not have a war so they wouldn't have to give out legs.

MORTY. Shame on you, Pop. Everybody knows war is necessary.

MOE. Don't make me laugh. Ask me—the first time you pick up a dead one in the trench—then you learn war ain't so damn necessary.

MORTY. Say, you should kick. The rest of your life Uncle Sam pays you ninety a month. Look, not a worry in the world.

MOE. Don't make me laugh. Uncle Sam can take his *seventy* bucks and— [*Finishes with a gesture.*] Nothing good hurts. [*He rubs his stump.*]

HENNIE. Use a crutch, Axelrod. Give the stump a rest.

MOE. Mind your business, Feinschreiber.

BESSIE. It's a sensible idea.

MOE. Who asked you?

BESSIE. Look, he's ashamed.

MOE. So's your Aunt Fanny.

BESSIE [*naïvely*]. Who's got an Aunt Fanny? [*She cleans a rubber plant's leaves with her apron.*]

MORTY. It's a joke!

MOE. I don't want my paper creased before I read it. I want it fresh. Fifty times I said that.

BESSIE. Don't get so excited for a five-cent paper—our star boarder.

MOE. And I don't want no one using my razor either. Get it straight. I'm not buying ten blades a week for the Berger family. [*Furious, he limps out.*]

BESSIE. Maybe I'm using his razor too.

HENNIE. Proud!

BESSIE. You need luck with plants. I didn't clean off the leaves in a month.

MORTY. You keep the house like a pin and I like your cooking. Any time Myron fires you, come to me, Bessie. I'll let the butler go and you'll be my housekeeper. I don't like Japs so much—sneaky.

BESSIE. Say, you can't tell. Maybe any day I'm coming to stay.

[HENNIE *exits.*]

JACOB. Finished.

MORTY. How much, Ed. Pinaud? [*Disengages self from chair.*]

JACOB. Five cents.

MORTY. Still five cents for a haircut to fit the face?

JACOB. Prices don't change by me. [*Takes a dollar.*] I can't change—

MORTY. Keep it. Buy yourself a Packard. Ha, ha, ha.

JACOB [*taking large envelope from pocket*]. Please, you'll keep this for me. Put it away.

MORTY. What is it?

JACOB. My insurance policy. I don't like it should lay around where something could happen.

MORTY. What could happen?

JACOB. Who knows, robbers, fire . . . they took next door. Fifty dollars from O'Reilly.

MORTY. Say, lucky a Berger didn't lose it.

JACOB. Put it downtown in the safe. Bessie don't have to know.

MORTY. It's made out to Bessie?

JACOB. No, to Ralph.

MORTY. To Ralph?

JACOB. He don't know. Some day he'll get three thousand.

MORTY. You got good years ahead.

JACOB. Behind.

[RALPH *enters.*]

RALPH. Cigarettes. Did a call come?

JACOB. A few minutes. She don't let me answer it.

RALPH. Did Mom say I was coming back?

JACOB. No.

[MORTY *is back at new jokes.*]

RALPH. She starting that stuff again? [BESSIE *enters.*] A call come for me?

BESSIE [*waters pot from milk bottle*]. A wrong number.

JACOB. Don't say a lie, Bessie.

RALPH. Blanche said she'd call me at two—was it her?

BESSIE. I said a wrong number.

RALPH. Please, Mom, if it was her tell me.

BESSIE. You call me a liar next. You got no shame—to start a scene in front of Uncle Morty. Once in a blue moon he comes—

RALPH. What's the shame? If my girl calls I wanna know it.

BESSIE. You made enough mish mosh with her until now.

MORTY. I'm surprised, Bessie. For the love of Mike tell him yes or no.

BESSIE. I didn't tell him? No!

MORTY [*to* RALPH]. No!

[RALPH *goes to a window and looks out.*]

BESSIE. Morty, I didn't say before—he runs around steady with a girl.

MORTY. Terrible. Should he run around with a foxie-woxie?

BESSIE. A girl with no parents.

MORTY. An orphan?

BESSIE. I could die from shame. A year already he runs around with her. He brought her once for supper. Believe me, she didn't come again, no!

RALPH. Don't think I didn't ask her.

BESSIE. You hear? You raise them and what's in the end for all your trouble?

JACOB. When you'll lay in a grave, no more trouble. [*Exits.*]

MORTY. Quack quack!

BESSIE. A girl like that he wants to marry. A skinny consumptive-looking . . . six months already she's not working—taking charity from an aunt. You should see her. In a year she's dead on his hands.

RALPH. You'd cut her throat if you could.

BESSIE. That's right! Before she'd ruin a nice boy's life I would first go to prison. Miss Nobody should step in the picture and I'll stand by with my mouth shut.

RALPH. Miss Nobody! Who am I? Al Jolson?

BESSIE. Fix your tie!

RALPH. I'll take care of my own life.

BESSIE. You'll take care? Excuse my expression, you can't even wipe your nose yet! He'll take care!

MORTY [*to* BESSIE]. I'm surprised. Don't worry so much, Bessie. When it's time to settle down he won't marry a poor girl, will you? In the long run common sense is thicker than love. I'm a great boy for live and let live.

BESSIE. Sure, it's easy to say. In the meantime he eats out my heart. You know I'm not strong.

MORTY. I know . . . a pussy cat . . . ha, ha, ha.

BESSIE. You got money and money talks. But without the dollar who sleeps at night?

RALPH. I been working for years, bringing in money here—putting it in your hand like a kid. All right, I can't get my teeth fixed. All right, that a new suit's like trying to buy the Chrysler Building. You never in your life bought me a pair of skates even—things I died for when I was a kid. I don't care about that stuff, see. Only just remember I pay some of the bills around here, just a few . . . and if my girl calls me on the phone I'll talk to her any time I please. [*He exits.* HENNIE *applauds.*]

BESSIE. Don't be so smart, Miss America! [*To* MORTY.] He didn't have skates! But when he got sick, a twelve-year-old boy, who called a big specialist for the last $25 in the house? Skates!

JACOB [*just in. Adjusts window shade*]. It looks like snow today.

MORTY. It's about time—winter.

BESSIE. Poppa here could talk like Samuel Webster, too, but it's just talk. He should try to buy a two-cent pickle in the Burland Market without money.

MORTY. I'm getting an appetite.

BESSIE. Right away we'll eat. I made chopped liver for you.

MORTY. My specialty!

BESSIE. Ralph should only be a success like you, Morty. I should only live to see the day when he rides up to the door in a big car with a chauffeur and a radio. I could die happy, believe me.

MORTY. Success she says. She should see how we spend thousands of dollars making up a winter line and winter don't come—summer in January. Can you beat it?

JACOB. Don't live, just make success.

MORTY. Chopped liver—ha!

JACOB. Ha! [Exits.]

MORTY. When they start arguing, I don't hear. Suddenly I'm deaf. I'm a great boy for the practical side. [*He looks over to* HENNIE *who sits rubbing her hands with lotion.*]

HENNIE. Hands like a raw potato.

MORTY. What's the matter? You don't look so well . . . no pep.

HENNIE. I'm swell.

MORTY. You used to be such a pretty girl.

HENNIE. Maybe I got the blues. You can't tell.

MORTY. You could stand a new dress.

HENNIE. That's not all I could stand.

MORTY. Come down to the place tomorrow and pick out a couple from the "eleven-eighty" line. Only don't sing me the blues.

HENNIE. Thanks. I need some new clothes.

MORTY. I got two thousand pieces of merchandise waiting in the stock room for winter.

HENNIE. I never had anything from life. Sam don't help.

MORTY. He's crazy about the kid.

HENNIE. Crazy is right. Twenty-one a week he brings in—a nigger don't have it so hard. I wore my fingers off on an Underwood for six years. For what? Now I wash baby diapers. Sure, I'm crazy about the kid too. But half the night the kid's up. Try to sleep. You don't know how it is, Uncle Morty.

MORTY. No, I don't know. I was born yesterday. Ha, ha, ha. Some day I'll leave you a little nest egg. You like eggs? Ha?

HENNIE. When? When I'm dead and buried?

MORTY. No, when *I'm* dead and buried. Ha, ha, ha.

HENNIE. You should know what I'm thinking.

MORTY. Ha, ha, ha, I know.

[MYRON *enters*.]

MYRON. I never take a drink. I'm just surprised at myself, I—

MORTY. I got a pain. Maybe I'm hungry.

MYRON. Come inside, Morty. Bessie's got some schnapps.

MORTY. I'll take a drink. Yesterday I missed the Turkish bath.

MYRON. I get so bitter when I take a drink, it just surprises me.

MORTY. Look how fat. Say, you live once. . . . Quack, quack. [*Both exit.* MOE *stands silently in the doorway.*]

SAM [*entering*]. I'll make Leon's bottle now!

HENNIE. No, let him sleep, Sam. Take away the diaper. [*He does. Exits.*]

MOE [*advancing into the room*]. That your husband?

HENNIE. Don't you know?

MOE. Maybe he's a nurse you hired for the kid—it looks it—how he tends it. A guy comes howling to your old lady every time you look cock-eyed. Does he sleep with you?

HENNIE. Don't be so wise!

MOE [*indicating newspaper*]. Here's a dame strangled her hubby with wire. Claimed she didn't like him. Why don't you brain Sam with an axe some night?

HENNIE. Why don't you lay an egg, Axelrod?

MOE. I laid a few in my day, Feinschreiber. Hard-boiled ones too.

HENNIE. Yeah?

MOE. Yeah. You wanna know what I see when I look in your eyes?

HENNIE. No.

MOE. Ted Lewis playing the clarinet—some of those high crazy notes! Christ, you coulda had a guy with some guts instead of a cluck stands around boilin' baby nipples.

HENNIE. Meaning you?

MOE. Meaning me, sweetheart.

HENNIE. Think you're pretty good.

MOE. You'd know if I slept with you again.

HENNIE. I'll smack your face in a minute.

MOE. You do and I'll break your arm. [*Holds up paper.*] Take a look. [*Reads.*] "Ten-day luxury cruise to Havana." That's the stuff you coulda had. Put up at ritzy hotels, frenchie soap, champagne. Now you're tied down to "Snake-Eye" here. What for? What's it get you? . . . a two by four flat on 108th Street . . . a pain in the bustle it gets you.

HENNIE. What's it to you?

MOE. I know you from the old days. How you like to spend it! What I mean! Lizard-skin shoes, perfume behind the ears. . . . You're in a mess, Paradise! Paradise—that's a hot one—yah, crazy to eat a knish at your own wedding.

HENNIE. I get it—you're jealous. You can't get me.

MOE. Don't make me laugh.

HENNIE. Kid Jailbird's been trying to make me for years. You'd give your other leg. I'm hooked? Maybe, but you're in the same boat. Only it's worse for you. I don't give a damn no more, but you gotta yen makes you—

MOE. Don't make me laugh.

HENNIE. Compared to you I'm sittin' on top of the world.

MOE. You're losing your looks. A dame don't stay young forever.

HENNIE. You're a liar. I'm only twenty-four.

MOE. When you comin' home to stay?

HENNIE. Wouldn't you like to know?

MOE. I'll get you again.

HENNIE. Think so?

MOE. Sure, whatever goes up comes down. You're easy —you remember—two for a nickel—a pushover! [*Suddenly she slaps him. They both seem stunned.*] What's the idea?

HENNIE. Go on . . . break my arm.

MOE [*as if saying "I love you"*]. Listen, lousy.

HENNIE. Go on, do something!

MOE. Listen—

HENNIE. You're so damn tough!

MOE. You like me. [*He takes her.*]

HENNIE. Take your hand off! [*Pushes him away.*] Come around when it's a flood again and they put you in the ark with the animals. Not even then—if you was the last man!

MOE. Baby, if you had a dog I'd love the dog.

HENNIE. Gorilla! [*Exits.* RALPH *enters.*]

RALPH. Were you here before?

MOE [*sits*]. What?

RALPH. When the call came for me?

MOE. What?

RALPH. The call came.

[JACOB *enters.*]

MOE [*rubbing his leg*]. No.

JACOB. Don't worry, Ralphie, she'll call back.

RALPH. Maybe not. I think somethin's the matter.

JACOB. What?

RALPH. I don't know. I took her home from the movie last night. She asked me what I'd think if she went away.

JACOB. Don't worry, she'll call again.

RALPH. Maybe not, if Mom insulted her. She gets it on both ends, the poor kid. Lived in an orphan asylum most of her life. They shove her around like an empty freight train.

JACOB. After dinner go see her.

RALPH. Twice they kicked me down the stairs.

JACOB. Life should have some dignity.

RALPH. Every time I go near the place I get heart failure. The uncle drives a bus. You oughta see him— like Babe Ruth.

MOE. Use your brains. Stop acting like a kid who still wets the bed. Hire a room somewhere—a club room for two members.

RALPH. Not that kind of proposition, Moe.

MOE. Don't be a bush leaguer all your life.

RALPH. Cut it out!

MOE [*on a sudden upsurge of emotion*]. Ever sleep with one? Look at 'im blush.

RALPH. You don't know her.

MOE. I seen her—the kind no one sees undressed till the undertaker works on her.

RALPH. Why give me the needles all the time? What'd I ever do to you?

MOE. Not a thing. You're a nice kid. But grow up! In life there's two kinds—the men that's sure of themselves and the ones who ain't! It's time you quit being a selling-plater and got in the first class.

JACOB. And you, Axelrod?

MOE [*to* JACOB]. Scratch your whiskers! [*To* RALPH.] Get independent. Get what-it-takes and be yourself. Do what you like.

RALPH. Got a suggestion?

[MORTY *enters, eating.*]

MOE. Sure, pick out a racket. Shake down the cocoanuts. See what that does.

MORTY. We know what it does—puts a pudding on your nose! Sing Sing! Easy money's against the law. Against the law don't win. A racket is illegitimate, no?

MOE. It's all a racket—from horse racing down. Marriage, politics, big business—everybody plays cops and robbers. You, you're a racketeer yourself.

MORTY. Who? Me? Personally I manufacture dresses.

MOE. Horse feathers!

MORTY [*seriously*]. Don't make such remarks to me

without proof. I'm a great one for proof. That's why I made a success in business. Proof—put up or shut up, like a game of cards. I heard this remark before —a rich man's a crook who steals from the poor. Personally, I don't like it. It's a big lie!

MOE. If you don't like it, buy yourself a fife and drum —and go fight your own war.

MORTY. Sweatshop talk. Every Jew and Wop in the shop eats my bread and behind my back says, "a sonofabitch." I started from a poor boy who worked on an ice wagon for two dollars a week. Pop's right here—he'll tell you. I made it honest. In the whole industry nobody's got a better name.

JACOB. It's an exception, such success.

MORTY. Ralph can't do the same thing?

JACOB. No, Morty, I don't think. In a house like this he don't realize even the possibilities of life. Economics comes down like a ton of coal on the head.

MOE. Red rover, red rover, let Jacob come over!

JACOB. In my day the propaganda was for God. Now it's for success. A boy don't turn around without having shoved in him he should make success.

MORTY. Pop, you're a comedian, a regular Charlie Chaplin.

JACOB. He dreams all night of fortunes. Why not? Don't it say in the movies he should have a personal steamship, pyjamas for fifty dollars a pair and a toilet like a monument? But in the morning he wakes up and for ten dollars he can't fix the teeth. And millions more worse off in the mills of the South— starvation wages. The blood from the worker's heart. [MORTY *laughs loud and long.*] Laugh, laugh . . . tomorrow not.

MORTY. A real, a real Boob McNutt you're getting to be.

JACOB. Laugh, my son. . . .

MORTY. Here is the North, Pop.

JACOB. North, south, it's one country.

MORTY. The country's all right. A duck quacks in every pot!

JACOB. You never heard how they shoot down men and women which ask a better wage? Kentucky 1932?

MORTY. That's a pile of chopped liver, Pop.

[BESSIE *and others enter.*]

JACOB. Pittsburgh, Passaic, Illinois—slavery—it begins where success begins in a competitive system.

[MORTY *howls with delight.*]

MORTY. Oh, Pop, what are you bothering? Why? Tell me why? Ha ha ha. I bought you a phonograph . . . stick to Caruso.

BESSIE. He's starting up again.

MORTY. Don't bother with Kentucky. It's full of moonshiners.

JACOB. Sure, sure—

MORTY. You don't know practical affairs. Stay home and cut hair to fit the face.

JACOB. It says in the Bible how the Red Sea opened and the Egyptians went in and the sea rolled over them. [*Quotes two lines of Hebrew.*] In this boy's life a Red Sea will happen again. I see it!

MORTY. I'm getting sore, Pop, with all this sweatshop talk.

BESSIE. He don't stop a minute. The whole day, like a phonograph.

MORTY. I'm surprised. Without a rich man you don't have a roof over your head. You don't know it?

MYRON. Now you can't bite the hand that feeds you.

RALPH. Let him alone—he's right!

BESSIE. Another county heard from.

RALPH. It's the truth. It's—

MORTY. Keep quiet, snotnose!

JACOB. For sure, charity, a bone for an old dog. But in Russia an old man don't take charity so his eyes turn black in his head. In Russia they got Marx.

MORTY [*scoffingly*]. Who's Marx?

MOE. An outfielder for the Yanks.

[MORTY *howls with delight.*]

MORTY. Ha ha ha, it's better than the jokes. I'm telling you. This is Uncle Sam's country. Put it in your pipe and smoke it.

BESSIE. Russia, he says! Read the papers.

SAM. Here is opportunity.

MYRON. People can't believe in God in Russia. The papers tell the truth, they do.

JACOB. So you believe in God . . . you got something for it? You! You worked for all the capitalists. You harvested the fruit from your labor? You got God! But the past comforts you? The present smiles on you, yes? It promises you the future something? Did you found a piece of earth where you could live like a human being and die with the sun on your face? Tell me, yes, tell me. I would like to know myself. But on these questions, on this theme—the struggle for existence—you can't make an answer. The answer I see in your face . . . the answer is your mouth can't talk. In this dark corner you sit and you die. But abolish private property!

BESSIE [*settling the issue*]. Noo, go fight City Hall!

MORTY. He's drunk!

JACOB. I'm studying from books a whole lifetime.

MORTY. That's what it is—he's drunk. What the hell does all that mean?

JACOB. If you don't know, why should I tell you.

MORTY [*triumphant at last*]. You see? Hear him? Like all those nuts, don't know what they're saying.

JACOB. I know, I know.

MORTY. Like Boob McNutt you know! Don't go in the park, Pop—the squirrels'll get you. Ha, ha, ha . . .

BESSIE. Save your appetite, Morty. [*To* MYRON.] Don't drop the duck.

MYRON. We're ready to eat, Momma.

MORTY [*to* JACOB]. Shame on you. It's your second childhood.

[*Now they file out.* MYRON *first with the duck, the others behind him.*]

BESSIE. Come eat. We had enough for one day. [*Exits.*]

MORTY. Ha, ha, ha. Quack, quack. [*Exits.*]

[JACOB *sits there trembling and deeply humiliated.* MOE *approaches him and thumbs the old man's nose in the direction of the dining room.*]

MOE. Give 'em five. [*Takes his hand away.*] They got you pasted on the wall like a picture, Jake. [*He limps out to seat himself at the table in the next room.*]

JACOB. Go eat, boychick. [RALPH *comes to him.*] He gives me eat, so I'll climb in a needle. One time I saw an old horse in summer . . . he wore a straw hat . . . the ears stuck out on top. An old horse for hire. Give me back my young days . . . give me fresh blood . . . arms . . . give me—

[*The telephone rings. Quickly* RALPH *goes to it.* JACOB *pulls the curtains and stands there, a sentry on guard.*]

RALPH. Hello? . . . Yeah, I went to the store and came right back, right after you called. [*Looks at* JACOB.]

JACOB. Speak, speak. Don't be afraid they'll hear.

RALPH. I'm sorry if Mom said something. You know how excitable Mom is. . . . Sure! What? . . . Sure, I'm listening. . . . Put on the radio, Jake. [JACOB *does so. Music comes in and up, a tango, grating with an insistent nostalgic pulse. Under the cover of the music* RALPH *speaks more freely*.] Yes . . . yes . . . What's the matter? Why're you crying? What happened? [*To* JACOB.] She's putting her uncle on. Yes? . . . Listen, Mr. Hirsch, what're you trying to do? What's the big idea? Honest to God. I'm in no mood for joking! Lemme talk to her! Gimme Blanche! [*Waits*.] Blanche? What's this? Is this a joke? Is that true? I'm coming right down! I know, but— You wanna do that? . . . I know, but— I'm coming down . . . tonight! Nine o'clock . . . sure . . . sure . . . sure. . . . [*Hangs up*.]

JACOB. What happened?

MORTY [*enters*]. Listen, Pop. I'm surprised you didn't— [*He howls, shakes his head in mock despair, exits*.]

JACOB. Boychick, what?

RALPH. I don't get it straight. [*To* JACOB]. She's leaving. . . .

JACOB. Where?

RALPH. Out West— To Cleveland.

JACOB. Cleveland?

RALPH. . . . In a week or two. Can you picture it? It's a put-up job. But they can't get away with that.

JACOB. We'll find something.

RALPH. Sure, the angels of heaven'll come down on her uncle's cab and whisper in his ear.

JACOB. Come eat. . . . We'll find something.

RALPH. I'm meeting her tonight, but I know—

[BESSIE *throws open the curtain between the two rooms and enters*.]

BESSIE. Maybe we'll serve for you a special blue plate supper in the garden?

JACOB. All right, all right.

[BESSIE *goes over to the window, levels the shade and on her way out, clicks off the radio*.]

MORTY [*within*]. Leave the music, Bessie.

[*She clicks it on again, looks at them, exits.*]

RALPH. I know. . . .

JACOB. Don't cry, boychick. [*Goes over to* RALPH.] Why
should you make like this? Tell me why you should
cry, just tell me. . . . [JACOB *takes* RALPH *in his arms
and both, trying to keep back the tears, trying fear-
fully not to be heard by the others in the dining
room, begin crying.*] You mustn't cry. . . .

[*The tango twists on. Inside the clatter of dishes and
the clash of cutlery sound.* MORTY *begins to howl
with laughter.*]

CURTAIN

SCENE II

That night. The dark dining room.
AT RISE JACOB *is heard in his lighted room, reading
from a sheet, declaiming aloud as if to an audience.*

JACOB. They are there to remind us of the horrors—
under those crosses lie hundreds of thousands of
workers and farmers who murdered each other in
uniform for the greater glory of capitalism. [*Comes
out of his room.*] The new imperialist war will send
millions to their death, will bring prosperity to the
pockets of the capitalist—aie, Morty—and will bring
only greater hunger and misery to the masses of
workers and farmers. The memories of the last
world slaughter are still vivid in our minds. [*Hearing a noise he quickly retreats to his room.* RALPH
comes in from the street. He sits with hat and coat
on. JACOB *tentatively opens the door and asks:*]
Ralphie?

RALPH. It's getting pretty cold out.

JACOB [*enters room fully, cleaning hair clippers*]. We should have steam till twelve instead of ten. Go complain to the Board of Health.

RALPH. It might snow.

JACOB. It don't hurt . . . extra work for men.

RALPH. When I was a kid I laid awake at nights and heard the sounds of trains . . . far-away lonesome sounds . . . boats going up and down the river. I used to think of all kinds of things I wanted to do. What was it, Jake? Just a bunch of noise in my head?

JACOB [*waiting for news of the girl*]. You wanted to make for yourself a certain kind of world.

RALPH. I guess I didn't. I'm feeling pretty, pretty low.

JACOB. You're a young boy and for you life is all in front like a big mountain. You got feet to climb.

RALPH. I don't know how.

JACOB. So you'll find out. Never a young man had such opportunity like today. He could make history.

RALPH. Ten p.m. and all is well. Where's everybody?

JACOB. They went.

RALPH. Uncle Morty too?

JACOB. Hennie and Sam he drove down.

RALPH. I saw her.

JACOB [*alert and eager*]. Yes, yes, tell me.

RALPH. I waited in Mount Morris Park till she came out. So cold I did a buck'n wing to keep warm. She's scared to death.

JACOB. They made her?

RALPH. Sure. She wants to go. They keep yelling at her—they want her to marry a millionaire, too.

JACOB. You told her you love her?

RALPH. Sure. "Marry me," I said. "Marry me tomorrow." On sixteen bucks a week. On top of that I had to admit Mom'd have Uncle Morty get me fired in a second. . . . Two can starve as cheap as one!

JACOB. So what happened?

RALPH. I made her promise to meet me tomorrow.

JACOB. Now she'll go in the West?

RALPH. I'd fight the whole goddam world with her, but not her. No guts. The hell with her. If she wantsa go—all right—I'll get along.

JACOB. For sure, there's more important things than girls. . . .

RALPH. You said a mouthful . . . and maybe I don't see it. She'll see what I can do. No one stops me when I get going. . . . [*Near to tears, he has to stop. JACOB examines his clippers very closely.*]

JACOB. Electric clippers never do a job like by hand.

RALPH. Why won't Mom let us live here?

JACOB. Why? Why? Because in a society like this today people don't love. Hate!

RALPH. Gee, I'm no bum who hangs around pool parlors. I got the stuff to go ahead. I don't know what to do.

JACOB. Look on me and learn what to do, boychick. Here sits an old man polishing tools. You think maybe I'll use them again! Look on this failure and see for seventy years he talked, with good ideas, but only in the head. It's enough for me now I should see your happiness. This is why I tell you—DO! Do what is in your heart and you carry in yourself a revolution. But you should act. Not like me. A man who had golden opportunities but drank instead a glass tea. No . . . [*A pause of silence.*]

RALPH [*listening*]. Hear it? The Boston air mail plane. Ten minutes late. I get a kick the way it cuts across the Bronx every night.

[*The bell rings: SAM, excited, disheveled, enters.*]

JACOB. You came back so soon?

SAM. Where's Mom?

JACOB. Mom? Look on the chandelier.

SAM. Nobody's home?

JACOB. Sit down. Right away they're coming. You went in the street without a tie?

SAM. Maybe it's a crime.

JACOB. Excuse me.

RALPH. You had a fight with Hennie again?

SAM. She'll fight once . . . some day. . . . [*Lapses into silence.*]

JACOB. In my day the daughter came home. Now comes the son-in-law.

SAM. Once too often she'll fight with me, Hennie. I mean it. I mean it like anything. I'm a person with a bad heart. I sit quiet, but inside I got a—

RALPH. What happened?

SAM. I'll talk to Mom. I'll see Mom.

JACOB. Take an apple.

SAM. Please . . . he tells me apples.

RALPH. Why hop around like a billiard ball?

SAM. Even in a joke she should dare say it.

JACOB. My grandchild said something?

SAM. To my father in the old country they did a joke . . . I'll tell you: One day in Odessa he talked to another Jew on the street. They didn't like it, they jumped on him like a wild wolf.

RALPH. Who?

SAM. Cossacks. They cut off his beard. A Jew without a beard! He came home—I remember like yesterday how he came home and went in bed for two days. He put like this the cover on his face. No one should see. The third morning he died.

RALPH. From what?

SAM. From a broken heart . . . Some people are like this. Me too. I could die like this from shame.

JACOB. Hennie told you something?

SAM. Straight out she said it—like a lightning from the sky. The baby ain't mine. She said it.

RALPH. Don't be a dope.

JACOB. For sure, a joke.

RALPH. She's kidding you.

SAM. She should kid a policeman, not Sam Feinschreiber. Please . . . you don't know her like me. I wake up in the nighttime and she sits watching me like I don't know what. I make a nice living from the store. But it's no use—she looks for a star in the sky. I'm afraid like anything. You could go crazy from less even. What I shall do I'll ask Mom.

JACOB. "Go home and sleep," she'll say. "It's a bad dream."

SAM. It don't satisfy me more, such remarks, when Hennie could kill in the bed. [JACOB *laughs*.] Don't laugh. I'm so nervous—look, two times I weighed myself on the subway station. [*Throws small cards to table*.]

JACOB [*examining one*]. One hundred and thirty-eight —also a fortune. [*Turns it and reads*.] "You are inclined to deep thinking, and have a high admiration for intellectual excellence and inclined to be very exclusive in the selection of friends." Correct! I think maybe you got mixed up in the wrong family, Sam.

[MYRON *and* BESSIE *now enter*.]

BESSIE. Look, a guest! What's the matter? Something wrong with the baby? [*Waits*.]

SAM. No.

BESSIE. Noo?

SAM [*in a burst*]. I wash my hands from everything.

BESSIE. Take off your coat and hat. Have a seat. Excitement don't help. Myron, make tea. You'll have a glass tea. We'll talk like civilized people. [MYRON *goes.*] What is it, Ralph, you're all dressed up for a party? [*He looks at her silently and exits. To* SAM.] We saw a very good movie, with Wallace Beery. He acts like life, very good.

MYRON [*within*]. Polly Moran too.

BESSIE. Polly Moran too—a woman with a nose from here to Hunts Point, but a fine player. Poppa, take away the tools and the books.

JACOB. All right. [*Exits to his room.*]

BESSIE. Noo, Sam, why do you look like a funeral?

SAM. I can't stand it. . . .

BESSIE. Wait. [*Yells.*] You took up Tootsie on the roof.

JACOB [*within*]. In a minute.

BESSIE. What can't you stand?

SAM. She said I'm a second fiddle in my own house.

BESSIE. Who?

SAM. Hennie. In the second place, it ain't my baby, she said.

BESSIE. What? What are you talking?

[MYRON *enters with dishes.*]

SAM. From her own mouth. It went like a knife in my heart.

BESSIE. Sam, what're you saying?

SAM. Please, I'm making a story? I fell in the chair like a dead.

BESSIE. Such a story you believe?

SAM. I don't know.

BESSIE. How you don't know?

SAM. She told me even the man.

BESSIE. Impossible!

SAM. I can't believe myself. But she said it. I'm a second fiddle, she said. She made such a yell everybody heard for ten miles.

BESSIE. Such a thing Hennie should say—impossible!

SAM. What should I do? With my bad heart such a remark kills.

MYRON. Hennie don't feel well, Sam. You see, she—

BESSIE. What then?—a sick girl. Believe me, a mother knows. Nerves. Our Hennie's got a bad temper. You'll let her she says anything. She takes after me —nervous. [*To* MYRON.] You ever heard such a remark in all your life? She should make such a statement! Bughouse.

MYRON. The little one's been sick all these months. Hennie needs a rest. No doubt.

BESSIE. Sam don't think she means it—

MYRON. Oh, I know he don't, of course—

BESSIE. I'll say the truth, Sam. We didn't half the time understand her ourselves. A girl with her own mind. When she makes it up, wild horses wouldn't change her.

SAM. She don't love me.

BESSIE. This is sensible, Sam?

SAM. Not for a nickel.

BESSIE. What do you think? She married you for your money? For your looks? You ain't no John Barrymore, Sam. No, she liked you.

SAM. Please, not for a nickel.

[JACOB *stands in the doorway.*]

BESSIE. We stood right here the first time she said it. "Sam Feinschreiber's a nice boy," she said it, "a boy he's got good common sense, with a business head." Right here she said it, in this room. You sent her two boxes of candy together, you remember?

MYRON. Loft's candy.

BESSIE. This is when she said it. What do you think?

MYRON. You were just the only boy she cared for.

BESSIE. So she married you. Such a world . . . plenty of boy friends she had, believe me!

JACOB. A popular girl . . .

MYRON. Y-e-s.

BESSIE. I'll say it plain out—Moe Axelrod offered her plenty—a servant, a house . . . she don't have to pick up a hand.

MYRON. Oh, Moe? Just wild about her . . .

SAM. Moe Axelrod? He wanted to—

BESSIE. But she didn't care. A girl like Hennie you don't buy. I should never live to see another day if I'm telling a lie.

SAM. She was kidding me.

BESSIE. What then? You shouldn't be foolish.

SAM. The baby looks like my family. He's got Fein-schreiber eyes.

BESSIE. A blind man could see it.

JACOB. Sure . . . sure. . . .

SAM. The baby looks like me. Yes . . .

BESSIE. You could believe me.

JACOB. Any day . . .

SAM. But she tells me the man. She made up his name too?

BESSIE. Sam, Sam, look in the phone book—a million names.

MYRON. Tom, Dick and Harry.

[JACOB *laughs quietly, soberly.*]

BESSIE. Don't stand around, Poppa. Take Tootsie on the roof. And you don't let her go under the water tank.

JACOB. Schmah Yisroeal. Behold! [*Quietly laughing he goes back into his room, closing the door behind him.*]

SAM. I won't stand he should make insults. A man eats out his—

BESSIE. No, no, he's an old man—a second childhood. Myron, bring in the tea. Open a jar of raspberry jelly.

[MYRON *exits.*]

SAM. Mom, you think—?

BESSIE. I'll talk to Hennie. It's all right.

SAM. Tomorrow, I'll take her by the doctor.

[RALPH *enters.*]

BESSIE. Stay for a little tea.

SAM. No, I'll go home. I'm tired. Already I caught a cold in such weather. [*Blows his nose.*]

MYRON [*entering with stuffs*]. Going home?

SAM. I'll go in bed. I caught a cold.

MYRON. Teddy Roosevelt used to say, "When you have a problem, sleep on it."

BESSIE. My Sam is no problem.

MYRON. I don't mean . . . I mean he said—

BESSIE. Call me tomorrow, Sam.

SAM. I'll phone supper time. Sometime I think there's something funny about me.

[MYRON *sees him out. In the following pause Caruso is heard singing within.*]

BESSIE. A bargain! Second fiddle. By me he don't even play in the orchestra—a man like a mouse. Maybe she'll lay down and die 'cause he makes a living?

RALPH. Can I talk to you about something?

BESSIE. What's the matter—I'm biting you?

RALPH. It's something about Blanche.

BESSIE. Don't tell me.

RALPH. Listen now—

BESSIE. I don't wanna know.

RALPH. She's got no place to go.

BESSIE. I don't want to know.

RALPH. Mom, I love this girl. . . .

BESSIE. So go knock your head against the wall.

RALPH. I want her to come here. Listen, Mom, I want you to let her live here for a while.

BESSIE. You got funny ideas, my son.

RALPH. I'm as good as anyone else. Don't I have some

rights in the world? Listen, Mom, if I don't do something, she's going away. Why don't you do it? Why don't you let her stay here for a few weeks? Things'll pick up. Then we can—

BESSIE. Sure, sure. I'll keep her fresh on ice for a wedding day. That's what you want?

RALPH. No, I mean you should—

BESSIE. Or maybe you'll sleep here in the same bed without marriage.

[JACOB *stands in his doorway, dressed.*]

RALPH. Don't say that, Mom. I only mean . . .

BESSIE. What you mean, I know . . . and what I mean I also know. Make up your mind. For your own good, Ralphie. If she dropped in the ocean I don't lift a finger.

RALPH. That's all, I suppose.

BESSIE. With me it's one thing—a boy should have respect for his own future. Go to sleep, you look tired. In the morning you'll forget.

JACOB. "Awake and sing, ye that dwell in dust, and the earth shall cast out the dead." It's cold out?

MYRON. Oh, yes.

JACOB. I'll take up Tootsie now.

MYRON [*eating bread and jam*]. He come on us like the wild man of Borneo, Sam. I don't think Hennie was fool enough to tell him the truth like that.

BESSIE. Myron!

[*A deep pause.*]

RALPH. What did he say?

BESSIE. Never mind.

RALPH. I heard him. I heard him. You don't needa tell me.

BESSIE. Never mind.

RALPH. You trapped that guy.

BESSIE. Don't say another word.

RALPH. Just have respect? That's the idea?

BESSIE. Don't say another word. I'm boiling over ten times inside.

RALPH. You won't let Blanche here, huh. I'm not sure I want her. You put one over on that little shrimp. The cat's whiskers, Mom?

BESSIE. I'm telling you something!

RALPH. I got the whole idea. I get it so quick my head's swimming. Boy, what a laugh! I suppose you know about this, Jake?

JACOB. Yes.

RALPH. Why didn't you do something?

JACOB. I'm an old man.

RALPH. What's that got to do with the price of bonds? Sits around and lets a thing like that happen! You make me sick too.

MYRON [*after a pause*]. Let me say something, son.

RALPH. Take your hand away! Sit in a corner and wag your tail. Keep on boasting you went to law school for two years.

MYRON. I want to tell you—

RALPH. You never in your life had a thing to tell me.

BESSIE [*bitterly*]. Don't say a word. Let him, let him run and tell Sam. Publish in the papers, give a broadcast on the radio. To him it don't matter nothing his family sits with tears pouring from the eyes. [*To* JACOB.] What are you waiting for? I didn't tell you twice already about the dog? You'll stand around with Caruso and make a bughouse. It ain't enough all day long. Fifty times I told you I'll break every record in the house. [*She brushes past him, breaks the records, comes out.*] The next time I say something you'll maybe believe it. Now maybe you learned a lesson.

[*Pause.*]

JACOB [*quietly*]. Bessie, new lessons . . . not for an old dog.

[MOE *enters.*]

MYRON. You didn't have to do it, Momma.

BESSIE. Talk better to your son, Mr. Berger! Me, I don't lay down and die for him and Poppa no more. I'll work like a nigger? For what? Wait, the day comes when you'll be punished. When it's too late you'll remember how you sucked away a mother's life. Talk to him, tell him how I don't sleep at night. [*Bursts into tears and exits.*]

MOE [*sings*]. "Good-bye to all your sorrows. You never hear them talk about the war, in the land of Yama Yama. . . ."

MYRON. Yes, Momma's a sick woman, Ralphie.

RALPH. Yeah?

MOE. We'll be out of the trenches by Christmas. Putt, putt, putt . . . here, stinker. . . . [*Picks up Tootsie, a small, white poodle that just then enters from the hall.*] If there's reincarnation in the next life I wanna be a dog and lay in a fat lady's lap. Barrage over? How 'bout a little pinochle, Pop?

JACOB. Nnno.

RALPH [*taking dog*]. I'll take her up. [*Conciliatory.*]

JACOB. No, I'll do it. [*Takes dog.*]

RALPH [*ashamed*]. It's cold out.

JACOB. I was cold before in my life. A man sixty-seven. . . . [*Strokes the dog.*] Tootsie is my favorite lady in the house. [*He slowly passes across the room and exits. A settling pause.*]

MYRON. She cried all last night—Tootsie—I heard her in the kitchen like a young girl.

MOE. Tonight I could do something. I got a yen . . . I don't know.

MYRON [*rubbing his head*]. My scalp is impoverished.

RALPH. Mom bust all his records.

MYRON. She didn't have to do it.

MOE. Tough tit! Now I can sleep in the morning. Who the hell wantsa hear a wop air his tonsils all day long!

RALPH [*handling the fragment of a record*]. "O Paradiso!"

MOE [*gets cards*]. It's snowing out, girls.

MYRON. There's no more big snows like in the old days. I think the whole world's changing. I see it, right under our very eyes. No one hardly remembers any more when we used to have gaslight and all the dishes had little fishes on them.

MOE. It's the system, girls.

MYRON. I was a little boy when it happened—the Great Blizzard. It snowed three days without a stop that time. Yes, and the horse cars stopped. A silence of death was on the city and little babies got no milk . . . they say a lot of people died that year.

MOE [*singing as he deals himself cards*].
    "Lights are blinking while you're drinking,
      That's the place where the good fellows go.
      Good-bye to all your sorrows,
      You never hear them talk about the war,
      In the land of Yama Yama.
      Funicalee, funicala, funicalo. . . ."

MYRON. What can I say to you, Big Boy?

RALPH. Not a damn word.

MOE [*goes "ta ra ta ra" throughout*.]

MYRON. I know how you feel about all those things, I know.

RALPH. Forget it.

MYRON. And your girl . . .

RALPH. Don't soft soap me all of a sudden.

MYRON. I'm not foreign born. I'm an American, and

yet I never got close to you. It's an American father's duty to be his son's friend.

RALPH. Who said that—Teddy R.?

MOE [*dealing cards*]. You're breaking his heart, "Litvak."

MYRON. It just happened the other day. The moment I began losing my hair I just knew I was destined to be a failure in life . . . and when I grew bald I was. Now isn't that funny, Big Boy?

MOE. It's a pisscutter!

MYRON. I believe in Destiny.

MOE. You get what-it-takes. Then they don't catch you with your pants down. [*Sings out.*] Eight of clubs. . . .

MYRON. I really don't know. I sold jewelry on the road before I married. It's one thing to— Now here's a thing the druggist gave me. [*Reads.*] "The Marvel Cosmetic Girl of Hollywood is going on the air. Give this charming little radio singer a name and win five thousand dollars. If you will send—"

MOE. Your old man still believes in Santy Claus.

MYRON. Someone's got to win. The government isn't gonna allow everything to be a fake.

MOE. It's a fake. There ain't no prizes. It's a fake.

MYRON. It says—

RALPH [*snatching it*]. For Christ's sake, Pop, forget it. Grow up. Jake's right—everybody's crazy. It's like a zoo in this house. I'm going to bed.

MOE. In the land of Yama Yama . . . [*Goes on with ta ra.*]

MYRON. Don't think life's easy with Momma. No, but she means for your good all the time. I tell you she does, she—

RALPH. Maybe, but I'm going to bed.

[*Downstairs doorbell rings violently.*]

MOE [*ring*]. Enemy barrage begins on sector eight seventy-five.

RALPH. That's downstairs.

MYRON. We ain't expecting anyone this hour of the night.

MOE. "Lights are blinking while you're drinking, that's the place where the good fellows go. Good-bye to ta ra tara ra," etc.

RALPH. I better see who it is.

MYRON. I'll tick the button. [*As he starts, the apartment doorbell begins ringing, followed by large knocking.* MYRON *goes out.*]

RALPH. Who's ever ringing means it.

[*A loud excited voice outside.*]

MOE. "In the land of Yama Yama, Funicalee, funicalo, funic—"

[MYRON *enters followed by* SCHLOSSER *the janitor.* BESSIE *cuts in from the other side.*]

BESSIE. Who's ringing like a lunatic?

RALPH. What's the matter?

MYRON. Momma . . .

BESSIE. Noo, what's the matter?

[*Downstairs bell continues.*]

RALPH. What's the matter?

BESSIE. Well, well . . . ?

MYRON. Poppa . . .

BESSIE. What happened?

SCHLOSSER. He shlipped maybe in de snow.

RALPH. Who?

SCHLOSSER [*to* BESSIE]. Your fadder fall off de roof. . . . Ja.

[*A dead pause.* RALPH *then runs out.*]

BESSIE [*dazed*]. Myron . . . Call Morty on the phone . . . call him. [MYRON *starts for phone.*] No. I'll do it myself. I'll . . . do it.

[MYRON *exits.*]

SCHLOSSER [*standing stupidly*]. Since I was in dis country . . . I was pudding out de ash can . . . The snow is vet. . . .

MOE [*to* SCHLOSSER]. Scram.

[SCHLOSSER *exits.*]

[BESSIE *goes blindly to the phone, fumbles and gets it.* MOE *sits quietly, slowly turning cards over, but watching her.*]

BESSIE. He slipped. . . .

MOE [*deeply moved*]. Slipped?

BESSIE. I can't see the numbers. Make it, Moe, make it. . . .

MOE. Make it yourself. [*He looks at her and slowly goes back to his game of cards with shaking hands.*]

BESSIE. Riverside 7— . . . [*Unable to talk she dials slowly. The dial whizzes on.*]

MOE. Don't . . . make me laugh. . . . [*He turns over cards.*]

CURTAIN

Act three

A week later in the dining room. MORTY, BESSIE *and* MYRON *eating. Sitting in the front room is* MOE *marking a "dope sheet," but really listening to the others.*

BESSIE. You're sure he'll come tonight—the insurance man?

MORTY. Why not? I shtupped him a ten-dollar bill. Everything's hot delicatessen.

BESSIE. Why must he come so soon?

MORTY. Because you had a big expense. You'll settle

once and for all. I'm a great boy for making hay
while the sun shines.

BESSIE. Stay till he'll come, Morty. . . .

MORTY. No, I got a strike downtown. **Business don't
stop for personal life.** Two times already in the past
week those bastards threw stink bombs in the show-
room. Wait! We'll give them strikes—in the kishkas
we'll give them. . . .

BESSIE. I'm a woman. I don't know about policies. Stay
till he comes.

MORTY. Bessie—sweetheart, leave me live.

BESSIE. I'm afraid, Morty.

MORTY. Be practical. They made an investigation.
Everybody knows Pop had an accident. Now we'll
collect.

MYRON. Ralphie don't know Papa left the insurance in
his name.

MORTY. It's not his business. And I'll tell him.

BESSIE. The way he feels. [*Enter* RALPH *into front
room.*] He'll do something crazy. He thinks Poppa
jumped off the roof.

MORTY. Be practical, Bessie. Ralphie will sign when I
tell him. Everything is peaches and cream.

BESSIE. Wait for a few minutes. . . .

MORTY. Look, I'll show you in black on white what the
policy says. *For God's sake, leave me live!* [*Angrily
exits to kitchen. In parlor,* MOE *speaks to* RALPH, *who
is reading a letter.*]

MOE. What's the letter say?

RALPH. Blanche won't see me no more, she says. I
couldn't care very much, she says. If I didn't come
like I said. . . . She'll phone before she leaves.

MOE. She don't know about Pop?

RALPH. She won't ever forget me she says. Look what
she sends me . . . a little locket on a chain . . . if she
calls I'm out.

MOE. You mean it?

RALPH. For a week I'm trying to go in his room. I guess he'd like me to have it, but I can't. . . .

MOE. Wait a minute! [*Crosses over.*] They're trying to rook you—a freeze-out.

RALPH. Who?

MOE. That bunch stuffin' their gut with hot pastrami. Morty in particular. Jake left the insurance—three thousand dollars—for you.

RALPH. For me?

MOE. Now you got wings, kid. Pop figured you could use it. That's why . . .

RALPH. That's why what?

MOE. It ain't the only reason he done it.

RALPH. He done it?

MOE. You think a breeze blew him off?

[HENNIE *enters and sits.*]

RALPH. I'm not sure what I think.

MOE. The insurance guy's coming tonight. Morty "shtupped" him.

RALPH. Yeah?

MOE. I'll back you up. You're dead on your feet. Grab a sleep for yourself.

RALPH. No!

MOE. Go on! [*Pushes boy into room.*]

SAM [*whom* MORTY *has sent in for the paper*]. Morty wants the paper.

HENNIE. So?

SAM. You're sitting on it. [*Gets paper.*] We could go home now, Hennie! Leon is alone by Mrs. Strasberg a whole day.

HENNIE. Go on home if you're so anxious. A full tub of diapers is waiting.

SAM. Why should you act this way?

HENNIE. 'Cause there's no bones in ice cream. Don't touch me.

SAM. Please, what's the matter. . . .

MOE. She don't like you. Plain as the face on your nose . . .

SAM. To me, my friend, you talk a foreign language.

MOE. A quarter you're lousy. [SAM *exits*.] Gimme a buck, I'll run it up to ten.

HENNIE. Don't do me no favors.

MOE. Take a chance. [*Stopping her as she crosses to doorway*.]

HENNIE. I'm a pushover.

MOE. I say lotsa things. You don't know me.

HENNIE. I know you—when you knock 'em down you're through.

MOE [*sadly*]. You still don't know me.

HENNIE. I know what goes in your wise-guy head.

MOE. Don't run away. . . . I ain't got hydrophobia. Wait. I want to tell you. . . . I'm leaving.

HENNIE. Leaving?

MOE. Tonight. Already packed.

HENNIE. Where?

MORTY [*as he enters followed by the others*]. My car goes through snow like a dose of salts.

BESSIE. Hennie, go eat. . . .

MORTY. Where's Ralphie?

MOE. In his new room. [*Moves into dining room*.]

MORTY. I didn't have a piece of hot pastrami in my mouth for years.

BESSIE. Take a sandwich, Hennie. You didn't eat all day. . . . [*At window*.] A whole week it rained cats and dogs.

MYRON. Rain, rain, go away. Come again some other days. [*Puts shawl on her*.]

MORTY. Where's my gloves?

SAM [*sits on stool*]. I'm sorry the old man lays in the rain.

MORTY. Personally, Pop was a fine man. But I'm a great

boy for an honest opinion. He had enough crazy ideas for a regiment.

MYRON. Poppa never had a doctor in his whole life. . . . [*Enter* RALPH.]

MORTY. He had Caruso. Who's got more from life?

BESSIE. Who's got more? . . .

MYRON. And Marx he had.

[MYRON *and* BESSIE *sit on sofa.*]

MORTY. Marx! Some say Marx is the new God today. Maybe I'm wrong. Ha ha ha . . . Personally I counted my ten million last night. . . . I'm sixteen cents short. So tomorrow I'll go to Union Square and yell no equality in the country! Ah, it's a new generation.

RALPH. You said it!

MORTY. What's the matter, Ralphie? What are you looking funny?

RALPH. I hear I'm left insurance and the man's coming tonight.

MORTY. Poppa didn't leave no insurance for you.

RALPH. What?

MORTY. In your name he left it—but not for you.

RALPH. It's my name on the paper.

MORTY. Who said so?

RALPH [*to his mother*]. The insurance man's coming tonight?

MORTY. What's the matter?

RALPH. I'm not talking to you. [*To his mother.*] Why?

BESSIE. I don't know why.

RALPH. He don't come in this house tonight.

MORTY. That's what *you* say.

RALPH. I'm not talking to you, Uncle Morty, but I'll tell you, too, he don't come here tonight when there's still mud on a grave. [*To his mother.*] Couldn't you give the house a chance to cool off?

MORTY. Is this a way to talk to your mother?

RALPH. Was that a way to talk to your father?

MORTY. Don't be so smart with me, Mr. Ralph Berger!

RALPH. Don't be so smart with *me*.

MORTY. What'll you do? I say he's coming tonight. Who says no?

MOE [*suddenly, from the background*]. Me.

MORTY. Take a back seat, Axelrod. When you're in the family—

MOE. I got a little document here. [*Produces paper.*] I found it under his pillow that night. A guy who slips off a roof don't leave a note before he does it.

MORTY [*starting for* MOE *after a horrified silence*]. Let me see this note.

BESSIE. Morty, don't touch it!

MOE. Not if you crawled.

MORTY. It's a fake. Poppa wouldn't—

MOE. Get the insurance guy here and we'll see how— [*The bell rings*]. Speak of the devil . . . Answer it, see what happens.

[MORTY *starts for the ticker.*]

BESSIE. Morty, don't!

MORTY [*stopping*]. Be practical, Bessie.

MOE. Sometimes you don't collect on suicides if they know about it.

MORTY. You should let . . . You should let him. . . . [*A pause in which* ALL *seem dazed. Bell rings insistently.*]

MOE. Well, we're waiting.

MORTY. Give me the note.

MOE. I'll give you the head off your shoulders.

MORTY. Bessie, you'll stand for this? [*Points to* RALPH.] Pull down his pants and give him with a strap.

RALPH [*as bell rings again*]. How about it?

BESSIE. Don't be crazy. It's not my fault. Morty said he should come tonight. It's not nice so soon. I didn't—

MORTY. I said it? Me?

BESSIE. Who then?

MORTY. You didn't sing a song in my ear a whole week to settle quick?

BESSIE. I'm surprised. Morty, you're a big liar.

MYRON. Momma's telling the truth, she is!

MORTY. Lissen. In two shakes of a lamb's tail, we'll start a real fight and then nobody won't like nobody. Where's my fur gloves? I'm going downtown. [*To* SAM.] You coming? I'll drive you down.

HENNIE [*to* SAM, *who looks questioningly at her*]. Don't look at me. Go home if you want.

SAM. If you're coming soon, I'll wait.

HENNIE. Don't do me any favors. Night and day he pesters me.

MORTY. You made a cushion—sleep!

SAM. I'll go home. I know . . . to my worst enemy I don't wish such a life—

HENNIE. Sam, keep quiet.

SAM [*quietly; sadly*]. No more free speech in America? [*Gets his hat and coat.*] I'm a lonely person. Nobody likes me.

MYRON. I like you, Sam.

HENNIE [*going to him gently; sensing the end*]. Please go home, Sam. I'll sleep here. . . . I'm tired and nervous. Tomorrow I'll come home. I love you. . . . I mean it. [*She kisses him with real feeling.*]

SAM. I would die for you. . . . [SAM *looks at her. Tries to say something, but his voice chokes up with a mingled feeling. He turns and leaves the room.*]

MORTY. A bird in the hand is worth two in the bush. Remember I said it. Good night. [*Exits after* SAM.]

[HENNIE *sits depressed.* BESSIE *goes up and looks at the picture calendar again.* MYRON *finally breaks the silence.*]

MYRON. Yesterday a man wanted to sell me a saxophone with pearl buttons. But I—

BESSIE. It's a beautiful picture. In this land, nobody works. . . . Nobody worries. . . . Come to bed, Myron. [*Stops at the door, and says to* RALPH.] Please don't have foolish ideas about the money.

RALPH. Let's call it a day.

BESSIE. It belongs for the whole family. You'll get your teeth fixed—

RALPH. And a pair of black and white shoes?

BESSIE. Hennie needs a vacation. She'll take two weeks in the mountains and I'll mind the baby.

RALPH. I'll take care of my own affairs.

BESSIE. A family needs for a rainy day. Times is getting worse. Prospect Avenue, Dawson, Beck Street— every day furniture's on the sidewalk.

RALPH. Forget it, Mom.

BESSIE. Ralphie, I worked too hard all my years to be treated like dirt. It's no law we should be stuck together like Siamese twins. Summer shoes you didn't have, skates you never had, but I bought a new dress every week. A lover I kept—Mr. Gigolo! Did I ever play a game of cards like Mrs. Marcus? Or was Bessie Berger's children always the cleanest on the block?! Here I'm not only the mother, but also the father. The first two years I worked in a stocking factory for six dollars while Myron Berger went to law school. If I didn't worry about the family who would? On the calendar it's a different place, but here without a dollar you don't look the world in the eye. Talk from now to next year—this is life in America.

RALPH. Then it's wrong. It don't make sense. If life made you this way, then it's wrong!

BESSIE. Maybe you wanted me to give up twenty years

ago. Where would you be now? You'll excuse my expression—a bum in the park!

RALPH. I'm not blaming you, Mom. Sink or swim—I see it. But it can't stay like this.

BESSIE. My foolish boy . . .

RALPH. No, I see every house lousy with lies and hate. He said it, Grandpa— Brooklyn hates the Bronx. Smacked on the nose twice a day. But boys and girls can get ahead like that, Mom. We don't want life printed on dollar bills, Mom!

BESSIE. So go out and change the world if you don't like it.

RALPH. I will! And why? 'Cause life's different in my head. Gimme the earth in two hands. I'm strong. There . . . hear him? The air mail off to Boston. Day or night, he flies away, a job to do. That's us and it's no time to die.

[*The airplane sound fades off as* MYRON *gives alarm clock to* BESSIE *which she begins to wind.*]

BESSIE. "Mom, what does she know? She's old-fashioned!" But I'll tell you a big secret: My whole life I wanted to go away too, but with children a woman stays home. A fire burned in *my* heart too, but now it's too late. I'm no spring chicken. The clock goes and Bessie goes. Only my machinery can't be fixed. [*She lifts a button: the alarm rings on the clock; she stops it, says "Good night" and exits.*]

MYRON. I guess I'm no prize bag. . . .

BESSIE [*from within*]. Come to bed, Myron.

MYRON [*tears page off calendar*]. Hmmm . . . [*Exits to her.*]

RALPH. Look at him, draggin' after her like an old shoe.

MOE. Punch drunk. [*Phone rings.*] That's for me. [*At*

phone.] Yeah? . . . Just a minute. [*To* RALPH.] Your
    girl . . .

RALPH. Jeez, I don't know what to say to her.

MOE. Hang up?

[RALPH *slowly takes phone.*]

RALPH. Hello. . . . Blanche, I wish. . . . I don't know
    what to say. . . . Yes . . . Hello? . . . [*Puts phone
    down.*] She hung up on me. . . .

MOE. Sorry?

RALPH. No girl means anything to me until . . .

MOE. Till when?

RALPH. Till I can take care of her. Till we don't look
    out on an airshaft. Till we can take the world in two
    hands and polish off the dirt.

MOE. That's a big order.

RALPH. Once upon a time I thought I'd drown to death
    in bolts of silk and velour. But I grew up these last
    few weeks. Jake said a lot.

MOE. Your memory's okay?

RALPH. But take a look at this. [*Brings armful of books
    from* JACOB'S *room—dumps them on table.*] His
    books, I got them too—the pages ain't cut in half of
    them.

MOE. Perfect.

RALPH. Does it prove something? Damn tootin'! A ten-
    cent nail-file cuts them. Uptown, downtown, I'll
    read them on the way. Get a big lamp over the bed.
    [*Picks up one.*] My eyes are good. [*Puts book in
    pocket.*] Sure, inventory tomorrow. Coletti to Dris-
    coll to Berger—that's how we work. It's a team down
    the warehouse. Driscoll's a show-off, a wiseguy, and
    Joe talks pigeons day and night. But they're like me,
    looking for a chance to get to first base too. Joe
    razzed me about my girl. But he don't know why. I'll
    tell him. Hell, he might tell me something I don't

know. Get teams together all over. Spit on your hands and get to work. And with enough teams together maybe we'll get steam in the warehouse so our fingers don't freeze off. Maybe we'll fix it so life won't be printed on dollar bills.

MOE. Graduation Day.

RALPH [*starts for door of his room, stops*]. Can I have . . . Grandpa's note?

MOE. Sure you want it?

RALPH. Please— [MOE *gives it.*] It's blank!

MOE [*taking note back and tearing it up*]. That's right.

RALPH. Thanks! [*Exits.*]

MOE. The kid's a fighter! [*To* HENNIE.] Why are you crying?

HENNIE. I never cried in my life. [*She is now.*]

MOE [*starts for door. Stops*]. You told Sam you love him. . . .

HENNIE. If I'm sore on life, why take it out on him?

MOE. You won't forget me to your dyin' day—I was the first guy. Part of your insides. You won't forget. I wrote my name on you—indelible ink!

HENNIE. One thing I won't forget—how you left me crying on the bed like I was two for a cent!

MOE. Listen, do you think—

HENNIE. Sure. Waits till the family goes to the open air movie. He brings me perfume. . . . He grabs my arms—

MOE. You won't forget me!

HENNIE. How you left the next week?

MOE. So I made a mistake. For Chris' sake, don't act like the Queen of Roumania!

HENNIE. Don't make me laugh!

MOE. What the hell do you want, my head on a plate? Was my life so happy? Chris', my old man was a bum. I supported the whole damn family—five kids and Mom. When they grew up they beat it the hell away like rabbits. Mom died. I went to the war; got clapped down like a bedbug; woke up in a room without a leg. What the hell do you think, anyone's got it better than you? I never had a home either. I'm lookin' too!

HENNIE. So what?

MOE. So you're it—you're home for me, a place to live! That's the whole parade, sickness, eating out your heart! Sometimes you meet a girl—she stops it— that's love. . . . So take a chance! Be with me, Paradise. What's to lose?

HENNIE. My pride!

MOE [*grabbing her*]. What do you want? Say the word —I'll tango on a dime. Don't gimme ice when your heart's on fire!

HENNIE. Let me go!

[*He stops her.*]

MOE. WHERE?!

HENNIE. What do you want, Moe, what do you want?

MOE. You!

HENNIE. You'll be sorry you ever started—

MOE. You!

HENNIE. Moe, lemme go— [*Trying to leave.*] I'm getting up early—lemme go.

MOE. No! . . . I got enough fever to blow the whole damn town to hell. [*He suddenly releases her and half stumbles backwards. Forces himself to quiet down.*] You wanna go back to him? Say the word. I'll know what to do. . . .

HENNIE [*helplessly*]. Moe, I don't know what to say.

MOE. Listen to me.

HENNIE. What?

MOE. Come away. A certain place where it's moonlight and roses. We'll lay down, count stars. Hear the big ocean making noise. You lay under the trees. Champagne flows like— [*Phone rings.* MOE *finally answers the telephone.*] Hello? . . . Just a minute. [*Looks at* HENNIE.]

HENNIE. Who is it?

MOE. Sam.

HENNIE [*starts for phone, but changes her mind*]. I'm sleeping. . . .

MOE [*in phone*]. She's sleeping. . . . [*Hangs up. Watches* HENNIE *who slowly sits.*] He wants you to know he got home O.K. . . . What's on your mind?

HENNIE. Nothing.

MOE. Sam?

HENNIE. They say it's a palace on those Havana boats.

MOE. What's on your mind?

HENNIE [*trying to escape*]. Moe, I don't care for Sam— I never loved him—

MOE. But your kid—?

HENNIE. All my life I waited for this minute.

MOE [*holding her*]. Me too. Made believe I was talkin' just bedroom golf, but you and me forever was what I meant! Christ, baby, there's one life to live! Live it!

HENNIE. Leave the baby?

MOE. Yeah!

HENNIE. I can't. . . .

MOE. You can!

HENNIE. No. . . .

MOE. But you're not sure!

HENNIE. I don't know.

MOE. Make a break or spend the rest of your life in a coffin.

HENNIE. Oh, God, I don't know where I stand.

MOE. Don't look up there. Paradise, you're on a big boat headed south. No more pins and needles in your heart, no snake juice squirted in your arm. The whole world's green grass and when you cry it's because you're happy.

HENNIE. Moe, I don't know. . . .

MOE. Nobody knows, but you do it and find out. When you're scared the answer's zero.

HENNIE. You're hurting my arm.

MOE. The doctor said it—cut off your leg to save your life! And they done it—one thing to get another.

[*Enter* RALPH.]

RALPH. I didn't hear a word, but do it, Hennie, do it!

MOE. Mom can mind the kid. She'll go on forever, Mom. We'll send money back, and Easter eggs.

RALPH. I'll be here.

MOE. Get your coat . . . get it.

HENNIE. Moe!

MOE. I know . . . but get your coat and hat and kiss the house good-bye.

HENNIE. The man I love. . . . [MYRON *entering*.] I left my coat in Mom's room. [*Exits.*]

MYRON. Don't wake her up, Beauty. Momma fell asleep as soon as her head hit the pillow. I can't sleep. It was a long day. Hmmm. [*Examines his tongue in a buffet mirror.*] I was reading the other day a person with a thick tongue is feebleminded. I can do anything with my tongue. Make it thick, flat. No fruit in the house lately. Just a lone apple. [*He gets apple and paring knife and starts paring.*] Must be something wrong with me—I say I won't eat but I eat. [HENNIE *enters dressed to go out.*] Where you going, little Red Riding Hood?

HENNIE. Nobody knows, Peter Rabbit.

MYRON. You're looking very pretty tonight. You were a beautiful baby too. 1910, that was the year you was born. The same year Teddy Roosevelt come back from Africa.

HENNIE. Gee, Pop; you're such a funny guy.

MYRON. He was a boisterous man, Teddy. Good night. [*He exits, paring apple.*]

RALPH. When I look at him, I'm sad. Let me die like a dog, if I can't get more from life.

HENNIE. Where?

RALPH. Right here in the house! My days won't be for nothing. Let Mom have the dough. I'm twenty-two and kickin'! I'll get along. Did Jake die for us to fight about nickels? No! "Awake and sing," he said. Right here he stood and said it. The night he died, I saw it like a thunderbolt! I saw he was dead and I was born! I swear to God, I'm one week old! I want the whole city to hear it—fresh blood, arms. We got 'em. We're glad we're living.

MOE. I wouldn't trade you for two pitchers and an out-fielder. Hold the fort!

RALPH. So long.

MOE. So long.

[*They go and* RALPH *stands full and strong in the door-way, seeing them off, as the curtain slowly falls.*]

CURTAIN

END OF SUMMER

by S. N. Behrman

For May and Harold Freedman

From *Four Plays by S. N. Behrman.*
Copyright 1936 by Samuel N. Behrman.
Reprinted by permission of Random House, Inc.

CAUTION: *Professionals and amateurs are hereby warned that End of Summer, being fully protected under the copyright laws of the United States of America, the British Empire, including the Dominion of Canada, and all other countries of the copyright union, is subject to royalty. All rights, including professional, amateur, motion picture, recitation, lecturing, public reading, radio broadcasting, and the rights of translation into foreign languages are strictly reserved. Particular emphasis is laid on the question of readings, permission for which must be secured from the author's agent in writing. All inquiries should be addressed to the author's agent, Harold Freedman, 101 Park Avenue, New York City.*

*First production, February 17, 1936,
at the Guild Theatre, New York,
with the following cast:*

WILL DEXTER, *Shepperd Strudwick*
MRS. WYLER, *Mildred Natwick*
PAULA FROTHINGHAM, *Doris Dudley*
ROBERT, *Kendall Clark*
LEONIE FROTHINGHAM, *Ina Claire*
SAM FROTHINGHAM, *Minor Watson*
DR. KENNETH RICE, *Osgood Perkins*
DENNIS MCCARTHY, *Van Heflin*
DR. DEXTER, *Herbert Yost*
BORIS, COUNT MIRSKY, *Tom Powers*

SCENE

*The action of the play takes place in the
living room of Bay Cottage, the Frothinghams'
summer place in Northern Maine.*

TIME—*The present.*

Act one

SCENE—*The verandah-living room of the Frothingham estate, Bay Cottage, in Northern Maine. It is a charmingly furnished room with beautiful old distinguished pieces. A chintz couch and chairs give the room an air of informality. Beyond the door back you see a spacious, more formal room. Through the series of glass windows over the curving window seat on the right wall you see the early budding lilac and sumach. Woodbine and Virginia creeper are sprawling over the fence of native stone. Silver birch and maple are beginning to put out their leaves. The tops of red pine and cedar are visible over the rocks which fall away to the sea.*

TIME. *The present. A lovely afternoon in May.*

AT RISE. MRS. WYLER, *a very old lady and* WILL DEXTER, *an attractive, serious boy, are engaged in conversation.* MRS. WYLER *is knitting.*

WILL. When you were a young girl in Cleveland, did you see much of Mr. Rockefeller?

MRS. WYLER. Not much. Of course my husband saw him every day at the office. But he never came to our house. We were young and worldly. He was strict and religious.

WILL. Did you suspect, in those days, how rich you were going to be?

MRS. WYLER. Mercy no! We debated a long time before
we moved up to Cleveland from Oil City. My
mother thought Oil City was no place to bring up a
young girl. She finally persuaded my father to let us
move up to Cleveland. But there was a lot of talk
about the expense.

WILL. Was Oil City lively?

MRS. WYLER [*demurely*]. It was pretty rough! I remember the celebration when they ran the first pipe-line
through to Pittsburgh. That was a celebration!

WILL. The oil just poured, didn't it? Gushed out of the
ground in great jets, and the people swarmed from
everywhere to scoop it up.

MRS. WYLER. I remember we had a gusher in our back-
yard. We put a fence around it to keep the cows
from lapping up the oil.

WILL. Were you excited?

MRS. WYLER. Not by the oil.

WILL. I should think you would have been!

MRS. WYLER [*dryly*]. We weren't. Oil was smelly. We
wanted to get away from it. We discovered bath-
salts.

WILL. You didn't know it was the true fountain of your
—dynasty?

MRS. WYLER. We left it to the men—as I look back over
my life the principal excitement came from houses—
buying and building houses. The shack in Oil City
to the mansion on Fifth Avenue. We had houses
everywhere—houses in London, houses in Paris, New-
port and this—and yet, it seemed to me, we were always checking in and out of hotels.

WILL. It seems strange to think—

MRS. WYLER. What?

WILL. This golden stream—that you stumbled on so
accidentally—it's flowing still—quenchless—and you

on it—all you dynastic families—floating along in it
—in luxurious barges!

MRS. WYLER. When I read these books about the early
days of oil—these debunking books, you call them—
they make me smile.

WILL. Do they? Why? I'd like to know that.

MRS. WYLER. They're so far from the truth.

WILL. Are they?

MRS. WYLER. Of course they are!

WILL. Why?

MRS. WYLER. Because they're written from a foreign
point of view—not *our* point of view. We did as well
as anybody could have done according to our lights.

WILL. Yes, but what sort of lights were they?

MRS. WYLER [*tolerantly*]. There you are!

WILL. How lucky you were!

MRS. WYLER [*teasing him*]. Our young men didn't moon
about. They made opportunities for themselves!

WILL. Or did the opportunities make them? All you
had to do was pack your week-end bag and pioneer.

MRS. WYLER. Is the world quite exhausted then?

WILL. Possibly not, but our pioneering might take a
form you would find—unpalatable.

MRS. WYLER. Yes yes. [*Benevolently.*] I suppose you're
one of those young radicals our colleges are said to
be full of nowadays. Tell me, what do you young
radicals stand for?

WILL. I haven't decided exactly what I'm for, but I'm
pretty certain what I'm against.

MRS. WYLER [*pumping him*]. Most young people are
bored by the past. You're full of curiosity. Why is
that?

WILL [*not committing himself*]. I'm interested.

MRS. WYLER. At my age to be permitted to talk of one's
youth is an indulgence. Ask me anything you like.
At my age also one has no reason for restraint. I have

had the bad judgment to survive most of my con-
temporaries.

WILL. I love talking to you, Mrs. Wyler. I think you're
very wise.

MRS. WYLER [with a sigh]. Go on thinking so—I'll try
not to disillusion you! [A moment's pause.] Are you
staying on here at Bay Cottage?

WILL. Oh, no, I have to go back to Amherst to get my
degree.

MRS. WYLER. And after that?

WILL [humorously]. The dole!

[The old lady laughs.]

MRS. WYLER. My daughter tells me she's invited your
father here.

WILL. Yes.

MRS. WYLER. I shall be so glad to meet him. He's an in-
ventor, isn't he?

WILL. He's a physicist. Specializes in—

MRS. WYLER. Don't tell me—in spite of my great wisdom
I can't keep up with science. Whenever anybody
makes a scientific explanation to me I find there are
two things I don't know instead of just one.

WILL [cheerfully]. Anyway, Dad's been fired.

MRS. WYLER. I am very sorry to hear that.

WILL. He's been working on a method for improving
high-speed steel.

MRS. WYLER. Did he fail?

WILL. He succeeded. [MRS. WYLER is surprised.] They
decided that his discovery, if perfected and mar-
keted, might increase the technological unemployment. They have decided therefore to call a halt on
scientific discovery—especially in those branches
where it might have practical results. That is one
of the differences, Mrs. Wyler, between my day—
and yours—in your day, you put a premium on in-
vention—we declare a moratorium on it.

[*The old lady gives him a shrewd look.*]

MRS. WYLER. Yes, yes. I am perfectly sure that you're in for a hard time, Will.

WILL [*lightly, shrugging his shoulders*]. As I have been elected by my class as the one most likely to succeed, I am not worrying, Mrs. Wyler. All I have to do is bide my time.

MRS. WYLER [*amused*]. I am perfectly certain you'll come out! Paula tells me you and your friend, Dennis McCarthy, want to start some kind of magazine.

WILL. Yes. A national magazine for undergraduate America. You see, Mrs. Wyler, before the rift in our so-called system, college men were supposed to live exclusively in a world of ukuleles, football slogans, and petting-parties—*College Humor* sort of thing. But it was never entirely true. Now it is less true than ever. This magazine—if we can get it going—would be a forum for intercollegiate thought. It would be the organ of critical youth as opposed—to the other.

MRS. WYLER. What other?

WILL. The R.O.T.C., the Vigilantes and the Fascists—the Youth Movement of guns and sabres—

MRS. WYLER. I see. Well, I wish you luck, Will.

WILL. Thank you.

[PAULA FROTHINGHAM *comes in, a lovely young girl in gay summer slacks.*]

PAULA [*to* WILL]. Aren't you swimming? Hello, Granny.

WILL. Your grandmother and I have been discussing life.

PAULA. With a capital L, I suppose?

WILL. Enormous! I've been getting data on the pioneer age. Your grandmother thinks the reason we're in the condition we're in is because we're lazy.

MRS. WYLER [*mildly*]. Lazy? Did I say that?

WILL. In a way.

MRS. WYLER. If I said it, it must be so. Everybody over seventy is infallible!

PAULA [*nestling to her*]. Darling.

MRS. WYLER. Survival is quite a knack. You children don't realize it.

WILL. Oh, don't we though! It's getting harder every day.

MRS. WYLER. Nonsense! At your age you can't help it.

WILL. In your stately opulence that's what you think, Mrs. Wyler. You just don't know!

MRS. WYLER. Nonsense! Do you think your generation has a monopoly on hard times?

WILL. Now please don't tell me we've had depressions before?

MRS. WYLER [*rising to go*]. Paula, your young man is impertinent. Don't have anything to do with him. [*She goes out.*]

PAULA. What a conquest you've made of Granny! Way and ahead of all my beaus!

WILL. That undistinguished mob! Who couldn't?

PAULA. As long as you admit there is a mob . . .

WILL. Why wouldn't there be? Everybody loves you for your money!

PAULA [*confidently*]. I know it! And of all the fortune-hunters I've had dangling after me you're easily the most . . .

WILL. Blatant!

PAULA. That's it! Blatant! Like my new slacks?

WILL. Love 'em.

PAULA. Love me?

WILL. Loathe you.

PAULA. Good! Kiss? [*They kiss quickly.*]

WILL. Funny thing about your grandmother . . .

PAULA. Now I won't have you criticizing Granny . . .

WILL. I'm crazy about her. You feel she's been through everything and that she understands everything. Not this though. Not the essential difference between her times and ours.

PAULA. Oh dear! Is it the end of the world then?

WILL. The end of this world.

PAULA [*goes to window seat right, with a sigh*]. Such a pretty world. [*She points through windows at the garden and sea beyond.*] Look at it! Too bad it has to go! Meantime before it quite dissolves let's go for a swim. [*She starts for door.*]

WILL [*abstracted*]. All right . . . [*Following her to window seat.*]

PAULA [*she turns back*]. What's on your mind?

WILL. Wanted to speak to you about something. . . .

PAULA. What?

WILL [*embarrassed slightly*]. Er—your mother. . . .

PAULA. What's Mother gone and done now? Out with it. Or is it you? My boy-friends are always in love with Mother. I've had to contend with that all my life. So if it's that you needn't even mention it . . . come on.

WILL. No, but really, Paula. . . .

PAULA. Well then, out with it! What is it!

WILL. This. [*He gives her note.*] Found it on my break-fast tray this morning in a sealed envelope marked "Confidential."

PAULA [*reading note aloud, rather bewildered*]. "To give my little girl a good time with. Leonie Frothing-ham."

WILL. And this! [*He hands her check. PAULA takes it and looks at it.*]

PAULA. A hundred dollars. Does Mother think her little girl can have a good time with *that?* She doesn't know her little girl!

WILL. But what'll I do with it? How'll I get it back to her?

PAULA. Over my dead body you'll get it back to her!

You'll spend it on Mother's little girl. Now come on swimming!

WILL. Does your mother put one of these on every breakfast tray?

PAULA. Argue it out with her.

WILL. I can't. It would seem ungracious. You must give it back to her for me.

PAULA. Catch me! Don't take it too seriously. She slips all the kids something every once in a while. She knows my friends are all stony. You overestimate the importance of money, Will—it's a convenience, that's all. You've got a complex on it.

WILL. I have! I've got to have. It's all right to be dainty about money when you've lots of it as you have. . . .

PAULA. Rotten with it is the expression, I believe. . . .

WILL. I repudiate that expression. It is genteel and moralistic. You can't be rotten with money—you can only be *alive* with it.

PAULA. You and the rest of our crowd make me feel it's bad taste to be rich. But what can I do? I didn't ask for it!

WILL. I know. But look here . . . I've got a brother out of college two years who's worked six weeks in that time and is broke and here I am in an atmosphere with hundred-dollar bills floating around!

PAULA [*with check*]. Send him that!

WILL. Misapplication of funds!

PAULA [*warmly*]. Mother would be only too . . .

WILL. I know she would—but that isn't the point. . . . You know, Paula—

PAULA. What?

WILL. Sometimes I think if we weren't in love with each other we should be irreconcilable enemies—

PAULA. Nothing but sex, eh?

WILL. That's all.

PAULA. In that case— [*They kiss.*]

WILL. That's forgiving. But seriously, Paula—

PAULA. Seriously what?

WILL. I can't help feeling I'm here on false pretenses. What am I doing with a millionaire family—with you? If your mother knew what I think, and what I've let you in for in college—she wouldn't touch me with a ten-foot pole. And you too—I'm troubled about the superficiality of your new opinions. Isn't your radicalism—acquired coloring?

PAULA. I hope not. But—so is all education.

WILL. I know but—!

PAULA. What are you bleating about? Didn't I join you on that expedition to Kentucky to be treated by that sovereign state as an offensive foreigner? My back aches yet when I remember that terrible bus ride. Didn't I get my name in the papers picketing? Didn't I give up my holiday to go with you to the Chicago Peace Congress? Didn't I?

WILL [*doubtfully*]. Yes, you did.

PAULA. But you're not convinced. Will darling, don't you realize that since knowing you and your friends, since I've, as you say, acquired your point of view about things, my life has had an excitement and a sense of reality it's never had before. I've simply come alive—that's all! Before then I was bored—terribly bored without knowing why. I wanted something more—fundamental—without knowing what. You've made me see. I'm terribly grateful to you, Will darling. I always shall be.

WILL. You are a dear, Paula, and I adore you—but—

PAULA. Still unconvinced?

WILL. This money of yours. What'll it do to us?

PAULA. I'll turn it over to you. Then you can give me an allowance—and save your pride.

WILL. I warn you, Paula—

PAULA. What?

WILL. If you turn it over to me, I'll use it in every way I can to make it impossible for anyone to have so much again.

PAULA. That's all right with me, Will.

WILL. Sometimes you make me feel I'm taking candy from babies.

PAULA. The candy is no good for the baby, anyway. Besides, let's cross that bridge when we come to it.

[ROBERT, *the butler, enters.*]

ROBERT. I beg your pardon, Miss Frothingham.

PAULA. Yes, Robert?

ROBERT. Telephone for you.

PAULA. Thank you, Robert. [*She crosses to table back of sofa for telephone. At phone.*] Yes—this is Paula—Dad!—Darling!—Where are you? . . . but how wonderful . . . I thought you were in New York . . . well, come right over this minute. . . . Will you stay the night? . . . Oh, too bad! . . . I'll wait right here for you. Hurry, darling! Bye! [*She hangs up.*] Imagine, Dad! He's motoring up to Selena Bryant's at Murray Bay—I'm dying to have you meet him. He's the lamb of the world.

WILL. Not staying long, is he?

PAULA. No. He wants to see Mother he says. I wonder . . . oh, dear!

WILL. What?

PAULA. I was so excited I forgot to tell him. . . .

WILL. What?

PAULA. That a new friend of Mother's is coming.

WILL. The Russian?

PAULA. The Russian's here. He dates from last winter. You're behind the times, Will.

WILL. Who's the new friend?

PAULA. I'm not sure about it all yet. Maybe Mother isn't either. But I've had some experience in watch-

ing them come and go and my instinct tells me Dr.
Rice is elected.

WILL. Who is Dr. Rice?

PAULA. Psychoanalyst from New York. [*Burlesquing
slightly.*] The last word, my dear—

[*At this point the object of* PAULA'S *maternal impulse
comes in, running a little and breathless, like a
young girl.* LEONIE FROTHINGHAM, *as she has a daughter of nearly twenty, must be herself forty, but, at
this moment, she might be sixteen. She is slim, girlish, in a young and quivering ecstasy of living and
anticipation. For* LEONIE, *her daughter is an agreeable phenomenon whom she does not specially relate
to herself biologically—a lovely apparition who hovers intermittently in the wild garden of her life.
There is something, for all her gaiety, heartbreaking
about* LEONIE, *something childish and childlike—an
acceptance of people instantly and uncritically at the
best of their own valuation. She is impulsive and
warm-hearted and generous to a fault. Her own fragile and exquisite loveliness she offers to the world
half shyly, tentatively, bearing it like a cup containing a precious liquid of which not a drop must be
spilled. A spirituelle amoureuse, she is repelled by
the gross or the voluptuary; this is not hypocrisy—it
is, in* LEONIE, *a more serious defect than that. In the
world in which she moves hypocrisy is merely a social lubricant but this myopia—alas for* LEONIE!—
*springs from a congenital and temperamental in-
ability to face anything but the pleasantest and the
most immediately appealing and the most flattering
aspects of things—in life and in her own nature.
At this moment, though, she is the loveliest fabri-
cation of Nature, happy in the summer sun and
loving all the world.*]

LEONIE. My darlings, did you ever know such a day?

WILL [*he is a shy boy with her*]. It's nice!

LEONIE. Nice! It's . . . [*Her gesture conveys her utter inadequacy to express the beauties of the day.*] It's— radiant! It knows it's radiant! The world is pleased with herself today. Is the world a woman? Today she is—a lovely young girl in blue and white.

WILL. In green and white.

LEONIE [*agreeing—warmly*]. In green and white!—it depends where you look, doesn't it? I'm just off to the station to meet Dr. Rice. Will, you'll be fascinated by him.

PAULA [*cutting in—crisply*]. Sam telephoned.

LEONIE. Sam!

PAULA. Your husband. My father. Think back, Leonie.

LEONIE. Darling! Where is he?

PAULA. He's on his way here. He telephoned from Miller's Point.

LEONIE. Is he staying?

PAULA. No.

LEONIE. Why not?

PAULA. He's going on to Selena Bryant's.

LEONIE. What is this deep friendship between Sam and Selena Bryant?

PAULA. Now, Leonie, don't be prudish!

LEONIE [*appealing for protection to* WILL]. She's always teasing me. She's always teasing everybody about everything. Developed quite a vein. I must warn you, Paula—sarcasm isn't feminine. In their hearts men don't like it. Do you like it, Will? Do you really like it?

WILL. I hate it!

LEONIE [*in triumph to* PAULA]. There you see! He hates it!

PAULA [*tersely*]. He doesn't always hate it!

LEONIE [*her most winning smile on* WILL]. Does she

bully you, Will? Don't let her bully you. The sad thing is, Paula, you're so charming. Why aren't you content to be charming? Are you as serious as Paula, Will? I hope not.

WILL. Much more.

LEONIE. I'm sorry to hear that. Still, for a man, it's all right, I suppose. But why are the girls nowadays so determined not to be feminine? Why? It's coming back you know—I'm sure of it—femininity is due for a revival.

PAULA. So are Herbert Hoover and painting on china.

LEONIE. Well I read that even in Russia . . . the women . . . [*She turns again to* WILL *whom she feels sympathetic.*] It isn't as if women had done such marvels with their—masculinity! Have they? Are things better because women vote? Not that I can see. They're worse. As far as I can see the women simply reinforce the men in their—mistakes.

WILL [*to* PAULA]. She has you there!

LEONIE [*with this encouragement warming to her theme*]. When I was a girl the calamities of the world were on a much smaller scale. It's because the women, who, after all, are half of the human race, stayed at home and didn't bother. Now they do bother—and look at us!

PAULA. Well, that's as Victorian as anything I ever—

LEONIE. I'd love to have been a Victorian. They were much happier than we are, weren't they? Of course they were.

PAULA [*defending herself to* WILL]. It's only Mother that brings out the crusader in me—[*to* LEONIE.] When you're not around I'm not like that at all. Am I, Will?

[*But* WILL *is given no chance to answer because* LEONIE *is holding a sprig of lilac to his nostrils.*]

LEONIE. Smell. [WILL *smells.*] Isn't it delicious?

WILL. It's lovely.

LEONIE. Here . . . . [*She breaks off a sprig and pins it into his lapel. While she is doing it she broaches a delicate subject quite casually to* PAULA.] Oh, by the way, Paula . . .

PAULA. Yes, Mother?

LEONIE. Did you mention to Sam that—that Boris—

PAULA. I didn't, no. It slipped my mind.

LEONIE. It doesn't matter in the least.

PAULA. Father isn't staying anyway. . . .

LEONIE. Well, why shouldn't he? You must make him. I want him to meet Dr. Rice. He's really a most extraordinary man.

PAULA. Where'd you find *him*?

LEONIE. I met him at a party at Sissy Drake's. He *saved* Sissy.

PAULA. From what?

LEONIE. From that awful eye-condition.

PAULA. Is he an oculist too?

LEONIE [*to* WILL]. She went to every oculist in the world—she went to Baltimore and she went to Vienna. Nobody could do a thing for her—her eyes kept blinking—twitching really in the most unaccountable way. It was an ordeal to talk to her—and of course she must have undergone agonies of embarrassment. But Dr. Rice psychoanalyzed her and completely cured her. How do you suppose? Well, he found that the seat of the trouble lay in her unconscious. It was too simple. She blinked in that awful way because actually she couldn't bear to look at her husband. So she divorced Drake and since she's married to Bill Wilmerding she's as normal as you or me. Now I'll take you into a little secret. I'm having Dr. Rice up to see Boris. Of course Boris mustn't know it's for him.

PAULA. What's the matter with Boris?

LEONIE. I'm not sure. I think he's working too hard.

WILL. What's he working at?

LEONIE. Don't you know? Didn't you tell him, Paula? His father's memoirs. He's the son, you know, of the great Count Mirsky!

WILL. I know.

LEONIE. I must show you the photographs of his father —wonderful old man with a great white beard like a snow-storm—looks like Moses—a Russian Moses— and Boris is sitting on his knees—couldn't be over ten years old and wearing a fur cap and boots— boots!—and they drank tea out of tall glasses with raspberry jelly in—people came from all over the world, you know, to see his father . . . !

WILL. Isn't it strange that Count Mirsky's son should find himself in this strange house on this odd headland of Maine—Maine of all places!—writing his father's life? It's fantastic!

PAULA [*with some malice*]. Is Dr. Rice going to help you acclimate him?

LEONIE. I hope so. You and Paula will have to enter- tain him—you young intellectuals. Isn't it a pity I have no mind? [*She rises and crosses to table right to arrange lily-of-the-valley sprigs in a vase.*]

PAULA [*to* WILL]. She knows it's her greatest asset. Be- sides she's a fake.

WILL [*gallantly*]. I'm sure she is.

LEONIE. Thank you, my dears. It's gallant of you. [*She crosses to* PAULA—*embraces her from behind.*] But I'm not deceived. I know what Paula thinks of me— she looks down on me because I won't get interested in sociology. There never were any such things about when I was a girl. The trouble is one gener- ation never has any perspective about another gen- eration.

WILL. That's what your mother was saying to me just a little while ago.

LEONIE. Was she? [*She sits left of* WILL.] I'm sure though Mother and I are much closer—that is, we understand each other better than Paula and I. Don't you think so, Paula?

PAULA [*considering it*]. Yes. I do think so.

LEONIE. I knew you'd agree. Something's happened between my generation and Paula's. New concepts. I don't know what they are exactly but I'm very proud that Paula's got them.

PAULA [*laughing helplessly*]. Oh, Mother! You·reduce everything to absurdity!

LEONIE [*innocently*]. Do I? I don't mean to. At any rate it's a heavenly day and I adore you and I don't care about anything so long as you're happy. I want you to be happy.

PAULA [*helplessly*]. Oh dear!

LEONIE. What's the matter?

PAULA. You're saying that!

LEONIE. Is that wrong? Will—did I say something wrong?

PAULA. You want me to be happy. It's like saying you want me to be eight feet tall and to sing like Lily Pons.

LEONIE. Is it like that? Why? Will . . .

WILL [*gravely feeling he must stand up for* PAULA, *but hating to*]. Paula means . . . [*Pause.*]

LEONIE. Yes . . . ?

WILL [*miserable*]. She means—suppose there isn't any happiness to be had? Suppose the supply's run out?

LEONIE. But, Will, really . . . ! On a day like this! Why don't you go swimming? [*Rises.*] Nothing like sea-water for—morbidity! Run out indeed! And today of all days! Really! [*Gets gloves.*] I'm disappointed in you, Will. I counted on you especially . . .

WILL [*abjectly*]. I was only fooling!

LEONIE. Of course he was. [*Sits on arm of sofa beside* WILL.] Will, I rely on you. Don't let Paula brood. Can't she drop the sociology in the summer? I think in the fall you're much better—braced—for things like that. Keep her happy, Will.

WILL. I'll do my best now that—thanks to you—I have the means.

LEONIE. Oh . . . [*Remembering.*] Oh, you didn't mind, did you? I hope you didn't mind.

WILL [*embarrassed*]. Very generous of you.

LEONIE. Generous! Please don't say that. After all— we who are in the embarrassing position nowadays of being rich must do something with our money, mustn't we? That's why I'm helping Boris to write this book. *Noblesse oblige.* Don't you think so, Will? Boris tells me that the Russians—the *present* Russians—

WILL. You mean the Bolsheviks?

LEONIE. Yes, I suppose I do. He says they don't like his father at all any more and won't read his works because in his novels he occasionally went on the assumption that rich people had souls and spirits too. You don't think like that too, do you, Will—that because I'm rich I'm just not worth bothering about at all— No, you couldn't! [*The appeal is tremulous.* WILL *succumbs entirely.*]

WILL [*bluntly*]. Mrs. Frothingham, I love you!

LEONIE [*rises from arm of sofa and sits in sofa beside* WILL. *To* PAULA]. Isn't he sweet? [*To* WILL.] And I love you, Will. Please call me Leonie. Do you know how Mother happened to name me Leonie? I was born in Paris, you know, and I was to be called Ruhama after my father's sister. But Mother said no. No child of mine, she said, shall be called Ruhama. She shall have a French name. And where do you think she got Leonie?

WILL. From the French version of one of those Gideon Bibles.

LEONIE [*as breathless as if it happened yesterday*]. Not at all. From a novel the nurse was reading. She asked the nurse what she was reading and the nurse gave her the paper book and Mother opened it and found Leonie!

WILL. What was the book?

LEONIE. Everyone wants to know that . . . But I don't know. Mother didn't know. She kept the book to give to me when I grew up. But one day she met M. Jusserand on a train—he was the French Ambassador to Washington, you know—and he picked up the book in Mother's compartment and he read a page of it and threw it out of the window because it was trash! You see what I've had to live down.

WILL. Heroic!

LEONIE. I hope you stay all summer, Will. I won't hear of your going anywhere else.

WILL. Don't worry. I have nowhere else to go!

LEONIE. Tell me—that magazine you and Dennis want to start—will it be gay?

WILL. Not exactly.

LEONIE. Oh, dear! I know. Columns and columns of reading matter and no pictures. Tell me—your father is coming to dine, isn't he? I am so looking forward to meeting him. I love scientific men. They're usually so nice and understanding. Now, I've really got to go. [*Rises and starts out.*]

PAULA. Dennis will be on that train.

LEONIE. Oh, good! I like Dennis. He makes me laugh and I like people around who make me laugh, but I do wish he'd dress better. Why can't radicals be chic? I saw a picture of Karl Marx the other day and he looks like one of those advertisements before you take something. I'll look after Dennis, Will —save you going to the station— [*To* PAULA.] And Paula, tell Sam—

PAULA. Yes?

LEONIE [*forgetting the message to* SAM]. You know, I asked Dr. Rice if he would treat me professionally and he said I was uninteresting to him because I was quite normal. Isn't that discouraging? Really, I must cultivate something. Good-bye, darlings. [*She runs out.*]

WILL. But what was the message to Sam? [*He sits.*]

PAULA [*helplessly*]. I'll never know. Neither will she. [WILL *laughs.*] What can you do with her? She makes me feel like an opinionated old woman. And I worry about her.

WILL. Do you?

PAULA. Yes. She arouses my maternal impulse.

WILL [*who feels he can be casual about* LEONIE *now that she is gone*]. She relies rather too much on charm!

PAULA [*turning on him bitterly*]. Oh, she does, does she! [*Goes over to sofa and sits right of* WILL.] You renegade. You ruin all my discipline with Mother. You're like a blushing schoolboy in front of her . . .

WILL [*protesting sheepishly*]. Now, Paula, don't exaggerate!

PAULA. You are! I thought in another minute you were going to ask her to the frat dance. And where was all that wonderful indignation about her leaving you the check? Where was the insult to your pride? Where was your starving brother in Seattle? Where? Where?

WILL. I don't know but somehow you can't face your mother with things like that. It seems cruel to face her with realities. She seems outside of all that.

PAULA [*conceding that*]. Well, you're going to be no help to me in handling Mother, I can see that!

WILL [*changing subject—a bit sensitive about having yielded so flagrantly to* LEONIE]. This Russian—

PAULA. What about him?

WILL [*gauche*]. Platonic, do you suppose?

PAULA. Don't be naïve!

[*Enter* SAM FROTHINGHAM, PAULA's *father, a very pleasant-faced, attractive man between forty-five and fifty.*]

SAM. Oh, hello.

[WILL *rises.*]

PAULA [*flying to him*]. Darling!—

SAM [*they meet center and embrace*]. Hello, Paula. Delighted to see you.

PAULA. This is Will Dexter.

SAM [*shaking hands with* WILL]. How do you do?

WILL. I'm delighted to meet you.

PAULA [*to* WILL]. Wait for me at the beach, will you, Will?

WILL. No, I'll run down to the station and ride back with the others.

PAULA. Okay.

[SAM *nods to him.* WILL *goes out.*]

SAM [*crosses to front of sofa*]. Nice boy. [*Follows her.*]

PAULA. Like him?

SAM. Do you?

PAULA. I think so.

SAM. Special?

PAULA. Sort of.

SAM. Very special?

PAULA [*sits right end of sofa*]. Well—not sure.

SAM. Wait till you are. You've lots of time.

PAULA. Oh, he's not exactly impulsive.

SAM. Then he's just a fool.

PAULA. How are you, darling?

SAM. Uneasy.

PAULA. With me!

SAM. Especially.

PAULA. Darling, why?

SAM. I'll tell you. That's why I've come.

PAULA. Everything all right?

SAM. Oh, fine.

PAULA [*mystified*]. Then . . . ?

SAM [*switching off*]. How's Leonie?

PAULA. Fine. Delighted you were coming.

SAM. Was she?

PAULA. She really was. She's off to Ellsworth to meet a
doctor.

SAM. Doctor?

PAULA. Psychoanalyst she's having up to massage her
Russian's complexes.

SAM [*laughing*]. Oh— [*With a sigh.*] What's going to
happen to Leonie?

PAULA. Why? She's on the crest!

SAM. She needs that elevation. Otherwise she sinks.

PAULA. Well—you know Mother . . .

SAM. Yes. [*A moment's pause.*] Paula?

PAULA. Yes, Dad.

SAM. The fact is—it's ridiculous I should feel so nervous about telling you—but the fact is . . .

PAULA. What?

SAM. I've fallen in love. I want to get married. There!
Well, thank God that's out! [*He wipes his forehead,
quite an ordeal.*] Romance at my age. It's absurd,
isn't it?

PAULA. Selena Bryant?

SAM. Yes.

PAULA. She has a grown son.

SAM [*smiling at her*]. So have I—a grown daughter.

PAULA. You'll have to divorce Mother.

SAM. Yes.

PAULA. Poor Leonie!

SAM. Well, after all—Leonie—you know how we've lived for years.

PAULA. Has Leonie hurt you?

SAM. Not for a long time. If this with Selena hadn't happened we'd have gone on forever, I suppose. But it has.

PAULA. You know, I have a feeling that, in spite of everything, this is going to be a shock to Leonie.

SAM. Paula?

PAULA. Yes.

SAM. Do you feel I'm deserting you?

[She turns her head away. She is very moved.]

PAULA. No—you know how fond I am of you—I want you to be . . .

SAM [deeply affected]. Paula . . . !

PAULA. Happy. [A silence. She is on the verge of tears.]

SAM. I must make you see my side, Paula.

PAULA [vehemently]. I do!

SAM. It isn't only that—you're so young—but somehow —we decided very soon after you were born, Leonie and I, that our marriage could only continue on this sort of basis. For your sake we've kept it up. I thought I was content to be an—appendage—to Leonie's entourage. But I'm not—do you know what Selena—being with Selena and planning with Selena for ourselves has made me see—that I've never had a home. Does that sound mawkish?

PAULA. I thought you loved Bay Cottage.

SAM. Of our various ménages this is my favorite—it's the simplest. And I've had fun here with you— watching you grow up. But very soon after I married Leonie I found this out—that when you marry a very rich woman it's always *her* house you live in. [A moment's pause.]

PAULA. I'm awfully happy for you, Sam, really I am. You deserve everything but I can't help it, I . . .

SAM. I know. [*A pause.*] Paula . . .

PAULA. Yes, Dad?

SAM. You and I get on so well together—always have—Selena adores you and really—when you get to know her . . .

PAULA. I like Selena enormously. She's a dear. Couldn't be nicer.

SAM. I'm sure you and she would get on wonderfully together. Of course, Leonie will marry again. She's bound to. Why don't you come to live with us? When you want to . . .

PAULA. Want to!

SAM. All the time then. Leonie has such a busy life.

PAULA. It's awfully sweet of you.

SAM. Sweet of me! Paula!

PAULA. Where are you going to live?

SAM. New York. Selena has her job to do.

PAULA. She's terribly clever, isn't she?

SAM. She's good at her job.

PAULA. It must be wonderful to be independent. I hope I shall be. I hope I can make myself.

SAM. No reason you can't.

PAULA. It seems to take so much—

SAM. What sort of independence?

PAULA. Leonie's independent, but that independence doesn't mean anything somehow. She's always been able to do what she likes.

SAM. So will you be.

PAULA. That doesn't count somehow. It's independence in a vacuum. No, it doesn't count.

SAM. Maybe it isn't independence you want then?

PAULA. Yes, it is. I want to be able to stand **on** my own feet. I want to be—justified.

SAM [*understandingly*]. Ah! That's something else. [*A little amused.*] That's harder!

PAULA. I mean it, really I do— [*Pause.*] It's curious— how—adrift—this makes me feel. As if something vital, something fundamental had smashed. I wonder how Mother'll take it. I think—unconsciously— she depends on you much more than she realizes. You were a stabilizing force, Sam, in spite of everything and now . . .

SAM [*seriously*]. *You* are the stabilizing force, if you ask me, Paula. . . .

PAULA. I don't know.

SAM. What's worrying you, Paula? Is it this Russian?

PAULA. Oh, I think he's harmless really.

SAM. What then?

PAULA. That one of these days—

SAM. What?

PAULA. That one of these days—now that you're going —somebody will come along—who won't be harmless.—You know, I really love Leonie.

[LEONIE *comes running in just ahead of* DR. KENNETH RICE, DENNIS *and* WILL. LEONIE *is in the gayest spirits.* DR. RICE *is handsome, dark, magnetic, quiet, masterful. He is conscious of authority and gives one the sense of a strange, genius-like intuition.* DENNIS *is a flamboyant Irishman, a little older than* WILL, *gawky, black-haired, slovenly, infinitely brash.* SAM *and* PAULA *rise.* LEONIE *comes down to center with* KENNETH *at her left.* WILL *remains back of sofa.* DENNIS *follows down to right center.*]

LEONIE. Oh, Sam, how perfectly . . . This is Dr. Rice— my husband Sam Frothingham—and my daughter Paula! Sam, Dennis McCarthy.

DENNIS. How do you do?

[*No one pays any attention to him.* DR. RICE *shakes*

hands with SAM *and* PAULA. LEONIE *keeps bubbling, her little laugh tinkling through her chatter.*]

LEONIE. It's courageous of me, don't you think, Dr. Rice, to display such a daughter? Does she look like me? I'll be very pleased if you tell me that she does. Sit down, sit down, everybody.

DENNIS [*holding up his pipe*]. You don't mind if I—?

LEONIE. No, no, not at all— [*She sits center chair,* PAULA *sits on right end sofa,* DENNIS *sinks into chair, right, by table.*] Sam! How well you're looking! Are you staying at Selena's? How is Selena?

SAM. She's very well.

LEONIE. Dr. Rice knows Selena.

KENNETH. Yes, indeed!

LEONIE. I envy Selena, you know, above all women. So brilliant, so attractive and so self-sufficient. That is what I envy in her most of all. I have no resources— I depend so much on other people. [*Turns to* RICE.] Do you think, Dr. Rice, you could make me self-sufficient?

KENNETH. I think I could.

LEONIE. How perfectly marvelous!

KENNETH. But I shouldn't dream of doing it!

LEONIE. But if I beg you to?

KENNETH. Not even if you beg me to.

LEONIE. But why?

KENNETH. It would deprive your friends of their most delightful avocation.

LEONIE. Now that's very grateful. You see, Sam, there are men who still pay me compliments.

SAM. I can't believe it!

LEONIE. You must keep it up, Dr. Rice, please. So good for my morale. [*To* PAULA.] Oh, my dear, we've been having the most wonderful argument— [*To* DENNIS.] Haven't we?

DENNIS. Yes.

LEONIE. All the way in from Ellsworth— [*To* RICE.] Really, Doctor, it's given me new courage. . . .

PAULA. New courage for what?

LEONIE. I've always been afraid to say it for fear of being old-fashioned—but Dr. Rice isn't afraid.

KENNETH [*explaining to* SAM]. It takes great courage, Mr. Frothingham, to disagree with the younger generation.

SAM. It does indeed.

PAULA. Well, what is it about?

LEONIE. Yes—what *was* it about, Dennis?

DENNIS. Statistics and theology. Some metaphysics thrown in.

SAM. Good heavens! [*Sits.*]

DENNIS. Statistics as a symbol.

WILL. Dr. Rice still believes in the individual career.

KENNETH. I hang my head in shame!

DENNIS. He doesn't know that as a high officer of the National Student Federation, I have at my fingers' ends the statistics which rule our future, the statistics which constitute our horizon. Not your future, Paula, because you are living parasitically on the stored pioneerism of your ancestors.

PAULA. Forgive me, Reverend Father!

DENNIS. I represent, Doctor, the Unattached Youth of America—

KENNETH. Well, that's a career in itself!

[*They laugh.*]

DENNIS [*imperturbable*]. When we presently commit the folly of graduating from a benevolent institution at Amherst, Massachusetts, there will be in this Republic two million like us. Two million helots. [*Leaning over* LEONIE.] But Dr. Rice pooh-poohs statistics.

LEONIE [*arranging his tie*]. Does he Dennis?

DENNIS. He says the individual can surmount statistics, violate the graphs. Superman!

WILL. Evidently Dr. Rice got in just under the wire.

KENNETH. I'd never submit to statistics, Mr. Dexter— I'd submit to many things but not to statistics.

LEONIE. Such dull things to submit to—

DENNIS. You must be an atheist, Dr. Rice.

KENNETH. Because I don't believe in statistics?—the new God?

LEONIE. Well, *I'm* a Protestant and I don't believe in them either.

DENNIS. Well, Protestant is a loose synonym for atheist —and I, as an Irishman—and a—

KENNETH. Young man—

DENNIS. Yes?

KENNETH. Have you ever heard Bismarck's solution of the Irish problem?

DENNIS. No. What?

KENNETH. Oh, it's entirely irrelevant.

LEONIE. Please tell us. I adore irrelevancies.

KENNETH. Well, he thought the Irish and the Dutch should exchange countries. The Dutch, he thought, would very soon make a garden out of Ireland, and the Irish would forget to mend the dikes.

[*They laugh.*]

LEONIE. That's not irrelevant—

DENNIS. It is an irrelevance, but pardonable in an adversary losing an argument.

KENNETH [*to* PAULA]. Miss Frothingham, you seem very gracious. Will you get me out of this?

PAULA. No, I'm enjoying it.

LEONIE. Whatever you may say, Dennis, it's an exciting time to be alive.

DENNIS. That is because your abnormal situation renders you free of its major excitement.

LEONIE. And what's that, Dennis?

DENNIS. The race with malnutrition.

KENNETH. But that race, Mr.—?

DENNIS. McCarthy.

KENNETH. Is the eternal condition of mankind. Perhaps mankind won't survive the solution of that problem.

WILL [*with heat*]. It's easy to sit in this living room— and be smug about the survival of the fittest—especially when you're convinced you're one of the fittest. But there are millions who won't concede you that superiority, Dr. Rice. There are millions who are so outrageously demanding that they actually insist on the right to live! They may demand it one day at the cost of your complacency.

LEONIE. Will! We were just chatting.

WILL. I'm sorry! The next thing Dr. Rice'll be telling us is that war is necessary also—to keep us stimulated —blood-letting for the other fellow.

KENNETH. Well, as a matter of fact, there's something to be said for that too. If you haven't settled on a career yet, Mr. Dexter, may I suggest evangelism?

DENNIS. But Dr. Rice—!

KENNETH. And now, Mrs. Frothingham, before these young people heckle me too effectively, may I escape to my room?

LEONIE [*rising*]. Of course. Though I don't think you need be afraid of their heckling, Doctor. You say things which I've always believed but never dared say.

KENNETH [*as they walk out*]. Why not?

LEONIE. I don't know—somehow—I lacked the—the authority. I want to show you your rooms myself. [*Leaving the room, followed by* RICE.] I'll be right back, Sam—[RICE *nods to them and follows her out. As they go out she keeps talking to him.*] I am giving you my father's rooms—he built the wing especially so that when he wanted to work he'd be away from the rest of the house—you have the sea *and* the garden— [*They are off. A moment's pause.*]

PAULA. Well, that's a new type for Leonie!

DENNIS. There's something Rasputinish about him. What's he doing in Maine?

WILL. What, for the matter of that, are you and I doing in Maine? We should be in New York, jockeying for position on the bread-line. Let's go to the beach, Dennis. Pep us up for the struggle.

DENNIS. In that surf? It looks angry. I can't face life today.

PAULA. Swim'll do you good.

DENNIS [*starting for garden*]. It's not a swim I want exactly but a float—a vigorous float. Lead me to the pool, Adonais—

WILL. All right.

[*As he starts to follow* DENNIS, DR. DEXTER, WILL's *father, comes in ushered by* ROBERT. *He is a dusty little man with a bleached yellow Panama hat. He keeps wiping his perspiring face with an old handkerchief. He doesn't hear very well.*]

DENNIS. Ah, the enemy—!

[PAULA *and* SAM *rise.*]

WILL. Hello, Dad. You remember Paula.

DEXTER. Yes . . . yes, I do.

WILL [*introducing* SAM]. My father—Mr. Frothingham.

SAM. Very glad to see you.

DEXTER [*shaking hands*]. Thank you.

DENNIS [*pointing dramatically at* DEXTER]. Nevertheless I repeat—the enemy!

PAULA. Dennis!

WILL. Oh, he's used to Dennis!

DEXTER [*wipes his forehead*]. Yes, and besides it was very dusty on the road.

PAULA. Won't you sit down?

[DEXTER *does so, in center chair. The others remain standing.*]

WILL. How long did it take you to drive over, Dad?

DEXTER. Let's see—left New Brunswick at two. . . .

WILL [*looks at watch*]. Three and one half hours— pretty good—the old tin Lizzie's got life in her yet.

DEXTER. You young folks having a good time, I suppose? [*He looks around him absent-mindedly.*]

PAULA. Dennis has been bullying us.

DEXTER. He still talking? [*Mildly.*] It's the Irish in him.

DENNIS [*nettled*]. You forgot to say shanty!

DEXTER [*surprised*]. Eh? Why should I say that?

WILL. Dennis is a snob. Wants all his titles.

DENNIS. You misguided children don't realize it—but here—in the guise of this dusty, innocent-seeming man—sits the enemy.

DEXTER [*turning as if stung by a fly—cupping his hand to his ear*]. What? What did he say?

DENNIS. The ultimate enemy, the true begetter of the fatal statistics—Science. You betray us, Paula, by having him in the house; *you* betray us, Will, by acknowledging him as a father.

DEXTER [*wiping his forehead*]. Gosh, it's hot!

SAM [*sensing a fight and urging it on—solemnly*]. Can all this be true, Dr. Dexter?

DEXTER. What be true?

SAM. Dennis's accusation.

DEXTER. I am slightly deaf and McCarthy's presence always fills me with gratitude for that affliction.

DENNIS. It's perfectly obvious. You've heard of technological unemployment. Well, here it sits, embodied in Will's father. Day and night with diabolical ingenuity and cunning he works out devices to unemploy us. All over the world, millions of us are being starved and broken on the altar of Science.

We Catholics understand that. We Catholics repudiate the new Moloch that has us by the throat.

WILL. Do you want us to sit in medieval taverns with
Chesterton and drink beer?

[DEXTER *turns to* DENNIS; *as if emerging suddenly from
an absent-minded daze, he speaks with great authority, casually but with clarity and precision.*]

DEXTER. The fact is, my voluble young friend, I am not
the Moloch who is destroying you but that you and
the hordes of the imprecise and the vaguely trained
—are destroying me! I have, you will probably be
pleased to learn, just lost my job. I have been interrupted in my work. And why? Because I am successful. Because I have found what, with infinite patience and concentration, I have been seeking to
discover. From the elusive and the indeterminate
and the invisible, I have crystallized a principle
which is visible and tangible and—predictable. From
the illimitable icebergs of the unknown I have
chipped off a fragment of knowledge, a truth which
so-called practical men may put to a use which will
make some of your numbers unnecessary in the
workaday world. Well—what of it, I say?—who de-
crees that you shall be supported? Of what importance are your lives and futures and your meander-
ing aspirations compared to the firmness and the
beauty and the cohesion of the principles I seek, the
truth I seek? None—none whatever! Whether you
prattle on an empty stomach or whether you prattle
on a full stomach can make no difference to anybody that I can see. [*To* PAULA *abruptly, rising.*]
And now, young woman, as I have been invited here
to spend the night, I'd like to see my room!

PAULA [*crossing to him*]. Certainly! Come with me. I'll
have Robert show you your room. [*They go to door*

back. She calls.] Robert! [ROBERT *enters.*] Will you take Dr. Dexter to his room?

[DEXTER *follows* ROBERT *out.*]

SAM. Gosh! I thought he was deaf!

WILL. He can hear when he wants to! [*To* DENNIS.] Now will you be good!

DENNIS. I'm sorry—I didn't know he'd lost his job or I wouldn't have . . .

WILL. Oh, that's all right. Well, Dennis, how does it feel to be superfluous?

DENNIS [*sourly*]. The man's childish! [*He goes out, door right through garden.*]

PAULA. Isn't he marvelous? Don't you love Will's father?

SAM. Crazy about him. He's swell.

WILL. He's a pretty good feller. He seems absent-minded but actually he's extremely present-minded. If you'll excuse me, I'm going out to soothe Dennis. [*He follows* DENNIS *out.*]

[*A pause.*]

SAM. That young man appears to have sound antecedents.

PAULA. Oh, yes—Will's all right, but—oh, Sam—!

SAM. What?

PAULA. With you gone—I'm terrified for Leonie. I really am! When I think of the foolish marriages Leonie would have made if not for you!

SAM. It's a useful function, but I'm afraid I'll have to give it up!

PAULA [*with new determination*]. Sam . . .

SAM. Yes, Paula.

PAULA. If Leonie goes Russian—

SAM. Well?

PAULA. Or if she goes Freudian—?

SAM. In any case you and this boy'll probably be getting married.

PAULA. That's far from settled yet.

SAM. Why?

PAULA. Will's scared.

SAM. Is he?

PAULA. Of getting caught in Leonie's silken web.

SAM. That's sensible of him.

[LEONIE *comes back, half running, breathless.*]

LEONIE. Well! Isn't Dr. Rice attractive?

SAM [*rising*]. Very.

PAULA [*rising*]. And so depressed about himself! [*She goes out—door right.*]

LEONIE. Isn't it extraordinary, Dr. Rice having achieved the position he has—at his age? He's amazing. And think of it, Sam—not yet forty.

SAM. Anybody under forty is young to me!

LEONIE. How old are you, Sam?

SAM. Forbidden ground, Leonie.

LEONIE. I should know, shouldn't I, but I don't. I know your birthday—I always remember your birthday. . . .

SAM. You do indeed!

LEONIE. It's June 14. But I don't know how old you are.

SAM. Knowledge in the right place—ignorance in the right place!

LEONIE [*meaning it*]. You're more attractive and charming than ever.

SAM. You're a great comfort.

LEONIE. It's so nice to see you!

SAM. And you too! [*He is not entirely comfortable— not as unself-conscious and natural as she is.*]

LEONIE. Sometimes I think Paula should see more of you. I think it would be very good for her. What do you think of her new friends?

SAM. They seem nice.

LEONIE. They're all poor and they're very radical. They

look on me—my dear, they have the most extraordinary opinion of me. . . .

SAM. What is that?

LEONIE. I'm fascinated by them. They think of me as a hopeless kind of spoiled Bourbon living away in a never-never land—a kind of Marie Antoinette. . . . [*She laughs.*] It's delicious!

SAM. Is Paula radical too?

LEONIE. I think she's trying to be. She's a strange child.

SAM. How do you mean?

LEONIE. Well, when I was a child I was brought up to care only if people were charming or attractive or . . .

SAM. Well-connected . . .

LEONIE. Yes . . . These kids don't care a hoot about that.

SAM. I think the difference between their generation and ours is that we were romantic and they're realistic.

LEONIE. Is that it?

SAM. I think so.

LEONIE. What makes that?

SAM. Changes in the world—the war—the depression . . .

LEONIE. What did people blame things on before—the war?

SAM [*smiling*]. Oh, on the tariff and on the Republicans—and on the Democrats! Leonie—

LEONIE. Yes, Sam.

SAM. I—I really have something to tell you.

LEONIE [*looks up at him curiously*]. What? [*Pause.*]

SAM. I am in love with Selena Bryant. We want to get married.

LEONIE [*pause—after a moment*]. Human nature is funny! Mine is!

SAM. Why?

LEONIE. I know I ought to be delighted to release you. Probably I should have spoken to you about it myself before long—separating. And yet—when you tell me—I feel—a pang. . . .

SAM. That's very sweet of you.

LEONIE. One's so possessive—one doesn't want to give up anything.

SAM. For so many years our marriage has been at its best—a friendship. Need that end?

LEONIE. No, Sam. It needn't. I hope truly that it won't.

SAM. What about Paula?

LEONIE. Did you tell Paula?

SAM. Yes . . .

LEONIE. Did she . . . ?

SAM [*rising*]. Leonie . . .

LEONIE [*pauses*]. Yes, Sam.

SAM. A little while ago you said—you thought Paula ought to see more of me.

LEONIE. Yes . . . I did. . . . [*She is quite agitated suddenly. The thought has crossed her mind that perhaps* PAULA *has told* SAM *that she would prefer to go with him. This hurts her deeply, not only for the loss of* PAULA *but because, from the bottom of her being, she cannot bear not to be loved.*]

SAM. Don't you think then . . . for a time at least . . .

LEONIE [*defeatist in a crisis*]. Paula doesn't like me! [*It is a sudden and completely accepted conviction.*]

SAM. Leonie!

LEONIE. She'd rather go with you!

SAM. Not at all—it's only that . . .

LEONIE. I know what Paula thinks of me. . . .

SAM. Paula adores you. It's only that . . .

LEONIE. It's only that what—

SAM. Well, for instance—if you should get married—

LEONIE. What if I did?

SAM [*coming to stand close to her left*]. It would mean

a considerable readjustment for Paula—wouldn't it? You can see that.

LEONIE [*rising*]. But it would too with you and Selena.

SAM [*taking step toward her*]. She knows Selena. She admires Selena.

LEONIE [*rising and walking down to front of sofa*]. What makes you think she wouldn't admire—whomever I married?

SAM [*after a moment, completely serious now*]. There's another aspect of it which I think for Paula's sake you should consider most carefully.

LEONIE. What aspect?

SAM [*coming down to her*]. Paula's serious. You know that yourself. She's interested in things. She's not content to be a Sunday-supplement heiress—floating along—she wants to do things. Selena's a working woman. Selena can help her.

LEONIE. I know. I'm useless.

SAM. I think you ought to be unselfish about this.

LEONIE. Paula can do what she likes, of course. If she doesn't love me . . .

SAM. Of course she loves you.

LEONIE. If she prefers to live with you and Selena I shan't stand in her way.

[*Her martyrish resignation irritates* SAM *profoundly. He feels that really* LEONIE *should not be allowed to get away with it.*]

SAM. You're so vain, Leonie.

LEONIE [*refusing to argue*]. I'm sorry.

[*This makes it worse.* SAM *goes deeper.*]

SAM. After all, you're Paula's mother. Can't you look at her problem—objectively?

LEONIE. Where my emotions are involved I'm afraid I never know what words like that mean.

[*He blunders in worse, farther than he really means to go.*]

SAM [*flatly*]. Well, this sort of thing isn't good for Paula.

LEONIE [*very cold, very hurt*]. What sort of thing? [*A moment's pause. He is annoyed with himself at the ineptitude of his approach.*] Be perfectly frank. You can be with me. What sort of thing?

SAM. Well—Leonie— [*With a kind of desperate bluntness.*] You've made a career of flirtation. Obviously Paula isn't going to. You know you and Paula belong to different worlds. [*With some heat.*] And the reason Paula is the way she is is because she lives in an atmosphere of perpetual conflict.

LEONIE. Conflict? Paula?

SAM. With herself. About you.

LEONIE [*rising*]. That's too subtle for me, I'm afraid.

SAM. Paula's unaware of it herself.

LEONIE. Where did you acquire this amazing psychological insight? You never used to have it. Of course! From Selena. Of course!

SAM. I've never discussed this with Selena.

LEONIE. No?

SAM. She's told me she'd be happy to have Paula but . . .

LEONIE. That's extremely generous of her—to offer without discussion. . . .

SAM [*she has him there; he loses his temper*]. It's impossible for you to consider anything without being personal.

LEONIE. I am afraid it is. I don't live on this wonderful rarefied, intellectual plane inhabited by Selena and yourself—and where you want to take Paula. I'm sorry if I've made Paula serious, I'm sorry she's in a perpetual conflict about me. I'm sorry I've let her in for—this sort of thing! I'm sorry! [*She is on the verge of tears. She runs out.*]

SAM. Leonie . . . ! [*He follows her to door back, call-*

ing.] Leonie! [*But it is too late. She is gone. He turns back into room.*] Damn!

[PAULA *comes in—from beach, door right.*]

PAULA. Where's Leonie?

SAM. She just went upstairs.

PAULA. I've been showing Dr. Rice our rock-bound coast.

SAM. What's he like?

PAULA. Hard to say. He's almost too sympathetic. At the same time—

SAM. What?

PAULA. At the same time—he is inscrutable! I can't tell whether I like him or dislike him. You say Selena knows him. What does she say about him?

SAM. Selena isn't crazy about him.

PAULA. Why not?

SAM. Brilliant charlatan, she says—also a charmer.

PAULA. I gather that, and I resent him. How'd you come out with Leonie?

SAM. I've made a mess of it. I'm a fool!

PAULA. My going with you, you mean?

SAM. Yes.

PAULA. Sam . . .

SAM. Yes?

PAULA. Will you mind very much . . .

SAM. What?

PAULA. If I don't go with Selena and you?

SAM. But I thought you said—and especially if she marries somebody—

PAULA [*slowly*]. That's just what I'm thinking of—

SAM. What's happened?

PAULA. There's no way out of it, Sam—I've got to stay.

SAM. But why?

PAULA [*simply, looking up at him*]. Somebody's got to look after Leonie. . . .

[KENNETH *enters.*]

KENNETH. My first glimpse of Maine. A masculine Riviera.

PAULA. It's mild now. If you want to see it really virile —come in the late fall.

KENNETH. You've only to crook your little finger. I'll be glad to look at more of Maine whenever you have the time. [*Sits, facing her.*]

PAULA. Of course. Tomorrow?

KENNETH. Yes. Tomorrow. [*To* SAM.] You know, from Mrs. Frothingham's description— [*Looking back at* PAULA, *intently.*] I never could have imagined her. Not remotely.

[ROBERT *enters.*]

SAM. What is it, Robert?

ROBERT. Mrs. Frothingham would like to see Dr. Rice in her study.

KENNETH [*rising*]. Oh, thank you. [*He walks to door back.*] Excuse me. [*He goes upstairs.*]

[PAULA *and* SAM *have continued looking front. As* KENNETH *starts upstairs they slowly turn and look at one another. The same thought has crossed both their minds—they both find themselves looking suddenly into a new and dubious vista.*]

CURTAIN

Act two

SCENE I

SCENE. *The same.*

TIME. *Midsummer—late afternoon.*

AT RISE: KENNETH *is at a bridge table working out a*

chess problem. He hears voices and footsteps ap-
proaching. Gets up, unhurried, and looks off into gar-
den. Sees BORIS *and* LEONIE *approaching. As they come*
in he strolls off—they do not see him. LEONIE'S *arms are*
full of flowers. She is looking for KENNETH. COUNT MIR-
SKY *follows her in.*

COUNT MIRSKY, *a Russian, is very good-looking, mon-*
goloid about the eyes. His English is beautiful, with a
slight and attractive accent. He is tense, jittery—a mass
of jangled nerves—his fingers tremble as he lights one
cigarette after another. He is very pale—his pallor ac-
centuated by a dark scarf he wears around his neck.

BORIS [*stopping center*]. It appears he is not here either.

LEONIE. He? Who? [*Crossing to table behind sofa to*
put some flowers in vase.]

BORIS. When you're in the garden with me you think—
perhaps he is in the house. When you are in the
house you think perhaps he is in the garden.

LEONIE. Boris, darling, you have the odd habit of referring to mysterious characters without giving me
any hint who they are. Is that Russian symbolism?
There will be a long silence; then you will say: He
would not approve, or they can't hear us. It's a bit
mystifying.

BORIS [*crossing to stand near her*]. You know who I
mean.

LEONIE [*going to table right to put flowers in vase*].
Really, you flatter me. I'm not a mystic, you know,
Boris. I'm a simple extrovert. When you say "he,"
why can't it refer to someone definite—and if possible to someone I know.

BORIS [*crossing to back of table, facing her across it*].
You know him, all right.

LEONIE. There you go again! *Really*, Boris!

BORIS [*moving closer to her around table*]. You've been

divorced now for several weeks. You're free. We were only waiting for you to be free—

LEONIE [*moving away, sitting in chair, right*]. Now that I am free you want to coerce me. It's a bit unreasonable, don't you think?

[BORIS *walks to end of windowseat and sits. Enter* KENNETH, *door back.*]

KENNETH [*strolling across stage toward* LEONIE]. Hello, Leonie. Count Mirsky—

LEONIE. Kenneth—I haven't seen you all day.

KENNETH. I've been in my room slaving away at a scientific paper.

LEONIE. My house hums with creative activity. I love it. It gives me a sense of vicarious importance. What's your paper on?

KENNETH. Shadow-neurosis.

LEONIE. Shadow-neurosis. How marvelous! What does it mean?

KENNETH [*looking at* BORIS]. It is a sensation of non-existence.

LEONIE. Is it common?

KENNETH. Quite. The victim knows that he exists and yet he feels that he does not!

LEONIE. In a curious way I can imagine a sensation like that- do you know I actually can. Isn't it amusing?

BORIS. The doctor is so eloquent. Once he describes a sensation it becomes very easy to feel it.

LEONIE. That's an entrancing gift. Why are you so antagonistic to Kenneth? He wants to help you but you won't let him. I asked him here to help you.

KENNETH [*to* BORIS]. Your skepticism about this particular disease is interesting, Count Mirsky, because, as it happens, you suffer from it.

BORIS [*bearing down on* KENNETH]. Has it ever occurred to you that you are a wasted novelist?

KENNETH. Though I have not mentioned you in my article I have described you.

LEONIE [*rising and crossing left to table behind sofa*]. You should be flattered, Boris.

BORIS. I am!

LEONIE. Another case history! I've been reading some of Kenneth's scientific textbooks. Most fascinating form of biography. Who was that wonderful fellow who did such odd things—Mr. X.? You'd never think you could get so interested in anonymous people. I'd have given anything to meet Mr. X.—though I must say I'd feel a bit nervous about having him in the house.

KENNETH. How is your book getting along, Count Mirsky?

BORIS. Very well. Oh—so—

KENNETH. Far along in it?

BORIS. Quite.

LEONIE. I'm crazy to see it. He's dedicating it to me but he hasn't let me see a word of it!

KENNETH. For a very good reason.

LEONIE. What do you mean?

KENNETH. Because there is no book. There never has been a book.

LEONIE [*she lets flowers drop*]. Kenneth!

KENNETH. Isn't that true, Count Mirsky?

BORIS. It is not!

KENNETH. Then why don't you let us see a bit of it?

LEONIE. Oh, do! At least the dedication page.

KENNETH. A chapter—

BORIS. Because it isn't finished yet.

LEONIE. Well, it doesn't have to be finished. We know the end, don't we? The end belongs to the world.

KENNETH. Let us see it, Count.

BORIS. I can't.

KENNETH. What are you calling the book?

BORIS. I haven't decided yet.

KENNETH. May I suggest a title to you—?

LEONIE. Oh, do! What shall we call it, Kenneth?

KENNETH. "The Memoirs of a Boy Who Wanted to Murder His Father."

LEONIE. What!

BORIS [*gripping arms of chair*]. I am not a hysterical woman, Doctor—and I'm not your patient!

LEONIE. But Kenneth—Boris worshipped his father.

KENNETH. No, he hated him. He hated him when he was alive and he hates him still. He grew up under the overwhelming shadow of this world-genius whom, in spite of an immense desire to emulate and even surpass—he felt he could never emulate and never surpass—nor even equal— Did you worship your father, Count Mirsky?

BORIS. It's true! I hated him!

LEONIE. Boris!

BORIS. I hated him!

KENNETH. Now you can let us see the book, can't you— now that we know the point of view—just a bit of it?

LEONIE. I'm more crazy than ever to see it now. I can tell you a little secret now, Boris. I was afraid—I was rather afraid—that your book would be a little like one of those statues of an ancestor in a frock-coat. Now it sounds really exciting. You hated him. But how perfectly marvelous! I can't wait to see it now. Do run up to your study and bring it down, Boris—do!

BORIS. No.

LEONIE. That's very unpleasant of you.

BORIS. You might as well know it then. There isn't any book. There never will be. Not by me.

LEONIE. But I don't understand—every day—in your room working—all these months!

BORIS [*facing her*]. One wants privacy! Possibly you can't realize that. You who always have to have a house full of people.

LEONIE [*goes back to flowers at table*]. Boris!

KENNETH [*rising*]. Why don't you write the book anyway, Count Mirsky? There is a vogue these days for vituperative biography.

BORIS. I am not interested in the vogue.

KENNETH. We are quite used nowadays to children who dislike their fathers. The public—

BORIS. To titillate the public would not compensate me for forcing myself to recall the atmosphere of saintly sadism in which my childhood was spent—I can still smell that living room, I can still smell those stinking, sexless pilgrims who used to come from all over the world to get my saintly father's blessing. I used to sit with my mother in a room no bigger than a closet to get away from the odor of that nauseating humanitarianism. There was no privacy in the Villa Mirskovitch. Oh, no—it was a Mecca—do you understand—a Mecca!

KENNETH. Yes, I think I understand.

BORIS. Well, I have been paying the haloed one back. I have been getting privacy at his expense at last.

LEONIE. Why have you never told me before that you felt this way about your father?

BORIS. I never said anything about him. It was you who did the talking. You always raved about the great man with that characteristic American enthusiasm for what you don't know.

LEONIE. Nevertheless, the world recognizes your father as a great man. The books are there to prove it. There they are. You can't write books like that without greatness—no matter what you say. You are a petulant child. Your father was a great man.

BORIS. It makes no difference how great he was—those pilgrims stank!

[LEONIE *turns away*.]

KENNETH. I suggest that to write that book, even if no one ever sees the manuscript but you, might amuse you—a kind of revenge which, when you were a boy, you were in no position to take.

BORIS. Are you trying to cure me, Doctor? Please don't trouble. I don't need your particular species of professionalism. I do not need any help from you. [*He goes to door back, turns to* LEONIE. LEONIE *looks bewilderedly at* KENNETH. BORIS *goes out*.]

LEONIE. How did you know? You're uncanny!

KENNETH. All in the day's work.

LEONIE. Why is it I always get myself involved with men weaker than myself? I certainly am no tower of strength.

KENNETH. Possibly not—but you are generous and impulsive. You have a tendency to accept people at the best of their own valuation.

LEONIE. I want to help them. I do help them. After they get used to my help, after they get to count on my help, I get impatient with them. Why, I ask myself, can't people help themselves?

KENNETH. And very natural.

LEONIE. I seem to attract people like that!

KENNETH. Leonie—you are the last woman on earth Count Mirsky should marry. He would only transfer his hatred of his father to you.

LEONIE. I don't think I understand you, Kenneth—really I don't—and I do so want to understand things.

KENNETH. Well—your charm, your gaiety, your position, your wealth, your beauty—these would oppress him. Again, he cannot be himself.—Or, if he

is himself, it is to reveal his nonentity, his infe-
riority—again the secondary role—Leonie Frothingham's husband—the son of Count Mirsky—the husband of Leonie Frothingham. Again the shadow—
again, eternally and always—non-existence. Poor
fellow. [*Pause.*]

LEONIE. I'm so grateful to you, Kenneth.

KENNETH. Nonsense. You mustn't be grateful to me
because I—exercise my profession.

LEONIE. I want to express my gratitude—in some tangible form. I've been thinking of nothing else lately.
I can't sleep for thinking of it.

KENNETH. Well, if it gives you insomnia, you'd better
tell me about it.

LEONIE. I want to make it possible for you to realize
your ambition.

KENNETH. Ambition? What ambition?

LEONIE. Ah! You've forgotten, haven't you? But you
let it slip out one day—you pump me professionally
—but I do the same to you—non-professionally.

KENNETH. You terrify me!

LEONIE. That night last winter when we went to dinner in that little restaurant where you go with your
doctor friends . . . you told me your dream.

KENNETH. My censor must have been napping.

LEONIE. He was. Or she was. What sex is your censor?

KENNETH. That's none of your business.

LEONIE. I'm sorry.

KENNETH. Which of my dreams was I so reckless as to
reveal to you?

LEONIE. To have a sanatorium of your own one day—
so you can carry out your own ideas of curing patients.

KENNETH. Oh, that! Out of the question.

LEONIE. Why?

KENNETH. To do it on the scale I visualize, would cost

more than I'm ever likely to save out of my practice.

LEONIE. I'll give you the sanatorium. I've never given anyone anything like that before. What fun!

KENNETH. Will I find it all wrapped up in silver foil on Christmas morning?

LEONIE. Yes. You will! You will! We'll have a suite in it for Mr. X.—for all your anonymous friends—we'll entertain the whole alphabet!

KENNETH. You see, Leonie!

LEONIE. What do you mean? I thought you'd be—

KENNETH. Of course, it's terribly generous of you. I'm deeply touched. But . . .

LEONIE. But . . . ?

KENNETH. I'm a stranger to you.

LEONIE. Kenneth!

KENNETH. Outside of my professional relation—such as I have with scores of patients—little more than that.

LEONIE. I thought—

KENNETH. And yet you are willing to back me in a venture that would cost a sizeable fortune—just on that. Leonie! Leonie!

LEONIE. It would be the best investment I've ever made. Paula's always telling me I have no social consciousness. Well, this would be.—It would keep me from feeling so useless. I do feel useless, Kenneth. Please!

KENNETH. I'm sorry. I couldn't hear of it. Of course, it's out of the question.

LEONIE. It isn't. I can afford it. Why shouldn't I? It would be helping so many people—you have no right to refuse. It's selfish of you to refuse.

KENNETH. I distrust impulsive altruism. You will forgive me, Leonie, but it may often do harm.

LEONIE. How do you mean, Kenneth?

KENNETH. I gather you are about to endow a radical magazine for the *boys*—

LEONIE. Will and Dennis! I thought it would be nice to give them something to do!

KENNETH. Yes. You are prepared to back them in a publication which, if it attained any influence, would undermine the system which makes you and your people like you possible.

LEONIE. But it never occurred to me anyone would read it.

KENNETH. There is a deplorably high literacy in this country. Unfortunately it is much easier to learn to read than it is to learn to think.

LEONIE. Well, if you don't think it's a good idea, Kenneth, I won't do it. But this sanatorium is different.

KENNETH. Why?

LEONIE. Because, if you must know it, it would be helping you—and that means everything in the world to me. There, I've said it. It's true! Kenneth —are you terrified?

KENNETH. You adorable child!

LEONIE. It's extraordinary, Kenneth—but you are the first strong man who's ever come into my life— [*Enter* PAULA, DENNIS, WILL, *door back.*] Oh, I'm very glad to see you! Will! Hullo, Dennis. You all know Dr. Rice. Mr. Dexter, Mr. McCarthy. Sit down, everybody. Well, children, how is New York?

[DENNIS *crosses down front of them to chair left by sofa and sits.*]

WILL. Stifling, thank you.

LEONIE. Any luck yet?

WILL. I am available, but New York is dead to its chief opportunity.

LEONIE. Then you can stay here for a bit. You can both stay here.

DENNIS. That was all right when we were in college, Mrs. Frothingham. Can't do it now.

LEONIE. Oh, you're working. I'm so glad!

DENNIS. I beg your pardon. Did you say working?

LEONIE. Well, then! I don't see why you can't stay here and take a holiday.

WILL. From what?

LEONIE. Since none of you are doing anything in town, you might as well stay here and do nothing and be comfortable.

DENNIS. Yes, but it's an ethical question. When we're in New York doing nothing, we belong to the most respectable vested group going! The unemployed. As such we have a status, position, authority. But if we stay here doing nothing—what are we? Low-down parasites.

KENNETH. No jobs about anywhere, eh?

WILL. Extinct commodity.

DENNIS. I did pretty well last week.

LEONIE. Really?

DENNIS. I was rejected by seven newspapers—including the *Bronx Home News* and the *Yonkers Herald*—six magazines and trade papers—a total of twenty-eight rejections in all, representing a net gain over the previous week of seven solid rejections. I submit to you, gentlemen, that's progress—pass the cigars, Will.

LEONIE. Couldn't you stay here and be rejected by mail?

DENNIS. Doesn't give you that same feeling somehow—that good, rich, dark-brown sensation of not being wanted!

LEONIE. You know, Kenneth, in a curious way, Dennis reminds me a bit of Mr. X.

DENNIS. And who's X.?

LEONIE. A sporting acquaintance.

DENNIS. There's one thing I'd like to ask Dr. Rice. . . . Do you mind?

KENNETH. At your service.

DENNIS [*turning chair and facing* KENNETH *upstage*]. In the psychoanalytic hierarchy Freud is the god, isn't he?

KENNETH. Of one sect, yes.

DENNIS. Well, the original sect—

KENNETH. Yes . . .

DENNIS. Now, every psychoanalyst has to have himself analyzed. That's true, isn't it, Doctor?

KENNETH. Generally speaking—yes.

DENNIS. As I understand it, the highest prices go to those nearest the Master himself.

KENNETH. This boy is irreverent . . .

DENNIS. I know whereof I speak. I prepared an article on the subject for *Fortune*.

WILL. Rejection number three hundred.

DENNIS. I am afraid, Will, that you are a success worshipper!

LEONIE. Dennis is an *enfant terrible,* and he exhausts himself keeping it up!

DENNIS. I have examined the racket with a microscopic patience and this I find to be true: at the top of the hierarchy is the Great Pan-Sexualist of Vienna. To be an orthodox and accepted Freudian, you must have been analyzed by another of the same. Now what I am burning to know is this: Who analyzed Sig Freud himself? Whom does he tell his repressions to? Why, the poor guy must be lonely as hell!

LEONIE. What would you do with him, Kenneth? He has no repressions whatever!

KENNETH. He needs some badly.

LEONIE. I wonder what Dennis would confess to his psychoanalyst that he isn't always shouting to the world?

DENNIS. I'd make the psychoanalyst talk. [*To* KENNETH. *Beckoning.*] Tell me, Doctor, what did you dream last night?

KENNETH [*behind his cupped hand*]. Not in public.

DENNIS [*rises and crosses straight right*]. You see—he's repressed! I tell you these psychoanalysts are repressed. They've got nobody to talk to! I'm going swimming. It's pathetic! [*He goes out.*]

LEONIE. I'm going too. He makes me laugh. How about you, Kenneth?

KENNETH. Oh, I'll watch.

LEONIE [*to others*]. Come along with us. There's plenty of time for a swim before dinner.

[KENNETH *starts out with* LEONIE, *stops on the way.*]

KENNETH. I suppose you and your Irish friend edited the comic paper at college?

WILL. No, we edited the serious paper.

KENNETH. Just the same it must have been very funny. [*He goes out after* LEONIE.]

WILL. Don't think that feller likes me much.

PAULA. You're psychic.

WILL. Well, for the matter of that I'm not crazy about him either.

PAULA. Don't bother about him. Concentrate on me!

WILL. How are you, darling?

PAULA. Missed you.

WILL [*pulls her to sofa and sits with her.* PAULA *left end sofa*]. And I you. Pretty lousy in town without you.

PAULA. Oh, poor darling!

WILL. Although my star is rising. I did some book-reviews for *The New York Times* and the *New Masses.*

PAULA. What a gamut!

WILL. I made, in fact, a total of eleven dollars. The student most likely to succeed in the first four months since graduation has made eleven dollars.

PAULA. Wonderful!

WILL. My classmates were certainly clairvoyant. As a matter of fact, I shouldn't have told you. Now I'll be tortured thinking you're after me for my money.

PAULA. You'll never know!

WILL [*putting arm around her shoulders and drawing her to him*]. What've you been doing?

PAULA. Lying in the sun mostly.

WILL. Poor little Ritz girl.

PAULA. Wondering what you do every night.

WILL. Forty-second Street Library mostly. Great fun! Voluptuary atmosphere!

PAULA. Is your life altogether so austere?

WILL. Well, frankly, no. Not altogether.

PAULA. Cad!

WILL. What do you expect?

PAULA. Loyalty.

WILL. I am loyal. But you go around all day job-hunting. You find you're not wanted. It's reassuring after that to find a shoulder to lean on, sort of haven where you *are* wanted. Even the public library closes at ten. You have to go somewhere. If I'm ever Mayor of New York, I'll have the public libraries kept open all night . . . the flop-houses of the intellectuals!

PAULA. Is it anyone special . . . ?

WILL. Just a generalized shoulder.

PAULA. Well, you're going to have a special one from now on—mine! You know, the way you're avoiding the issue is all nonsense.

WILL. You mean my gallant fight against you?

PAULA. I've decided that you are conventional and bourgeois. You're money-ridden.

WILL. Eleven dollars. They say a big income makes you conservative.

PAULA. I don't mean your money. I mean—my money. It's childish to let an artificial barrier like that stand between us. It's also childish to ignore it.

WILL [*rising*]. I don't ignore it. That's what worries me. I count on it. Already I find myself counting on it. I can't help it. Sitting and waiting in an office for some bigwig who won't see me or for some underling who won't see me I think: "Why the hell should I wait all day for this stuffed shirt?" I don't wait. Is it because of you I feel in a special category? Do I count on your money? Is that why I don't wait as long as the other fellow? There's one consolation: the other fellow doesn't get the job either. But the point is disquieting!

PAULA. What a Puritan you are!

WILL [*sitting beside her again*]. Will I become an appendage to you—like your mother's men?

PAULA. You're bound to—money or no money.

WILL [*taking her into his arms*]. I suppose I might as well go on the larger dole—

PAULA. What?

WILL. Once you are paid merely for existing—you are on the dole. I rather hoped, you know—

PAULA. What?

WILL. It's extraordinary the difference in one's thinking when you're in college and when you're out—

PAULA. How do you mean?

WILL. Well, when I was in college, my interest in the— "movement"—was really impersonal. I imagined myself giving my energies to the poor and the downtrodden in my spare time. I didn't really believe I'd be one of the poor and down-trodden myself. In my heart of hearts, I was sure I'd break through the iron law of Dennis's statistics and land a job somewhere. But I can't—and it's given a tremendous jolt to my self-esteem.

PAULA. But you'll come through. I'm sure of it. I wish you could learn to look at my money as a means rather than an end.

WILL. I'd rather use my own.

PAULA. You're proud.

WILL. I am.

PAULA. It's humiliating but I'm afraid I've got to ask you to marry me, Will.

WILL. It's humiliating but considering my feelings I see no way out of accepting you.

PAULA. You submit?

WILL [*kissing her hand*]. I submit.

PAULA. After a hard campaign—victory!

WILL. You *are* a darling.

PAULA [*getting up and crossing to center*]. I can't tell you what a relief it'll be to get away from this house.

WILL. Why?

PAULA. I don't know. It's getting very complicated.

WILL. Leonie?

PAULA. *And* Boris. *And* Dr. Rice. Funny thing how that man . . .

WILL. What?

PAULA. Makes you insecure somehow.

WILL. Supposed to do just the opposite.

PAULA. He answers every question—and yet he's secretive. I've never met a man who—who—

WILL. Who what?

PAULA. Really, I can't stand Dr. Rice.

WILL. I believe he fascinates you.

PAULA. He does. I don't deny that. And I can't tell

you how I resent it. Isn't it silly? [*The old lady* WYLER *in a wheel chair is propelled in by a nurse. The old lady is much wasted since the preceding summer; she is touched with mortality.*] Granny!

MRS. WYLER. Paula! How are you, my dear?

PAULA. I came up to see you before, but you were asleep.

MRS. WYLER. Nurse told me.

[*Exit* NURSE, *door left.*]

PAULA. You remember Will?

WILL. How do you do, Mrs. Wyler?

MRS. WYLER. Of course. How do you do, young man?

PAULA. Well, this is quite an adventure for you, isn't it, Granny?

MRS. WYLER. You're the boy who was always so curious about my youth.

WILL. Yes.

MRS. WYLER. I've forgotten most of it. Now I just live from day to day. The past is just this morning. [*A moment's pause.*] And I don't always remember that very well. Aren't there insects who live only one day? The morning is their youth and the afternoon their middle age. . . .

PAULA. You don't seem yourself today. Not as cheerful as usual.

MRS. WYLER. Can't I have my moods, Paula? I am pleased to be reflective today. People are always sending me funny books to read. I've been reading one and it depressed me.

PAULA. Well, I'll tell you something to cheer you up, Granny— Will and I are going to be married.

MRS. WYLER. Have you told your mother?

PAULA. Not yet. It's a secret.

[*Enter* KENNETH.]

KENNETH. Well, Mrs. Wyler! Wanderlust today?

MRS. WYLER. Yes! Wanderlust!

KENNETH. Paula, if you're not swimming, what about our walk, and our daily argument?

MRS. WYLER. What argument?

KENNETH. Paula is interested in my subject. She hovers between skepticism and fascination.

PAULA. No chance to hover today, Kenneth. Will's improving his tennis. Sorry.

KENNETH. So am I.

MRS. WYLER. I've a surprise for you, Paula.

PAULA. What?

MRS. WYLER. Your father's coming.

PAULA. No!

MRS. WYLER. Yes.

PAULA. But how—! How do you know?

MRS. WYLER. Because I've sent for him, and he wired me he's coming. He's driving from Blue Hill. He should be here now.

PAULA. That's too—! Oh, Granny, that's marvelous! Will, let's drive out to meet him, shall we? Does Mother know?

MRS. WYLER. I only had Sam's wire an hour ago.

PAULA. Granny, you're an angel.

MRS. WYLER. Not quite yet. Don't hurry me, child.

PAULA. Come on, Will. [*Exit* PAULA *and* WILL.]

MRS. WYLER. I can see you are interested in Paula. You are, aren't you, Dr. Rice?

KENNETH. Yes. She's an extraordinary child. Adores her father, doesn't she?

MRS. WYLER. How would you cure that, Doctor?

KENNETH. It's quite healthy.

MRS. WYLER. Really? I was hoping for something juicy in the way of interpretation.

KENNETH. Sorry!

MRS. WYLER. What an interesting profession yours is, Dr. Rice.

KENNETH. Why particularly?

MRS. WYLER. Your province is the soul. Strange region.

KENNETH. People's souls, I find are, on the whole, infinitely more interesting than their bodies. I have been a general practitioner and I know.

MRS. WYLER. These young people—don't they frighten you?

KENNETH. Frighten!

MRS. WYLER. They are so radical—prepared to throw everything overboard—every tradition—

KENNETH. Paula's friends have nothing to lose, any change would be—in the nature of velvet for them.

MRS. WYLER. What do you think of Will?

KENNETH. I'm afraid I've formed no strongly defined opinion on Will.

MRS. WYLER. Oh, I see— That is a comment in itself.

KENNETH. He's nondescript.

MRS. WYLER. Do you mean to point that out to Paula?

KENNETH. I don't think so. That won't be necessary.

MRS. WYLER. Why not?

KENNETH. Blood will tell.

MRS. WYLER. That's very gracious of you, Doctor. [*Pause.*] And what do you think of Leonie?

KENNETH. Very endearing—and very impulsive.

MRS. WYLER. For example—I mean of the latter—

KENNETH. She offered to build me a sanatorium—a fully equipped modern sanatorium.

MRS. WYLER. Did she? Convenient for you.

KENNETH. Except that I refused.

MRS. WYLER. Wasn't that quixotic?

KENNETH. Not necessarily.

[PAULA *and* SAM *enter, door back.*]

PAULA. Here he is!

MRS. WYLER. Sam!

SAM. Louise!

PAULA. He wouldn't come if I'd ask him. He said so shamelessly. You know Dr. Rice?

SAM. Of course.

KENNETH. Excuse me. [KENNETH *goes out.*]

SAM. Well, Louise!

MRS. WYLER. Hello, Sam.

[SAM *kisses her.*]

SAM. How's she behaving?

PAULA. Incorrigible. Dr. Prentiss tells her to rest in her room. You see how she obeys him. She'll obey you though.

SAM. Well, I'll sneak her away from Dr. Prentiss and take her abroad.

MRS. WYLER. I want to go to Ethiopia. Run along, dear. I want to talk to Sam.

PAULA. Keep him here, Granny. Pretend you're not feeling well.

MRS. WYLER. I'll try. [*Exit* PAULA *door back.*] Well, Sam—

SAM. I got your wire last night. Here I am.

MRS. WYLER. It's nice of you.

SAM. Oh, now, Louise. You know you're the love of my life.

MRS. WYLER. Yes, Sam, I know—but how is Selena?

SAM. Flourishing.

MRS. WYLER. You're all right then?

SAM. Unbelievably.

MRS. WYLER. I knew you would be.

SAM. And you?

MRS. WYLER. I'm dying, Sam.

SAM. Not you—

MRS. WYLER. Don't contradict me. Besides, I'm rather looking forward to it.

SAM. Is Dr. Prentiss—?

MRS. WYLER. Dr. Prentiss soft-soaps me. I let him. It relieves his mind. But that's why I've sent for you.

SAM. You know, my dear—

MRS. WYLER. Yes, Sam. I know I can count on you. I'm

dying. And I'm dying alone. I have to talk to somebody. You're the only one.

SAM. Is anything worrying you?

MRS. WYLER. Plenty.

SAM. What, dear?

MRS. WYLER. The future. Not my own. That's fixed or soon will be. But Leonie's—Paula's—

SAM. Aren't they all right?

MRS. WYLER. I am surrounded by aliens. The house is full of strangers. That Russian upstairs; this doctor.

SAM. Rice? Are you worried about him?

MRS. WYLER. What is he after? What does he want? He told me Leonie offered to build him a sanatorium—

SAM. Did he accept it?

MRS. WYLER. No. He refused. But something tells me he will allow himself to be persuaded.

SAM. I don't think Rice is a bad feller really. Seems pretty sensible. Are you worried about this boy—Dexter, and Paula?

MRS. WYLER. Not in the same way. I like the boy. But Paula—I'm worried about what the money'll do to her. We know what it's done to Leonie. You know, Sam, in spite of all her romantic dreams Leonie has a kind of integrity. But I often wonder if she's ever been really happy.

SAM. Oh, now, Louise, this pessimism's unlike you—

MRS. WYLER. This money we've built our lives on—it used to symbolize security—but there's no security in it any more.

SAM. Paula'll be all right. I count on Paula.

MRS. WYLER. In the long run. But that may be too late. One can't let go of everything, Sam. It isn't in nature. That's why I've asked you to come. I want you to remain as executor under my will.

SAM. Well, I only resigned because—since I'm no longer married to Leonie—

MRS. WYLER. What has that got to do with it?

SAM. All right.

MRS. WYLER. Promise?

SAM. Certainly.

MRS. WYLER. I feel something dark ahead, a terror—

SAM. Now, now, you've been brooding.

MRS. WYLER. Outside of you—Will is the soundest person I'll leave behind me, the healthiest—but in him too I feel a recklessness that's just kept in—I see a vista of the unknown—to us the unknown was the West, land—physical hardship—but he's hard and bitter underneath his jocularity—he isn't sure, he says, what he is— Once he is sure, what will he do?—I want you to watch him, Sam, for Paula's sake.

SAM. I will.

MRS. WYLER. They're all strange and dark. . . . And this doctor. A soul doctor. We didn't have such things—I am sure that behind all this is a profound and healing truth. But sometimes truths may be perverted, and this particular doctor—how are we to know where his knowledge ends and his pretension begins? Now that I am dying, for the first time in my life I know fear. Death seems easy and simple, Sam—a self-indulgence—but can I afford it? [*She smiles up at him. He squeezes her hand.*]

SAM. Everything will be all right. Trust me.

MRS. WYLER. I do. [*A pause.*] You'll stay the night?

SAM. Of course.

MRS. WYLER. Now I feel better.

SAM. That's right. [*Pause.*]

MRS. WYLER. I'd like to live till autumn.

SAM. Of course you will. Many autumns.

MRS. WYLER. Heaven forbid. But this autumn. The color—the leaves turn. [*Looking out window.* SAM *looks too.*] The expression seems strange. What do they turn to?

SAM [*softly, helping her mood*]. Their mother. The earth.

MRS. WYLER. I'm happy now. I'm at peace.

SAM [*puts arm around her and draws her to him*]. That's better.

MRS. WYLER [*smiling up at him*]. It's very clever of me to have sent for you, Sam. I'm pleased with myself. Now, Sam, let 'em do their worst—

SAM [*smiling back at her and patting her hands*]. Just let 'em . . . !

CURTAIN

SCENE II

SCENE. *The same.*

TIME. *A few hours later—before dinner.* LEONIE *is standing in doorway looking out.* BORIS *center; he is fatalistically quiet at first.*

BORIS. What it comes to is this then! You're through with me. You want me to go!

LEONIE. I'm no good to you! I can no longer help you.

BORIS. Frustrated altruist!

LEONIE. You hate me!

BORIS. That would be encouraging!

LEONIE. We have nothing more for each other.

BORIS. Less than we had in the beginning!

LEONIE. Less than I thought we had.

BORIS [*walking toward her*]. And the man of science?

LEONIE. What?

BORIS [*still bearing down on her*]. This intricate man of science. You fluctuate so, Leonie. [*Facing her.*]

LEONIE. Please, Boris. I've failed. Can't we part—beautifully?

BORIS. What do you want to do? Go out on the bay and say farewell before the villagers in a barge drawn by a flock of swans? Shall we have a little orchestra to play—with the strings sobbing—and the bassoon off key?

LEONIE. You are bitter and cruel. Why? I've tried to help you. Why are you bitter?

BORIS [*moving close to her*]. At least I'm honest. Can you say the same?

LEONIE [*breaking away from him*]. I don't know what you mean by that.

BORIS [*getting in front of her*]. Yes, you do.

LEONIE. You're eating yourself up. You're killing yourself. There's the great lovely world outside and you sit in your room hating—

BORIS. What do you recommend? Cold showers and Swedish massage? What does the man of science prescribe for me?

LEONIE. Why do you hate Kenneth so?

BORIS. I'm jealous, my dear!

LEONIE. Poor Boris. You're beyond a simple emotion like that, aren't you?

BORIS. I envy you, Leonie. All like you.

LEONIE. Do you?

BORIS. I envy all sentimental liars who gratify their desires on high principle. It makes all your diversions an exercise in piety. You're sick of me and want to sleep with the man of science. [LEONIE *turns away. He seizes her arms and turns her to him.*] Does this suffice for you? No. It must be that you can no longer help me. [*Little silent laugh.*] My sainted father was like that! God!

LEONIE. This is the end, Boris.

BORIS. Of course it is. I tell you this though: Beware of him, Leonie. Beware of him.

LEONIE. Your hatred of Kenneth—like all your hatreds

—they're unnatural, frightening. I'm frightened of you. [*Turning from him.*]

BORIS [*crossing before her, closing door so she can't escape*]. Much better to be frightened of him. You know what I think. What does he think? Does he tell you? Do you know?

LEONIE. Yes, I know.

BORIS. You know what he tells you. This clairvoyant who gets rich profoundly analyzing the transparent.

[*Enter* KENNETH, *door back.*]

KENNETH. Your mother would like to see you, Leonie.

LEONIE. Is she all right?

[BORIS *goes upstage to small table. Gets cigarette.*]

KENNETH. Oh, very chipper, Mr. Frothingham is with her.

LEONIE. She sent for Sam, didn't she? I wonder why.

BORIS. Perhaps she felt the situation too complicated —even for *you*, Dr. Rice.

KENNETH. I don't think so.

BORIS. You are so Olympian, Dr. Rice. Would it be possible to anger you?

KENNETH. Symptoms, my dear Count, never anger me. I study them.

BORIS. Really, you are in a superb position. I quite envy you. One might cut oneself open in front of you—and it would be a symptom. Wouldn't it?

LEONIE. Boris, please—what's the good?

BORIS [*crossing slowly to* LEONIE]. You are quite right, my dear, no good—no good in the world. Give your mother this message for me. Tell her that under the circumstances I shall simplify the situation by withdrawing.

LEONIE. You make me very unhappy, Boris.

BORIS. How agreeable then that you have Dr. Rice here —to resolve your unhappiness. [*Crosses quickly to table behind sofa and puts out cigarette.*]

LEONIE [*following him*]. Where will you be in case I— in case you—Boris?

BORIS. Don't worry about me. A magazine syndicate has offered me a great deal for *sentimental* reminiscences of my father. Imagine that, sentimental! They have offered me—charming Americanism—a ghost-writer. It will be quaint—one ghost collaborating with another ghost. [*Raising hand like Greek priest.*] My blessings, Leonie. [*Kisses her hand.*] You have been charming. Dr. Rice— [*He bows formally. Exit* BORIS.]

LEONIE. Poor Boris— [*She sinks into a chair, overcome.*]

KENNETH. He's part of the past. You must forget him.

LEONIE. Poor Boris!

KENNETH. You will forget him.

LEONIE. I'll try.

KENNETH. Exorcised!

LEONIE. You know, Kenneth, I feel you are the only one in the world I can count on.

KENNETH. Not me.

LEONIE. Whom else?

KENNETH. Yourself!

LEONIE. Light reed! Fragile! Fragile!

KENNETH. Pliant but unbreakable.

LEONIE. No. Don't think much of myself, Kenneth. Really I don't. My judgment seems to be at fault somehow. Paula thinks so too. She's always lecturing me. [*Sits right end of sofa.*]

KENNETH. Paula can't abide me.

LEONIE. It's not true!

KENNETH. You know, Leonie, I have an instinct in these matters—so, also, has your daughter.

LEONIE. Don't you like Paula?

KENNETH. I love her. Everyone connected with you.

LEONIE. Kenneth! How dear of you! Of course Paula and I are poles apart. Look at her friends!

KENNETH. Raffish!

LEONIE [*a little taken aback by this*]. Oh, do you think so? All of them? Don't you like Will?

KENNETH. Nice enough. Clever in his way. With an eye to the main chance.

LEONIE. Really?

KENNETH. Naturally—penniless boy.

LEONIE. I've always encouraged Paula to be independent. I've never tried to impose my ideals or my standards on her. Have I done wrong to give her her own head this way? She's such a darling, really. She's killing, you know. So superior, so knowing. The other day—the other day, Kenneth . . . I took her to lunch in town and she criticized me—now what do you think about?

KENNETH [*sitting on arm of chair*]. For once my intuition fails me.

LEONIE. About my technique with men. She said it was lousy. Isn't it delicious?

KENNETH. Not more specific than simply lousy?

LEONIE. She said I threw myself at men instead of reversing the process.

KENNETH. But I should think she would have approved of that. She makes such a fetish of being candid!

LEONIE. That's just what I said—exactly. I said I couldn't pretend—that I couldn't descend to—technique. I said that when my feelings were involved I saw no point in not letting the other person see it. I reproached her for deviousness. Strange ideas that child has—strange!

KENNETH. I'm afraid her generation is theory-ridden! [*Pause.*]

LEONIE. Kenneth?

KENNETH. Yes, Leonie?

LEONIE. It's true of course.

KENNETH. What?

LEONIE. Paula's—criticism. I can't conceal my feelings, Least of all—from you. [*Slight pause.*]

KENNETH. Why should you?

LEONIE. Oh, Kenneth, I'm so useless! You know how useless I am!

KENNETH. I know only that you are gracious and lovely —and that you have the gift of innocence.

LEONIE. I hate my life. It's been so scattered—emotionally.

KENNETH. Whose isn't?

LEONIE. You are such a comfort. Really it's too much now to expect me to do without you. Kenneth?

KENNETH. Yes . . . Leonie.

LEONIE. Will you be a darling—and marry me?

KENNETH. Leonie?

LEONIE [*returning his gaze*]. Yes, Kenneth.

KENNETH. Have you thought this over?

LEONIE. It's the first time—the very first time—that I've ever been sure.

KENNETH. You are so impulsive, Leonie.

LEONIE. Kenneth, don't you think we'd have a chance —you and I—don't you think?

[*Enter* PAULA, *door back.*]

PAULA [*realizes she has interrupted a tête-à-tête*]. Oh, sorry—!

LEONIE. Paula dear, have you been with Mother?

PAULA. Yes. Granny wants to see you, as a matter of fact.

LEONIE. Oh, I forgot! Is she all right? Cheerful?

PAULA. Oh, very.

LEONIE. I'll be right there. Stay and talk to Kenneth, Paula. He thinks you don't like him. Prove to him it isn't true. Do you think you could be gracious, Paula? Or is that too old-fashioned? [*Exit* LEONIE *door back.*]

[*In the following scene* PAULA *determines to get rid of*

*the tantalizing and irritating mixed feelings she has
about* KENNETH, *her sense of distrusting, disliking
and simultaneously being fascinated by him—she
feels he has something up his sleeve; she is playing a
game to discover what it is and yet she becomes increasingly conscious that game is not unpleasant to
her because of her interest in her victim.*]

PAULA. Leonie's all a-flutter. What is it?

KENNETH. She was just telling me—she envies you your
poise.

PAULA. Your intentions are honorable, I hope.

KENNETH. Old hat, Paula.

PAULA. I beg your pardon.

KENNETH. Undergraduate audacity. Scott Fitzgerald.
Old hat.

PAULA. We don't like each other much, do we?

KENNETH. That's regrettable.

PAULA. And yet—I'm very curious about you.

KENNETH. What would you like to know?

PAULA. Your motive.

KENNETH. Ah!

PAULA. And yet even if you told me—

KENNETH. You wouldn't believe it?

PAULA [*facing him*]. No. Now why is that? Even when
you are perfectly frank, your frankness seems to me
—a device. Now why is that?

KENNETH. I'll tell you.

PAULA. Why?

KENNETH. Because you yourself are confused, muddled,
unsure, contradictory. I am simple and co-ordinated.
You resent that. You dislike it. You envy it You
would like such simplicity for yourself. But, as you
are unlikely to achieve it, you soothe yourself by
distrusting me.

PAULA. You say I'm muddled. Why am I muddled?

KENNETH. You've accepted a set of premises without

examining them or thinking about them. You keep
them like jewels in a box and dangle them. Then
you put them back in the box, confident that they
belong to you. But as they don't you feel an occasional twinge of insecurity—

PAULA. Do you mind dropping the parables—?

KENNETH. Not at all—

PAULA. Why am I muddled? For example—

KENNETH. You're a walking contradiction in terms—

PAULA. For example?

KENNETH. For example—for example—your radicalism.
Your friends. Your point of view. Borrowed. Unex-
amined. Insincere.

PAULA. Go on.

KENNETH. You are rich and you are exquisite. Why are
you rich and exquisite? [*Walking back to face her.*]
Because your forebears were not moralistic but ruthless. Had they been moralistic, had they been concerned, as you pretend to be, with the "predatory
system"—this awful terminology—you'd be working
in a store somewhere wrapping packages or waiting
on querulous housewives with bad skins or teaching
school. Your own origins won't bear a moralistic investigation. You must know that. Your sociology
and economics must teach you that.

PAULA. Suppose I repudiate my origins?

KENNETH. That takes more courage than you have.

PAULA. Don't be so sure.

KENNETH. But why should you? If you had a special
talent or were a crusader there might be some sense
in it. But you have no special talent and you are
not a crusader. Much better to be decorative. Much
better for a world starving for beauty. Instead of
repudiating your origins you should exult in them
and in that same predatory system that made you

possible. [*Crossing to table behind sofa for cigarette.*]

[*Pause.*]

PAULA. What were your origins?

KENNETH [*lighting cigarette*]. Anonymous.

PAULA. What do you mean?

KENNETH. I was discovered on a doorstep.

PAULA. Really?

KENNETH. Like Moses.

PAULA. Where were you brought up?

KENNETH. In a foundling asylum in New England. The place lacked charm. This sounds like an unpromising beginning but actually it was more stimulating than you might imagine. I remember as a kid of twelve going to the library at Springfield and getting down the *Dictionary of National Biography* and hunting out the bastards. Surprising how many distinguished ones there were and are. I allied myself early with the brilliant and variegated company of the illegitimate.

PAULA. You don't know who your parents were?

KENNETH. No.

PAULA. Did you get yourself through college?

KENNETH. *And* medical school.

PAULA. Did you practice medicine?

KENNETH. For a bit. I devoted myself—when the victims would let me—to their noses and throats. It was a starveling occupation. But I gave up tonsillectomy for the soul. The poor have tonsils but only the rich have souls. My instinct was justified—as you see.

PAULA. You've gone pretty far.

KENNETH. Incredible journey!

PAULA. Having come from—from—

KENNETH. The mud—?

PAULA. Well—I should think you'd be more sympathetic to the under-dogs.

KENNETH. No, why should I? The herd bores me. It interests me only as an indication of the distance I've traveled.

PAULA. Will would say that you are a lucky individual who—

KENNETH. Yes, that is what Will would say. It always satisfies the mediocrity to call the exceptional individual lucky.

PAULA. You don't like Will?

KENNETH. I despise him.

PAULA. Why?

KENNETH. I detest these young firebrands whose incandescence will be extinguished by the first job! I detest radicals who lounge about in country-houses.

PAULA. You're unfair to Will.

KENNETH. I have no interest in being fair to him. We were discussing you.

PAULA. You are too persuasive. I don't believe you.

KENNETH. My advice to you is to find out what you want before you commit yourself to young Mr. Dexter.

PAULA. But I have committed myself.

KENNETH. Too bad.

PAULA. For him or for me?

KENNETH. For both of you; but for him particularly.

PAULA. Why?

KENNETH. I see precisely the effect your money will have on him. He will take it and the feeling will grow in him that in having given it you have destroyed what he calls his integrity. He will even come to believe that if not for this quenching of initiative he might have become a flaming leader of the people. At the same time he will be aware that both these comforting alibis are delusions—because he has no integrity to speak of nor any initiative to speak of. Knowing they are lies he will only proclaim them the louder, cling to them the harder. He will hate you as the thief of his character—petty larceny, I must say.

PAULA [*jumping up, taking several steps away from him*]. That's a lie.

KENNETH. Will is an American Puritan. A foreigner— Boris, for example—marries money, feeling that he gives value received. Very often he does. But young Dexter will never feel that—and maybe he'll be right.

PAULA. You hate Will.

KENNETH. You flatter him.

PAULA. How did you get to know so much about people? About what they feel and what they will do?

KENNETH. I began by knowing myself—but not lying to myself. [*A silence. He looks at her. He takes in her loveliness. He speaks her name, in a new voice, softly.*] Paula—

PAULA [*she looks at him fixedly*]. What?

KENNETH. Paula—

PAULA. What?

KENNETH. Do you know me any better now? Do you trust me any better now?

PAULA. I don't know.

[*Enter* WILL.]

KENNETH. Paula, Paula, Paula— [PAULA *starts toward door back.*] Don't go, Paula!

WILL. Oughtn't you to be changing for dinner? [PAULA *stops upstage.*] Hello, Doctor. What's the matter?

KENNETH. May I congratulate him?

WILL. What's he been saying?

KENNETH. Paula told me she is going to marry you.

PAULA. The doctor is a cynic.

KENNETH. We were discussing the European and American points of view toward money marriages— There's a great difference. The European fortune hunter, once he has landed the bag, has no more twinge of conscience than a big-game hunter when he has made his kill. The American—

WILL. Is that what you think I am, Doctor?

KENNETH [to PAULA amiably]. You see. He resents the mere phrase. But, my dear boy, that is no disgrace. We are all fortune hunters—

PAULA [pointedly]. Not all, Kenneth—!

KENNETH. But I see no difference at all between the man who makes a profession of being charming to rich ladies—or any other—specialist. The former is more arduous.

PAULA. Are you defending Will or yourself?

KENNETH. I am generalizing. [To WILL.] Congratulations! I admit that to scatter congratulations in this way is glib, but we live in a convention of glibness. Good God, we congratulate people when they marry and when they produce children—we skim lightly over these tremendous hazards— Excuse me. [Exit KENNETH.]

WILL. God damn that man!

PAULA. Will!

WILL. I can't stand him—not from the moment I saw him—because he's incapable of disinterestedness himself, he can't imagine it in others. He's the kind of cynical, sneering— He's a marauder. The adventurer with the cure-all. This is just the moment for him. And this is just the place!

PAULA. I've never seen you lose your temper before, Will.

WILL. You know why, don't you?

PAULA. Why?

WILL. Because he's right! While he was talking I felt like hitting him. At the same time a voice inside me said: Can you deny it? When I came in here he was saying your name. He was looking at you—it seems he hasn't quite decided, has he?

PAULA. I'm worried about him and Leonie—

WILL. He's got Leonie hook, line and sinker. That's obvious.

PAULA. She mustn't! Will, she mustn't!

WILL. You can't stop it—you can't do anything for Leonie. Nobody can do anything for anybody. Nobody should try.

PAULA. Will—you mustn't go back to New York. You must stay and help me.

WILL. Sorry. Nothing doing.

PAULA. Will!

WILL. I have a feeling you'll rather enjoy saving Leonie from the doctor.

PAULA. Will! That's not fair, Will!

WILL. It may not be fair but it is obvious. Also, it is obvious that the doctor won't mind being saved.

PAULA. It's lucky for both of us that one of us has some self-control.

WILL. No, I won't stay here. I hate the place, I hate Dr. Rice, I hate myself for being here!

PAULA. Don't let me down, Will—I need you terribly just now—

WILL [at white heat]. I haven't quite the technique of fortune hunting yet—in the European manner. Which of the two is he after—you or Leonie? Will he flip a coin?

PAULA. I hate you! I hate you!

WILL. Well, we know where we are at any rate.

PAULA. Yes. We do!

[LEONIE *comes running in. She wears an exquisite summer evening frock. She is breathless with happiness.*]

LEONIE. Paula! Why aren't you dressed? I want you to wear something especially lovely tonight! Do you like this? It's new. I haven't worn it before. [*She twirls for them.*] I've a surprise for you, Will. You'll know what it is in a minute. I was thinking of you and it popped into my mind. You know, Will, I'm very, very fond of you. And I think you are equally fond of me. I can't help liking people who like me. I suppose you think I'm horribly vain. But then, everybody's vain about something. [BUTLER *comes in with cocktails and sandwiches, to table right of fireplace.*] If they're not, they're vain about their lack of vanity. I believe that's a mot! Pretty good for a brainless— Here, Will, have a cocktail— [WILL *takes cocktail.*] Paula—what's your pet vanity? She thinks mine's my looks but it's not. If I had my way I shouldn't look at all the way I look.

[*Enter* DR. DEXTER, *door back. He wears a sea-green baggy dinner-suit; he looks as "hicky" and uncertain as ever.*]

DEXTER. Good evening, Mrs. Frothingham.

LEONIE. Dr. Dexter—how good of you to come. Delighted to see you.

DEXTER. Good evening. Hello, Will.

WILL. Dad!

DEXTER. Mrs. Frothingham invited me. Didn't you know?

LEONIE [*takes* DEXTER's *arm and goes to* WILL]. You told me you had to leave tomorrow to visit your father in Brunswick so I just called him up in Brunswick—

DEXTER. She sent the car all the way for me. Nice car. Great springs.

LEONIE [*to* WILL]. Now you won't have to leave tomorrow. You can both spend the week-end here.

WILL [*walking away a little right*]. Awfully nice of you, Leonie.

LEONIE [*following him.* DEXTER *sits on sofa*]. You see, Will, I leave the big issues to the professional altru-

ists. I just do what I can toward making those
around me happy. And that's *my* vanity!

[*Enter* DENNIS, *door back.*]

DENNIS. Well! Well! Fancy that now, Hedda!

LEONIE. Oh, hello, Dennis, just in time for a cocktail.
[LEONIE *leads him over to sofa.* WILL *is isolated down
right center.*]

DENNIS [*to* DEXTER]. How are you?

DEXTER [*not friendly*]. I'm all right.

DENNIS. Complicated week-end! You and the Healer!
Faraday and Cagliostro. That'll be something.

LEONIE [*takes* DENNIS's *arm*]. Everybody tells me to like
you, Dennis. I'm in such a mood that I'm going to
make the effort.

DENNIS. I've been waiting for this. I'm thrilled!

LEONIE [*strolling with him across stage front*]. Something tells me you could be very charming if you
wanted to. Tell me, Dennis, have you ever tried
being lovable and sweet?

DENNIS. For you, Mrs. Frothingham, I would willingly
revive the age of chivalry!

LEONIE. But there's no need of that. I just want you to
be nice. Here, have a cocktail. Give you courage.

DENNIS. Just watch me from now on, Mrs. Frothingham.

LEONIE. I will. Passionately. [*Hands him cocktail.*] I'll
be doing nothing else.

[BUTLER *crosses back of sofa, offers* DEXTER *and* PAULA
cocktails. DR. RICE *comes in.*]

DENNIS [*stage sigh*]. A-h-h! The doctor! Just in time to
look at my tongue, Doctor.

KENNETH. That won't be necessary, young man. I can
tell— It's excessive.

LEONIE [*crossing to* KENNETH]. Kenneth—you remember
Will's father—Dr. Dexter.

KENNETH. How do you do?

[*They shake hands. A second* BUTLER *has come in and he and* ROBERT *are passing cocktails and hors d'oeuvres.* LEONIE *keeps circulating among her guests.* KENNETH *and* DEXTER *are in the center—*DENNIS, *obeying a malicious impulse, presides over them. Announces a theme on which he eggs them on to utter variations.*]

DENNIS. A significant moment, ladies and gentlemen— the magician of Science meets the magician of Sex— The floating libido bumps the absolute! What happens?

DEXTER [*cupping his hand to his ear*]. What?

[WILL *crosses to door and looks out moodily.*]

DENNIS. The absolute hasn't got a chance. Isn't that right, Dr. Rice?

KENNETH. I shouldn't venture to contradict a young intellectual. Especially a very young intellectual.

LEONIE [*crosses front of* KENNETH, *to* DENNIS]. There, you see, I'm afraid, after all, I'll have to give you up, Dennis. You can't be lovable. You can't be sweet.

DENNIS. But I didn't promise to be winsome to everybody, only to you.

LEONIE. You really must treat him, Kenneth. He has no censor at all.

DENNIS. My censor is the Catholic tradition. We Catholics anticipated both Marx and Freud by a little matter of nineteen centuries. Spiritually, we have a Communion in the Holy Ghost—Communion. As for Dr. Rice, he offers confession without absolution. He is inadequate.

[LEONIE *returns with tray of canapes.*]

LEONIE. It seems such bad taste to discuss religion at cocktail time. Try a stuffed olive.

DEXTER. By the time you get your beautiful new world, true science will have perished.

LEONIE. Aren't you too pessimistic, Dr. Dexter? Too

much science has made you gloomy. Kenneth, the
depression hasn't stopped your work, has it? Depression or no depression—

[WILL *springs up.*]

WILL [*tensely*]. That's right, Leonie. [*Everyone faces*
WILL.] Depression or no depression—war or peace—
revolution or reaction—Kenneth will reign supreme!

[KENNETH *stares at him.* WILL *confronts him.*]

LEONIE. Will!

WILL. Yes, Leonie. His is the power and the glory!

LEONIE. Dennis, this is your influence—

WILL. I admire you unreservedly, Doctor. Of your kind
you are the best. You are the essence.

KENNETH. You embarrass me.

WILL. Some men are born ahead of their time, some behind, but you are made pat for the instant. Now is
the time for you—when people are unemployed and
distrust their own capacities—when people suffer
and may be tempted—when integrity yields to despair—now is the moment for you!

KENNETH [*strolling closer to him so they are face to
face*]. When, may I ask, is the moment for you—
when if ever?

WILL. After your victory. When you are stuffed and
inert with everything you want, then will be the
time for me. [*He goes out.*]

PAULA [*running after* WILL]. Will . . . Will . . . Will . . .
[*She follows him out.*]

LEONIE [*devastated by this strange behavior*]. What is
it? I don't like it when people stand in the middle
of the floor and make speeches. What's the matter
with him? Dennis, do you know?

DENNIS [*with a look at* KENNETH]. I can guess.

LEONIE. Has he quarreled with Paula? Paula is so in-
ept. She doesn't know how to . . . At the same time,

if he had a grievance, why couldn't he have kept it until after dinner?

[*Enter* ROBERT.]

ROBERT. Dinner is served. [*Exit* ROBERT.]

LEONIE. Well, we'll do what we can. Sam is dining with Mother in her room, Boris has a headache. Dennis, you and Dr. Dexter—

DENNIS. You've picked me, Dr. Dexter. I congratulate you.

DEXTER. Thank God, I can't hear a word you say. [*Exit* DEXTER, *door back*.]

DENNIS [*sadistically*]. Oh, yes, he can. And we'll fight it out on these lines if it takes all dinner. [*He follows* DEXTER *out*.]

LEONIE. What extraordinary behavior! What do you suppose, Kenneth—shall I go after them?

KENNETH. I wouldn't. It's their problem. Give them time.

LEONIE [*reassured*]. You are so wise, Kenneth. How did I ever get on without you? I have that secure feeling that you are going to be my last indiscretion. When I think how neatly I've captured you—I feel quite proud. I guess my technique isn't so lousy after all. [*She takes his arm and swings along beside him as they waltz in to dinner.*]

CURTAIN

Act three

SCENE. *The same.*

TIME. *Late that fall. The trees have turned. The sumach have put out the brilliant red flowers of autumn.*

AT RISE. WILL *and* DENNIS *have just arrived, and are standing at fireplace, back.* LEONIE *comes in to greet them.* SAM *strolls in with her.*

LEONIE. I'm so glad to see you! [*She shakes hands with each of them warmly.*] Will! How are you? [*To* DENNIS.] It's so good of you to come.

SAM [*shaking hands with* WILL]. Very glad to see you.

WILL. Thanks.

[SAM *shakes hands with* DENNIS.]

LEONIE. Sam drove over for a few hours from Blue Hill to talk business to me. He hasn't had much luck so far. It's simply wonderful having you boys here—it's like old times. I didn't tell Paula. [*To* SAM.] I did all this on my own. It's a surprise for Paula.

DENNIS. She'll be overcome when she sees me. Maybe you should prepare her.

WILL. Where is Paula?

LEONIE. Isn't it provoking! She and Kenneth went for a walk. They should have been back long before this. [*Turning back to them.*] Paula hasn't been at all herself, Will. I thought you would cheer her up.

DENNIS. I will be very glad to do what I can, of course. Several very stubborn cases have yielded to my charm.

LEONIE. I'm sure! Do sit down. [*She sits.*]

DENNIS [*taking out his pipe*]. Do you mind?

[WILL *sits.*]

LEONIE. Oh, please—I can't tell you how I appreciate your coming—

DENNIS [*the harassed business man*]. Well, as a matter of fact, Leonie, it wasn't easy to get away from the office—

LEONIE. Are you in an office?

DENNIS. Sometimes as many as fifteen in a day. [LEONIE

laughs.] But when I got your appealing letter—*and*
the return tickets—I'm chivalrous at heart, you
know, Leonie—

LEONIE. I know you are!

SAM. How's town?

WILL. Very hot.

SAM. I'm just on my way down. Stopped by to go over
several things with Leonie—

LEONIE. Poor Sam's been having an awful time with
me. He keeps putting things in escrow. Where is
escrow?

DENNIS. It's where squirrels put nuts in the winter-
time.

LEONIE. I see! Dennis is much more lucid than you,
Sam.

DENNIS. I have a knack for making the abstruse trans-
lucent. Especially in economics. Now, would you
like to know why England went off gold?

LEONIE. No, I wouldn't.

DENNIS. I shall yield to your subconscious demand and
tell you.

LEONIE [*to others*]. Help!

DENNIS. I see that there is no audience for my peculiar
gift.

LEONIE. You know, Will, I've thought perhaps you
were angry with us.

WILL. Why?

LEONIE. You haven't been here for so long. [*To* SAM.]
Since Granny died—none of them have been here.
Did Paula write you about Granny's funeral?

WILL. No. She didn't.

LEONIE. Of course I hate funerals—I can't bear them—
but this was so—natural. Mother wanted to live till
the fall and she did. It was a dreaming blue sky and
there was that poignant haze over the hills and over
the bay, and the smell of burning wood from some-

where. Burning wood never smells at any other time the way it does in Indian summer. And the colors that day! Did you ever, Sam, see such a day?

SAM. It was beautiful.

LEONIE. They say the colors of autumn are the colors of death, but I don't believe that. They were in such strength that day. I cried—but not on account of Mother—that kind of day always makes me cry a little bit anyway. You couldn't cry over consigning anyone you loved to an earth like that—on a day like that. I put some blazing leaves over her, but when I passed there the other day, they were withered and brown—

SAM [*chiding her*]. Now, Leonie—

LEONIE. Sam thinks I shouldn't talk about Mother. But I don't see why. She doesn't depress me. I think of her with joy. She had a wonderful life.

SAM. She was a wonderful woman.

LEONIE [*to* WILL]. Imagine, Will—when Sam was here last time—you were here that week-end—she *knew*. She asked Sam to be executor of her will.

SAM [*very annoyed at her for bringing this up*]. Leonie—

LEONIE. Why didn't you tell me, Sam, then?

SAM. Seemed no point.

LEONIE. She didn't want me to know, did she?

SAM. No. She didn't want to distress you. [*A moment's pause.*]

LEONIE. What can be keeping Paula? [*She glances out of the window.*] Sam, do you want to talk business to me some more?

SAM. I'd like to talk to Will a minute.

LEONIE. Oh—yes. Well, Dennis, wouldn't you like me to show you to your room? [*She rises, goes to door into hallway.* DENNIS *follows.*]

DENNIS. Thanks. I've got to answer a chain letter.

LEONIE. I've given you a room you've never had. The tower room.

DENNIS. Is it ivory? I won't be comfortable if it isn't ivory.

LEONIE. Well just this once you're going to be uncomfortable—and like it! [*She goes out.*]

DENNIS [*tragically*]. And for this I gave up a superb view of the gas-house on 149th Street. [*He goes out.*]

SAM [*rises and goes up toward fireplace*]. Will—

WILL. Yes, Mr. Frothingham.

SAM. Oh—call me Sam.

WILL. All right.

SAM. I'll have to be pushing off in an hour or so. I rather wanted to talk to you.

WILL. Yes—

SAM [*wipes his forehead*]. Gosh, Leonie's a difficult woman to talk business to. [*Sits.*]

WILL. I can imagine that. She's not interested in business.

SAM. *She—is—not!!!*

WILL. What do you want to speak to me about?

SAM. Paula.

WILL. What about Paula?

SAM. As I'm her father—I hope you won't think me—

WILL. Of course not—

SAM. It's not altogether easy—

WILL. Do you want me to help you?

SAM. Yes. I wish you would!

WILL. You're worried about Paula and me, aren't you? So was her grandmother. You think me irresponsible. Less responsible for example—[*as if making a random comparison*] than Dr. Rice?

SAM. Well, as a matter of fact, I've rather gotten to know Dr. Rice, and in many respects, he's a pretty sound feller. [*Rising and going to stand above*

WILL.] Hang it all, Will, I like you, and I don't like to preach to you, you know.

WILL. Go on.

SAM. Well, there are—from my point of view at least—a lot of nonsensical ideas knocking about. I'd like to point out just one thing to you. Your radicalism and all that— Well, the point is this—if you marry Paula —and I hope you do, because I like you—and, what is more important, Paula likes you—you'll have responsibilities. Paula will be rich. Very rich. Money means responsibility. Now, I shouldn't, for example, like you to start radical magazines with it. I shouldn't like you to let money drift through your fingers in all sorts of aimless, millennial directions that won't get anywhere.

WILL. Who told you that was my intention?

SAM. A little bird.

WILL. With a black moustache?

SAM. Does that matter?

WILL. No.

SAM [*putting hand on* WILL's *shoulder*]. As a matter of fact, I'm not worried about you at all. Money, I expect, will do to you what getting power does to radical opposition, once it gets office—

WILL. Emasculate me, you mean?

SAM. Well, hardly. Mature you. Once you're rich, I have no doubt you'll be—

WILL. Sound.

SAM. Yes. Sound. But your friends—this McCarthy boy—

WILL. Well, I can easily cut Dennis—all my poor and unsound friends—

SAM [*quietly*]. I'm sorry you're taking this tone with me, Will. I'm the last person in the world to ask you to drop anybody. I'd be ashamed of you if you did. Only—

WILL. Only?

SAM. I must tell you that I am in position—by virtue of the will left by Mrs. Wyler—to keep Paula's money from being used for any purpose that might be construed as—subversive.

WILL. From whose point of view?

SAM [*quietly*]. From mine.

WILL. I see.

SAM. Possibly you may not believe this—but I trust you, Will. Mrs. Wyler trusted you.

WILL. You needn't worry. Paula seems to have other interests apparently.

SAM. What do you mean?

WILL. Sounder interests—

[DENNIS *enters, through door back.*]

DENNIS. The tower room lets in light on four sides, but nothing to look at. Just the sea and the landscape.

SAM. What did you do with Leonie?

DENNIS. She's gone to her mother's room to potter around.

SAM. Maybe I can get her attention while she's pottering. Excuse me. [SAM *goes out.*]

DENNIS. Poor Leonie—she's the last of the lovely ladies. The inheritance taxes'll get 'em soon. You know we were by way of getting our magazine from Leonie when Dr. Rice spiked our guns. So I'm leaving. My time is too valuable. But the Healer won't last forever, and when he goes, I shall return. Take heart, my good man. I know you feel a little tender about this, but remember, my lad, it's the Cause that counts. Remember what Shaw says: "There is no money but the devil's money. It is all tainted and it might as well be used in the service of God." [*A moment*—WILL *is obviously thinking of something else.*] What's the matter?

WILL. Nothing.

DENNIS [*bringing down chair to sit left of* WILL, *he imitates* RICE'S *manner*]. Now you must speak, young man—how can I sublimate your subconscious troubles, if you won't speak? Are you unhappy about Paula, my lad? [*No answer.*] Tell me what's happened between you—relieve your soul, and, as a reward, I may make you co-editor of our magazine. [*No response. He rises and walks to opposite side of table.*] No? Assistant editor you remain. I may even fire you. Yes, I think I will fire you. [*Crossing in front of* WILL *to fireplace.*] Dexter—you're through. Go upstairs and get your check. [*Rubs his hands together in glee.*] God, it gives me a sense of power to fire a man—especially an old friend!

[PAULA *and* KENNETH *come in door right from the garden.*]

PAULA [*amazed to see them*]. Will! But how—! Dennis!

WILL [*rather coolly*]. Hello, Paula.

DENNIS. We came to surprise you. Now that we have surprised you, we can go home.

WILL. Leonie asked me to come.

PAULA. Oh. Well, it's very nice to see you.

WILL. Thanks.

PAULA. When I wired you to come a few weeks ago, you were too busy. It takes Leonie, doesn't it?

DENNIS. You should have tried me, Paula. Hello, Dr. Rice. How's business? Any suppressions today?

KENNETH [*significantly*]. Apparently not.

DENNIS. Well, come on up to my room, Doctor, and we'll play Twenty Questions. [*He goes out.*]

WILL. Hello, Dr. Rice.

KENNETH. How are you?

PAULA. Will—I'm awfully glad to see you. I was just going to write you to thank you for the sweet letter you sent me after Granny died.

KENNETH. I'm afraid it's my fault, Dexter. I do my best

to keep Paula so busy that she finds no time to write letters.

WILL. I was sure I could count on you, Doctor. [WILL *goes out.*]

PAULA. You enjoy hurting Will, don't you?

KENNETH. When there is an obstacle in my path, I do my best to remove it.

PAULA. What makes you think it is only Will that stands between us— That if left to myself I—

KENNETH. Because it is true. Were it not for the squids of idealistic drivel spouted around you by Will and his friends, there would be no issue at all between us. I resent even an imputed rivalry with someone I despise.

PAULA. Rivalry?

KENNETH. Paula— There's no reason any longer why I shouldn't tell you the truth.

PAULA. What is it, Kenneth?

KENNETH [*after a moment—slowly*]. Do you know what I feel like? I feel like a man on a great height, irresistibly tempted to jump over. Do you want the truth really? [*She says nothing. Somehow his words, his voice, his attitude make her feel that really now he may reveal something which before he wouldn't have revealed. He is in a trance-like state almost; she feels it; she is rather horribly fascinated—somehow, though she distrusts him utterly, some instinct tells her that at this moment actually he is tempted by a force, disruptive to himself, to tell her the truth.*] Don't you know it? Don't you feel it? [*Pause.*] Haven't you known it? Haven't you felt it? [*A moment's pause.*] I love you.

PAULA. What?

KENNETH. I love you.

[*A pause. She is too stupefied to speak. She too is under a spell. She is fascinated by him—by the enor-*

mity of this. She rises, walks away from him to stand by sofa.]

PAULA. I suppose I should be afraid of you. I am not afraid of you.

KENNETH. I am afraid of you. You tempt me to venture the impossible. That is impractical. And I have always been eminently practical.

PAULA. I'm sure you have. [*She feels herself talking automatically, as if out of a hypnotic state—at the same time some vanity and shrewdness keeps pounding inside her: "See how far he will go—see how far he will go!"*]

KENNETH. I have lived by a plan. The plan has matured. But I have yearned for a face that would give me joy, for the voice that would soothe me. It is your face. It is your voice.

[PAULA *is fighting not to scream; at the same time she is caught in a nightmarish fascination.*]

PAULA [*very faintly*]. Don't you love Mother?

KENNETH. No. [*A moment's pause.*] You are the youth I have never had, the security I have never had—you are the home I have hungered for. [*Moves toward her—stands over her and a little back.*] That I am standing near you now, that I have achieved a share in your life, that you are listening to me, that you are thinking of me and of what I am, to the exclusion of everything else in the whirling universe— this is a miracle so devastating, that it makes any future possible—Paula—

PAULA. What?

KENNETH. Paula?

PAULA. What *is* it?

KENNETH [*bending over her*]. Paula . . . [*It is as if he got a sexual joy from saying her name.*] I love your name. I love to say your name.

PAULA. I *am* afraid of you. I'm sorry for you.

KENNETH. Do you think me insane?

PAULA. Yes.

KENNETH. Because I am ambitious, because I am forthright, because I deal scientifically with the human stuff around me—you think me insane. Because I am ruthless and romantic, you think me insane. This boy you think you love—who spends his time sniveling about a system he is not strong enough to dominate—is he sane?

PAULA. I don't expect you to—

KENNETH. When I hear the chatter of your friends, it makes me sick. While they and their kind prate of co-operative commonwealths, the strong man takes power, and rides over their backs—which is all their backs are fit for. Never has the opportunity for the individual career been so exalted, so infinite in its scope, so horizontal. House-painters and minor journalists become dictators of great nations. [With puckish humor—leaning on arm of her chair.] Imagine what a really clever man could do? See what he has done! [He smiles, makes a gesture of modest self-assertion, indicating the room as part of his conquest. She laughs, rather choked and embarrassed. He goes on.] And this I have done alone. From an impossible distance—I have come to you, so that when I speak, you can hear. What might we not do together, Paula—you and I—

[To her surprise, PAULA finds herself arguing an inconceivable point. She loathes the strange fascination she feels in this man, and yet is aware that it might turn to her advantage.]

PAULA. We don't want the same things.

KENNETH. You want what everyone wants who has vitality and imagination—new forms of power—new domains of knowledge—the ultimate sensations.

PAULA. You are romantic, aren't you?

KENNETH. Endlessly. And endlessly—realistic. [*Staring at her.*] What are you thinking?

PAULA [*shrewd against him—against herself*]. I keep thinking—what you want now—what you're after now?

KENNETH [*moving toward her*]. You don't believe then —that I love you?

PAULA [*leaning back in chair—not looking at him*]. You are a very strange man.

KENNETH. I am simple really. I want everything. That's all!

PAULA. And you don't care how you get it.

KENNETH. Don't be moralistic, Paula—I beg you. I am directly in the tradition of your own marauding ancestors. They pass now for pioneers—actually they fell on the true pioneers, and wrested what they had found away from them, by sheer brutal strength. I am doing the same thing—but more adroitly.

PAULA. Why are you so honest with me?

KENNETH [*with his most charming smile*]. Perhaps because I feel that, in your heart, you too are an adventurer.

[*A pause. During these half-spellbound instants a thought has been forming slowly in* PAULA'S *mind that crystallizes now. This man is the enemy. This man is infinitely cunning, infinitely resourceful. Perhaps—just the possibility—he really feels this passion for her. If so, why not use this weakness in an antagonist so ruthless? She will try.*]

PAULA. I shouldn't listen to you—

[*A moment. He senses her cunning. He looks at her.*]

KENNETH. You don't trust me?

PAULA. Have I reason to trust you?

KENNETH. What reason would you like? What proof would you like?

PAULA. Aren't you going to marry Mother?

KENNETH. Only as an alternative.

PAULA. Will you—tell her so? Will you give up the alternative?

KENNETH. And if I do?

PAULA. What shall I promise you?

KENNETH. Yourself.

PAULA [*looks at him—speaks*]. And if I do?

KENNETH. Then . . .

PAULA [*taking fire*]. You say you love me! If you feel it —really feel it— You haven't been very adventurous for all your talk! Taking in Mother and Sam! Give up those conquests. Tell her! Tell Mother! Then perhaps I will believe you.

KENNETH. And then?

PAULA. Take your chances!

KENNETH [*quietly*]. Very well.

PAULA. You will?

KENNETH. I will.

PAULA. You'll tell Mother—you love me?

KENNETH. Yes.

PAULA [*going to the foot of the stairs, calls*]. Mother! Mother!

LEONIE [*offstage*]. Yes, Paula. I'm coming right down! I've the most marvelous surprise for you! Wait and see!

[PAULA *walks to end of sofa—looking at* KENNETH. LEONIE *comes in. She is wearing an exquisite old-fashioned silk wedding-dress which billows around her in an immense shimmering circle. She is a vision of enchantment.*]

LEONIE [*in a great flurry of excitement*]. Children, look what I found! It's Mother's. It's the dress she was married in. I was poking around in Granny's room while Sam was talking to me about bonds, and I came upon it. Do you like it, Kenneth? Isn't it adorable? Have you ever . . . What's the matter? Don't you like it?

PAULA. It's very pretty.

LEONIE [*overwhelmed by the inadequacy of this word*]. Pretty! Pretty! [*She hopes for more from* KENNETH.] Kenneth . . . ?

KENNETH. It's exquisite.

LEONIE. Isn't it? [*She whirls around in the dress.*] Isn't it? Yes. Exquisite. Can you imagine the scene? Can you imagine Granny walking down the aisle—and all the august spectators in mutton-chop whiskers and Prince Alberts? We've lost something these days —a good deal—oh, I don't miss the mutton-chops— but in ceremony, I mean—in punctilio and grace. . . .

PAULA [*cutting ruthlessly through the nostalgia*]. Mother!

LEONIE. What is it, Paula?

PAULA. Kenneth has something to tell you.

LEONIE. Kenneth?

PAULA. Yes. He has something to tell you.

LEONIE. Have you, Kenneth?

KENNETH. Yes.

LEONIE. What is it?

KENNETH [*quietly*]. I love Paula. I want to marry Paula.

[*A pause. Granny's wedding dress droops.*]

LEONIE. Do you mean that, Kenneth?

KENNETH. Yes.

LEONIE [*piteously*]. This isn't very nice of you, Paula.

PAULA. I had nothing to do with it. I loathe Kenneth. But I wanted you to know him. Now you see him, Mother, your precious Lothario—there he is! Look at him!

LEONIE. These clothes are picturesque, but I think our modern ones are more comfortable. I think—I feel quite faint—isn't it ridiculous? [*She sways.*]

PAULA. I'm sorry, Mother. I had to. But I love you. I really do.

LEONIE [*very faint*]. Thank you, Paula.

PAULA. You'd better go up and lie down. I'll come to you in a moment.

LEONIE. Yes. I think I'd better. Yes. [*She begins to sob; she goes out, hiding her face in the lace folds of her dress.* PAULA, *having gone with her to the door, rings bell for* ROBERT, *turns to* KENNETH.]

PAULA. I suppose you're going to tell me this isn't cricket. Well, don't, because it will only make me laugh. To live up to a code with people like you is only to be weak and absurd.

KENNETH [*his voice is low and even but tense with hate*]. You, Miss Frothingham, are my *last* miscalculation. I might even say my first. Fortunately, not irreparable!

[ROBERT *enters.*]

PAULA. Robert.

ROBERT. Yes, Miss Frothingham.

PAULA [*still staring fixedly at* KENNETH]. Dr. Rice is leaving. Will you see that his bags are packed, please?

ROBERT. Yes, Miss. [*He goes out.*]

KENNETH. Forgive me—for having overestimated you. [*He goes out door right.*]

[PAULA *comes slowly down and sits on sofa. She gets a reaction herself now from all she has been through; this game hasn't been natural to her; she is trembling physically; she is on the verge of tears.* WILL *comes in.*]

PAULA. Will—Will darling— [*She clings to* WILL.]

WILL [*worried*]. Paula!

PAULA. Put your arms around me, Will—hold me close—

[WILL *obeys*.]

WILL. What's happened?

PAULA. I've tricked him. I made him say in front of Mother that he loved me, that he wanted to marry me. Poor Leonie! But it had to be done! And do you know, Will—at the end I felt—gosh, one has so many selves, Will. I must tell you—for the—well, for the completeness of the record—

WILL [*curious*]. What?

PAULA. At the end I felt I had to do it—not only to save Leonie—but to save myself. Can you understand that? I felt horribly drawn to him, and by the sordid thing I was doing— But it's over. Thank God it's over. Will, darling, these six weeks have been hell without you. When I got your letter about Granny, I sat down and cried. I wanted to go right to New York to be with you. And yet I couldn't. How could I? But now, Will—I don't want to wait for you any longer. I've done what I can. It's cost me almost— Will—I need you terribly—

WILL. And I you, Paula. But listen, darling—I've decided during the weeks I've been away from you— I can't marry you now— I can't face what I'd become—

PAULA. But, Will, I— [*Springing up*.] But, Will, I'll give up the money. I'll live with you anywhere.

WILL. I know that, Paula. But I mustn't. You mustn't let me. I've thought it all out. You say you'd live with me anywhere. But what would happen? Supposing I didn't get a job? Would we starve? We'd take fifty dollars a week from your grandmother's estate. It would be foolish not to. Taking fifty, why not seventy-five? Why not two hundred? I can't let myself in for it, Paula. [*A long pause*.] Paula, darling—do you hate me?

PAULA. No.

WILL. Supposing you weren't rich? Is it a world in which, but for this, I'd have to sink? If it is, I'm going to damn well do what I can to change it. I don't have to scrabble for the inheritance of dead men. That's for Kenneth—one robber baron—after the lapse of several generations—succeeding another. I don't want this damn fortune to give me an unfair advantage over people as good as I am who haven't got it. [*Torn with pity for her.*] Paula—my dearest—what can I do?

PAULA. I see that you can't do anything. I quite see. Still—

WILL. I love you, Paula, and I'll be longing for you terribly, but I can't marry you—not till there's somebody for you to marry. When I've struck my stride, I won't care about Sam, or the money, or anything, because I'll be on my own. If you feel the way I do, you'll wait.

PAULA [*very still voice*]. Of course, Will. I'll wait.

WILL [*overcome with gratitude and emotion—seizes her in his arms passionately*]. Darling—darling—

[LEONIE *comes in.* WILL, *overcome with emotion, goes out.*]

LEONIE. It's easy to say "lie down." But what happens then? Thoughts assail you. Thoughts . . .

PAULA. Mother . . .

LEONIE. Kenneth's going. He's leaving. I suppose you're happy. It's the end—the end of summer.

PAULA [*herself shaken with emotion*]. Mother— [*She wants to talk to* LEONIE, *to tell her what has happened, but* LEONIE *is lost in her own maze.*]

LEONIE. It's cold here. I hate this place. I'm going to sell it. [*She sits, in chair, right of fireplace.*] I've always wanted things around me to be gay and warm and happy. I've done my best. I must be wrong. Why do I find myself this way? With nothing. With nothing.

PAULA [*running to her mother and throwing herself on her knees beside her*]. Mother—Mother darling—

LEONIE [*not responding, reflectively*]. I suppose the thing about me that is wrong is that love is really all I care about. [*A moment's pause.*] I suppose I should have been interested in other things. Good works. Do they sustain you? But I couldn't somehow. I think when you're not in love—you're dead. Yes, that must be why I'm . . . [*Her voice trails off rather.* PAULA *drops her head in her mother's lap and begins to cry.*]

LEONIE [*surprised*]. Paula—what is it? What's the matter? Are you sorry? It's all right, child.

PAULA [*through her tears*]. It's Will—

LEONIE. Will?

PAULA. He's going away.

LEONIE. Why don't you go with him?

PAULA. He doesn't want me.

LEONIE. That's not true. It must be something else.

PAULA. The money.

LEONIE. Oh, the money. Yes, the money. The money won't do anything for you. It'll work against you. It's worked against me. It gives you the illusion of escape—but always you have to come back to yourself. At the end of every journey—you find yourself.

PAULA. What shall I do, Mother?

LEONIE. You and Will want the same things. In the end you will find them. But don't let him find them with someone else. Follow him. Be near him. When he is depressed and discouraged, let it be your hand that he touches, your face that he sees.

PAULA [*breathless*]. Mother—you're right—he told me

last summer—"you must have a shoulder to lean on"—

LEONIE. Let it be your shoulder, Paula; follow him. Be near him.

PAULA. Thank you, Mother.

LEONIE [*ruefully*]. I am telling you what *I* should do. It must be bad advice.

PAULA [*gratefully*]. Darling!

[DENNIS *and* WILL *come in.*]

DENNIS. Here you are! We're off to the boat! Thirty minutes! Why don't you and Paula come too? What do you say, Leonie?

LEONIE. You know, all these years I've been coming up here, and I've never been on the Bar Harbor boat.

DENNIS. It may be said, Mrs. Frothingham, if you have never been on the Bar Harbor boat, that you have not lived!

LEONIE. Really! I'd always heard it was poky.

DENNIS. Poky! The *Normandie* of the Kennebec poky! Mrs. Frothingham!

LEONIE. It's fun, is it? But doesn't it get into New York at some impossible hour?

DENNIS. At seven a.m.

LEONIE. Seven! [*She shudders.*]

DENNIS [*the brisk executive*]. Seven! Yes, sir! At my desk at nine! All refreshed and co-ordinated and ready to attack my South American correspondence.

LEONIE. I must learn not to believe him, mustn't I?

DENNIS. I am my own master, Leonie. All day for nine mortal hours I grind out escape fiction for the pulp magazines. But one day I shall become famous and emerge into the slicks and then I doubt very much whether I shall come here.

LEONIE. I shall miss you.

DENNIS. Then I'll come.

LEONIE. I hate to have you go, Dennis. You cheer me up. Why don't you stay?

DENNIS. Impossible, Leonie. I must go to New York to launch the magazine. But for the moment, good-bye, Leonie. As a reward for your hospitality I shall send you the original copy of one of my stories. Would you like to escape from something?

LEONIE [*smiling wanly*]. I would indeed!

DENNIS. Think no more about it. You're as good as free. The story is yours, typed personally on my Underwood. Those misplaced keys—those inaccuracies—how they will bemuse posterity! [*He goes out.*]

WILL [*awkwardly*]. Good-bye, Leonie.

LEONIE. Good-bye, Will. [*He goes out without looking at* PAULA. *In pantomime,* LEONIE *urges* PAULA *to go after him.* PAULA *kisses her quickly and runs after* WILL. *Left alone,* LEONIE *walks to the chair in which her mother sat so often—she looks through the glowing autumn at the darkening sea.* KENNETH *comes in. There is a pause.*]

KENNETH. Leonie—

LEONIE. Yes, Kenneth.

KENNETH. I don't expect you to understand this. I shall not try to make you understand it.

LEONIE. Perhaps I'd better not.

KENNETH. Really I am amused at myself—highly entertained. That I should have almost had to practice on myself what hitherto I have reserved for my patients—that I who have made such a fetish of discipline and restraint so nearly succumbed to an inconsistency. I must revise my notion of myself.

LEONIE. And I too.

KENNETH. Why? Why you?

LEONIE. I seem to be a survival—Paula's directness— and your calculations—they are beyond me.

KENNETH. Nevertheless, it's curious how you and Paula

are alike—no wonder that, for a moment at least, you seemed to me—interchangeable.

LEONIE. Did you know it from the beginning—that it was Paula?

KENNETH. I was attracted by her resemblance to you—for exercising this attraction I hated her. She felt it too—from the beginning and she must have hated me from the beginning. Between us there grew up this strange, unnatural antagonism—

LEONIE. What?

KENNETH. This fused emotion of love and hate. It had to be brought out into the open. It's a familiar psychosis—the unconscious desire of the daughter to triumph over the mother.

LEONIE. But I don't understand—

KENNETH. There is so much in these intricate relationships that the layman can't understand—

LEONIE. You mean that you—felt nothing for Paula?

KENNETH. No, I don't mean that at all. But I saw that what I felt for her was some twisted reflection of what I felt for you. And I saw there was only one way out of it—to let her triumph over you. I told her that I loved her. But this was not enough. I must repeat it in front of you. You must witness her triumph. I made it possible. I gave her her great moment. Well, you see what it's done. It freed her so beautifully that she was able to go to Will. They've gone away together. Perfect cure for her as well as for myself. [*A moment's pause.*]

LEONIE. It all sounds almost too perfect, Kenneth.

KENNETH. I said I didn't expect you to understand it—you have lived always on your emotions. You have never bothered to delve beneath them. You are afraid to, aren't you?

LEONIE. I know this, Kenneth. I heard you say that you loved Paula. I heard your voice. No, I can't accept this, Kenneth! It's not good enough. I've never done that before. I only think now that everything you did, everything you said, was to cover what you felt. And I'd end by telling myself that I believed you. I'd end by taking second best from you. No, I must guard myself from that. I felt this a month ago—that's why I sent for Will.

KENNETH. Some day, Leonie, you will learn that feeling is not enough.

LEONIE. But I trust my instinct, Kenneth.

KENNETH. That, Leonie, is your most adorable trait—

LEONIE. What?

KENNETH. That trust—that innocence. If it weren't for that, you wouldn't be you—and everyone wouldn't love you—

LEONIE. Oh, no, Kenneth—

[DENNIS *comes in.*]

DENNIS. Oh, excuse me. But I left my brief-case. Oh, here it is. [*He picks it up.*] Without my brief-case I am a man without a Destiny. With it I am—

KENNETH. A man with a brief-case.

LEONIE [*crossing rather desperately to* DENNIS—*this straw in the current*]. What's in it—your stories?

DENNIS. Stories—no, that wouldn't matter. I am fertile; I can spawn stories. But the plans for the magazine are in here—the future of Young America is here—

LEONIE. Will you stay and have a whiskey and soda?

DENNIS. Thanks, but if I do, I shall miss the boat.

LEONIE. Suppose you do?

KENNETH. Leonie—that would delay the millenium one day.

DENNIS. The doctor's right. That would be selfish.

LEONIE. Be selfish. Please stay.

DENNIS. No. Once you are enlisted in a cause, you can't live a personal life. It is a dedication.

LEONIE. Kenneth is leaving. I shall be lonely, Dennis. I can't bear to be alone.

KENNETH. Your need for people is poignant, isn't it, Leonie?

LEONIE. Stay for dinner. After dinner we can talk about your magazine.

DENNIS. Oh, well—that makes it possible for me to stay. Thank you, Kenneth. [*He goes to sofa, sits, busying himself with brief-case.*]

[*She goes to console to make highball.*]

KENNETH. Send me your magazine, Dennis. I shall be honored to be the first subscriber.

DENNIS. I'll be glad to. Your patients can read it in the waiting-room instead of the *National Geographic.*

KENNETH. Your first subscriber—and very possibly your last. [*He crosses to door and turns back.*] Good-bye, Leonie. Good luck, Dennis. We who are about to re-tire—salute you. [*She does not look at him. He bows formally to* DENNIS'S *back, makes a gesture of "good luck" and exits.*]

DENNIS. Trouble with that fellow is—he lives for himself. No larger interest. That's what dignifies human beings, Leonie—a dedication to something greater than themselves.

LEONIE [*coming down to hand him his highball*]. Yes? Here's your whiskey and soda. I envy you, Dennis. I wish I could dedicate myself to something—something outside myself.

DENNIS [*rising to sit beside her*]. Well, here's your op-portunity, Leonie—it's providential. You couldn't do better than this magazine. It would give you a new interest—impersonal. It would emancipate you, Leo-nie. It would be a perpetual dedication to Youth—to the hope of the world. The world is middle-aged and tired. But we—

LEONIE [*wistfully*]. Can you refresh us, Dennis?

DENNIS. Refresh you? Leonie, we can rejuvenate you!

LEONIE [*grateful there is someone there—another human being she can laugh with*]. That's an awfully amusing idea. You make me laugh.

DENNIS [*eagerly selling the idea*]. In the youth of any country, there is an immense potentiality—

LEONIE. You're awfully serious about it, aren't you, Dennis?

DENNIS. Where the magazine is concerned, Leonie, I am a fanatic.

LEONIE. I suppose if it's really successful—it'll result in my losing everything I have—

DENNIS. It'll be taken from you anyway. You'll only be anticipating the inevitable.

LEONIE. Why—how clever of me!

DENNIS. Not only clever but grateful.

LEONIE. Will you leave me just a little to live on—?

DENNIS. Don't worry about that—come the Revolution —you'll have a friend in high office.

[LEONIE *accepts gratefully this earnest of security. They touch glasses in a toast as the curtain falls.*]

IDIOT'S DELIGHT

by Robert E. Sherwood

*This play is lovingly dedicated to
Lynn Fontanne and Alfred Lunt*

Copyright 1935, 1936, by Robert E. Sherwood.
Used by permission of Charles Scribner's Sons.

*First production, March 9th, 1936,
at the National Theatre, Washington, D.C.,
with the following cast:*

DUMPTSY, *George Meader*
ORCHESTRA LEADER, *Stephen Sandes*
DONALD NAVADEL, *Barry Thompson*
PITTALUGA, *S. Thomas Gomez*
AUGUSTE, *Edgar Barrier*
CAPTAIN LOCICERO, *Edward Raquello*
DR. WALDERSEE, *Sydney Greenstreet*
MR. CHERRY, *Bretaigne Windust*
MRS. CHERRY, *Jean Macintyre*
HARRY VAN, *Alfred Lunt*
SHIRLEY, *Jacqueline Paige*
BEULAH, *Connie Crowell*
BEBE, *Ruth Timmons*
FRANCINE, *Etna Ross*
ELAINE, *Marjorie Baglin*
EDNA, *Frances Foley*
MAJOR, *George Greenberg*
FIRST OFFICER, *Alan Hewitt*
SECOND OFFICER, *Winston Ross*
THIRD OFFICER, *Gilmore Bush*
FOURTH OFFICER, *Tomasso Tittoni*
QUILLERY, *Richard Whorf*
SIGNOR ROSSI, *Le Roi Operti*
SIGNORA ROSSI, *Ernestine de Becker*
MAID, *Una Val*
ACHILLE WEBER, *Francis Compton*
IRENE, *Lynn Fontanne*

*The scene of the play is the cocktail lounge
of the Hotel Monte Gabriele, in the Italian Alps,
near the frontiers of Switzerland and Austria.*

ACT I
Afternoon of a winter day in any imminent year.
ACT II
Scene 1. *Eight o'clock that evening.*
Scene 2. *Eleven o'clock that evening.*
Scene 3. *After midnight.*
ACT III
The following afternoon.

Act one

The cocktail lounge of the Hotel Monte Gabriele.

The hotel is a small one, which would like to consider itself a first-class resort. It was originally an Austrian sanatorium. Its Italian management has refurnished it and added this cocktail lounge and a few modern bedrooms with baths, in the hope that some day Monte Gabriele may become a rival for St. Moritz. So far, this is still a hope. Although the weather is fine, the supply of winter sports enthusiasts at Monte Gabriele is negligible, and the hotel is relying for its trade upon those itinerants who, because of the current political situation, are desirous of leaving Italy.

Near at hand are a railway line into Switzerland, highways into Switzerland and Austria, and an Italian army airport.

At the left, up-stage, is a large doorway, leading to the lobby, in which we can just see the Reception Desk.

At the upper right is a staircase. A few steps up is a landing, above which is a high window with a fine view of the Alpine scenery to the North and West. The panes are fringed with frost. From the landing, the stairs continue up to a gallery which leads to bedrooms off to the upper left.

Downstairs left is a swinging door marked with the word "BAR."

Over this bar entrance are crossed skis and the head of a mountain goat. On the wall at the right is a Fascist emblem with crossed Italian flags. About the Reception Desk, off to the left, are signs assuring the guest that this hotel has been approved by all the automobile associations of Europe and that Travelers' Cheques may be cashed here. Somewhere on the walls are pictures of the Coliseum and the S.S. "Conte de Savoia."

There are small tables and chairs about, with perhaps a couch or two. At the left is a piano, and when the first curtain rises a dismal little four-piece orchestra is playing "June in January."

Note a line in the dialogue along toward the end of Act One: there is something about this place that suggests "a vague kind of horror." This is nothing definite, or identifiable, or even, immediately, apparent. Just an intimation.

Behind the Reception Desk, PITTALUGA *is occasionally visible. He is the proprietor of the hotel—a fussy, worried little Italian in the conventional morning coat and striped pants.*

On the landing at the upper right, looking dolefully out the window, is DONALD NAVADEL, *a rather precious, youngish American, suitably costumed for winter sports by Saks Fifth Avenue. Experienced in the resort business, he was imported this year to organize sporting and social life at Monte Gabriele with a view to making it a Mecca for American tourists. He is not pleased with the way things have turned out.*

DUMPTSY *comes in from the left. He is an humble, gentle little bell-boy, aged about forty, born in this district when it was part of Austria, but now a subject of the Fascist Empire. He has come in to clean the ashtrays. He listens to the music.*

DUMPTSY. Come si chiama questa musica che suonate?

ORCHESTRA LEADER. Il pezzo si chiama: "Giugno in Gennaio."

DUMPTSY. Oh, com'e bello! Mi piace! [*To* DON.] It's good.

DON. Will you please for God's sake stop playing that same damned tiresome thing?

DUMPTSY. You don't like it, Mr. Navadel?

DON. I'm so sick of it, I could scream!

DUMPTSY. I like it. To me, it's good.

DON. Go on, and clean the ash-trays.

DUMPTSY. But they're not dirty, sir. Because there's nobody using them.

DON. There's no need to remind me of *that!* Do as you're told!

DUMPTSY. If you please, sir. [*He whistles the tune and goes out.*]

DON [*to the* LEADER]. You've played enough. Get out!

LEADER. But it is not yet three o'clock.

DON. Never mind what time it is. There's nobody here to listen to you, is there? You can just save the wear and tear on your harpsichord and go grab yourselves a smoke.

LEADER. Very good, Mr. Navadel. [*To the other* MUSICIANS.] E inutile continuare a suonare. La gente non ascolta più. Si potrà invece far quattro chiachiere e fumare una sigaretta.

[*They put away instruments and music and start to go out, as* PITTALUGA *appears bristling.*]

PITTALUGA [*to* LEADER]. Eh, professori? Perchè avete cessato di suonare? Non sono ancora le tre.

LEADER. Il Signor Navadel ci ha detta di andare a fumare egli ne ha avuto abbastanza della nostra musica.

[*The* MUSICIANS *have gone.*]

PITTALUGA [*going to* DON]. You told my orchestra it would stop?

DON [*untroubled*]. I did.

PITTALUGA. My orders to them are they play in here until three o'clock. Why do you take it to yourself to countermand my orders?

DON. Because their performance was just a little too macabre to be bearable.

PITTALUGA. So! You have made yourself the manager of this hotel, have you? You give orders to the musicians. Next you will be giving orders to me—and to the guests themselves, I have no doubt. . . .

DON. The guests! [*He laughs drily.*] That's really very funny. Consult your room chart, my dear Signor Pittaluga, and let me know how many guests there are that I can give orders to. The number when last I counted . . .

PITTALUGA. And you stop being insolent, you—animale fetente. I pay you my money, when I am plunging myself into bankruptcy. . . .

DON. Yes, yes, Signor—we know all about that. You pay me your money. And you have a right to know that I'm fed to the teeth with this little pension that you euphemistically call a high-grade resort hotel. Indeed, I'm fed to the teeth with you personally.

PITTALUGA [*in a much friendlier tone*]. Ah! So you wish to leave us! I'm very sorry, my dear Donald. We shall miss you.

DON. My contract expires on March the first. I shall bear it until then.

PITTALUGA. You insult me by saying you are fed with me, but you go on taking my money?

DON. Yes!

PITTALUGA. Pezzo mascalzone farabutto prepotente canaglia . . .

DON. And it will do you no good to call me names in

your native tongue. I've had a conspicuously successful career in this business, all the way from Santa Barbara to St. Moritz. And you lured me away from a superb job . . .

PITTALUGA [*as* DON *continues*]. Lazzarone, briccone, bestione. Perdio.

DON. . . . with your glowing descriptions of this handsome place, and the crowds of sportlovers, gay, mad, desperately chic, who were flocking here from London, Paris, New York. . . .

PITTALUGA. Did *I* know what was going to happen? Am *I* the king of Europe?

DON. You are the proprietor of this obscure tavern. You're presumably responsible for the fact that it's a deadly, boring dump!

PITTALUGA. Yes! And I engaged you because I thought you had friends—rich friends—and they would come here after you instead of St. Moritz, and Muerren, and Chamonix. And where are your friends? What am I paying for you? To countermand my orders and tell me you are fed . . . [*Wails from warning sirens are heard from off-stage right.* PITTALUGA *stops short. Both listen.*] Che cosa succede?

DON. That's from down on the flying field.

PITTALUGA. It is the warning for the air raids!

[AUGUSTE, *the barman, is heard in bar off-stage, left.*]

AUGUSTE'S VOICE. Che cosa?

[PITTALUGA *and* DON *rush to the window.*]

PITTALUGA. Segnali d'incursione. La guerra e incominiciata e il nemico viene.

[*Airplane motors are heard off right.*]

DON [*looking through window*]. Look! The planes are taking off. They're the little ones—the combat planes.

[CAPTAIN LOCICERO *enters from the lobby. He is the officer in charge of the frontier station. He is tired, quiet, nice.* AUGUSTE *enters from the bar.* DUMPTSY *follows the* CAPTAIN.]

AUGUSTE. Signor Capitano!

CAPTAIN. Buona sera!

[AUGUSTE *helps him take off his coat.*]

DUMPTSY. Che cosa succede, Signor Capitano? È la guerra?

CAPTAIN. No—no—datemi cognac.

[DUMPTSY *puts coat on chair right of table and goes up and exits through arch center.* CAPTAIN *sits chair left of table.*]

AUGUSTE [*as he goes out*]. Si, Signor Capitano.

[*The* CAPTAIN *sits down at a table.* PITTALUGA *and* DON *cross to him.* DUMPTSY *goes.*]

PITTALUGA. Che cosa significano quei terribili segnali? È, forse, il nemico che arriva?

DON. What's happened, Captain? Is there an air raid? Has the war started?

CAPTAIN [*smiling*]. Who knows? But there is no raid. [*The porter's hand-bell in the lobby is heard.*] They're only testing the sirens, to see how fast the combat planes can go into action. You understand—it's like lifeboat drill on a ship.

[DUMPTSY *enters.*]

DUMPTSY. Scusi, padrone. Due Inglesi arrivati. [*He hurries out.*]

PITTALUGA. Scusi. Vengo subito. Presto, presto! [*He goes.*]

CAPTAIN. Have a drink, Mr. Navadel?

DON. Thank you very much—but some guests are actually arriving. I must go and be very affable. [*He goes.*]

[DR. WALDERSEE *appears on the gallery above and comes down the stairs as* AUGUSTE *enters from the bar and serves the* CAPTAIN *with brandy and soda.*

The DOCTOR *is an elderly, stout, crotchety, sad German.*]

CAPTAIN. Good afternoon, Doctor. Have a drink?

DOCTOR. Thank you very much—no. What is all that aeroplanes?

[AUGUSTE *goes.*]

CAPTAIN. This is a crucial spot, Dr. Waldersee. We must be prepared for visits from the enemy.

DOCTOR. Enemy, eh? And who is that?

CAPTAIN. I don't quite know, yet. The map of Europe supplies us with a wide choice of opponents. I suppose, in due time, our government will announce its selection—and we shall know just whom we are to shoot at.

DOCTOR. Nonsense! Obscene nonsense!

CAPTAIN. Yes—yes. But the taste for obscenity is incurable, isn't it?

DOCTOR. When will you let me go into Switzerland?

CAPTAIN. Again I am powerless to answer you. My orders are that no one for the time being shall cross the frontiers, either into Switzerland or Austria.

DOCTOR. And when will this "time being" end?

CAPTAIN. When Rome makes its decision between friend and foe.

DOCTOR. I am a German subject. I am not your foe.

CAPTAIN. I am sure of that, Dr. Waldersee. The two great Fascist states stand together, against the world.

DOCTOR [*passionately*]. Fascism has nothing to do with it! I am a scientist. I am a servant of the whole damn stupid human race. [*He crosses toward the* CAPTAIN.] If you delay me any longer here, my experiments will be ruined. Can't you appreciate that? I must get my rats at once to the laboratory in Zurich, or all my months and years of research will have gone for nothing.

[DON *enters, followed by* MR. *and* MRS. CHERRY—*a pleas-*

ant young English couple in the first flush of their honeymoon.]

DON. This is our cocktail lounge. There is the American bar. We have a *thé dansant* here every afternoon at 4:30—supper dancing in the evening.

CHERRY. Charming.

DON. All this part of the hotel is new. Your rooms are up there. [*He crosses to the window.*] I think you'll concede that the view from here is unparalleled. We can look into four countries. [*The* CHERRYS *follow him to the window.*] Here in the foreground, of course, is Italy. This was formerly Austrian territory, transferred by the treaty of Versailles. It's called Monte Gabriele in honor of D'Annunzio, Italian poet and patriot. Off there is Switzerland and there is Austria. And far off, you can just see the tip of a mountain peak that is in the Bavarian Tyrol. Rather gorgeous, isn't it?

CHERRY. Yes.

MRS. CHERRY. Darling—*look* at that sky!

CHERRY. I say, it *is* rather good.

DON. Do you go in for winter sports, Mrs. Cherry?

MRS. CHERRY. Oh, yes—I—we're very keen on them.

DON. Splendid! We have everything here.

CHERRY. I've usually gone to Kitzbuhel.

[PITTALUGA *and* DUMPTSY *appear up-stage and speak in Italian through the dialogue.*]

PITTALUGA. Dumptsy, il bagaglio è stato portato su?

DUMPTSY. Si, signore, è già sopra.

PITTALUGA. Sta bene, vattene.

DON. It's lovely there, too.

CHERRY. But I hear it has become much too crowded there now. I—my wife and I hoped it would be quieter here.

DON. Well—at the moment—it is rather quiet here.

PITTALUGA [*coming down*]. Your luggage has been sent

up, Signor. Would you care to see your room now?

CHERRY. Yes. Thank you.

PITTALUGA. If you will have the goodness to step this way. [*He goes up the stairs.*] 'Scuse me.

CHERRY [*pauses at the window on the way up*]. What's that big bare patch down there?

DON [*casually*]. Oh, that's the airport. [PITTALUGA *coughs discreetly.*] We have a great deal of flying here.

PITTALUGA. Right this way, please.

CHERRY. Oh—I see.

[*They continue on up, preceded by* PITTALUGA.]

DON. And do come down for *thé dansant.*

MRS. CHERRY. We should love to.

PITTALUGA. Right straight ahead, please. [*They exit through gallery.*]

DON [*standing on first step*]. Honeymooners.

CAPTAIN. Yes—poor creatures.

DON. They wanted quiet.

DOCTOR [*rises*]. Ach Gott! When will you know when I can cross into Switzerland?

CAPTAIN. The instant that word comes through from Rome. [*The hand-bell is heard.*] You understand that I am only an obscure frontier official. And here in Italy, as in your own Germany, authority is centralized.

DOCTOR. But you can send a telegram to Rome, explaining the urgency of my position.

[DUMPTSY *appears, greatly excited.*]

DUMPTSY. More guests from the bus, Mr. Navadel. Seven of them! [*He goes.*]

DON. *Good God!* [*He goes out.*]

DOCTOR. Ach, es gibt kein Ruhe hier.

CAPTAIN. I assure you, Dr. Waldersee, I shall do all in my power.

DOCTOR. They must be made to understand that time is of vital importance.

CAPTAIN. Yes, I know.

DOCTOR. I have no equipment here to examine them properly—no assistant for the constant observation that is essential if my experiments are to succeed . . .

CAPTAIN [*a trifle wearily*]. I'm so sorry . . .

DOCTOR. Yes! You say you are so sorry. But what do you *do?* You have no comprehension of what is at stake. You are a soldier and indifferent to death. You say you are sorry, but it is nothing to you that hundreds of thousands, *millions,* are dying from a disease that it is within my power to cure!

CAPTAIN. Again, I assure you, Dr. Waldersee, that I . . .

DON'S VOICE. Our Mr. Pittaluga will be down in a moment. In the meantime, perhaps you and the—the others . . . [*He comes in, followed by* HARRY VAN, *a wan, thoughtful, lonely American vaudevillian promoter, press agent, book-agent, crooner, hoofer, barker or shill, who has undertaken all sorts of jobs in his time, all of them capitalizing his powers of salesmanship, and none of them entirely honest. He wears a snappy, belted, polo coat and a brown felt hat with brim turned down on all sides*] . . . would care to sit here in the cocktail lounge. We have a *thé dansant* here at 4:30 . . . supper dancing in the evening. . . .

HARRY. Do you run this hotel?

DON. I'm the Social Manager.

HARRY. What?

DON. The Social Manager.

HARRY. Oh! American, aren't you?

DON. I am. Santa Barbara's my home, and Donald Navadel is my name.

HARRY. Happy to know you. My name's Harry Van. [*They shake hands.*]

DON. Glad to have you here, Mr. Van. Are you—staying with us long?

DOCTOR [*rising*]. I shall myself send a telegram to Rome, to the German Embassy.

CAPTAIN. They might well be able to expedite matters. [*The* DOCTOR *goes.*]

HARRY. I've got to get over that border. When I came in on the train from Fiume, they told me the border is closed, and the train is stuck here for tonight and maybe longer. I asked them why, but they either didn't know or they refused to divulge their secrets to me. What seems to be the trouble?

DON. Perhaps Captain Locicero can help you. He's the commander of Italian Headquarters here. This is Mr. Van, Captain.

CAPTAIN [*rising*]. Mr. Van, my compliments.

HARRY. And mine to you, Captain. We're trying to get to Geneva.

CAPTAIN. You have an American passport?

HARRY. I have. Several of them. [*He reaches in his pocket and takes out seven passports, bound together with elastic. He fans them like a deck of cards and hands them to the* CAPTAIN.]

CAPTAIN. You have your family with you?

HARRY. Well—it isn't exactly a family. [*He goes to the right.*] Come in here, girls!

SHIRLEY [*from off-stage*]. Come on in, kids. Harry wants us.

[*Six blonde chorus girls come in. They are named:* SHIRLEY, BEULAH, BEBE, FRANCINE, EDNA *and* ELAINE. *Of these,* SHIRLEY *is the principal, a frank, knowing fan dancer.* BEULAH *is a bubble dancer, and therefore ethereal.* BEBE *is a hard, harsh little number who shimmies.* DON *doesn't know quite how to take this surprising troupe, but the* CAPTAIN *is impressed, favorably.*]

HARRY. Allow me to introduce the girls, Captain. We call them "Les Blondes." We've been playing the Balkan circuit—Budapest, Bucharest, Sofia, Belgrade, and Zagreb. [*He turns to* DON.] Back home, that would be the equivalent of "Pan Time." [*He laughs nervously, to indicate that the foregoing was a gag.*]

CAPTAIN [*bowing*]. How do you do?

HARRY. The Captain is head man, girls.

GIRLS. How do you do? . . . Pleased to meet you. . . . Etc.

HARRY. The situation in brief is this, Captain. We've got very attractive bookings at a night spot in Geneva. Undoubtedly they feel that the League of Nations needs us. [*Another laugh.*] It's important that we get there at once. So, Captain, I'll be grateful for prompt action.

CAPTAIN [*looking at the first passport*]. Miss Shirley Laughlin.

HARRY. Laughlin. This is Shirley. Step up, honey. [*Shirley steps forward.*]

CAPTAIN [*pleased with* SHIRLEY]. How do you do?

SHIRLEY. Pleased to meet you.

CAPTAIN. This photograph hardly does you justice.

SHIRLEY. I know. It's terrible, isn't it!

HARRY [*interrupting*]. Who's next, Captain?

CAPTAIN. Miss Beulah Tremoyne.

HARRY. Come on, Beulah. [*She comes forward in a wide sweep, as* SHIRLEY *goes up and joins the group.*] Beulah is our bubble dancer, a product of the aesthetic school, and therefore more of a dreamer.

CAPTAIN. Exquisite!

BEULAH. Thank you *ever* so much. [*She starts to sit down by the* CAPTAIN. *She is turning it on.*]

HARRY. That'll be all, Beulah.

CAPTAIN. Miss Elaine Messiger—

HARRY. Come on, babe.

CAPTAIN. Miss Francine Merle—

HARRY. No tricks, Francine. This is just identification.

CAPTAIN. Miss Edna Creesh—

HARRY. Turn it off, honey.

CAPTAIN. And Miss Bebe Gould.

HARRY. You'll find Bebe a very, very lovely girl.

BEBE [*remonstrating*]. *Harry!*

HARRY. A shimmy artiste, and incorrigibly unsophisticated.

CAPTAIN [*summing up*]. Very beautiful. Very, very beautiful. Mr. Van, I congratulate you.

HARRY. That's nice of you, Captain. Now, can we . . .

CAPTAIN. And I wish I, too, were going to Geneva. [*He hands back the passports to* HARRY.]

HARRY. Then it's O.K. for us to pass?

CAPTAIN. But won't you young ladies sit down?

SHIRLEY. Thanks, Captain.

BEULAH. We'd love to.

FRANCINE. He's cute.

EDNA. I'll say. [*They all sit.*]

HARRY. I don't want to seem oblivious of your courtesy, Captain, but the fact is we can't afford to hang around here any longer. That train may pull out and leave us.

CAPTAIN. I give you my word, that train will not move tonight, and maybe not tomorrow night, and maybe never. [*He bows deeply.*] It is a matter of the deepest personal regret to me, Mr. Van, but—

HARRY. Listen, pal. Could you stop being polite for just a moment, and tell us how do we get to Geneva?

CAPTAIN. That is not for me to say. I am as powerless as you are, Mr. Van. I, too, am a pawn. [*He picks up his coat and hat.*] But, speaking for myself, I shall not be sorry if you and your beautiful companions are forced to remain here indefinitely. [*He salutes the girls, smiles and goes out.*]

HARRY. Did you hear that? He says he's a pawn.

BEBE. He's a Wop.

BEULAH. But he's cute!

SHIRLEY. Personally, I'd just as soon stay here. I'm sick of the slats on those stinking day coaches.

HARRY. After the way we've been betrayed in the Balkans, we can't afford to stay any place. [*He turns to* DON.] What's the matter, anyway? Why can't decent respectable people be allowed to go about their legitimate business?

DON. Evidently you're not fully aware of the international situation.

HARRY. I'm fully aware that the international situation is always regrettable. But what's wrong now?

DON. Haven't you been reading the papers?

HARRY. In Bulgaria and Jugo-Slavia? [*He looks around at the girls, who laugh.*] No.

DON. It may be difficult for you to understand, Mr. Van, but we happen to be on the brink of a frightful calamity.

HARRY. What?

DON. We're on the verge of war.

SHIRLEY. War?

BEBE. What about?

HARRY. You mean—that business in Africa?

DON. Far more serious than that! *World* war! All of them!

HARRY. No lie! You mean—it'll be started by people like that? [*Points after the* CAPTAIN.] Italians?

DON. Yes. They've reached the breaking point.

HARRY. I don't believe it. I don't believe that people like that would take on the job of licking the world. They're too romantic. [PITTALUGA *steps forward.*]

PITTALUGA. You wish rooms, Signor?

HARRY. What have you got?

PITTALUGA. We can give you grande luxe accommodations, rooms with baths. . . .

HARRY. What's your scale of prices?

PITTALUGA. From fifty lira up.

DON. That's about five dollars a day.

HARRY [*wincing*]. What?

DON. Meals included.

HARRY. I take it there's the usual professional discount.

PITTALUGA [*to* DON]. Che cosa significa?

DON. Mr. Van and the young ladies are artists.

PITTALUGA. Ebbene?

DON [*scornfully*]. In America we give special rates to artists.

PITTALUGA [*grimly*]. Non posso, non posso.

[*The* CHERRYS *appear on the balcony above.*]

DON. I'm sure Mr. Pittaluga will take care of you nicely, Mr. Van. He will show you attractive rooms on the *other* side of the hotel. They're delightful.

HARRY. No doubt. But I want to see the accommodations.

PITTALUGA. Step this way, please.

HARRY. Come on, girls. Now—I want two girls to a room, and a single room for me adjoining. I promised their mothers I'd always be within earshot. Put on your shoes, Beulah. [*He goes out right, followed by the* GIRLS *and* DON.]

BEULAH [*as they go*]. Why's he kicking? I think this place is *attractive!*

SHIRLEY. Oh—you know Harry. He's always got to have something to worry about. [*They have gone.*]

MRS. CHERRY [*coming down*]. What an extraordinary gathering!

CHERRY. There's something I've never been able to understand—the tendency of Americans to travel en masse. [*They pause to admire the view and each other. He takes her in his arms and kisses her.*] Darling!

MRS. CHERRY. What?

CHERRY. Nothing. I just said, "Darling"! [*He kisses her again.*] My sweet. I love you.

MRS. CHERRY. That's right. [*She kisses him.*]

CHERRY. I think we're going to like it here, aren't we, darling?

MRS. CHERRY. Yes. You'll find a lot to paint.

CHERRY. No doubt. But I'm not going to waste any time painting.

MRS. CHERRY. Why not, Jimmy? You've got to work and—

CHERRY. Don't ask "why not" in that laboriously girlish tone! You know damned well why not!

MRS. CHERRY [*laughing*]. Now really darling. We don't have to be maudlin. We're old enough to be sensible about it, aren't we!

CHERRY. God forbid that we should spoil everything by being sensible! This is an occasion for pure and beautiful foolishness. So don't irritate me by any further mention of work.

MRS. CHERRY. Very well, darling. If you're going to be stinking about it . . . [*He kisses her again.*]

[*The* DOCTOR *comes in from the right and regards their love-making with scant enthusiasm. They look up and see him. They aren't embarrassed.*]

CHERRY. How do you do?

DOCTOR. Don't let me interrupt you. [*He rings a bell and sits down.*]

CHERRY. It's quite all right. We were just starting out for a walk.

MRS. CHERRY. The air is so marvelous up here, isn't it?

DOCTOR [*doubtfully*]. Yes.

[DUMPTSY *comes in from the right.*]

CHERRY. Yes—we think so. Come on, darling. [*They go out at the back.*]

DOCTOR. Mineral water.

DUMPTSY. Yes, sir.

[QUILLERY *comes in and sits at the left. He is small, dark, brooding and French—an extreme-radical-socialist, but still, French.*]

DOCTOR. Not iced—warm.

DUMPTSY. If you please, sir. [*He goes out, left.*]

[*A group of five Italian flying corps officers come in, talking gaily in Italian. They cross to the bar entrance and go out.*]

FIRST OFFICER. Sono Americane.

SECOND OFFICER. Sono belle, proprio da far strabiliare.

THIRD OFFICER. Forse sarranno stelle cinematografiche di Hollyvood.

SECOND OFFICER. E forse ora non ci rincrescerà che abbiano cancellato la nostra licenza. [*They go into the bar.*]

HARRY [*coming in*]. Good afternoon.

DOCTOR. Good afternoon.

HARRY. Have a drink?

DOCTOR. I am about to have one.

HARRY. Mind if I join you? [*He sits down near the* DOCTOR.]

DOCTOR. This is a public room.

HARRY [*whistles a snatch of a tune*]. It's a funny kind of situation, isn't it?

DOCTOR. To what situation do you refer?

HARRY. All this stopping of trains . . . [DUMPTSY *enters from the bar and serves the* DOCTOR *with a glass of mineral water.*] and orders from Rome and we are on the threshold of calamity.

DOCTOR. To me it is not funny. [*He rises with his mineral water.*]

HARRY. Get me a Scotch.

DUMPTSY. With soda, sir?

HARRY. Yes.

DUMPTSY. If you please, sir.

QUILLERY. I will have a beer.

DUMPTSY. We have native or imported, sir.

QUILLERY. Native will do.

DUMPTSY. If you please, sir. [*He goes out.*]

DOCTOR. I repeat—to me it is *not* funny! [*He bows.*] You will excuse me.

HARRY. Certainly. . . . See you later, pal. [*The* DOCTOR *goes.* HARRY *turns to* QUILLERY.] Friendly old bastard!

QUILLERY. Quite! But you were right. The situation *is* funny. There is always something essentially laughable in the thought of a lunatic asylum. Although, it may perhaps seem less funny when you are inside.

HARRY. I guess so. I guess it isn't easy for Germans to see the comical side of things these days. Do you mind if I join you? [*He rises and crosses to the left.*]

QUILLERY. I beg of you to do so, my comrade.

HARRY. I don't like to thrust myself forward—[*He sits down.*]—but, you see, I travel with a group of blondes, and it's always a relief to find somebody to talk to. Have you seen the girls?

QUILLERY. Oh, yes.

HARRY. Alluring, aren't they?

QUILLERY. Very alluring.

[DUMPTSY *comes in with the drinks and goes.* HARRY *takes out his chewing gum, wraps it in paper, places it in a silver snuff box, which he shows to* QUILLERY.]

HARRY. That's a genuine antique snuff box of the period of Louis Quinze.

QUILLERY. Very interesting.

HARRY. It's a museum piece. [*Puts the box in his pocket.*] You've got to hoard your gum here in Europe.

QUILLERY. You've traveled far?

HARRY. Yeah—I've been a long way with that gorgeous array of beautiful girls. I took 'em from New York to Monte Carlo. To say we were a sensation in Monte Carlo would be to state a simple incontrovertible fact. But then I made the mistake of accepting an offer from the manager of the Club Arizona in Budapest. I found that conditions in the South-East are not so good.

QUILLERY. I traveled on the train with you from Zagreb.

HARRY. Zagreb! A plague spot! What were you doing there?

QUILLERY. I was attending the Labor Congress.

HARRY. Yeah—I heard about that. The night club people thought that the congress would bring in a lot of business. They were wrong. But—excuse me— [*Rises.*] My name is Harry Van.

QUILLERY [*rises*]. Quillery is my name.

HARRY. Glad to know you, Mr.—?

QUILLERY. Quillery.

HARRY. Quillery. [*Sits.*] I'm an American. What's your nationality?

QUILLERY. I have no nationality. [*Sits.*] I drink to your good health.

HARRY. And to your lack of nationality, of which I approve. [*They drink.*]

[SIGNOR *and* SIGNORA ROSSI *come in and cross to the bar.* ROSSI *is a consumptive.*]

ROSSI. Abbiamo trascorso una bella giornata, Nina. Beviamo un po'?

SIGNORA ROSSI. Dopo tutto quell' esercizio ti farebbe male. Meglio che tu ti riposi per un'oretta.

ROSSI. Ma, no, mi sento proprio bene. Andiamo. Mi riposerò più tardi. [*They go into the bar.*]

HARRY. I get an awful kick hearing Italian. It's beautiful. Do you speak it?

QUILLERY. Only a little. I was born in France. And I love my home. Perhaps if I had raised pigs—like my father, and all his fathers, back to the time when Caesar's Roman legions came—perhaps, if I had done that, I should have been a Frenchman, as they were. But I went to work in a factory—and machinery is international.

HARRY. And I suppose pigs are exclusively French?

QUILLERY. My father's pigs are! [HARRY *laughs.*] The factory where I have worked made artificial limbs— an industry that has been prosperous the last twenty years. But sometimes—in the evening—after my work —I would go out into the fields and help my father. And then, for a little while, I would become again a Frenchman.

HARRY [*takes out his cigarette case*]. That's a nice thought, pal. [*Offers* QUILLERY *a cigarette.*] Have a smoke?

QUILLERY. No, thank you.

HARRY. I don't blame you. These Jugo-Slav cigarettes are not made of the same high-grade quality of manure to which I grew accustomed in Bulgaria.

QUILLERY. You know, my comrade—you seem to have a long view of things.

HARRY. So long that it gets very tiresome.

QUILLERY. The long view is not easy to sustain in this short-sighted world.

HARRY. You're right about that, pal.

QUILLERY. Let me give you an instance: There we were—gathered in Zagreb, representatives of the workers of all Europe. All brothers, collaborating harmoniously for the United Front! And now—we are rushing to our homes to prevent our people from plunging into mass murder—mass suicide!

HARRY. You're going to try to stop the war?

QUILLERY. Yes.

HARRY. Do you think you'll succeed?

QUILLERY. Unquestionably! This is not 1914, remember! Since then, some new voices have been heard in this world—loud voices. I need mention only one of them—Lenin—Nikolai Lenin!

[*A ferocious looking* MAJOR *of the Italian flying corps comes in and goes quickly to the bar. As he opens the door, he calls "Attention!" He goes into the bar, the door swinging to behind him.*]

HARRY. Yes—but what are you going to do about people like *that*?

QUILLERY. Expose them! That's all we have to do. Expose them—for what they are—atavistic children! Occupying their undeveloped minds playing with outmoded toys.

HARRY. Have you *seen* any of those toys?

QUILLERY. Yes! France is full of them. But there is a force more potent than all the bombing planes and submarines and tanks. And that is the mature intelligence of the workers of the world! There is one. antidote for war—Revolution! And the cause of Revolution gains steadily in strength. Even here in Italy, despite all the repressive power of Fascism, sanity has survived, and it becomes more and more articulate. . . .

HARRY. Well, pal—you've got a fine point there. And I hope you stick to it.

QUILLERY. I'm afraid you think it is all futile idealism!

HARRY. No—I don't. And what if I did? I am an idealist myself.

QUILLERY. You too believe in the revolution?

HARRY. Not necessarily in *the* revolution. I'm just in favor of any revolution. Anything that will make people wake up, and get themselves some convictions. Have you ever taken cocaine?

QUILLERY. Why—I imagine that I have—at the dentist's.

HARRY. No—I mean, for pleasure. You know—a vice.

QUILLERY. No! I've never indulged in that folly.

HARRY. I have—during a stage of my career when luck was bad and confusion prevailed.

QUILLERY. Ah, yes. You needed delusions of grandeur.

HARRY. That's just what they were.

QUILLERY. It must have been an interesting experience.

HARRY. It was illuminating. It taught me what is the precise trouble with the world today. We have become a race of drug addicts—hopped up with false beliefs—false fears—false enthusiasms. . . .

[*The four* OFFICERS *emerge from the bar, talking excitedly.*]

SECOND OFFICER. Ma, è state fatta la dichiarazone di guerra attuale?

FIRST OFFICER. Caricheremo delle bombe esplosive?

THIRD OFFICER. Se la guerra è in cominciata, allora vuol dire che noi. . . .

FOURTH OFFICER. La guerra è in cominciata.

MAJOR. Silenzio! Solo il vostro commandante conosce gli ordini. Andiamo! [*All five go out hurriedly.*]

QUILLERY [*jumps up*]. Mother of God! Did you hear what they were saying?

HARRY [*rises*]. I heard, but I couldn't understand.

QUILLERY. It was about war. I know only a little Italian—but I thought they were saying that war has already been declared. [*He grabs his hat.*] I *must* go and demand that they let me cross the border! At once! [*He starts to go.*]

HARRY. That's right, pal. There's no time to lose.

QUILLERY. Wait – I haven't paid. . . . [*He is fumbling for money.*]

HARRY. No, no. This was my drink. You've got to hurry!

QUILLERY. Thank you, my comrade. [*He goes out quickly.*]

[*Airplane motors are heard, off at the right.* HARRY *crosses to the window.* DUMPTSY *comes in to remove the empty glasses.*]

DUMPTSY. Fine view, isn't it, sir?

HARRY. I've seen worse.

DUMPTSY. Nothing quite like it, sir. From here, we look into four nations. Where you see that little village, at the far end of the valley—that is Austria. Isn't that beautiful over there?

HARRY. Are you Italian?

DUMPTSY. Well, yes, sir. That is to say, I didn't used to be.

HARRY. What did you used to be?

DUMPTSY. Austrian. All this part was Austria, until after the big war, when they decided these mountains must go to Italy, and I went with them. In one day, I became a foreigner. So now, my children learn only Italian in school, and when I and my wife talk our own language they can't understand us. [*He gets* HARRY's *drink and brings it over to him.*] They changed the name of this mountain. Monte Gabriele—that's what it is now. They named it after an Italian who dropped poems on Vienna. Even my old father—he's dead—but all the writing on the gravestones was in German, so they rubbed it out and translated it. So now he's Italian, too. But they didn't get my sister. She married a Swiss. She lives over there, in Schleins.

HARRY. She's lucky.

DUMPTSY. Yes—those Swiss are smart.

HARRY. Yeah, they had sense enough to get over there in the first place.

DUMPTSY [*laughs*]. But it doesn't make much difference who your masters are. When you get used to
them, they're all the same.

[*The porter's bell rings.* PITTALUGA *appears.*]

PITTALUGA. Dumptsy! Dumptsy! Una gentildonna arriva. Prendi i suoi bagagli. Affretati!

DUMPTSY. Si, Signore. Vengo subito. [*He goes.*]

PITTALUGA [*claps his hands*]. Sciocco! Anna, Per Dio!
Dove sei stata, va sopra a preparare la stanza. [ANNA,
the maid, enters with towels.] Presto, presto!

[ANNA *runs up the steps, exits.* PITTALUGA *goes back
into the lobby.*]

IRENE'S VOICE. Vieni, Achille.

DON [*coming in*]. This is our cocktail lounge, madame.

[IRENE *enters. She is somewhere between thirty and
forty, beautiful, heavily and smartly furred in the
Russian manner. Her hair is blonde and quite
straight. She is a model of worldly wisdom, chic,
and carefully applied graciousness. Her name is
pronounced* "EAR-RAY-NA." . . . *She surveys the
room with polite appreciation, glancing briefly at*
HARRY.]

DON. Your suite is up there, madame. All this part of
the hotel is quite new.

IRENE. How very nice!

DON. We have our best view from this side of the
hotel. [*He goes to the window.* IRENE *follows slowly.*]
You can see four countries—Italy, Switzerland, Austria and Bavaria.

IRENE. Magnificent!

DON. Yes—we're very proud of it.

IRENE. All those countries. And they all look so very
much alike, don't they!

DON. Yes—they do really—from this distance.

IRENE. All covered with the beautiful snow. I think
the whole world should be always covered with

snow. It would be so much more clean, wouldn't it?

DON. By all means!

IRENE. Like in my Russia. White Russia. [*Sighs, and goes up to the next landing.*] Oh, and—how exciting! A flying field. Look! They're bringing out the big bombers.

DON. Madame is interested in aviation?

IRENE. No, no. Just ordinary flying bores me. But there is no experience in life quite so thrilling as a parachute jump, is there!

DON. I've never had that thrill, I'm ashamed to say.

IRENE. Once I had to jump when I was flying over the jungle in Indo-China. It was indescribable. Drifting down, sinking into that great green sea of enchantment and hidden danger.

[DUMPTSY *comes in.*]

DON. And you weren't afraid?

IRENE. No—no—I was not afraid. In moments like that, one is given the sense of eternity.

HARRY [*viciously*]. Dumptsy! Get me another Scotch.

DUMPTSY. Yes, sir.

HARRY. And put ice in it, this time. If you haven't got any ice, go out and scoop up some snow.

DUMPTSY. If you please, sir. [*He goes into the bar.*]

IRENE [*her gaze wandering about the room*]. But your place is really charming.

DON. You're very kind.

IRENE. I must tell everyone in Paris about it. There's something about this design—it suggests a—an amusing kind of horror.

DON [*not knowing quite how to interpret that*]. Madame is a student of decoration?

IRENE. No, no. Only an amateur, my friend. An amateur, I'm afraid, in everything.

[*The siren sounds from off at the right.* IRENE, *near the top of the staircase, stops to listen.*]

IRENE. What is that?

DON. Oh—it's merely some kind of warning. They've been testing it.

IRENE. Warning? Warning against what?

DON. I believe it's for use in case of war.

IRENE. War? But there will be no war.

[PITTALUGA *enters from the lobby, escorting* ACHILLE WEBER—*which is pronounced* "VAY-BAIR." *He is a thin, keen executive, wearing a neat little mustache and excellent clothes. In his lapel is the rosette of the Legion of Honor. He carries a brief case.*]

PITTALUGA [*as they come in*]. Par ici, Monsieur Weber. Vous trouverez Madame ici . . .

IRENE [*leaning over the railing*]. Achille!

WEBER [*pausing and looking up*]. Yes, my dear?

IRENE. Achille—there will be no war, will there?

WEBER [*amused*]. No, no—Irene. There will be no war. They're all much too well prepared for it. [*He turns to* PITTALUGA.] Where are our rooms?

PITTALUGA. Votre suite est par ici, Monsieur. La plus belle de la maison! La vue est superbe!

IRENE [*to* DON]. There, you see! They will not fight. They are all much too much afraid of each other.

[WEBER *is going up the staircase, ignoring the view.* PITTALUGA *is following.*]

IRENE [*to* WEBER]. Achille—I am mad about this place! Je rafolle de cette place!

WEBER [*calmly*]. Yes, my dear.

IRENE. We must be sure to tell the Maharajah of Raj-pipla, Achille. Can't you imagine how dear little "Pip" would love this? [*They go out on the landing above.*]

HARRY. Who was that?

DON [*impressed*]. That was Achille Weber. One of the biggest men in France. I used to see him a lot at St. Moritz.

[*There is a sound of airplane motors off at the right.*]

HARRY. And the dame? Do you assume that is his wife?

DON [*curtly*]. Are you implying that she's not?

HARRY. No, no—I'm not implying a thing. [*He wanders to the piano.*] I'm just kind of—kind of baffled.

DON. Evidently. [*He goes out.*]

[HARRY *at the piano strikes a chord of the Russian song, "Kak Stranna."* DUMPTSY *enters from the bar and serves* HARRY *with Scotch. The off-stage noise increases as more planes take the air.*]

DUMPTSY [*at the window*]. Do you see them—those aeroplanes—flying up from the field down there?

HARRY [*glances toward window, without interest*]. Yes —I see them.

DUMPTSY. Those are the big ones. They're full of bombs, to drop on people. Look! They're going north. Maybe Berlin. Maybe Paris.

[*Harry strikes a few chords.*]

HARRY. Did you ever jump with a parachute?

DUMPTSY. Why, no—sir. [*He looks questioningly at* HARRY.]

HARRY. Well, I have—a couple of times. And it's nothing. But—I didn't land in any jungle. I landed where I was supposed to—in the Fair Grounds.

DUMPTSY [*seriously*]. That's interesting, sir.

[*The* ROSSIS *enter from the bar. He is holding a handkerchief to his mouth. She is supporting him as they cross.*]

SIGNORA ROSSI. Non t'ho detto che dovevi fare attenzione? Te l'ho detto, te l'ho detto che sarebbe accaduto ciò. Vedi, ora ti piglia un accesso di tosse.

ROSSI. 'Scusatemi, Mina. [*Another coughing fit.*]

SIGNORA ROSSI. Va a sdraiarti. Dovresti riposarti a lungo. E adopera il termometro. Scommetto che t'è aumentata la temperatura. [*They go out.*]

DUMPTSY. That Signor Rossi—he has tuberculosis.

HARRY. Is he getting cured up here?

[*The* DOCTOR *appears on the landing above.*]

DUMPTSY. Ja. This used to be a sanatorium, in the old days. But the Fascisti—they don't like to admit that anyone can be sick! [*He starts to go.*]

DOCTOR. Dumptsy!

DUMPTSY. Herr Doctor.

DOCTOR [*coming down*]. Mineral water.

DUMPTSY. Ja wohl, Herr Doctor. [DUMPTSY *goes out, left.*]

[*The* DOCTOR *sits down.* HARRY *takes one more look toward the gallery, where* IRENE *had been. He then looks at the* DOCTOR, *and decides not to suggest joining him. He starts to play "Kak Stranna." The* DOCTOR *turns and looks at him, with some surprise. The uproar of planes is now terrific, but it starts to dwindle as the planes depart.*]

DOCTOR. What is that you are playing?

HARRY. A Russian song, entitled "Kak Stranna," meaning "how strange!" One of those morose ballads about how once we met, for one immortal moment, like ships that pass in the night. Or maybe like a couple of trucks, side-swiping each other. And now we meet again! How strange!

DOCTOR. You are a musician?

HARRY. Certainly. I used to play the piano in picture theatres—when that was the only kind of sound they had—except the peanuts.

[DUMPTSY *brings the mineral water and stops to listen, admiringly.*]

DOCTOR. Do you know Bach?

HARRY. With pleasure. [*He shifts into something or other by Bach.*]

DOCTOR [*after a moment*]. You have good appreciation, but not much skill.

HARRY. What do you mean, not much skill? Listen to

this. [*He goes into a trick arrangement of* "The Waters of the Minnetonka."] "The Waters of the Minnetonka"—Cadman. [*He goes on playing.*] Suitable for Scenics—Niagara Falls by moonlight. Or—if you play it this way—it goes fine with the scene where the young Indian chief turns out to be a Yale man, so it's O.K. for him to marry Lillian "Dimples" Walker. [*Starts playing* "Boola Boola."]

DOCTOR. Will you have a drink?

HARRY. Oh! So you want me to stop playing?

DOCTOR. No, no! I like your music very much.

HARRY. Then, in that case, I'd be delighted to drink with you. Another Scotch, Dumptsy.

DUMPTSY. If you please, sir. [*He goes out.*]

DOCTOR. I'm afraid I was rude to you.

HARRY. That's all right, pal. I've been rude to lots of people, and never regretted it. [*He plays on, shifting back into* "Kak Stranna."]

DOCTOR. The fact is, I am a man who is very gravely distressed.

HARRY. I can see that, Doctor. And I sympathize with you.

DOCTOR [*fiercely*]. You cannot sympathize with me, because you do not know!

HARRY. No—I guess I don't know—except in a general way.

DOCTOR. You are familiar with the writings of Thomas Mann. [*It is a challenge, rather than a question.*]

HARRY. I'm afraid not, pal.

[*The* DOCTOR *opens* "The Magic Mountain," *which he has been reading.*]

DOCTOR. "Backsliding"—he said—"spiritual backsliding to that dark and tortured age—that, believe me, is disease! A degradation of mankind—a degradation painful and offensive to conceive." True words, eh?

HARRY. Absolutely!

[DUMPTSY *comes in with the Scotch.* HARRY *gets up from the piano and crosses.* DUMPTSY *goes.* HARRY *sits down with the* DOCTOR.]

DOCTOR. Have you had any experience with cancer?

HARRY. Certainly. I once sold a remedy for it.

DOCTOR [*exploding*]. There *is* no remedy for it, so far!

HARRY. Well—this was kind of a remedy for everything.

DOCTOR. I am within *that* of finding the cure for cancer! You probably have not heard of Fibiger, I suppose?

HARRY. I may have. I'm not sure.

DOCTOR. He was a Dane—experimented with rats. He did good work, but he died before it could be completed. I carry it on. I have been working with Oriental rats, in Bologna. But because of this war scare, I must go to neutral territory. You see, nothing must be allowed to interfere with my experiments. Nothing!

HARRY. No. They're important.

DOCTOR. The laboratory of the University of Zurich has been placed at my disposal—and in Switzerland, I can work, undisturbed. I have twenty-eight rats with me, all in various carefully tabulated stages of the disease. It is the disease of civilization—and I can cure it. And now they say I must not cross the border.

HARRY. You know, Doctor, it *is* funny.

DOCTOR. What's funny? To you, everything is funny!

HARRY. No—it's just that you and I are in the same fix. Both trying to get across that line. You with rats—me with girls. Of course—I appreciate the fact that civilization at large won't suffer much if *we* get stuck in the war zone. Whereas with you, there's a lot at stake. . . .

DOCTOR. It is for me to win one of the greatest victories of all time. And the victory belongs to Germany.

HARRY. Sure it does!

DOCTOR. Unfortunately, just now the situation in Germany is not good for research. They are infected with the same virus as here. Chauvinistic nationalism! They expect all bacteriologists to work on germs to put in bombs to drop from airplanes. To fill people with death! When we've given our lives to *save* people. Oh—God in heaven—why don't they let me do what is good? Good for the whole world? Forgive me. I become excited.

HARRY. I know just how you feel, Doctor. Back in 1918, I was a shill with a carnival show, and I was doing fine. The boss thought very highly of me. He offered to give me a piece of the show, and I had a chance to get somewhere. And then what do you think happened? Along comes the United States Government and they drafted me! You're in the army now! They slapped me into a uniform and for three whole months before the Armistice, I was parading up and down guarding the Ashokan Reservoir. They were afraid your people might poison it. I've always figured that that little interruption ruined my career. But I've remained an optimist, Doctor.

DOCTOR. *You* can afford to.

HARRY. I've remained an optimist because I'm essentially a student of human nature. You dissect corpses and rats and similar unpleasant things. Well—it has been my job to dissect suckers! I've probed into the souls of some of the God-damnedest specimens. And what have I found? Now, don't sneer at me, Doctor—but above everything else I've found faith. Faith in peace on earth and good will to men and faith that "Muma," "Muma" the three-legged girl, really has got three legs. All my life, Doctor, I've been selling phony goods to people of meager intelligence and great faith. You'd think that would make me contemptuous of the human race, wouldn't you? But—on the contrary—it has given *me* faith. It has made me sure that no matter how much the meek may be bulldozed or gypped they *will* eventually inherit the earth.

[SHIRLEY *and* BEBE *come in from the lobby.*]

SHIRLEY. Harry!

HARRY. What is it, honey?

[SHIRLEY *goes to* HARRY *and hands him a printed notice.*]

SHIRLEY [*excited*]. Did you see this?

HARRY. Doctor—let me introduce, Miss Shirley Laughlin and Miss Bebe Gould.

SHIRLEY. How do you do?

DOCTOR [*grunts*]. How do you do.

BEBE. Pleased to know you, Doctor.

[HARRY *looks at the notice.*]

SHIRLEY. They got one of those put up in every one of our rooms.

HARRY [*showing it to the* DOCTOR]. Look— "What to do in case of air raids"—in all languages.

DOCTOR. Ja—I saw that.

SHIRLEY. Give it back to me, Harry. I'm going to send it to Mama.

HARRY [*handing it to her*]. Souvenir of Europe.

SHIRLEY. It'll scare the hell out of her.

BEBE. What's the matter with these people over here? Are they all screwy?

HARRY. Bebe—you hit it right on the nose! [*Turns to the* DOCTOR.] I tell you, Doctor—these are very wonderful, profound girls. The mothers of tomorrow! [*He beams on them.* BEULAH *comes in.*]

SHIRLEY. Oh—shut up!

BEULAH. Say—Harry . . .

HARRY. What is it, honey?

BEULAH. Is it all right if I go out with Mr. Navadel and try to learn how to do this ski-ing?

[WEBER *comes out on the gallery and starts down.*]

HARRY. What? And risk those pretty legs? Emphatically—no!

BEULAH. But it's healthy.

HARRY. Not for me, dear. Those gams of yours are my bread and butter. [WEBER *crosses. They look at him. He glances briefly at them.*] Sit down, girls, and amuse yourselves with your own thoughts.

[*The* GIRLS *sit.* WEBER, *at the left, lights his cigar. The* CAPTAIN *comes in, quickly, obviously worried.*]

CAPTAIN. I have been trying to get through to headquarters, Monsieur Weber.

WEBER. And when can we leave?

CAPTAIN. Not before tomorrow, I regret to say.

[IRENE *appears on the gallery.*]

WEBER. Signor Lanza in Venice assured me there would be no delay.

CAPTAIN. There would be none, if only I could get into communication with the proper authorities. But—the wires are crowded. The whole nation is in a state of uproar.

WEBER. It's absurd lack of organization.

[*The* PIANIST *and* DRUMMER *come in from the lobby. The* VIOLINIST *and* SAXOPHONIST *follow.*]

CAPTAIN [*with tense solemnity*]. There is good excuse for the excitement now, Monsieur Weber. The report has just come to us that a state of war exists between Italy and France.

HARRY. What?

CAPTAIN. There is a rumor of war between Italy and France!

HARRY. Rumors—rumors—everything's rumors! When are we going to *know*?

CAPTAIN. Soon enough, my friend.

DOCTOR. And what of Germany?

CAPTAIN. Germany has mobilized. [IRENE *pauses to listen.*] But I don't know if any decision has been reached. Nor do I know anything of the situation anywhere else. But—God help us—it will be serious enough for everyone on this earth.

[IRENE *joins* WEBER, *who has sat down at the left.*]

IRENE [*to* WEBER, *and straight at him*]. But I thought they were all too well prepared, Achille. Has there been some mistake somewhere?

WEBER [*confidentially*]. We can only attribute it to spontaneous combustion of the dictatorial ego.

IRENE [*grimly*]. I can imagine how thrilling it must be in Paris at this moment. Just like 1914. All the lovely soldiers—singing—marching! We must go at once to Paris, Achille.

HARRY [*rises*]. What's the matter with the music, professor? Us young folks want to dance.

[ELAINE *and* FRANCINE *come in.*]

ELAINE. Can we have a drink now, Harry?

HARRY. Sure. Sit down.

[DON *enters, exuding gratification at the sight of this gay, chic throng. The* ORCHESTRA *starts to play "Valencia."*]

WEBER. Will you have a drink, Irene?

IRENE. No, thank you.

WEBER. Will you, Captain Locicero?

CAPTAIN. Thank you. Brandy and soda, Dumptsy.

DUMPTSY. Si, Signor.

BEBE [*yells*]. Edna! We're going to have a drink!

[EDNA *comes in.*]

WEBER. For me, Cinzano.

DUMPTSY. Oui, Monsieur. [*He goes into the bar.*]

DOCTOR. It is all incredible.

HARRY. Nevertheless, Doctor, I remain an optimist. [*He looks at* IRENE.] Let doubt prevail throughout this night—with dawn will come again the light of truth! [*He turns to* SHIRLEY.] Come on, honey—let's dance. [*They dance.*]

[DON *dances with* BEULAH. *The* ORCHESTRA *continues with its spirited but frail performance of* "Valencia." *There are probably* "border incidents" *in Lorraine, the Riviera, Poland, Czecho-Slovakia and Mongolia.*]

CURTAIN

Act two

SCENE I

It is about 7:30 in the evening of the same day.

The CHERRYS *are seated, both of them dressed for dinner.* AUGUSTE *is serving them cocktails.*

CHERRY. Thank you.

AUGUSTE. Thank you, Signor.

CHERRY. Has any more news come through?

AUGUSTE. No, Signor. They permit the wireless to say nothing.

CHERRY. I suppose nothing really will happen.

AUGUSTE. Let us pray that is so, Signor. [AUGUSTE *goes into the bar.* CHERRY *leans over and kisses his wife.*]

CHERRY. My sweet . . . you're really very lovely.

MRS. CHERRY. Yes. [*He kisses her again, then lifts his glass.*]

CHERRY. Here's to us, darling.

MRS. CHERRY. And to hell with all the rest.

CHERRY. And to hell with all the rest. [*They drink, solemnly.*]

MRS. CHERRY. Jimmy—

CHERRY. What is it, darling?

MRS. CHERRY. Were you just saying that—or do you believe it?

CHERRY. That you're lovely? I can give you the most solemn assurance. . . .

MRS. CHERRY. No—that nothing is going to happen.

CHERRY. Oh.

MRS. CHERRY. Do you believe that?

CHERRY. I know this much: they can't start any real war without England. And no matter how stupid and blundering our government may be, our people simply won't stand for it.

MRS. CHERRY. But people can be such complete fools.

CHERRY. I know it, darling. Why can't they all be like us?

MRS. CHERRY. You mean—nice.

CHERRY. Yes—nice—and intelligent—and happy.

MRS. CHERRY. We're very conceited, aren't we?

CHERRY. Of course. And for good and sufficient reason.

MRS. CHERRY. I'm glad we're so superior, darling. It's comforting.

[HARRY *comes in from bar.*]

CHERRY. Oh—good evening, Mr. Van.

HARRY. Good evening. Pardon me— [*He starts to go.*]

CHERRY. Oh—don't run away, Mr. Van. Let's have some music.

MRS. CHERRY. Won't you have a drink with us?

HARRY. No, thanks, Mrs. Cherry—if you don't mind. [*Sits down at the piano.*] I'm afraid I put down too many Scotches this afternoon. As a result of which, I've just had to treat myself to a bicarbonate of soda. [*Starts playing* "Some of These Days."]

MRS. CHERRY. I love that.

HARRY. Thanks, pal—always grateful for applause from the discriminating. [*Finishes the chorus and stops.*]

CHERRY. Do play some more.

HARRY. No. The mood isn't right.

MRS. CHERRY. I can't tell you what a relief it is to have you here in this hotel.

HARRY. It's kind of you to say that, Mrs. Cherry. But I don't deserve your handsome tribute. Frequently, I can be an asset to any gathering—contributing humorous anecdotes and bits of homely philosophy. But here and now, I'm far from my best.

CHERRY. You're the only one here who seems to have retained any degree of sanity.

MRS. CHERRY. You and your young ladies.

HARRY. The girls are lucky. They don't know anything. And the trouble with me is that I just don't give a damn.

MRS. CHERRY. We've been trying hard not to know anything—or not to give a damn. But it isn't easy.

HARRY. You haven't been married very long, have you? I hope you don't mind my asking. . . .

CHERRY. We were married the day before yesterday.

HARRY. Let me offer my congratulations.

CHERRY. Thank you very much.

HARRY. It's my purely intuitive hunch that you two ought to get along fine.

CHERRY. That's our intention, Mr. Van.

MRS. CHERRY. And we'll do it, what's more. You see— we have one supreme thing in common:

HARRY. Yeah?

MRS. CHERRY. We're both independent.

CHERRY. We're like you Americans, in that respect.

HARRY. You flatter us.

MRS. CHERRY. Jimmy's a painter.

HARRY. You don't say!

MRS. CHERRY. He's been out in Australia, doing colos-

sal murals for some government building. He won't
show me the photographs of them, but I'm sure
they're simply awful. [*She laughs fondly.*]

CHERRY. They're allegorical. [*He laughs, too.*]

HARRY. I'll bet they're good, at that. What do you
do, Mrs. Cherry?

MRS. CHERRY. Oh, I work in the gift department at
Fortnum's—

HARRY. Behind a counter, eh!

MRS. CHERRY. Yes—wearing a smock, and disgracing
my family.

HARRY. Well, what d'ye know!

MRS. CHERRY. Both our families hoped we'd be married in some nice little church, and settle down in
a nice little cottage, in a nice little state of decay.
But when I heard Jimmy was on the way home I
just dropped everything and rushed down here to
meet him—and we were married, in Florence.

CHERRY. We hadn't seen each other for nearly a year
—so, you can imagine, it was all rather exciting.

HARRY. I can imagine.

MRS. CHERRY. Florence is the most perfect place in the
world to be married in.

HARRY. I guess that's true of any place.

CHERRY. We both happen to love Italy. And—I suppose—we're both rather on the romantic side.

HARRY. You stay on that side, no matter what happens.

MRS. CHERRY [*quickly*]. What do you think is going to
happen?

HARRY. Me? I haven't the slightest idea.

CHERRY. We've looked forward so much to being here
with no one bothering us, and plenty of winter
sports. We're both keen on ski-ing. And now—we
may have to go dashing back to England at any moment.

MRS. CHERRY. It's rotten luck, isn't it?

HARRY. Yes, Mrs. Cherry. That's what it is—it's rotten. [QUILLERY *enters from the bar, reading a newspaper.*] So they wouldn't let you cross?

QUILLERY. No!

HARRY. Is there any news?

QUILLERY [*glaring*]. News! Not in this patriotic journal. "Unconfirmed rumors"—from Vienna, London, Berlin, Moscow, Tokyo. And a lot of confirmed lies from Fascist headquarters in Rome. [*He slaps the paper down and sits.*] If you want to know what is really happening, ask *him*—up there! [*Indicates the rooms above.*]

CHERRY. Who?

QUILLERY. Weber! The great Monsieur Achille Weber, of the Comité des Forges! He can give you all the war news. Because he *made* it. You don't know who he is, eh? Or what he has been doing here in Italy? I'll tell you. [*He rises and comes close to them.*] He has been organizing the arms industry. Munitions. To kill French babies. And English babies. France and Italy are at war. England joins France. Germany joins Italy. And that will drag in the Soviet Union and the Japanese Empire and the United States. In every part of the world, the good desire of men for peace and decency is undermined by the dynamite of jingoism. And it needs only one spark, set off anywhere by one egomaniac, to send it all up in one final, fatal explosion. Then love becomes hatred, courage becomes terror, hope becomes despair. [*The* DOCTOR *appears on the gallery above.*] But—it will all be very nice for Achille Weber. Because he is a master of the one *real* League of Nations— [*The* DOCTOR *slowly comes down steps.*] The League of Schneider-Creusot, and Krupp, and Skoda, and Vickers and Dupont. The League of Death! And the workers of the world are expected to pay him for it, with their sweat, and their life's blood.

DOCTOR. Marxian nonsense!

QUILLERY. Ah! Who speaks?

DOCTOR. *I* speak.

QUILLERY. Yes! The eminent Dr. Hugo Waldersee. A wearer of the sacred swastika. Down with the Communists! Off with their heads! So that the world may be safe for the Nazi murderers.

DOCTOR. So that Germany may be safe from its oppressors! It is the same with all of you—Englishmen, Frenchmen, Marxists—you manage to forget that Germany, too, has a right to live! [*Rings handbell on the table.*]

QUILLERY. If you love Germany so much, why aren't you there, now—with your rats?

DOCTOR [*sitting*]. I am not concerned with politics. [AUGUSTE *enters from the bar.*] I am a scientist. [*To* AUGUSTE.] Mineral water!

[AUGUSTE *bows and exits into the bar.*]

QUILLERY. That's it, Herr Doctor! A scientist—a servant of humanity! And you know that if you were in your dear Fatherland, the Nazis would make you abandon your cure of cancer. It might benefit too many people outside of Germany—even maybe some Jews. They would force you to devote yourself to breeding malignant bacteria—millions of little germs, each one trained to give the Nazi salute and then go out and poison the enemy. You—a fighter against disease and death—you would become a Judas goat in a slaughter house.

[DON *has appeared during this.*]

CHERRY. I say, Quillery, old chap—do we have to have so much blood and sweat just before dinner?

QUILLERY [*turning on him*]. Just before dinner! And now we hear the voice of England! The great, well-fed, pious hypocrite! The grabber—the exploiter—the immaculate butcher! It was *you* forced this war, because miserable little Italy dared to drag its black shirt across your trail of Europe. What do *you* care if civilization goes to pieces—as long as you have your dinner—and your dinner jacket!

CHERRY [*rising*]. I'm sorry, Quillery—but I think we'd better conclude this discussion out on the terrace.

MRS. CHERRY. Don't be a damned fool, Jimmy. You'll prove nothing by thrashing him.

QUILLERY. It's the Anglo-Saxon method of proving everything! Very well—I am at your disposal.

DON. No! I beg of you, Mr. Cherry. We mustn't have any of that sort of thing. [*He turns to* QUILLERY.] I must ask you to leave. If you're unable to conduct yourself as a gentleman, then . . .

QUILLERY. Don't say any more. Evidently I cannot conduct myself properly! I offer my apologies, Mr. Cherry.

CHERRY. That's quite all right, old man. Have a drink. [*He extends his hand. They shake.*]

QUILLERY. No, thank you. And my apologies to you, Herr Doctor.

DOCTOR. There is no need for apologizing. I am accustomed to all that.

QUILLERY. If I let my speech run away with me, it is because I have hatred for certain things. And you should hate them, too. They are the things that make us blind—and ignorant—and—and dirty. [*He turns and goes out quickly.* DON *goes with him.*]

MRS. CHERRY. He's so right about everything.

CHERRY. I know, poor chap. Will you have another cocktail, darling?

MRS. CHERRY. I don't think so. Will you, Doctor? [*He shakes his head, indicates the mineral water. She rises.*] Let's dine.

CHERRY. It will be a bit difficult to summon up much relish. [*They go out, hand in hand.*]

HARRY. I find them very appealing, don't you, Doctor? [*The* DOCTOR *doesn't announce his findings.*] Did you know they were married only the day before yesterday? Yeah—they got themselves sealed in Florence—because they love Italy. And they came here hoping to spend their honeymoon on skis. . . . Kind of pathetic, isn't it?

DOCTOR. What did you say?

HARRY. Nothing, pal. [DON *comes in.*] Only making conversation.

DOCTOR [*rising*]. That Communist! Making me a criminal because I am a German!

DON. I'm dreadfully sorry, Dr. Waldersee. We never should have allowed the ill-bred little cad to come in here.

DOCTOR. Oh— It's no matter. I have heard too many hymns of hate before this. To be a German is to be used to insults, and injuries. [*He goes out.* DON *starts to go out left.*]

HARRY. Just a minute, Don.

DON. Well?

HARRY. Have you found out yet who that dame is?

DON. What "dame"?

HARRY. That Russian number with Weber.

DON. I have not inquired as to her identity.

HARRY. But did he register her as his wife?

DON. They registered separately! And if it's not too much to ask, might I suggest that you mind your own damned business?

HARRY. You might suggest just that. And I should still be troubled by one of the most tantalizing of questions—namely, "Where have I seen that face before?" Generally, it turns out to be someone who was in the second row one night, yawning.

DON. I'm sure that such is the case now. [*He starts again to go.*]

HARRY. One moment, Don. There's something else.

DON [*impatiently*]. What is it?

HARRY. I take it that your job here is something like that of a professional greeter.

DON. You're at liberty to call it that, if you choose.

HARRY. You're a sort of Y.M.C.A. secretary—who sees to it that all the guests get together and have a good time.

DON. Well?

HARRY. Well—do you think you're doing a very good job of it right now?

DON [*simply furious*]. Have you any suggestions for improving the performance of my duties?

HARRY. Yes, Don—I have.

DON. And I'd very much like to know just exactly who the hell do you think you are to be offering criticism of my work?

HARRY. Please, please! You needn't scream at me. I'm merely trying to be helpful. I'm making you an offer.

DON. What is it?

HARRY [*looking around*]. I see you've got a color wheel here. [*Referring to the light.*]

DON. We use it during the supper dance. But—if you don't mind, I—

HARRY. I see—well—how would it be if I and the girls put on part of our act here, tonight? For purposes of wholesome merriment and relieving the general tension?

DON. What kind of an act is it?

HARRY. And don't say, "What kind of an act," in that tone of voice. It's good enough for this place. Those girls have played before the King of Rumania. And if some of my suspicions are correct—but I won't pursue that subject. All that need concern you is that we can adjust ourselves to our audience, and tonight we'll omit the bubble dance and the number in which little Bebe does a shimmy in a costume composed of detachable gardenias, unless there's a special request for it.

DON. Do you expect to be paid for this?

HARRY. Certainly not. I'm making this offer out of the goodness of my heart. Of course, if you want to make any appropriate adjustment on our hotel bill . . .

DON. And you'll give me your guarantee that there'll be no vulgarity?

[IRENE *appears on the gallery and starts to come down. She is wearing a dinner dress.*]

HARRY. Now be careful, Don. One more word like that and the offer is withdrawn . . .

[DON *cautions him to silence.*]

DON. It's a splendid idea, Mr. Van. We'll all greatly appreciate your little entertainment, I'm sure. [*To* IRENE]. Good evening, madame.

IRENE [*with the utmost graciousness*]. Good evening, Mr. Navadel. [*She pauses at the window.*] It *is* a lovely view. It's like a landscape on the moon.

DON. Yes—yes. That's exactly what it's like.

[*She comes down.*]

HARRY. You understand, we'll have to rehearse with the orchestra.

DON. Oh, yes—Mr. Van. Our staff will be glad to co-operate in every way. . . Do sit down, madame.

IRENE [*sitting*]. What became of those planes that flew off this afternoon? I haven't heard them come back. [*Takes out a cigarette.*]

DON. I imagine they were moving to some base farther from the frontier. I hope so. They always made the most appalling racket. [*Lights her cigarette for her.*]

HARRY. About eleven o'clock?

[WEBER *appears on the gallery.*]

DON. Yes, Mr. Van. Eleven will do nicely. You'll have a cocktail, madame?

[HARRY *goes into the lobby.*]

IRENE. No, no. Vodka, if you please.

DON. I shall have it sent right in. [*He goes off at the left into bar.*]

[IRENE *looks slowly off, after* HARRY. *She smiles slightly.* WEBER *comes down the stairs quickly. He is not in evening dress. He too pauses at the window.*]

WEBER. A perfectly cloudless night! They're very lucky. [*He comes on down.*]

IRENE. Did you get your call?

WEBER. Yes. I talked to Lanza.

IRENE. I gather the news is, as usual, good.

WEBER. It is extremely serious! You saw those bombers that left here this afternoon?

IRENE. Yes.

WEBER. They were headed for Paris. Italy is evidently in a great hurry to deliver the first blow.

IRENE. How soon may we leave here?

WEBER. None too soon, I can assure you. The French high command will know that the bombers come from this field. There will be reprisals—probably within the next twenty-four hours.

IRENE. That will be exciting to see.

WEBER. An air raid?

IRENE. Yes—with bombs bursting in the snow. Sending up great geysers of diamonds.

WEBER. Or perhaps great geysers of us.

IRENE [*after a moment*]. I suppose many people in Paris are being killed now.

WEBER. I'm afraid so. Unless the Italians bungle it.

IRENE. Perhaps your sister—Madame d'Hilaire—perhaps she and her darling little children are now dying.

WEBER [*sharply*]. My sister and her family are in Montbeliard.

IRENE. But you said the Italians might bungle it. They might drop their bombs on the wrong place.

WEBER. I appreciate your solicitude, my dear. But you can save your condolences until they are needed. [DUMPTSY *comes in from the bar and serves the vodka.* WEBER *rises.*] I must telegraph to Joseph to have the house ready. It will be rather cold in Biarritz now—but far healthier than Paris. You are going in to dinner now?

IRENE. Yes.

WEBER. I shall join you later. [*He goes out.*]

[DUMPTSY *picks up the* CHERRYS' *glasses.*]

DUMPTSY. We will have a great treat tonight, madame.

IRENE. Really?

DUMPTSY. That American impresario, that Mr. Harry Van—he will give us an entertainment with his dancing girls.

IRENE. Is he employed here regularly?

DUMPTSY. Oh, no, madame. He is just passing, like you. This is a special treat. It will be very fine.

IRENE. Let us hope so. [*She downs the vodka.*]

DUMPTSY. Madame is Russian, if I may say so.

IRENE [*pleased*]. How did you know that I am Russian? Just because I am having vodka?

DUMPTSY. No, madame. Many people try to drink vodka. But only true Russians can do it gracefully. You see—I was a prisoner with your people in the war. I liked them.

IRENE. You're very charming. What is your name?

DUMPTSY. I am called Dumptsy, madame.

IRENE. Are you going again to the war, Dumptsy?

DUMPTSY. If they tell me to, madame.

IRENE. You will enjoy being a soldier?

DUMPTSY. Yes—if I'm taken prisoner soon enough.

IRENE. And who do you think will win?

DUMPTSY. I can't think, madame. It is all very doubtful. But one thing I can tell you: whoever wins, it will be the same as last time—Austria will lose.

IRENE. They will all lose, Dumptsy. [*The* CHERRYS *come in. She greets them pleasantly.*] Good evening.

CHERRY. Good evening, madame. [*The* CHERRYS *start to sit, across from* IRENE.]

IRENE. Bring some more vodka, Dumptsy. Perhaps Mr. and Mrs. Cherry will have some, too.

CHERRY. Why, thank you—we . . .

MRS. CHERRY. I'd love to. I've never tasted vodka.

IRENE. Ah—then it's high time. Bring in the bottle, Dumptsy.

DUMPTSY. Yes, madame. [*He goes in to the bar.*]

IRENE. Come, sit down here. [*The* CHERRYS *sit by her.*] You will find vodka a perfect stimulant to the appetite. So much better than that hybrid atrocity, the American cocktail!

CHERRY. To tell you the truth, madame—we've already dined.

IRENE. It is no matter. It is just as good as a liqueur.

MRS. CHERRY. We didn't really dine at all. We merely looked at the minestrone and the Parmesan cheese—and we felt too depressed to eat anything.

IRENE. It's the altitude. After the first exhilaration there comes a depressive reaction, especially for you, who are accustomed to the heavy, Pigwiggian atmosphere of England.

CHERRY. Pigwiggian?

IRENE. Yes, Pigwig—Oliver Twist—you know, your Dickens?

[DUMPTSY *enters from bar with a bottle of vodka and*

two more glasses, which he places on the table. He returns to the bar.]

CHERRY. You know England, madame?

IRENE [*fondly*]. Of course I know England! My governess was a sweet old ogre from your north country—and when I was a little girl I used to visit often at Sandringham.

CHERRY [*impressed*]. Sandringham?

MRS. CHERRY. The palace?

IRENE. Yes. That was before your time. It was in the reign of dear, gay King Edward, and the beautiful Alexandra. [*She sighs a little for those days.*] I used to have such fun playing with my cousin David. He used to try to teach me to play cricket, and when I couldn't swing the bat properly, he said, "Oh, you Russians will never be civilized!" [*Laughs.*] When I went home to Petersburg I told my uncle, the Tsar, what David had said, and he was so amused! But now—you must drink your vodka. [*They rise, and lift their glasses.*] A toast! To his most gracious Majesty the King. [*They clink glasses.*] God bless him.

CHERRY. Thank you, madame. [*All three drink and* MRS. CHERRY *coughs violently.*]

IRENE [*to* MRS. CHERRY]. No—no! Drink it right down. Like this. [*She swallows it in a gulp.*] So! [*Refills the glasses from the bottle.*] The second glass will go more easily. [*They sit.*] I used to laugh so at your funny British Tommies in Archangel. They all hated vodka until one of them thought of mixing it with beer.

MRS. CHERRY. How loathsome!

IRENE. It was! But I shall be forever grateful to them—those Tommies. They saved my life when I escaped from the Soviets. For days and nights—I don't know how many I was driving through the snow- snow—

snow—snow—in a little sleigh, with the body of my
father beside me, and the wolves running along like
an escort of dragoons. You know—you always think
of wolves as howling constantly, don't you?

CHERRY. Why, yes—I suppose one does.

IRENE. Well, they don't. No, these wolves didn't howl!
They were horribly, confidently silent. I think silence is much more terrifying, don't you?

CHERRY. You must have been dreadfully afraid.

IRENE. No, I was not afraid for myself. It was the
thought of my father. . . .

MRS. CHERRY. Please! I know you don't want to talk
about it any more.

IRENE. Oh, no—it is so far away now. I shall never forget the moment when I came through the haze of
delirium, and saw the faces of those Tommies.
Those simple, friendly faces. And the snow—and the
wolves—and the terrible cold—they were all gone—
and I was looking at Kew Gardens on a Sunday
afternoon, and the sea of golden daffodils—"flutter-
ing and dancing in the breezes."

[WEBER *has come in with the daffodils.*]

WEBER. Shall we go in to dinner now, Irene?

IRENE. Yes, yes, Achille. In a minute. I am coming.
[WEBER *goes.* IRENE *rises.*] Now—we must finish our
vodka. [CHERRY *rises.*] And you must make another
try to eat something.

CHERRY. Thank you so much, madame. [*They drink.*]

IRENE. And later on, we must all be here for Mr. Van's
entertainment—and we must all applaud vigorously.

MRS. CHERRY. We shall, madame.

CHERRY. He's such a nice chap, isn't he?

IRENE [*going*]. Yes—and a real artist, too.

CHERRY. Oh—you've seen him?

IRENE. Why—yes—I've seen him, in some *café chantant,*
somewhere. I forget just where it was.

[*The three of them have gone out together. The light is dimmed to extinction. The curtain falls.*]

SCENE II

About two hours later.
WEBER *is drinking brandy. The* CAPTAIN *is standing.*

CAPTAIN. I have been listening to the radio. Utter bedlam! Of course, every government has imposed the strictest censorship—but it is very frightening—like one of those films where ghostly hands suddenly reach in and switch off all the lights.

WEBER. Any suggestions of air raids?

CAPTAIN. None. But there is ominous quiet from Paris. Think of it—Paris—utterly silent! Only one station there is sending messages, and they are in code.

WEBER. Probably instructions to the frontier.

CAPTAIN. I heard a man in Prague saying something that sounded interesting, but him I could not understand. Then I turned to London, hopefully, and listened to a gentleman describing the disastrous effects of ivy upon that traditional institution, the oak.

WEBER. Well—we shall soon know. . . . There'll be no trouble about crossing the frontier tomorrow?

CAPTAIN. Oh, no. Except that I am still a little worried about madame's passport.

WEBER. We'll arrange about that. Have a cigar, Captain?

CAPTAIN. Thank you.

[*Irene comes in as the* CAPTAIN *starts to light the cigar.*]

IRENE. Do you hear the sound of airplanes?

[*All stop to listen, intently. The sound becomes audi-*

ble. *The* CAPTAIN *shakes out the match, throws the unlit cigar on the table, and dashes to the window and looks upward.*]

CAPTAIN. It is our bombers. One—two—three. Seven of them. Seven out of eighteen. You will excuse me? [*He salutes and dashes out.*]

WEBER. Seven out of eighteen! Not bad, for Italians.

[IRENE *has gone to the window to look out.*]

IRENE. I'm so happy for you, Achille.

WEBER. What was that, my dear?

IRENE. I said—I'm so happy for you.

WEBER. But—just why am I an object of congratulation?

IRENE. All this great, wonderful death and destruction, everywhere. And you promoted it!

WEBER. Don't give me too much credit, Irene.

IRENE. But I *know* what you've done.

WEBER. Yes, my dear. You know a great deal. But don't forget to do honor to Him—up there—who put fear into man. I am but the humble instrument of His divine will.

IRENE [*looking upward, sympathetically*]. Yes—that's quite true. We don't do half enough justice to Him. Poor, lonely old soul. Sitting up in heaven, with nothing to do, but play solitaire. Poor, dear God. Playing Idiot's Delight. The game that never means anything, and never ends.

WEBER. You have an engaging fancy, my dear.

IRENE. Yes.

WEBER. It's the quality in you that fascinates me most. Limitless imagination! It is what has made you such an admirable, brilliant liar. And so very helpful to me! Am I right?

IRENE. Of course you are right, Achille. Had I been bound by any stuffy respect for the truth, I should never have escaped from the Soviets.

WEBER. I'm sure of it.

IRENE. Did I ever tell you of my escape from the Soviets?

WEBER. You have told me about it at least eleven times. And each time it was different.

IRENE. Well, I made several escapes. I am always making escapes, Achille. When I am worrying about you, and your career, I have to run away from the terror of my own thoughts. So I amuse myself by studying the faces of the people I see. Just ordinary, casual, dull people. [*She is speaking in a tone that is sweetly sadistic.*] That young English couple, for instance. I was watching them during dinner, sitting there, close together, holding hands, and rubbing their knees together under the table. And I saw him in his nice, smart, British uniform, shooting a little pistol at a huge tank. And the tank rolls over him. And his fine strong body, that was so full of the capacity for ecstasy, is a mass of mashed flesh and bones—a smear of purple blood—like a stepped-on snail. But before the moment of death, he consoles himself by thinking, "Thank God *she* is safe! She is bearing the child I gave her, and he will live to see a better world." [*She walks behind* WEBER *and leans over his shoulder.*] But I know where she is. She is lying in a cellar that has been wrecked by an air raid, and her firm young breasts are all mixed up with the bowels of a dismembered policeman, and the embryo from her womb is splattered against the face of a dead bishop. That is the kind of thought with which I amuse myself, Achille. And it makes me so proud to think that I am so close to you—who make all this possible.

[WEBER *rises and walks about the room. At length he turns to her.*]

WEBER. Do you talk in this whimsical vein to many people?

IRENE. No. I betray my thoughts to no one but you. You know that I am shut off from the world. I am a contented prisoner in your ivory tower.

WEBER. I'm beginning to wonder about that.

IRENE. What? You think I could interest myself in someone else—?

WEBER. No—no, my dear. I am merely wondering whether the time has come for you to turn commonplace, like all the others?

IRENE. The others?

WEBER. All those who have shared my life. My former wife, for instance. She now boasts that she abandoned me because part of my income is derived from the sale of poison gas. Revolvers and rifles and bullets she didn't mind—because they are also used by sportsmen. Battleships too are permissible; they look so splendid in the news films. But she couldn't stomach poison gas. So now she is married to an anemic duke, and the large fortune that she obtained from me enables the duke to indulge his principal passion, which is the slaughtering of wild animals, like rabbits, and pigeons and rather small deer. My wife is presumably happy with him. I have always been glad you are not a fool as she was, Irene.

IRENE. No. I don't care even for battleships. And I shall not marry an anemic duke.

WEBER. But—there was something unpleasantly reminiscent in that gaudy picture you painted. I gather that this silly young couple has touched a tender spot, eh?

IRENE. Perhaps, Achille. Perhaps I am softening.

WEBER. Then apply your intelligence, my dear. Ask yourself: why shouldn't they die? And who are the greater criminals—those who sell the instruments of death, or those who buy them, and use them? You know there is no logical reply to that. But all these little people—like your new friends—all of them consider me an arch-villain because I furnish them with what they want, which is the illusion of power. That is what they vote for in their frightened governments—what they cheer for on their national holidays—what they glorify in their anthems, and their monuments, and their waving flags! Yes—they shout bravely about something they call "national honor." And what does it amount to? Mistrust of the motives of everyone else! Dog in the manger defense of what they've got, and greed for the other fellow's possessions! Honor among thieves! I assure you, Irene—for such little people the deadliest weapons are the most merciful.

[*The* CHERRYS *enter. He is whistling* "Minnie the Moocher."]

IRENE. Ah! Mr. and Mrs. Cherry!

CHERRY. Hello there. [*They come down.*]

IRENE. You have dined well!

MRS. CHERRY. Superbly!

CHERRY. We ate everything—up to and including the zabaglione.

IRENE. You can thank the vodka for that. Vodka never fails in an emergency.

CHERRY. And we can thank you, madame, and do so.

IRENE. But—permit me to introduce Monsieur Weber. [WEBER *rises.*] Mrs. Cherry—Mr. Cherry. [*They are exchanging greetings as* DON *comes in.*]

DON. We're going to have a little cabaret show for you now, madame.

WEBER. I don't think I shall wait for it, my dear.

IRENE. But you must—

WEBER. I really should look over Lanza's estimates—

IRENE. Please, Achille—Mr. Van is an artist. You will be so amused.

WEBER [*resuming seat*]. Very well, Irene.

DON [*his tone blandly confidential*]. Between ourselves, I don't vouch for the quality of it. But it may be unintentionally amusing.

IRENE. I shall love it.

CHERRY. This is the most marvelous idea, Mr. Navadel.

DON. Oh, thank you. We try to contrive some novelty each evening. If you'll be good enough to sit here— [DON *goes up to usher in the* ROSSIS *and direct them to their seats.*]

[*The* MUSICIANS *come in and take their places. The* DOCTOR *comes in.* DUMPTSY *is busily moving chairs about, clearing a space for the act.* IRENE *and the* CHERRYS *chat pleasantly.* ANNA, *the maid, appears on the gallery above to watch the entertainment.* HARRY *comes in. He is wearing a tight-fitting dinner jacket, and carries a cane and a straw hat.*]

HARRY. All set, Don?

DON. Quite ready, whenever you are.

HARRY. Okey-doke. Give us a fanfare, professor. [*He goes out. The* BAND *obliges with a fanfare.* HARRY *returns, all smiles.*] Before we start, folks, I just want to explain that we haven't had much chance to rehearse with my good friend, Signor Palota, and his talented little team here. [*He indicates the* ORCHESTRA *with a handsome gesture.*] So we must crave your indulgence and beg you to give us a break if the rhythm isn't all kosher. [*He waits for his laugh.*] All we ask of you, kind friends, is "The Christian pearl of charity," to quote our great American poet, John Greenleaf Whittier. We thank you. Take it away! [*He bows. All applaud. He then sings a song— The* GIRLS *come on in costume and dance.*]

[*During the latter part of the act, the* CAPTAIN, *the*

MAJOR, *and four flying corps* OFFICERS *come in. The latter are dirty and in a fever of heroically restrained excitement. They survey the scene with wonderment and then with delight, saying, in Italian, "What's all this?" and "What brought these blonde bambinos to Monte Gabriele?" etc.* HARRY *interrupts the act and orders the orchestra to play the Fascist anthem, "Giovinezza." The officers acknowledge this graceful gesture with the Fascist salute. The* GIRLS *wave back. The* CAPTAIN *gets the* OFFICERS *seated and then goes to order drinks.* HARRY *and the* GIRLS *resume.*]

[*At the end of the act, all applaud and the* OFFICERS *shout "Brava—Bravissima" and stamp their feet with enthusiasm. The* GIRLS *take several bows and go.* HARRY *returns for a solo bow, waving his straw hat. One of the* OFFICERS *shouts, in Italian, "We want the young ladies!"*]

CAPTAIN [*to* HARRY]. My friends wish to know respectfully if the young ladies will care to join them in a little drink?

HARRY. Certainly! Come back in, girls. Get over there and join the army! [*The* GIRLS *do so.*] Now, folks—with your kind permission—I shall give the girls an interlude of rest and refreshment and treat you to a little piano specialty of my own. Your strict attention is not obligatory. [*He starts his specialty, assisted by* SHIRLEY *and* EDNA. *The* OFFICERS *don't pay much attention. Bottles of champagne are brought for them and the* GIRLS.]

[WEBER *goes and speaks to the* CAPTAIN. *He beckons him up to the landing of the stairs where they converse in low tones, the* CAPTAIN *telling him about the air raid.*]

[HARRY'S *act is interrupted by the entrance of* QUILLERY.]

QUILLERY [*to* HARRY]. Do you know what has happened?

DON. I told you we didn't want you here.

PITTALUGA. We're having an entertainment here.

QUILLERY. Yes! An entertainment!

HARRY. If you'll just sit down, pal . . . [*He and the* GIRLS *continue with their singing.*]

QUILLERY. An entertainment—while Paris is in ruins!

CHERRY [*rises*]. What?

DOCTOR. What are you saying?

QUILLERY. They have bombed Paris! The Fascisti have bombed Paris!

DON. What? It can't be possible—

HARRY. Go on, Shirley. Keep on singing.

QUILLERY. I tell you—tonight their planes flew over and—

CHERRY. But how do you know this?

QUILLERY. It is on the wireless—everywhere. And I have just talked to one of their mechanics, who was on the flight, and saw, with his own eyes—

HARRY. Won't you please sit down, pal? We're trying to give you a little entertainment— [*Stops playing.*]

QUILLERY. For the love of God—listen to me! While you sit here eating and drinking, tonight, Italian planes dropped twenty thousand kilos of bombs on Paris. God knows how many they killed. God knows how much of life and beauty is forever destroyed! And you sit here, drinking, laughing, with *them*— the murderers. [*Points to the* FLYERS, *who ask each other, in Italian, what the hell is he talking about.*] They did it! It was their planes, from that field down there. Assassins!

[*The* OFFICERS *make a move toward* QUILLERY—*one of them arming himself with a champagne bottle.*]

HARRY [*comes down from the piano*]. We can't have any skull-cracking in this club. Hey, Captain, speak to your men before anything starts.

[*The* CAPTAIN *comes down to the* OFFICERS *and pacifies them.* CHERRY *comes down to stand by* QUILLERY.]

MRS. CHERRY. Jimmy! . . . You keep out of this!

MAJOR *and* FIRST *and* THIRD OFFICERS [*jump up*]. Assassini!

HARRY. Now listen, pal . . .

SHIRLEY. Harry! Don't get yourself mixed up in this mess!

QUILLERY. You see, we stand together! France—England—America! Allies!

HARRY. Shut up, France! It's O.K., Captain. We can handle this—

QUILLERY. They don't dare fight against the power of England and France! The free democracies against the Fascist tyranny!

HARRY. Now, for God's sake stop fluctuating!

QUILLERY. England and France are fighting for the hopes of mankind!

HARRY. A minute ago, England was a butcher in a dress suit. Now we're Allies!

QUILLERY. We stand together. We stand together forever. [*Turns to* OFFICERS.] I say God damn you. God damn the villains that sent you on this errand of death.

CAPTAIN [*takes a few steps toward* QUILLERY]. If you don't close your mouth, Frenchman, we shall be forced to arrest you.

QUILLERY. Go on, Fascisti! Commit national suicide. That's the last gesture left to you toy soldiers.

HARRY. It's all right, Captain. Mr. Quillery is for peace. He's going back to France to stop the war.

QUILLERY [*turns on* HARRY]. You're not authorized to speak for me. I am competent to say what I feel. And what I say is "Down with Fascism! Abbasso Fascismo!"

[*There is an uproar from the* OFFICERS.]

CAPTAIN [*ordinarily gentle, is now white hot with rage*]. Attenzione!

QUILLERY. Vive la France! Viv—

CAPTAIN. E agli arresti.

QUILLERY. Call out the firing squad! Shoot me dead! But do not think you can silence the truth that's in me.

CAPTAIN [*grabs* QUILLERY *from the left and calls the* FIRST OFFICER]. Molinari! [FIRST OFFICER *grabs* QUILLERY *from the right. They start to take him out.*]

QUILLERY [*as he is being led out*]. The Empire of the Fascisti will join the Empire of the Caesars in smoking ruins. Vive la France! Vive la France!

[WEBER *goes upstairs and exits. They have gone.*]

CHERRY [*to* HARRY]. You'd better carry on with your turn, old boy.

HARRY. No, pal. The act is cold. [*To the* ORCHESTRA LEADER.] Give us some music, Signor. [*The* ORCHESTRA *starts playing.*] Let dancing become general.

CHERRY. Let's dance, my sweet.

MRS. CHERRY. I can't bear to, Jimmy.

CHERRY. I think we should.

MRS. CHERRY. Very well, darling. [*They dance. The* OFFICERS *dance with the* GIRLS.]

HARRY [*goes over to* IRENE]. Would you care to dance?

IRENE. Why—why, thank you. [*She stands up, and they join the slowly moving mob.*]

[SHIRLEY *is singing as loud as she can. The color wheel turns so that the dancers are bathed in blue, then amber, then red.*]

CURTAIN

SCENE III

Later that night.

IRENE *and* HARRY *are alone. She is sitting, telling the story of her life. He is listening with fascination and doubt.*

IRENE. My father was old. The hardships of that terrible journey had broken his body. But his spirit was strong—the spirit that is Russia. He lay there, in that little boat, and he looked up at me. Never can I forget his face, so thin, so white, so beautiful, in the starlight. And he said to me, "Irene—little daughter," and then—he died. For four days I was alone, with his body, sailing through the storms of the Black Sea. I had no food—no water—I was in agony from the bayonet wounds of the Bolsheviki. I knew I must die. But then—an American cruiser rescued me. May God bless those good men! [*She sighs.*] I've talked too much about myself. What about you, my friend?

HARRY. Oh—I'm not very interesting. I'm just what I seem to be.

IRENE. C'est impossible!

HARRY. C'est possible! The facts of my case are eloquent. I'm a potential genius—reduced to piloting six blondes through the Balkans.

IRENE. But there is something that you hide from the world—even, I suspect, from yourself. Where did you acquire your superior education?

HARRY. I worked my way through college selling encyclopedias.

IRENE. I knew you had culture! What college was it?

HARRY. Oh—just any college. But my sales talk was so

good that I fell for it myself. I bought the God-
damned encyclopedia. And I read it all, traveling
around, in day coaches, and depot hotels, and Fox-
time dressing rooms. It was worth the money.

IRENE. And how much of all this have you retained?

HARRY [*significantly*]. I? I—never forget anything.

IRENE. How unfortunate for you! Does your encyclopedia help you in your dealings with the girls?

HARRY. Yes, Mrs. Weber. . . . I got considerable benefit
from studying the lives of the great courtesans, and
getting to understand their technique. . . .

IRENE. Forgive me for interrupting you—but that is
not my name.

HARRY. Oh—pardon me, I thought . . .

IRENE. I know what you thought. Monsieur Weber and
I are associated in a sort of business way.

HARRY. I see.

IRENE. He does me the honor to consult me in matters
of policy.

HARRY. That's quite an honor! Business is pretty good,
isn't it!

IRENE. I gather that you are one of those noble souls
who does not entirely approve of the munitions industry?

HARRY. Oh, no—I'm not noble. Your friend is just another salesman. And I make it a point never to criticize anybody else's racket.

IRENE. Monsieur Weber is a very distinguished man.
He has rendered very distinguished services to all
the governments of the world. He is decorated with
the Legion of Honor, the Order of the White Eagle,
the Order of St. James of the Sword, and the Military Order of Christ!

HARRY. The Military Order of Christ. I never heard of
that one.

IRENE. It is from Portugal. He has many orders.

HARRY. Have you ever been in America?

IRENE. Oh, yes—I've seen it all—New York, Washington, Palm Beach . . .

HARRY. I said America. Have you ever been in the West?

IRENE. Certainly I have. I flew across your continent. There are many White Russians in California.

HARRY. Did you ever happen to make any parachute landings in any places like Kansas, or Iowa, or Nebraska?

IRENE [*laughing*]. I have seen enough of your countrymen to know that you are typical.

HARRY. Me? I'm not typical of anything.

IRENE. Oh, yes, you are. You are just like all of them—an ingenuous, sentimental idealist. You believe in the goodness of human nature, don't you?

HARRY. And what if I do? I've known millions of people, intimately—and I never found more than one out of a hundred that I didn't like, once you got to know them.

IRENE. That is very charming—but it *is* naïve.

HARRY. Maybe so. But experience prevents me from working up much enthusiasm over anyone who considers the human race as just so many clay pigeons, even if he does belong to the Military Order of Christ.

IRENE. If you came from an older culture, you would realize that men like Monsieur Weber are necessary to civilization.

HARRY. You don't say.

IRENE. I mean, of course, the sort of civilization that we have got. [*She smiles upon him benevolently. It is as though she were explaining patiently but with secret enjoyment the facts of life to a backward nephew.*] Stupid people consider him an arch-villain because it is his duty to stir up a little trouble here and there to stimulate the sale of his products. Do you understand me, my friend?

HARRY. I shouldn't wonder.

IRENE. Monsieur Weber is a true man of the world. He is above petty nationalism; he can be a Frenchman in France—a German in Germany—a Greek—a Turk —whatever the occasion demands.

HARRY. Yes—that little Quillery was an Internationalist, too. He believed in brotherhood, but the moment he got a whiff of gunpowder he began to spout hate and revenge. And now those nice, polite Wops will probably have to shut him up with a firing squad.

IRENE [*takes out a cigarette from her case*]. It is a painful necessity.

HARRY. And it demonstrates the sort of little trouble that your friend stirs up. [*He takes out his lighter and lights her cigarette.*]

IRENE. Do you know that you can be extremely rude?

HARRY. I'm sorry if I've hurt your feelings about Mr. Weber, but he just happens to be a specimen of the one per cent that I *don't* like.

IRENE. I was not referring to that. Why do you stare at me so?

HARRY. Have I been staring?

IRENE. Steadily. Ever since we arrived here this afternoon. Why do you do it?

HARRY. I've been thinking I could notice a funny resemblance to someone I used to know.

IRENE. You should know better than to tell any woman that she resembles somebody else. We none of us like to think that our appearance is commonplace.

HARRY. The one you look like wasn't commonplace.

IRENE. Oh! She was someone near and dear to you?

HARRY. It was somebody that occupies a unique shrine in the temple of my memory.

IRENE. That *is* a glowing tribute. The temple of your memory must be so crowded! But I am keeping you from your duties.

HARRY. What duties?

IRENE. Shouldn't you be worrying about your young ladies?

HARRY. They're all right; they've gone to bed.

IRENE. Yes—but there are several Italian officers about. Aren't you supposed to be the chaperon?

HARRY. I leave the girls to their own resources, of which they have plenty. [*He stares hard at her.*] Have you always been a blonde?

IRENE. Yes—as far as I can remember.

HARRY. You don't mind my asking?

IRENE. Not at all. And now, may I ask you something?

HARRY. Please do so.

IRENE. Why do you waste yourself in this degraded work? Touring about with those obvious little harlots?

HARRY. You mean you think I'm fitted for something that requires a little more mentality?

IRENE. Yes.

HARRY. How do you know so much about me? [*It should be remembered that all through this scene* HARRY *is studying her, trying to fit together the pieces of the jigsaw puzzle of his memory.*]

IRENE. For one thing, I saw your performance tonight.

HARRY. You thought it was punk?

IRENE. I thought it was unworthy.

HARRY. It was unfortunately interrupted. You should have seen . . .

IRENE. I saw enough. You are a very bad dancer.

HARRY. The King of Rumania thought I was pretty good.

IRENE. He is entitled to his opinion—and I to mine.

HARRY. I'll admit that I've done better things in my

time. Would it surprise you to know that I was once with a mind-reading act?

IRENE. Really?

HARRY. Yeah.

IRENE. Now you're staring at me again.

HARRY. Have you ever been in Omaha?

IRENE. Omaha? Where is that? Persia?

HARRY. No. Nebraska. That's one of our states. I played there once with the greatest act of my career. I was a stooge for Zuleika, the Mind Reader. At least she called me her stooge. But I was the one who had to do all the brain work.

IRENE. And she read people's minds?

HARRY. I did it for her. I passed through the audience and fed her the cues. We were sensational, playing the finest picture houses in all the key cities. Zuleika sat up on the stage, blindfolded—and usually blind drunk.

IRENE. Oh, dear. And was *she* the one that I resemble?

HARRY. No! There was another act on the same bill. A troupe of Russians . . .

IRENE. Russians?

HARRY. Singers, mandolin players, and squat dancers. One of them was a red-headed girl. She was fascinated by our act, and she kept pestering me to teach her the code. She said she could do it better than Zuleika.

IRENE. Those poor Russians. There are so many of them all over the world. And so many of them completely counterfeit!

HARRY. This dame was counterfeit all right. In fact, she was the God-damnedest liar I ever saw. She lied just for the sheer artistry of it. She kept after me so much that I told her finally to come up to my hotel room one night, and we'd talk it over.

IRENE. I hope you didn't tell her the code.

HARRY. No. After the week in Omaha the bill split. The Russians went to Sioux Falls and we went on the Interstate Time. I played with Zuleika for another year and then the drink got her and she couldn't retain. So the act busted up. I've always hoped I'd catch up with that red-headed Russian again sometime. She might have been good. She had the voice for it, and a kind of overtone of mystery.

IRENE. It's a characteristic Gypsy quality. And you never saw her again?

HARRY. No.

IRENE. Perhaps it is just as well. She couldn't have been so clever—being duped so easily into going to your room.

HARRY. She wasn't being duped! She knew what she was doing. If there was any duping going on, she was the one that did it.

IRENE. She *did* make an impression!

HARRY [*looking straight at her*]. I was crazy about her. She was womanhood at its most desirable—and most unreliable.

IRENE. And you such a connoisseur. But—it's getting late.

HARRY [*rises*]. Do you know any Russian music? [*He crosses to the piano.*]

IRENE [*rises*]. Oh, yes. When I was a little girl my father used to engage Chaliapin to come often to our house. He taught me many songs.

HARRY. Chaliapin, eh? Your father spared no expense. [*He sits at the piano.*]

IRENE. That was in *old* Russia. [*He plays a few bars of* "Kak Stranna."] "Kak Stranna!"

HARRY. Yeah! How strange! [*He starts to play* "Prostchai."] Do you know this one? [IRENE *sings some of it in Russian.*] How do you spell that name—Irene?

IRENE. I-R-E-N-E. [HARRY *pounds the piano and jumps up.*] What's the matter?

HARRY. That's it! Irene! [*He pronounces it* I-REEN.]

IRENE. But what—?

HARRY. I knew it! You're the one!

IRENE. What one?

HARRY. That red-headed liar! Irene! I knew I could never be mistaken. . . .

IRENE. Irene is a very usual name in Russia. [*She laughs heartily.*]

HARRY. I don't care how usual it is. Everything fits together perfectly now. The name—the face—the voice —Chaliapin for a teacher! Certainly it's you! And it's no good shaking your head and looking amazed! No matter how much you may lie, you can't deny the fact that you slept with me in the Governor Bryan Hotel in Omaha in the fall of 1925. [IRENE *laughs heartily again.*] All right—go ahead and laugh. That blonde hair had me fooled for a while —but now I know it's just as phony as the bayonet wounds, and the parachute jumps into the jungle. . . .

IRENE [*still laughing*]. Oh—you amuse me.

HARRY. It's a pleasure to be entertaining. But you can't get away with it.

IRENE. You amuse me very much indeed. Here we are —on a mountain peak in Bedlam. Tonight, the Italians are bombing Paris. At this moment, the French may be bombing Rome, and the English bombing Germany—and the Soviets bombing Tokyo, and all you worry about is whether I am a girl you once met casually in Omaha.

HARRY. Did I say it was casual?

IRENE [*laughing*]. Oh—it *is* amusing!

HARRY [*angrily*]. I know you're amused. I admit it's all

very funny. I've admitted everything. I told you I was crazy about you. Now when are you going to give me a break and tell me—

IRENE. You! You are so troubled—so—so uncertain about everything.

HARRY. I'm not uncertain about it any more, babe. I had you tagged from the start. There was something about you that was indelible . . . something I couldn't forget all these years.

[WEBER *appears on the gallery, wearing his Sulka dressing gown.*]

WEBER. Forgive me for intruding, my dear. But I suggest that it's time for you to go to bed.

IRENE. Yes, Achille. At once. [WEBER *treats* HARRY *to a rather disparaging glance and exits.* IRENE *starts upstairs.*] Poor Achille! He suffers with the most dreadful insomnia—it is something on his mind. [*She goes up a few more steps.*] He is like Macbeth. Good night, my friend—my funny friend.

HARRY. Good night.

IRENE. And thank you for making me laugh so much—tonight.

HARRY. I could still teach you that code.

IRENE. Perhaps—we shall meet again in—what was the name of the hotel?

HARRY. It was the Governor Bryan.

IRENE. Oh, yes! The Governor Bryan! [*Laughing heartily, she exits.*]

[HARRY *goes to the piano, sits down and starts to play* "Kak Stranna." DUMPTSY *enters from the bar.*]

DUMPTSY. That was wonderful—that singing and dancing.

HARRY [*still playing*]. Thanks, pal. Glad you enjoyed it.

DUMPTSY. Oh, yes, Mr. Van—that was good.

HARRY [*bangs a chord*]. Chaliapin—for God's *sake!*

DUMPTSY. I beg your pardon, sir?

HARRY [*rises*]. It's nothing. Good night, Dumptsy. [*He goes out into the lobby.*]

DUMPTSY. Good night, sir. [*He starts for the bar.*]

CURTAIN

Act three

The following afternoon.

HARRY *is at the piano, idly playing the "Caprice Viennoise," or something similar. His thoughts are elsewhere.*

SHIRLEY *is darning some stockings and humming the tune.* BEBE *is plucking her eyebrows.*

BEULAH, ELAINE, FRANCINE *and* EDNA *are seated at a table.* BEULAH *is telling* ELAINE'S *fortune with cards. The others are watching. All are intensely serious, and all chewing gum.*

SHIRLEY. What's that number, Harry?

HARRY. The "Caprice Viennoise"—Kreisler.

SHIRLEY. It's pretty.

HARRY. You think so? [*He shifts to something jazzier.*]

BEULAH. You are going to marry.

ELAINE. Again?

BEULAH. The cards indicate dis*tinctly* two marriages, and maybe a third.

ELAINE [*chewing furiously*]. For *God's* sake!

SHIRLEY [*to* HARRY]. We certainly need some new stockings.

HARRY. We'll renovate the wardrobe in Geneva.

BEULAH. Now—let's see what the fates tell us next.

BEBE. Say, Harry—when do we lam it out of here?

HARRY. Ask Beulah. Maybe she can get it out of the cards.

BEBE. I hate this place. It's spooky.

BEULAH [*to* HARRY]. What'd you say, honey?

ELAINE. Ah—don't pay any attention to him. What else do they say about me?

BEULAH. Well . . . you'll enter upon a period of very poor health.

ELAINE. When?

BEULAH. Along about your thirty-seventh year.

SHIRLEY. That means any day now. [*She winks broadly at* BEBE, *who laughs.*]

HARRY [*vehemently*]. Listen to me, you nymphs! We can't be wasting our time with card tricks. We've got to do a little rehearsing.

SHIRLEY. Why, Harry—what are you mad about now?

HARRY. Who said I was mad about anything?

SHIRLEY. Well—every time you get yourself into a peeve, you take it out on us. You start in hollering, "Listen, girls—we got to rehearse."

HARRY. I am not peeved. Merely a little disgusted. The act needs brushing up.

BEBE. Honestly, Harry—don't you think we know the routine by now?

HARRY. I'm not saying you don't know it. I'm just saying that your performance last night grieved me and shocked me. You had your eyes on those officers and not on your work. That kind of attitude went big in Rumania, but now we're going to a town where artistry counts. Some day, I'll take the whole bunch of you to watch the Russian ballet, just to give you an idea of what dancing is.

[CAPTAIN LOCICERO *comes in.*]

CAPTAIN. Your pardon, Mr. Van.

HARRY. Ah, Captain. Good afternoon. . . . Rest, girls.

CAPTAIN [*to the* GIRLS]. Good afternoon.

GIRLS. Good afternoon, Captain.

HARRY. You bring us news?

CAPTAIN. Good news, I hope. May I have your pass-ports?

HARRY. Certainly. [*He gets them out of his coat and hands them to the* CAPTAIN.]

CAPTAIN. Thank you. I hope to have definite word for you very shortly. [*He salutes and starts to go.*]

HARRY. What about Mr. Quillery, Captain? What's happened to him?

CAPTAIN. Mr. Quillery was very injudicious. Very inju-dicious. I am glad that you are so much more intelli-gent. [*He goes out.*]

SHIRLEY. I don't think they could have done anything cruel to him. They're awfully sweet boys, those Wops.

HARRY. So I observed. . . . Now listen to me, girls. Ge-neva's a key spot, and we've got to be good. Your audiences there won't be a lot of hunkies who don't care what you do as long as you don't wear practic-ally any pants. These people are accustomed to the best. They're mains—big people, like prime min-isters, and maharajahs and archbishops. If we click with them, we'll be set for London and Paris. We may even make enough money to get us home!

BEBE. Oh—don't speak of such a thing! Home!

EDNA. To get a real decent henna wash again!

HARRY. The trouble with all of you is, you're thinking too much about your own specialties. You're trying to steal the act, and wreck it. Remember what the late Knute Rockne said: "Somebody else can have the all-star, all-American aggregations. All *I* want is a team!" Now, you—Beulah. You've got plenty of chance to score individually in the bubble number. But when we're doing the chorus routine, you've got to submerge your genius in the mass.

BEULAH. What do I do wrong, honey?

HARRY. Your Maxie Ford is lackluster. Here—I'll show you. . . . [HARRY *gets up to demonstrate the Maxie Ford.*]

SHIRLEY [*laughs*]. If you do it that way, Beulah, you'll go flat on your face. Here—*I'll* show you.

HARRY. Just a minute, Miss Laughlin. Who's the director of this act, you or me?

SHIRLEY [*amiably*]. You are, you old poop. But you just don't know the steps.

ELAINE. Don't let her get fresh, Harry.

BEBE. Slap her down!

SHIRLEY. Give us the music, Harry.

BEULAH. Please, Harry. Shirley just wants to be helpful.

HARRY. I feel I should resent this—but— [*He returns to the piano.*] Go ahead, Miss Laughlin. Carry on. [*He plays.* SHIRLEY *demonstrates.* BEULAH *tries it.*]

BEULAH. Have I got it right?

SHIRLEY. Sure! He's just shooting his face off!

[*During this, the following conversation goes on.*]

ELAINE. You know that Wop that was giving me a play last night?

FRANCINE. You mean the one with the bent nose?

BEBE. I thought he was terrible. But that boy I had is a Count.

ELAINE. Well, look what he gave me.

EDNA. What is it?

BEBE. Let me see it.

ELAINE. I don't know what it is.

BEBE. Looks like money. What kind of money is that, Harry.

HARRY. It's an old Roman coin.

SHIRLEY. How much is it worth?

HARRY. I haven't looked up the latest rate of exchange on dinars. But I think, dear, you've been betrayed. Now, pay attention, girls. . . . As I said, we've got to improve the act, and with that in view, I'm going to retire from all the dance routine.

BEBE. What?

BEULAH. Why, *Harry*—we couldn't. . . .

SHIRLEY. Oh! I hurt you, didn't I! [*She rushes to him, coos over him.*] Yes, I did, you poor baby. I hurt his feelings—and I'm sorry—I'm very, very sorry.

HARRY. All right, Shirley. We can dispense with the regrets. Save your lipstick. [*He thrusts her away.*]

SHIRLEY. But why . . . ?

HARRY. I've decided that I'm a thinker, rather than a performer. From now on, I shall devote myself to the purely creative end of the act, and, of course, the negotiation of contracts.

BEULAH. But when did you make up your mind to this, honey?

HARRY. I've been considering it for a long time.

SHIRLEY. Say! What were you talking about to that Russian dame?

HARRY. We discussed world politics.

FRANCINE. Oh!

SHIRLEY. And how are politics these days?

BEBE. Did you get anywheres near to first base, Harry?

HARRY. I find it impossible to explain certain things to you girls. You're children of nature.

SHIRLEY. We're *what*?

BEULAH. He means we're natural.

HARRY. Never mind, sweetheart. You'll sing the number, Shirley.

SHIRLEY. Me?

BEBE. With that terrible voice?

HARRY. She handled it fine that time I had bronchitis in Belgrade. And with a little rehearsal, you'll have the whole League of Nations rooting for you. Now— let's have it. [*He plays,* SHIRLEY *sings,* BEBE *disapproves.*]

[DON *comes in, dressed for traveling.*]

DON. Captain Locicero has got the orders to let us through and the train is due to leave about four o'clock. What a relief to be out of this foul place!

HARRY. You going too, Don?

DON. Yes. There's nothing for me here. In fact, I'm sick and tired of Europe as a whole. I was in town this morning when they shot Quillery.

BEBE. Who?

SHIRLEY. It was that little guy that bawled out the Wops.

BEULAH. They *shot* him? Why did they have to do that?

DON. Of course, he asked for it. But even so, it's pretty sickening to see one of your fellow human beings crumpled up in horrible, violent death. Well— there'll be plenty more like him, and right here, too. The French know all about this air base, and they'll be over any minute with their bombs. So—it's California here I come!

HARRY. And run right into the Japs? Better stop off at Wichita.

DON. I'll see you all on the train. [*He goes up the stairs.*]

HARRY. You girls go get yourselves ready.

[*The* CHERRYS *appear on the gallery.* DON *speaks to them, then goes out. The* CHERRYS *come down.*]

ELAINE. O.K., Harry.

EDNA [*going*]. I'm surprised at those Wops. They seemed like such sweet boys.

BEBE. Sure—when they talk they sound like opera. But they're awful excitable.

[BEBE, ELAINE, EDNA *and* FRANCINE *have gone out.*]

BEULAH. But I can't understand—why did they have to shoot that poor boy?

HARRY. It's hard to explain, Beulah. But it seems

there's some kind of argument going on over here, and the only way they can settle it is by murdering a lot of people.

BEULAH. You don't need to tell *me* what it's like. I was in the Club Grotto the night the Purple Gang shot it out with the G's. And was that terrible! Blood all over everything!

[SHIRLEY *and* BEULAH *have gone out.*]

HARRY. You heard what they did to Quillery?

CHERRY. Yes. It seems that he died like a true patriot, shouting "Vive La France."

HARRY. Better if he died like a man—sticking to what he knew was right.

CHERRY. He was a nice little chap.

MRS. CHERRY. The Italians are swine!

[DON *reappears on the balcony and comes down.*]

CHERRY. Oh, they had a perfect right to do it.

MRS. CHERRY. But to kill a man for saying what he thinks!

CHERRY. Many people will be killed for less than that.

HARRY. I'll have to be saying good-bye pretty soon. Did you say the train goes at four, Don?

DON. Four o'clock. Correct! [*He goes.*]

HARRY. I hope all this unpleasantness won't spoil your winter sports.

CHERRY. Oh, that's all washed up. We're going, too—if they'll let us cross the border.

HARRY. So the honeymoon has ended already?

MRS. CHERRY. Yes—I suppose so.

CHERRY. England is coming into this business. We have to stand by France, of course. And so there's nothing for it but . . .

MRS. CHERRY. And so Jimmy will have to do his bit, manning the guns, for civilization. Perhaps he'll join in the bombardment of Florence, where we were married.

CHERRY. You know—after the ceremony we went into the Baptistery and prayed to the soul of Leonardo da Vinci that we might never fail in our devotion to that which is beautiful and true. I told you we were a bit on the romantic side. We forgot what Leonardo said about war. Bestial frenzy, he called it. And bestial frenzy it is.

MRS. CHERRY. But we mustn't think about that now. We have to stand by France. We have to make the world a decent place for heroes to live in. Oh, Christ! [*She starts to sob.* CHERRY *rushes to her.*]

CHERRY. Now, now, darling. We've got to make a pretense of being sporting about it. Please, darling. Don't cry.

HARRY. Let her cry, the poor kid. Let her sob her heart out—for all the God-damned good it will do her. You know what I often think? [*He is trying to be tactful.*] I often think we ought to get together and elect somebody else God. Me, for instance. I'll bet I'd do a much better job.

MRS. CHERRY. You'd be fine, Mr. Van.

HARRY. I believe I would. There'd be a lot of people who would object to my methods. That Mr. Weber, for instance. I'd certainly begin my administration by beating the can off him.

CHERRY. Let's start the campaign now! Vote for good old Harry Van, and his Six Angels!

[*The* CAPTAIN *comes in with a brief-case full of papers and passports. He takes these out and puts them on a table.*]

CAPTAIN. Good afternoon, Mrs. Cherry. Gentlemen.

HARRY. Do we get across?

CAPTAIN. Here is your passport, Mr. Van—and the young ladies', with my compliments. They have been duly stamped. [*He hands them over.*]

HARRY. Thanks, Captain. And how about Mr. Weber

and his—friend? Are they going, too?

CAPTAIN. I have their passports here. I advise you to make ready, Mr. Van. The train will leave in about forty-five minutes.

HARRY. O.K., Captain. See you later, Mr. and Mrs. Cherry. [*He goes.*]

CHERRY. O.K., Harry.

MRS. CHERRY. And what about us, Captain?

CAPTAIN. Due to a slight technicality, you will be permitted to cross the frontier. Here are your passports.

CHERRY. I can't tell you how grateful we are.

[WEBER *appears on the gallery.*]

CAPTAIN. You needn't be grateful to me, Mr. Cherry. The fact that you are allowed to pass is due to the superb centralization of authority in my country. The telegram authorizing your release was filed at 11:43 today, just seventeen minutes before a state of war was declared between Great Britain and Italy. I must obey the order of Rome, even though I know it's out of date. Is your luggage ready?

CHERRY. It's all out here in the hall. We're off now, Captain. Well, good-bye and good luck!

CAPTAIN. And good luck to you—both of you.

CHERRY. I need hardly say that I'm sorry about all this. It's really a damned rotten shame.

CAPTAIN. It is. All of that. Good-bye, my friend. [*He extends his hand and Cherry shakes it.*] Madame. . . . [*He extends his hand to* MRS. CHERRY.]

MRS. CHERRY. Don't call *me* your friend, because I say what Quillery said—damn you—damn your whole country of mad dogs for having started this horror.

CAPTAIN [*bows*]. It is not my fault, Mrs. Cherry.

CHERRY. It's utterly unfair to talk that way, darling. The Captain is doing his miserable duty as decently as he possibly can.

CAPTAIN [*tactfully*]. In this unhappy situation, we are

all in danger of losing our heads.

MRS. CHERRY. I know . . . I know. Forgive me for the outburst. [*She extends her hand to the* CAPTAIN *and they shake.*] I should have remembered that it's everybody's fault.

CHERRY. That's right, my sweet. Come along. [*They go out.*]

CAPTAIN [*to* WEBER]. Frankly, my heart bleeds for them.

WEBER. They're young. They'll live through it, and be happy.

CAPTAIN. Will they? I was their age, and in their situation, twenty years ago, when I was sent to the Isonzo front. And people said just that to me: "Never mind, you are young—and youth will survive and come to triumph." And I believed it. That is why I couldn't say such deceiving words to them now.

WEBER. The cultivation of hope never does any immediate harm. Is everything in order?

CAPTAIN [*rises*]. Quite, Monsieur Weber. Here it is. [*He hands over* WEBER'S *passport.*]

WEBER. And Madame's?

[*The* CAPTAIN *picks up a document on foolscap.*]

CAPTAIN. This is an unusual kind of passport. It has given us some worry.

WEBER. The League of Nations issues documents like that to those whose nationality is uncertain.

CAPTAIN. I understand—but the attitude of Italy toward the League of Nations is not at the moment cordial.

WEBER. Then you refuse to honor Madame's passport?

CAPTAIN. My instructions are to accord you every consideration, Monsieur Weber. In view of the fact that Madame is traveling with you, I shall be glad to approve her visa.

WEBER. Madame is not traveling with me. She has her own passport.

CAPTAIN. But it is understood that you vouch for her, and that is enough to satisfy the authorities.

WEBER [*with cold authority*]. Vouch for her? It is not necessary for anyone to vouch for Madame! She is entirely capable of taking care of herself. If her passport is not entirely in order, it is no affair of mine.

CAPTAIN [*genuinely distressed*]. But—I must tell you, Monsieur Weber—this is something I do not like. This places me in a most embarrassing position. I shall be forced to detain her.

WEBER. You are a soldier, my dear Captain, and you should be used to embarrassing positions. Undoubtedly you were embarrassed this morning, when you had to shoot that confused pacifist, Quillery. But this is war, and unpleasant responsibilities descend upon you and on me as well. However . . . [*He sees* HARRY, *who is coming in.*] I shall attend to my luggage. Thank you, Captain. [*He goes out.*]

CAPTAIN. Don't mention it. [*To* HARRY.] The young ladies are ready?

HARRY. Yes—they're ready. And some of your aviators are out there trying to talk them into staying here permanently.

CAPTAIN [*smiling*]. And I add my entreaties to theirs.

HARRY. We won't have any more trouble, will we?

[*The* DOCTOR *appears on the gallery with coat, hat, books done in a bundle, and umbrella. He comes downstairs.*]

CAPTAIN. Oh, no, Mr. Van. Geneva is a lovely spot. All of Switzerland is beautiful, these days. I envy you going there, in such charming company.

HARRY. Hi, Doctor. Have you got the rats all packed?

DOCTOR. Good afternoon. I am privileged to go now? [*He puts down all of his belongings and crosses.*]

CAPTAIN. Yes, Dr. Waldersee. Here is your passport.

DOCTOR. Thank you. [*He examines the passport carefully.*]

HARRY. I can tell you, Doctor—I'm going to be proud to have known you. When I read in the papers that you've wiped out cancer and won the Nobel prize, and you're the greatest hero on earth, I'll be able to say, "He's a personal friend of mine. He once admired my music."

DOCTOR [*solemnly*]. Thank you very much. [*To the* CAPTAIN.] This visa is good for crossing the Austrian border?

CAPTAIN. Certainly. But you are going to Zurich?

DOCTOR [*rises*]. I have changed my plans. I am going back into Germany. Germany is at war. Perhaps I am needed. [*He crosses to pick up his coat.*]

HARRY. Needed for what?

DOCTOR. I shall offer my services for what they are worth.

[HARRY *goes to help him on with his coat.*]

HARRY. But what about the rats?

DOCTOR [*fiercely*]. Why should I save people who don't want to be saved—so that they can go out and exterminate each other? Obscene maniacs! [*Starts to put on his gloves.*] Then I'll be a maniac, too. Only I'll be more dangerous than most of them. For I know all the tricks of death! And—as for my rats, maybe they'll be useful. Britain will put down the blockade again, and we shall be starving—and maybe I'll cut my rats into filets and eat them. [*He laughs, not pleasantly, and picks up his umbrella and books.*]

HARRY. Wait a minute, Doctor. You're doing this without thinking. . . .

DOCTOR. I'm thinking probably that remedy you sold is better than mine. Hasten to apply it. We are all diseased. . . .

HARRY. But you can't change around like this! Have you forgotten all the things you told me? All that about backsliding?

DOCTOR. No, I have not forgotten the degradation of mankind—that is painful and offensive to conceive. [*He is going out.*] I am sorry to disappoint you about the Nobel prize. [*He has gone.*]

HARRY. Good-bye, Doctor. [*He sits down, wearily.*] Why in the name of God can't somebody answer the question that everybody asks? Why? Why? Oh—I know the obvious answers, but they aren't good enough. Weber—and a million like him—they can't take credit for *all* of this! Who is it that did this dirty trick on a lot of decent people? And why do you let them get away with it? That's the thing that I'd like to know!

CAPTAIN. We have avalanches up here, my friend. They are disastrous. They start with a little crack in the ice, so tiny that one cannot see it, until, suddenly, it bursts wide open. And then it is too late.

HARRY. That's very effective, Captain. But it don't satisfy me, because this avalanche isn't made out of ice. It's made out of flesh and blood—and—and *brains.* . . . It's God-damned bad management—that's what it is! [*This last is half to himself.*]

[IRENE *has appeared on the gallery and started to come down.*]

IRENE. Still upset about the situation, Mr. Van? Ah—good afternoon, my dear Captain Locicero.

CAPTAIN. Good afternoon, madame.

IRENE. I have had the most superb rest here. The atmosphere is so calm, and impersonal, and soothing. I can't bear to think that we're going to Biarritz, with the dull, dismal old sea pounding in my ears.

[WEBER *comes in.*]

IRENE. We are leaving now, Achille?

WEBER. I believe that some difficulties have arisen. [*He looks toward the* CAPTAIN.]

IRENE. Difficulties?

CAPTAIN. I regret, madame, that there must be some further delay.

IRENE. Oh! Then the train is not going through, after all?

CAPTAIN. The train is going, madame. But this passport of yours presents problems which, under the circumstances—

IRENE. Monsieur Weber will settle the problems, whatever they are. Won't you, Achille?

WEBER. There is some question about your nationality, Irene.

CAPTAIN [*referring to the passport*]. It states here, madame, that your birthplace is uncertain, but assumed to be Armenia.

IRENE. That is a province of Russia!

CAPTAIN. You subsequently became a resident of England, then of the United States, and then of France.

IRENE [*angrily*]. Yes—it's all there—clearly stated. I have never before had the slightest difficulty about my passport. It was issued by the League of Nations.

WEBER. I'm afraid the standing of the League of Nations is not very high in Italy at this moment.

CAPTAIN. The fact is, madame, the very existence of the League is no longer recognized by our government. For that reason, we can not permit you to cross the frontier at this time. [*She looks at him and then at* WEBER. *The* CAPTAIN *hands her the passport.*] I'm sure you will appreciate the delicacy of my position. Perhaps we shall be able to adjust the matter tomorrow. [*He salutes and goes out, glad to escape.* HARRY *goes with him, asking,* "What's the trouble, Captain? Can't something be done about it?"]

WEBER. I should of course wait over, Irene. But you

know how dangerous it is for me to delay my return to France by so much as one day. I have been in touch with our agents. The premier is demanding that production be doubled—trebled—at once.

IRENE. Of course.

WEBER. Here— [*He takes out an envelope containing money.*] This will cover all possible expenses. [*He gives her the envelope.*] There is a train for Venice this evening. You must go there and see Lanza. I have already sent him full instructions.

IRENE. Yes, Achille. And I thank you for having managed this very, very tactfully.

WEBER [*smiles*]. You are a genuinely superior person, my dear. It is a privilege to have known you.

IRENE. Thank you again, Achille. Good-bye.

WEBER. Good-bye, Irene. [*He kisses her hand.* HARRY *returns.*] Coming, Mr. Van?

HARRY. In a minute. [WEBER *goes.* IRENE *puts the money in her handbag.*] Tough luck, babe.

IRENE. It's no matter.

HARRY. I just talked to the Captain and he isn't going to be as brutal as the Bolsheviks were. I mean, you won't suffer any bayonet wounds. He'll fix it for you to get through tomorrow.

IRENE. You want to be encouraging, my dear friend. But it's no use. The Italian government has too many reasons for wishing to detain me. They'll see to it that I disappear—quietly—and completely.

HARRY. Yes—I know all about that.

IRENE. All about what?

HARRY. You're a person of tremendous significance. You always were.

[SHIRLEY *appears at the left.*]

SHIRLEY. Hey, Harry! It's time for us to go.

HARRY. I'll be right out.

[SHIRLEY *goes.*]

IRENE. Go away—go away with your friends. If I am to die, it is no concern of yours!

HARRY. Listen, babe—I haven't any wish to . . .

IRENE [*flaming*]. And please don't call me *babe!* [*She stands up and walks away from him. He follows her.*]

HARRY. My apologies, madame. I just call everybody "babe."

IRENE. Perhaps that's why I do not like it!

HARRY. Even if I don't believe anything you say, I can see pretty plainly that you're in a tough spot. And considering what we were to each other in the old Governor Bryan Hotel—

IRENE. Must you always be in Omaha?

HARRY. I'd like to help you, Irene. Isn't there something I can do?

IRENE. I thank you, from my heart, I thank you, for that offer. But it's useless. . . .

HARRY. You don't have to thank me. Tell me—what can I do?

IRENE. You're very kind, and very gallant. But, unfortunately, you're no match for Achille Weber. He has decided that I shall remain here and his decision is final!

HARRY. Is he responsible for them stopping you?

IRENE. Of course he is. I knew it the moment I saw that ashamed look on Captain Locicero's face, when he refused to permit me . . .

HARRY. So Weber double-crossed you, did he! What has the son of a bitch got against you?

IRENE. He's afraid of me. I know too much about his methods of promoting his own business.

HARRY. Everybody knows about his methods. Little Quillery was talking about them last night. . . .

IRENE. Yes—and what happened to Quillery? That's what happens to everyone who dares to criticize him. Last night I did the one thing he could never forgive. I told him the truth! At last I told him just what I think. And now—you see how quickly he strikes back!

[SHIRLEY *and* BEBE *appear.*]

SHIRLEY. Harry! The bus is going to leave.

HARRY. All right—all right!

BEBE. But we got to go this *minute!*

HARRY. I'll be with you. Get out!

SHIRLEY [*as they go*]. Can you imagine? He stops everything to make another pass at that Russian. [*They have gone.*]

IRENE. Go ahead—go ahead! You can't help me! No one can! [*He picks up his coat and hat.*] But—if it will make you any happier in your future travels with Les Blondes, I'll tell you, yes—I did know you, slightly, in Omaha!

HARRY [*peering at her*]. Are you lying again?

IRENE. It was room 974. Does that convince you?

HARRY [*ferociously*]. How can I remember what room it was?

IRENE [*smiling*]. Well, then—you'll never be sure, Mr. Van.

BEBE'S VOICE. Harry!

SHIRLEY'S VOICE. For God's sake, Harry!

DON [*appearing*]. We can't wait another instant!
[DON *goes.*]

SHIRLEY'S VOICE. Come *on!*

HARRY [*he turns and starts for the door, addressing the* GIRLS *en route*]. All right, God damn it! [*He goes out.*]

[IRENE *takes out her vanity case, and does something to her face. She takes off her hat and cloak.* DUMPTSY *comes in from the back. He is wearing the uniform of a private in the Italian army, with gas mask at the alert, and a full pack on his back.*]

DUMPTSY. Good afternoon, madame.

IRENE [*turning*]. Why, Dumptsy—what is that costume?

DUMPTSY. They called me up. Look! I'm an Italian soldier.

IRENE. You look splendid!

DUMPTSY. If you please, madame. But why didn't you go on that bus?

IRENE. I've decided to stay and enjoy the winter sports.

DUMPTSY. I don't think this is a good place any more, madame. They say the war is very big—bigger than last time.

IRENE. Yes—I hear that on all sides.

DUMPTSY. The French will be here to drop bombs on everybody.

IRENE. It will be thrilling for us if they do. Won't it, Dumptsy?

DUMPTSY. Maybe it will, madame. But—I came to say good-bye to Auguste, the barman, and Anna, the maid. They're both cousins of mine. They'll laugh when they see me in these clothes. [*He goes to the left.*] Can I get you anything, madame?

IRENE. Yes, Dumptsy. I'll have a bottle of champagne. Bring two glasses. We'll have a drink together.

DUMPTSY. If you please, madame. [DUMPTSY *goes into the bar.*]

[IRENE *lights a cigarette and goes up to the window to look out.* PITTALUGA *comes in.*]

PITTALUGA. Your luggage is in the hall, madame. Will you wish it taken to the same suite?

IRENE. No—I didn't really care much for those rooms. Have you anything smaller?

PITTALUGA [*in a less deferential tone*]. We have smaller rooms on the other side of the hotel.

IRENE. I'll have the smallest. It will be cozier.

PITTALUGA. You wish to go to it now?

IRENE. No. You can send up the luggage. I'll look at it later.

[PITTALUGA *bows and goes.* DUMPTSY *returns with the champagne.*]

DUMPTSY. I was right, madame. Auguste laughed very much.

IRENE [*coming down*]. What will happen to your wife and children, Dumptsy?

DUMPTSY. Oh—I suppose the Fascisti will feed them. They promised to feed all the families with a man who is out fighting for their country. [*He has filled her glass. She sits down.*]

IRENE. Go ahead and pour yourself one, Dumptsy.

DUMPTSY. Thank you so much, madame. I wasn't sure I heard correctly.

IRENE. Here's to you, Dumptsy—and to Austria.

DUMPTSY. And to you, madame, if you please.

IRENE. Thank you. [*They drink.*]

DUMPTSY. And may you soon be restored to your home in Petersburg.

IRENE. Petersburg?

DUMPTSY. Yes, madame. Your home.

IRENE [*with a slight smile*]. Ah, yes. My home! [*They drink again.*] And have no fear for the future, Dumptsy. Whatever happens—have no fear!

DUMPTSY. If you please, madame. [*He finishes his drink.*] And now I must go find Anna, if you will excuse me.

IRENE. Here, Dumptsy. [*She hands him a note of money.*] Good-bye, and God bless you.

DUMPTSY. Thank you so much, madame. [DUMPTSY *leans over and kisses her hand.*] Kiss die hand, madame.

[*The* CAPTAIN *and* MAJOR *come in from the lobby.* DUMPTSY *salutes, strenuously, and goes out. The* MA-

JOR *goes across and into the bar. The* CAPTAIN *is following him.*]

IRENE. Some champagne, Captain?

CAPTAIN. No, thank you very much.

IRENE. You needn't be anxious to avoid me, Captain. I know perfectly well that it wasn't your fault.

CAPTAIN. You are very understanding, madame.

IRENE. Yes—that's true. I am one of the most remarkably understanding people on earth. [*She swallows her drink.*] I understand so damned much that I am here, alone, on this cold mountain, and I have no one to turn to, nowhere to go. . . .

CAPTAIN. If I can be of service to you in any way . . .

IRENE. I know you'll be kind, Captain Locicero. And faultlessly polite.

CAPTAIN [*with genuine sympathy*]. I realize, madame, that politeness means nothing now. But—under these tragic circumstances—what else can I do?

IRENE [*deliberately*]. What else can you do? I'll tell you what else you can do in these tragic circumstances. You can refuse to fight! Have you ever thought of that possibility? You can refuse to use those weapons that they have sold you! But—you were going into the bar. Please don't let me detain you.

CAPTAIN. You will forgive me, madame?

IRENE. Fully, my dear Captain. . . . Fully.

CAPTAIN. Thank you. [*He salutes and goes into the bar.*]

[IRENE *pours herself another drink. Then she picks it up, goes to the piano, and starts to play a sketchy accompaniment for "Kak Stranna." She seems to be pretty close to tears. Perhaps she does cry a little, thoroughly enjoying the emotion.* HARRY *comes in wearing his snappy overcoat and his hat. He pays no attention to her, as he takes off his coat and hat and throws them down somewhere.*]

IRENE. Did you have some trouble?

HARRY. No. Whose is that champagne?

IRENE. Mine. Won't you have some?

HARRY. Thanks.

IRENE. Dumptsy used that glass.

HARRY. That's all right. [*He fills the glass and drinks.*]

IRENE. What happened? Didn't the train go?

HARRY. Yes—the train went. . . . I got the girls on board. Mr. and Mrs. Cherry promised to look out for them. They'll be O.K.

IRENE. And you came back—to me?

HARRY [*curtly*]. It seems fairly obvious that I did come back. [*He refills his glass.*]

IRENE. You meant it when you said that you wanted to help me.

HARRY. You said I'd never be sure. Well—I came back to tell you I *am* sure! I got thinking back, in the bus, and I came to the conclusion that it *was* Room 974 or close to it, anyway. And somehow or other, I couldn't help feeling rather flattered, and touched, to think that with all the sordid hotel rooms you've been in, you should have remembered that one. [*He has some more champagne.*]

IRENE [*after a moment*]. Bayard is not dead!

HARRY. Who?

IRENE. The Chevalier Bayard.

HARRY. Oh?

IRENE. Somewhere in that funny, music-hall soul of yours is the spirit of Leander, and Abelard, and Galahad. You give up everything—risk your life—walk unafraid into the valley of the shadow—to aid and comfort a damsel in distress. Isn't that the truth?

HARRY. Yes—it's the truth—plainly and simply put. [*He pours himself more champagne and drinks it quickly.*] Listen to me, babe—when are you going to break down and tell me who the hell are you?

IRENE. Does it matter so very much who I am?

HARRY. No.

IRENE. Give me some more champagne. [HARRY *goes to her and pours.*] My father was not one of the Romanoffs. But for many years, he was their guest—in Siberia. From him I learned that it is no use telling the truth to people whose whole life is a lie. But you —Harry—you are different. You are an honest man.

HARRY [*after a short pause*]. I am—am I? [*He crosses to the bar.*] Another bottle of champagne. . . . Hi, Captain.

CAPTAIN'S VOICE [*offstage in bar*]. What has happened, Mr. Van? Did you miss the train?

HARRY. No—just a God-damned fool. [*He closes the bar door.* IRENE *is gazing at him. He goes to her and kisses her.*]

IRENE. All these years—you've been surrounded by blondes—and you've loved only me!

HARRY. Now listen—we don't want to have any misunderstanding. If you're hooking up with me, it's only for professional reasons—see?

IRENE. Yes—I see.

HARRY. And what's more, I'm the manager. I'll fix it with the Captain for us to cross the border tomorrow, or the next day, or soon. We'll join up with the girls in Geneva—and that's as good a place as any to rehearse the code.

IRENE. The code! Of *course*—the code! I shall learn it easily.

HARRY. It's a very deep complicated scientific problem.

IRENE. You must tell it to me at once.

HARRY. At once! If you're unusually smart and apply yourself you'll have a fairly good idea of it after six months of study and rehearsal.

IRENE. A mind reader! Yes—you're quite right. I shall be able to do that very well!

[AUGUSTE *enters from the bar with a bottle of champagne. He refills their glasses, then refills* HARRY'S *glass, gives* HARRY *the bottle and goes back in to the bar.*]

HARRY. And, another thing, if you're going to qualify for this act with me, you've got to lay off liquor. I mean, after we finish this. It's a well-known fact that booze and science don't mix. [*He has another drink.* IRENE *is as one in a trance.*]

IRENE. I don't think I shall use my own name. No—Americans would mispronounce it horribly. No, I shall call myself—Namoura . . . Namoura the Great —assisted by Harry Van.

HARRY. You've got nice billing there.

IRENE. I shall wear a black velvet dress—very plain— My skin, ivory white. I must have something to hold. One white flower. No! A little white prayer book. That's it. A little white . . . [*The warning siren is heard.*] What's that?

HARRY. Sounds like a fire. [*The* CAPTAIN *and* MAJOR *burst out of the bar and rush to the big window, talking excitedly in Italian and pointing to the northwestern sky. The siren shrieks continue. The* MAJOR *then rushes out, the* CAPTAIN *about to follow him.*] What's up, Captain?

CAPTAIN. French aeroplanes. It is reprisal for last night. They are coming to destroy our base here.

HARRY. I see.

CAPTAIN. They have no reason to attack this hotel. But —there may easily be accidents. I advise the cellar.

[AUGUSTE *rushes in from the bar,* PITTALUGA *from the lobby. The latter orders* AUGUSTE *to lower the Venetian blinds.*]

IRENE. Oh, no, Captain. We must stay here and watch the spectacle.

CAPTAIN. I entreat you not to be reckless, madame. I have enough on my conscience now, without adding to it your innocent life!

IRENE. Don't worry, Captain. Death and I are old friends.

CAPTAIN. God be with you, madame. [*He goes out.*]

[HARRY *and* IRENE *empty their glasses.* HARRY *refills them. Airplane motors are heard, increasing. Then the sound of machine guns. Bombs are heard bursting at some distance.* AUGUSTE *and* PITTALUGA *go.*]

IRENE. Those are bombs.

HARRY. I guess so.

IRENE. We're in the war, Harry.

HARRY. What do you think we ought to do about it? Go out and say "Boo"?

IRENE. Let them be idiotic if they wish. We are sane. Why don't you try singing something?

HARRY. The voice don't feel appropriate. Too bad we haven't got Chaliapin here. [*She laughs.*] You know, babe—you look better blonde.

IRENE. Thank you.

[PITTALUGA *runs in.*]

PITTALUGA. The French beasts are bombing us! Everyone goes into the cellar.

HARRY. Thanks very much, Signor.

PITTALUGA. You have been warned! [*He rushes out.*]

IRENE. Ridiculous! Here we are, on top of the world— and he asks us to go down into the cellar. . . . Do you want to go into the cellar?

HARRY. Do you?

IRENE. No. If a bomb hits, it will be worse in the cellar. [*He holds her close to him. She kisses him.*] I love you, Harry.

HARRY. You do, eh!

IRENE. Ever since that night—in the Governor Bryan Hotel—I've loved you. Because I knew that you have a heart that I can trust. And that whatever I would say to you, I would never—*never* be misunderstood.

HARRY. That's right, babe. I told you I had you tagged, right from the beginning.

IRENE. And you adore me, don't you, darling?

HARRY. No! Now lay off—

IRENE. No—of course not—you mustn't admit it!

HARRY. Will you please stop pawing me? [*She laughs and lets go of him.*]

[HARRY *pours more champagne, as she crosses to the window, opens the slats of the blinds, and looks out. There is now great noise of planes, machine guns and bombs.*]

IRENE. Oh, you must see this! It's superb! [*He crosses to the window with his glass and looks out. The light on the stage is growing dimmer, but a weird light comes from the window. The scream of many gas bombs is heard.*] It's positively Wagnerian—isn't it?

HARRY. It looks to me exactly like "Hell's Angels." Did you ever see that picture, babe?

IRENE. No. I don't care for films.

HARRY. I *do*. I love 'em—every one of them. [*He is dragging her to the piano—a comparatively safe retreat.*] Did you know I used to play the piano in picture theatres? Oh, sure—I know all the music there is. [*They are now at the piano—*HARRY *sitting,* IRENE *standing close by him. She is looking toward the window. He starts to accompany the air raid with the* "Ride of the Valkyries." *There is a loud explosion.*]

IRENE. Harry . . .

HARRY. Yes, babe?

IRENE. Harry—do you realize that the whole world has gone to war? The *whole world!*

HARRY. I realize it. But don't ask me why. Because I've stopped trying to figure it out.

IRENE. I know why it is. It's just for the purpose of killing *us* . . . you and me. [*There is another loud explosion.* HARRY *stops playing.*] Because we are the little people—and for us the deadliest weapons are the most merciful. . . .

[*Another loud explosion.* HARRY *drinks.*]

HARRY. They're getting closer.

IRENE. Play some more. [*He resumes the* "Valkyrie."] Harry—do you know any hymns?

HARRY. What?

IRENE. Do you know any hymns?

HARRY. Certainly. [*He starts to play* "Onward, Christian Soldiers" *in furious jazz time, working in strains of* "Dixie." *There is another fearful crash, shattering the pane of the big window. He drags her down beside him at the piano.* HARRY *resumes* "Onward, Christian Soldiers" *in a slow, solemn tempo.*]

HARRY [*sings*]. Onward, Christian Soldiers—

[IRENE *joins the loud singing.*]

BOTH [*singing*].

> Marching as to war—
> With the Cross of Jesus
> Going on before. . . .

[*The din is now terrific. Demolition-bombs, gas-bombs, airplanes, shrapnel, machine guns.*]

CURTAIN

OF MICE AND MEN

by John Steinbeck

Copyright, 1937, by John Steinbeck
Published by The Viking Press, Inc., New York

*Reprinted by arrangement with the publishers. No profes-
sional performance or public reading of this play may be
given without permission in writing obtained from McIn-
tosh & Otis, Inc., 18 East 41st Street, New York 17, N.Y.
No amateur performance may be given without the permission of Dramatists Play Service, 14 East 38th Street,
New York 16, New York.*

First production, November 23, 1937,
at the Music Box Theatre, New York,
with the following cast·

GEORGE, *Wallace Ford*
LENNIE, *Broderick Crawford*
CANDY, *John F. Hamilton*
THE BOSS, *Thomas Findlay*
CURLEY, *Sam Byrd*
CURLEY'S WIFE, *Claire Luce*
SLIM, *Will Geer*
CARLSON, *Charles Slattery*
WHIT, *Walter Baldwin*
CROOKS, *Leigh Whipper*

SYNOPSIS OF SCENES

ACT I

Scene 1. *A Sandy bank of the Salinas River.*
          Thursday night.
Scene 2. *The interior of a bunkhouse. Late Friday*
          morning.

ACT II

Scene 1. *The same as Act I, Scene 2. About seven-thirty*
          Friday evening.
Scene 2. *The room of the stable buck, a lean-to.*
          Ten o'clock Saturday evening.

ACT III

Scene 1. *One end of a great barn. Mid-afternoon, Sunday.*
Scene 2. *Same as Act I, Scene 1.*

TIME: *The present.*
PLACE: *An agricultural valley in Southern California.*

Act one

Thursday night.

A sandy bank of the Salinas River sheltered with willows—one giant sycamore right, upstage.

The stage is covered with dry leaves. The feeling of the stage is sheltered and quiet.

Stage is lit by a setting sun.

Curtain rises on an empty stage. A sparrow is singing. There is a distant sound of ranch dogs barking aimlessly and one clear quail call. The quail call turns to a warning call and there is a beat of the flock's wings. Two figures are seen entering the stage in single file, with GEORGE, *the short man, coming in ahead of* LENNIE. *Both men are carrying blanket rolls. They approach the water. The small man throws down his blanket roll, the large man follows and then falls down and drinks from the river, snorting as he drinks.*

GEORGE [*irritably*]. Lennie, for God's sake, don't drink so much. [*Leans over and shakes* LENNIE.] Lennie, you hear me! You gonna be sick like you was last night.

LENNIE [*dips his whole head under, hat and all. As he sits upon the bank, his hat drips down the back*]. That's good. You drink some, George. You drink some too.

GEORGE [*kneeling and dipping his finger in the water*]. I ain't sure it's good water. Looks kinda scummy to me.

LENNIE [*imitates, dipping his finger also*]. Look at them wrinkles in the water, George. Look what I done.

GEORGE [*drinking from his cupped palm*]. Tastes all right. Don't seem to be runnin' much, though. Lennie, you oughtn' to drink water when it ain't running. [*Hopelessly.*] You'd drink water out of a gutter if you was thirsty. [*He throws a scoop of water into his face and rubs it around with his hand, pushes himself back and embraces his knees.* LENNIE, *after watching him, imitates him in every detail.*]

GEORGE [*beginning tiredly and growing angry as he speaks*]. God damn it, we could just as well of rode clear to the ranch. That bus driver didn't know what he was talkin' about. "Just a little stretch down the highway," he says. "Just a little stretch" —damn near four miles. I bet he didn't want to stop at the ranch gate. . . . I bet he's too damn lazy to pull up. Wonder he ain't too lazy to stop at Soledad at all! [*Mumbling.*] Just a little stretch down the road.

LENNIE [*timidly*]. George?

GEORGE. Yeh . . . what you want?

LENNIE. Where we goin', George?

GEORGE [*jerks down his hat furiously*]. So you forgot that already, did you? So I got to tell you again! Jeez, you're a crazy bastard!

LENNIE [*softly*]. I forgot. I tried not to forget, honest to God, I did!

GEORGE. Okay, okay, I'll tell you again. . . . [*With sarcasm.*] I ain't got nothin' to do. Might just as well spen' all my time tellin' you things. You forgit 'em and I tell you again.

LENNIE [*continuing on from his last speech*]. I tried

and tried, but it didn't do no good. I remember about the rabbits, George!

GEORGE. The hell with the rabbits! You can't remember nothing but them rabbits. You remember settin' in that gutter on Howard Street and watchin' that blackboard?

LENNIE [*delightedly*]. Oh, sure! I remember that . . . but . . . wha'd we do then? I remember some girls come by, and you says—

GEORGE. The hell with what I says! You remember about us goin' in Murray and Ready's and they give us work cards and bus tickets?

LENNIE [*confidently*]. Oh, sure, George . . . I remember that now. [*Puts his hand into his side coat-pocket; his confidence vanishes. Very gently.*] . . . George?

GEORGE. Huh?

LENNIE [*staring at the ground in despair*]. I ain't got mine. I musta lost it.

GEORGE. You never had none. I got both of 'em here. Think I'd let you carry your own work card?

LENNIE [*with tremendous relief*]. I thought I put it in my side pocket. [*Puts his hand in his pocket again.*]

GEORGE [*looking sharply at him; and as he looks,* LENNIE *brings his hand out of his pocket*]. Wha'd you take out of that pocket?

LENNIE [*cleverly*]. Ain't a thing in my pocket.

GEORGE. I know there ain't. You got it in your hand now. What you got in your hand?

LENNIE. I ain't got nothing, George! Honest!

GEORGE. Come on, give it here!

LENNIE [*holds his closed hand away from* GEORGE]. It's on'y a mouse!

GEORGE. A mouse? A live mouse?

LENNIE. No . . . just a dead mouse. [*Worriedly.*] I didn't kill it. Honest. I found it. I found it dead.

GEORGE. Give it here!

LENNIE. Leave me have it, George.

GEORGE [*sternly*]. Give it here! [LENNIE *reluctantly gives him the mouse.*] What do you want of a dead mouse, anyway?

LENNIE [*in a propositional tone*]. I was petting it with my thumb while we walked along.

GEORGE. Well, you ain't pettin' no mice while you walk with me. Now let's see if you can remember where we're going. [GEORGE *throws it across the water into the brush.*]

LENNIE [*looks startled and then in embarrassment hides his face against his knees*]. I forgot again.

GEORGE. Jesus Christ! [*Resignedly.*] Well, look, we are gonna work on a ranch like the one we come from up north.

LENNIE. Up north?

GEORGE. In Weed!

LENNIE. Oh, sure I remember—in Weed.

GEORGE [*still with exaggerated patience*]. That ranch we're goin' to is right down there about a quarter mile. We're gonna go in and see the boss.

LENNIE [*repeats as a lesson*]. And see the boss!

GEORGE. Now, look! I'll give him the work tickets, but you ain't gonna say a word. You're just gonna stand there and not say nothing.

LENNIE. Not say nothing!

GEORGE. If he finds out what a crazy bastard you are, we won't get no job. But if he sees you work before he hears you talk, we're set. You got that?

LENNIE. Sure, George . . . sure, I got that.

GEORGE. Okay. Now when we go in to see the boss, what you gonna do?

LENNIE [*concentrating*]. I . . . I . . . I ain't gonna say nothing . . . jus' gonna stand there.

GEORGE [*greatly relieved*]. Good boy, that's swell! Now

say that over two or three times so you sure won't forget it.

LENNIE [*drones softly under his breath*]. I ain't gonna say nothing . . . I ain't gonna say nothing. . . . [*Trails off into a whisper.*]

GEORGE. And you ain't gonna do no bad things like you done in Weed neither.

LENNIE [*puzzled*]. Like I done in Weed?

GEORGE. So you forgot that too, did you?

LENNIE [*triumphantly*]. They run us out of Weed!

GEORGE [*disgusted*]. Run us out, hell! We run! They was lookin' for us, but they didn't catch us.

LENNIE [*happily*]. I didn't forget that, you bet.

GEORGE [*lies back on the sand, crosses his hands under his head. And again* LENNIE *imitates him*]. God, you're a lot of trouble! I could get along so easy and nice, if I didn't have you on my tail. I could live so easy!

LENNIE [*hopefully*]. We gonna work on a ranch, George.

GEORGE. All right, you got that. But we're gonna sleep here tonight, because . . . I want to. I want to sleep out.

[*The light is going fast, dropping into evening. A little wind whirls into the clearing and blows leaves. A dog howls in the distance.*]

LENNIE. Why ain't we goin' on to the ranch to get some supper? They got supper at the ranch.

GEORGE. No reason at all. I just like it here. Tomorrow we'll be goin' to work. I seen thrashing machines on the way down; that means we'll be buckin' grain bags. Bustin' a gut liftin' up them bags. Tonight I'm gonna lay right here an' look up! Tonight there ain't a grain bag or a boss in the world.

Tonight, the drinks is on the . . . house. Nice house we got here, Lennie.

LENNIE [*gets up on his knees and looks down at* GEORGE, *plaintively*]. Ain't we gonna have no supper?

GEORGE. Sure we are. You gather up some dead willow sticks. I got three cans of beans in my bindle. I'll open 'em up while you get a fire ready. We'll eat 'em cold.

LENNIE [*companionably*]. I like beans with ketchup.

GEORGE. Well, we ain't got no ketchup. You go get the wood, and don't you fool around none. Be dark before long. [LENNIE *lumbers to his feet and disappears into the brush.* GEORGE *gets out the bean cans, opens two of them, suddenly turns his head and listens. A little sound of splashing comes from the direction that* LENNIE *has taken.* GEORGE *looks after him; shakes his head.* LENNIE *comes back carrying a few small willow sticks in his hand.*] All right, give me that mouse.

LENNIE [*with elaborate pantomime of innocence*]. What, George? I ain't got no mouse.

GEORGE [*holding out his hand*]. Come on! Give it to me! You ain't puttin' nothing over. [LENNIE *hesitates, backs away, turns and looks as if he were going to run. Coldly*]. You gonna give me that mouse or do I have to take a sock at you?

LENNIE. Give you what, George?

GEORGE. You know goddamn well, what! I want that mouse!

LENNIE [*almost in tears*]. I don't know why I can't keep it. It ain't nobody's mouse. I didn' steal it! I found it layin' right beside the road. [GEORGE *snaps his fingers sharply, and* LENNIE *lays the mouse in his hand.*] I wasn't doin' nothing bad with it. Just stroking it. That ain't bad.

GEORGE [*stands up and throws the mouse as far as he can into the brush, then he steps to the pool, and washes his hands*]. You crazy fool! Thought you could get away with it, didn't you? Don't you think I could see your feet was wet where you went in the water to get it? [LENNIE *whimpers like a puppy.*] Blubbering like a baby. Jesus Christ, a big guy like you! [LENNIE *tries to control himself, but his lips quiver and his face works with an effort.* GEORGE *puts his hand on* LENNIE's *shoulder for a moment.*] Aw, Lennie, I ain't takin' it away just for meanness. That mouse ain't fresh. Besides, you broke it pettin' it. You get a mouse that's fresh and I'll let you keep it a little while.

LENNIE. I don't know where there is no other mouse. I remember a lady used to give 'em to me. Ever' one she got she used to give it to me, but that lady ain't here no more.

GEORGE. Lady, huh! . . . Give me them sticks there. . . . Don't even remember who that lady was. That was your own Aunt Clara. She stopped givin' 'em to you. You always killed 'em.

LENNIE [*sadly and apologetically*]. They was so little. I'd pet 'em and pretty soon they bit my fingers and then I pinched their head a little bit and then they was dead . . . because they was so little. I wish we'd get the rabbits pretty soon, George. They ain't so little.

GEORGE. The hell with the rabbits! Come on, let's eat. [*The light has continued to go out of the scene so that when* GEORGE *lights the fire, it is the major light on the stage.* GEORGE *hands one of the open cans of beans to* LENNIE.] There's enough beans for four men.

LENNIE [*sitting on the other side of the fire, speaks patiently*]. I like 'em with ketchup.

GEORGE [*explodes*]. Well, we ain't got any. Whatever we ain't got, that's what you want. God Almighty, if I was alone, I could live so easy. I could go get a job of work and no trouble. No mess . . . and when the end of the month come, I could take my fifty bucks and go into town and get whatever I want. Why, I could stay in a cat-house all night. I could eat any place I want. Order any damn thing.

LENNIE [*plaintively, but softly*]. I didn't want no ketchup.

GEORGE [*continuing violently*]. I could do that every damn month. Get a gallon of whiskey or set in a pool room and play cards or shoot pool. [LENNIE *gets up to his knees and looks over the fire, with frightened face.*] And what have I got? [*Disgustedly.*] I got *you*. You can't keep a job and you lose me every job I get!

LENNIE [*in terror*]. I don't mean nothing, George.

GEORGE. Just keep me shovin' all over the country all the time. And that ain't the worst—you get in trouble. You do bad things and I got to get you out. It ain't bad people that raises hell. It's dumb ones. [*He shouts.*] You crazy son-of-a-bitch, you keep me in hot water all the time. [LENNIE *is trying to stop* GEORGE's *flow of words with his hands. Sarcastically.*] You just wanta feel that girl's dress. Just wanta pet it like it was a mouse. Well, how the hell'd she know you just wanta feel her dress? How'd she know you'd just hold onto it like it was a mouse?

LENNIE [*in panic*]. I didn't mean to, George!

GEORGE. Sure you didn't mean to. You didn't mean for her to yell bloody hell, either. You didn't mean for us to hide in the irrigation ditch all day with guys out lookin' for us with guns. Alla time it's something you didn't mean. God damn it, I wish I could put you in a cage with a million mice and let them pet *you*. [GEORGE's *anger leaves him suddenly. For the first time he seems to see the expression of terror on* LENNIE's *face. He looks down ashamedly at the fire, and maneuvers some beans onto the blade of his pocket-knife and puts them into his mouth.*]

LENNIE [*after a pause*]. George! [GEORGE *purposely does not answer him.*] George?

GEORGE. What do you want?

LENNIE. I was only foolin', George. I don't want no ketchup. I wouldn't eat no ketchup if it was right here beside me.

GEORGE [*with a sullenness of shame*]. If they was some here you could have it. And if I had a thousand bucks I'd buy ya a bunch of flowers.

LENNIE. I wouldn't eat no ketchup, George. I'd leave it all for you. You could cover your beans so deep with it, and I wouldn't touch none of it.

GEORGE [*refusing to give in from his sullenness, refusing to look at* LENNIE]. When I think of the swell time I could have without you, I go nuts. I never git no peace!

LENNIE. You want I should go away and leave you alone?

GEORGE. Where the hell could you go?

LENNIE. Well, I could . . . I could go off in the hills there. Some place I could find a cave.

GEORGE. Yeah, how'd ya eat? You ain't got sense enough to find nothing to eat.

LENNIE. I'd find things. I don't need no nice food with ketchup. I'd lay out in the sun and nobody would hurt me. And if I found a mouse—why, I could keep it. Wouldn't nobody take it away from me.

GEORGE [*at last he looks up*]. I been mean, ain't I?

LENNIE [*presses his triumph*]. If you don't want me, I can go right in them hills, and find a cave. I can go away any time.

GEORGE. No. Look! I was just foolin' ya. 'Course I want you to stay with me. Trouble with mice is you always kill 'em. [*He pauses.*] Tell you what I'll do, Lennie. First chance I get I'll find you a pup. Maybe you wouldn't kill it. That would be better than mice. You could pet it harder.

LENNIE [*still avoiding being drawn in*]. If you don't want me, you only gotta say so. I'll go right up on them hills and live by myself. And I won't get no mice stole from me.

GEORGE. I want you to stay with me. Jesus Christ, somebody'd shoot you for a coyote if you was by yourself. Stay with me. Your Aunt Clara wouldn't like your runnin' off by yourself, even if she is dead.

LENNIE. George?

GEORGE. Huh?

LENNIE [*craftily*]. Tell me—like you done before.

GEORGE. Tell you what?

LENNIE. About the rabbits.

GEORGE [*near to anger again*]. You ain't gonna put nothing over on me!

LENNIE [*pleading*]. Come on, George . . . tell me! Please! Like you done before.

GEORGE. You get a kick out of that, don't you? All right, I'll tell you. And then we'll lay out our beds and eat our dinner.

LENNIE. Go on, George. [*Unrolls his bed and lies on his side, supporting his head on one hand.* GEORGE *lays out his bed and sits cross-legged on it.* GEORGE *repeats the next speech rhythmically, as though he had said it many times before.*]

GEORGE. Guys like us that work on ranches is the loneliest guys in the world. They ain't got no family. They don't belong no place. They come to a ranch and work up a stake and then they go in to town and blow their stake. And then the first thing you know they're poundin' their tail on some other ranch. They ain't got nothin' to look ahead to.

LENNIE [*delightedly*]. That's it, that's it! Now tell how it is with us.

GEORGE [*still almost chanting*]. With us it ain't like that. We got a future. We got somebody to talk to that gives a damn about us. We don't have to sit in no barroom blowin' in our jack, just because we got no place else to go. If them other guys gets in jail, they can rot for all anybody gives a damn.

LENNIE [*who cannot restrain himself any longer. Bursts into speech.*] But not us! And why? Because . . . because I got you to look after me . . . and you got me to look after you . . . and that's why! [*He laughs.*] Go on, George!

GEORGE. You got it by heart. You can do it yourself.

LENNIE. No, no. I forget some of the stuff. Tell about how it's gonna be.

GEORGE. Some other time.

LENNIE. No, tell how it's gonna be!

GEORGE. Okay. Some day we're gonna get the jack together and we're gonna have a little house, and a couple of acres and a cow and some pigs and . . .

LENNIE [*shouting*]. And live off the fat of the land! And have rabbits. Go on, George! Tell about what we're gonna have in the garden. And about the rabbits in the cages. Tell about the rain in the winter . . . and about the stove and how thick the cream is on the milk, you can hardly cut it. Tell about that, George!

GEORGE. Why don't you do it yourself—you know all of it!

LENNIE. It ain't the same if I tell it. Go on now. How I get to tend the rabbits.

GEORGE [*resignedly*]. Well, we'll have a big vegetable patch and a rabbit hutch and chickens. And when it rains in the winter we'll just say to hell with goin' to work. We'll build up a fire in the stove, and set around it and listen to the rain comin' down on the roof— Nuts! [*Begins to eat with his knife.*] I ain't got time for no more. [*He falls to eating.* LENNIE *imitates him, spilling a few beans from his mouth with every bite.* GEORGE, *gesturing with his knife.*] What you gonna say tomorrow when the boss asks you questions?

LENNIE [*stops chewing in the middle of a bite, swallows painfully. His face contorts with thought*]. I . . . I ain't gonna say a word.

GEORGE. Good boy. That's fine. Say, maybe you're gettin' better. I bet I can let you tend the rabbits . . . specially if you remember as good as that!

LENNIE [*choking with pride*]. I can remember, by God!

GEORGE [*as though remembering something, points his knife at* LENNIE's *chest*]. Lennie, I want you to look around here. Think you can remember this place? The ranch is 'bout a quarter mile up that way. Just follow the river and you can get here.

LENNIE [*looking around carefully*]. Sure, I can remember here. Didn't I remember 'bout not gonna say a word?

GEORGE. 'Course you did. Well, look, Lennie, if you just happen to get in trouble, I want you to come right here and hide in the brush.

LENNIE [*slowly*]. Hide in the brush.

GEORGE. Hide in the brush until I come for you. Think you can remember that?

LENNIE. Sure I can, George. Hide in the brush till you come for me!

GEORGE. But you ain't gonna get in no trouble. Because if you do I won't let you tend the rabbits

LENNIE. I won't get in no trouble. I ain't gonna say a word.

GEORGE. You got it. Anyways, I hope so. [GEORGE *stretches out on his blankets. The light dies slowly out of the fire until only the faces of the two men can be seen.* GEORGE *is still eating from his can of beans.*] It's gonna be nice sleeping here. Lookin' up . . . and the leaves . . . Don't build no more fire. We'll let her die. Jesus, you feel free when you ain't got a job—if you ain't hungry.

[*They sit silently for a few moments. A night owl is heard far off. From across the river there comes the sound of a coyote howl and on the heels of the howl all the dogs in the country start to bark.*]

LENNIE [*from almost complete darkness*]. George?

GEORGE. What do you want?

LENNIE. Let's have different color rabbits, George.

GEORGE. Sure. Red rabbits and blue rabbits and green rabbits. Millions of 'em!

LENNIE. Furry ones, George. Like I seen at the fair in Sacramento.

GEORGE. Sure. Furry ones.

LENNIE. 'Cause I can jus' as well go away, George, and live in a cave.

GEORGE [*amiably*]. Aw, shut up.

LENNIE [*after a long pause*]. George?

GEORGE. What is it?

LENNIE. I'm shutting up, George.

[*A coyote howls again.*]

CURTAIN

SCENE II

Late Friday morning.
  The interior of a bunkhouse.

Walls, white-washed board and bat. Floors un-painted.

There is a heavy square table with upended boxes around it used for chairs. Over each bunk there is a box nailed to the wall which serves as two shelves on which are the private possessions of the working men.

On top of each bunk there is a large noisy alarm clock ticking madly.

The sun is streaking through the windows. Note: Articles in the boxes on wall are soap, talcum powder, razors, pulp magazines, medicine bottles, combs, and from nails on the sides of the boxes a few neckties.

There is a hanging light from the ceiling over the table, with a round dim reflector on it.

The curtain rises on an empty stage. Only the ticking of the many alarm clocks is heard.

CANDY, GEORGE *and* LENNIE *are first seen passing the open window of the bunkhouse.*

CANDY. This is the bunkhouse here. Door's around this side. [*The latch on the door rises and* CANDY *enters, a stoop-shouldered old man. He is dressed in blue jeans and a denim coat. He carries a big push broom in his left hand. His right hand is gone at the wrist. He grasps things with his right arm between arm and side. He walks into the room followed by* GEORGE *and* LENNIE. *Conversationally.*] The boss was expecting you last night. He was sore as hell when you wasn't here to go out this morning. [*Points with his handless arm.*] You can have them two beds there.

GEORGE. I'll take the top one . . . I don't want you falling down on me. [*Steps over to the bunk and throws his blankets down. He looks into the nearly empty box shelf over it, then picks up a small yellow can.*] Say, what the hell's this?

CANDY. I don't know.

GEORGE. Says "positively kills lice, roaches and other scourges." What the hell kinda beds you givin' us, anyway? We don't want no pants rabbits.

CANDY [*shifts his broom, holding it between his elbow and his side, takes the can in his left hand and studies the label carefully*]. Tell you what . . . last guy that had this bed was a blacksmith. Helluva nice fellow. Clean a guy as you'd want to meet. Used to wash his hands even *after* he et.

GEORGE [*with gathering anger*]. Then how come he got pillow-pigeons?

[LENNIE *puts his blankets on his bunk and sits down, watching* GEORGE *with his mouth slightly open.*]

CANDY. Tell you what. This here blacksmith, name of Whitey, was the kinda guy that would put that stuff around even if there wasn't no bugs. Tell you what he used to do. He'd peel *his* boiled potatoes and take out every little spot before he et it, and if there was a red splotch on an egg, he'd scrape it off. Finally quit about the food. That's the kind of guy Whitey was. Clean. Used to dress up Sundays even when he wasn't goin' no place. Put on a necktie even, and then set in the bunkhouse.

GEORGE [*skeptically*]. I ain't so sure. What da' ya say he quit for?

CANDY [*puts the can in his pocket, rubs his bristly white whiskers with his knuckles*]. Why . . . he just quit the way a guy will. Says it was the food. Didn't give no other reason. Just says "give me my time" one night, the way any guy would.

[GEORGE *lifts his bed tick and looks underneath, leans over and inspects the sacking carefully.* LENNIE *does the same with his bed.*]

GEORGE [*half satisfied*]. Well, if there's any gray-backs in this bed, you're gonna hear from me!

[*He unrolls his blankets and puts his razor and bar of soap and comb and bottle of pills, his liniment and leather wristband in the box.*]

CANDY. I guess the boss'll be out here in a minute to write your name in. He sure was burned when you wasn't here this morning. Come right in when we was eatin' breakfast and says, "Where the hell's them new men?" He give the stable buck hell, too. Stable buck's a nigger.

GEORGE. Nigger, huh!

CANDY. Yeah. [*Continues.*] Nice fellow too. Got a crooked back where a horse kicked him. Boss gives him hell when he's mad. But the stable buck don't give a damn about that.

GEORGE. What kinda guy is the boss?

CANDY. Well, he's a pretty nice fella for a boss. Gets mad sometimes. But he's pretty nice. Tell you what. Know what he done Christmas? Brung a gallon of whiskey right in here and says, "Drink hearty, boys, Christmas comes but once a year!"

GEORGE. The hell he did! A whole gallon?

CANDY. Yes, sir. Jesus, we had fun! They let the nigger come in that night. Well, sir, a little skinner named Smitty took after the nigger. Done pretty good too. The guys wouldn't let him use his feet so the nigger got him. If he could a used his feet Smitty says he would have killed the nigger. The guys says on account the nigger got a crooked back Smitty can't use his feet. [*He smiles in reverie at the memory.*]

GEORGE. Boss the owner?

CANDY. Naw! Superintendent. Big land company. . . . Yes, sir, that night . . . he comes right in here with a whole gallon . . . he set right over there and says, "Drink hearty, boys," . . . he says. . . . [*The door opens. Enter the* BOSS. *He is a stocky man, dressed in blue jean trousers, flannel shirt, a black unbuttoned vest and a black coat. He wears a soiled brown Stetson hat, a pair of high-heeled boots and spurs. Ordinarily he puts his thumbs in his belt.* CANDY, *shuffling towards the door, rubbing his whiskers with his knuckles as he goes.*] Them guys just come. [CANDY *exits and shuts the door behind him.*]

BOSS. I wrote Murray and Ready I wanted two men this morning. You got your work slips?

GEORGE [*digs in his pockets, produces two slips, and hands them to the* BOSS]. Here they are.

BOSS [*reading the slips*]. Well, I see it wasn't Murray and Ready's fault. It says right here on the slip, you was to be here for work this morning.

GEORGE. Bus driver give us a bum steer. We had to walk ten miles. That bus driver says we was here when we wasn't. We couldn't thumb no rides. [GEORGE *scowls meaningly at* LENNIE *and* LENNIE *nods to show that he understands.*]

BOSS. Well, I had to send out the grain teams short two buckers. It won't do any good to go out now until after dinner. You'd get lost. [*Pulls out his time book, opens it to where a pencil is stuck between the leaves. Licks his pencil carefully.*] What's your name?

GEORGE. George Milton.

BOSS. George Milton. [*Writing.*] And what's yours?

GEORGE. His name's Lennie Small.

BOSS. Lennie Small. [*Writing.*] Le's see, this is the twentieth. Noon the twentieth . . . [*Makes positive mark. Closes the book and puts it in his pocket.*] Where you boys been workin'?

GEORGE. Up around Weed.

BOSS [*to* LENNIE]. You too?

GEORGE. Yeah. Him too.

BOSS [*to* LENNIE]. Say, you're a big fellow, ain't you?

GEORGE. Yeah, he can work like hell, too.

BOSS. He ain't much of a talker, though, is he?

GEORGE. No, he ain't. But he's a hell of a good worker. Strong as a bull.

LENNIE [*smiling*]. I'm strong as a bull.

[GEORGE *scowls at him and* LENNIE *drops his head in shame at having forgotten.*]

BOSS [*sharply*]. You are, huh? What can you do?

GEORGE. He can do anything.

BOSS [*addressing* LENNIE]. What can you do?

[LENNIE, *looking at* GEORGE, *gives a high nervous chuckle.*]

GEORGE [*quickly*]. Anything you tell him. He's a good skinner. He can wrestle grain bags, drive a cultivator. He can do anything. Just give him a try.

BOSS [*turning to* GEORGE]. Then why don't you let *him* answer? [LENNIE *laughs.*] What's he laughing about?

GEORGE. He laughs when he gets excited.

BOSS. Yeah?

GEORGE [*loudly*]. But he's a goddamn good worker. I ain't saying he's bright, because he ain't. But he can put up a four hundred pound bale.

BOSS [*hooking his thumbs in his belt*]. Say, what you sellin'?

GEORGE. Huh?

BOSS. I said what stake you got in this guy? You takin' his pay away from him?

GEORGE. No. Of course I ain't!

BOSS. Hell, I never seen one guy take so much trouble for another guy. I just like to know what your percentage is.

GEORGE. He's my . . . cousin. I told his ole lady I'd take care of him. He got kicked in the head by a horse when he was a kid. He's all right. . . . Just ain't bright. But he can do anything you tell him.

BOSS [*turning half away*]. Well, God knows he don't need no brains to buck barley bags. [*He turns back.*]

But don't you try to put nothing over, Milton. I got my eye on you. Why'd you quit in Weed?

GEORGE [*promptly*]. Job was done.

BOSS. What kind of job?

GEORGE. Why . . . we was diggin' a cesspool.

BOSS [*after a pause*]. All right. But don't try to put nothing over 'cause you can't get away with nothing. I seen wise guys before. Go out with the grain teams after dinner. They're out pickin' up barley with the thrashin' machines. Go out with Slim's team.

GEORGE. Slim?

BOSS. Yeah. Big, tall skinner. You'll see him at dinner. [*Up to this time the* BOSS *has been full of business. He has been calm and suspicious. In the following lines he relaxes, but gradually, as though he wanted to talk but felt always the burden of his position. He turns toward the door, but hesitates and allows a little warmth into his manner.*] Been on the road long?

GEORGE [*obviously on guard*]. We was three days in 'Frisco lookin' at the boards.

BOSS [*with heavy jocularity*]. Didn't go to no night clubs, I 'spose?

GEORGE [*stiffly*]. We was lookin' for a job.

BOSS [*attempting to be friendly*]. That's a great town if you got a little jack, Frisco.

GEORGE [*refusing to be drawn in*]. We didn't have no jack for nothing like that.

BOSS [*realizes there is no contact to establish; grows rigid with his position again*]. Go out with the grain teams after dinner. When my hands work hard they get pie and when they loaf they bounce down the road on their can. You ask anybody about me. [*He turns and walks out of the bunkhouse.*]

GEORGE [*turns to* LENNIE]. So you wasn't gonna say a word! You was gonna leave your big flapper shut. I was gonna do the talkin'. . . . You goddamn near lost us the job!

LENNIE [*stares hopelessly at his hands*]. I forgot.

GEORGE. You forgot. You always forget. Now, he's got his eye on us. Now, we gotta be careful and not make no slips. You keep your big flapper shut after this.

LENNIE. He talked like a kinda nice guy towards the last.

GEORGE [*angrily*]. He's the boss, ain't he? Well, he's the boss first an' a nice guy afterwards. Don't you have nothin' to do with no boss, except do your work and draw your pay. You can't never tell whether you're talkin' to the nice guy or the boss. Just keep your goddamn mouth shut. Then you're all right.

LENNIE. George?

GEORGE. What you want now?

LENNIE. I wasn't kicked in the head with no horse, was I, George?

GEORGE. Be a damn good thing if you was. Save everybody a hell of a lot of trouble!

LENNIE [*flattered*]. You says I was your cousin.

GEORGE. Well, that was a goddamn lie. And I'm glad it was. Why, if I was a relative of yours— [*He stops and listens, then steps to the front door, and looks out.*] Say, what the hell you doin', listenin'?

CANDY [*comes slowly into the room. By a rope, he leads an ancient drag-footed, blind sheep dog. Guides it from running into a table leg, with the rope. Sits down on a box, and presses the hind quarters of the old dog down*]. Naw . . . I wasn't listenin'. . . . I was just standin' in the shade a minute, scratchin' my dog. I jest now finished swamping out the washhouse.

GEORGE. You was pokin' your big nose into our business! I don't like nosey guys.

CANDY [*looks uneasily from* GEORGE *to* LENNIE *and then back*]. I jest come there . . . I didn't hear nothing you guys was sayin'. I ain't interested in nothing you was sayin'. A guy on a ranch don't never listen. Nor he don't ast no questions.

GEORGE [*slightly mollified*]. Damn right he don't! Not if the guy wants to stay workin' long. [*His manner changes.*] That's a helluva ole dog.

CANDY. Yeah. I had him ever since he was a pup. God, he was a good sheep dog, when he was young. [*Rubs his cheek with his knuckles.*] How'd you like the boss?

GEORGE. Pretty good! Seemed all right.

CANDY. He's a nice fella. You got ta take him right, of course. He's runnin' this ranch. He don't take no nonsense.

GEORGE. What time do we eat? Eleven-thirty?

[CURLEY *enters. He is dressed in working clothes. He wears brown high-heeled boots and has a glove on his left hand.*]

CURLEY. Seen my ole man?

CANDY. He was here just a minute ago, Curley. Went over to the cookhouse, I think.

CURLEY. I'll try to catch him. [*Looking over at the new men, measuring them. Unconsciously bends his elbow and closes his hand and goes into a slight crouch. He walks gingerly close to* LENNIE.] You the new guys my ole man was waitin' for?

GEORGE. Yeah. We just come in.

CURLEY. How's it come you wasn't here this morning?

GEORGE. Got off the bus too soon.

CURLEY [*again addressing* LENNIE]. My ole man got to get the grain out. Ever bucked barley?

GEORGE [*quickly*]. Hell, yes. Done a lot of it.

CURLEY. I mean him. [*To* LENNIE.] Ever bucked barley?

GEORGE. Sure he has.

CURLEY [*irritatedly*]. Let the big guy talk!

GEORGE. 'Spose he don't want ta talk?

CURLEY [*pugnaciously*]. By Christ, he's gotta talk when he's spoke to. What the hell you shovin' into this for?

GEORGE [*stands up and speaks coldly*]. Him and me travel together.

CURLEY. Oh, so it's that way?

GEORGE [*tense and motionless*]. What way?

CURLEY [*letting the subject drop*]. And you won't let the big guy talk? Is that it?

GEORGE. He can talk if he wants to tell you anything. [*He nods slightly to* LENNIE.]

LENNIE [*in a frightened voice*]. We just come in.

CURLEY. Well, next time you answer when you're spoke to, then.

GEORGE. He didn't do nothing to you.

CURLEY [*measuring him*]. You drawin' cards this hand?

GEORGE [*quietly*]. I might.

CURLEY [*stares at him for a moment, his threat moving to the future*]. I'll see you get a chance to ante, anyway. [*He walks out of the room.*]

GEORGE [*after he has made his exit*]. Say, what the hell's he got on his shoulder? Lennie didn't say nothing to him.

CANDY [*looks cautiously at the door*]. That's the boss's son. Curley's pretty handy. He done quite a bit in the ring. The guys say he's pretty handy.

GEORGE. Well, let 'im be handy. He don't have to take after Lennie. Lennie didn't do nothing to him.

CANDY [*considering*]. Well . . . tell you what, Curley's like a lot a little guys. He hates big guys. He's alla time pickin' scraps with big guys. Kinda like he's mad at 'em because *he* ain't a big guy. You seen little guys like that, ain't you—always scrappy?

GEORGE. Sure, I seen plenty tough little guys. But this here Curley better not make no mistakes about Lennie. Lennie ain't handy, see, but this Curley punk's gonna get hurt if he messes around with Lennie.

CANDY [*skeptically*]. Well, Curley's pretty handy. You know, it never did seem right to me. 'Spose Curley jumps a big guy and licks him. Everybody says what a game guy Curley is. Well, 'spose he jumps 'im and gits licked, everybody says the big guy oughta pick somebody his own size. Seems like Curley ain't givin' nobody a chance.

GEORGE [*watching the door*]. Well, he better watch out for Lennie. Lennie ain't no fighter. But Lennie's strong and quick and Lennie don't know no rules. [*Walks to the square table, and sits down on one of the boxes. Picks up scattered cards and pulls them together and shuffles them.*]

CANDY. Don't tell Curley I said none of this. He'd slough me! He jus' don't give a damn. Won't ever get canned because his ole man's the boss!

GEORGE [*cuts the cards. Turns over and looks at each one as he throws it down*]. This guy Curley sounds like a son-of-a-bitch to me! I don't like mean little guys!

CANDY. Seems to me like he's worse lately. He got married a couple of weeks ago. Wife lives over in the boss's house. Seems like Curley's worse'n ever since he got married. Like he's settin' on a ant-hill an' a big red ant come up an' nipped 'im on the turnip. Just feels so goddamn miserable he'll strike at anything that moves. I'm kinda sorry for 'im.

GEORGE. Maybe he's showin' off for his wife.

CANDY. You seen that glove on his left hand?

GEORGE. Sure I seen it!

CANDY. Well, that glove's full of vaseline.

GEORGE. Vaseline? What the hell for?

CANDY. Curley says he's keepin' that hand soft for his wife.

GEORGE. That's a dirty kind of a thing to tell around.

CANDY. I ain't quite so sure. I seen such funny things a guy will do to try to be nice. I ain't sure. But you jus' wait till you see Curley's wife!

GEORGE [*begins to lay out a solitaire hand, speaks casually*]. Is she purty?

CANDY. Yeah. Purty, but—

GEORGE [*studying his cards*]. But what?

CANDY. Well, she got the eye.

GEORGE [*still playing at his solitaire hand*]. Yeah? Married two weeks an' got the eye? Maybe that's why Curley's pants is fulla ants.

CANDY. Yes, sir, I seen her give Slim the eye. Slim's a jerkline skinner. Hell of a nice fella. Well, I seen her give Slim the eye. Curley never seen it. And I seen her give a skinner named Carlson the eye.

GEORGE [*pretending a very mild interest*]. Looks like we was gonna have fun!

CANDY [*stands up*]. Know what I think? [*Waits for an answer.* GEORGE *doesn't answer.*] Well, I think Curley's married himself a tart.

GEORGE [*casually*]. He ain't the first. Black queen on a red king. Yes, sir . . . there's plenty done that!

CANDY [*moves towards the door, leading his dog out with him*]. I got to be settin' out the wash basins for the guys. The teams'll be in before long. You guys gonna buck barley?

GEORGE. Yeah.

CANDY. You won't tell Curley nothing I said?

GEORGE. Hell, no!

CANDY [*just before he goes out the door, he turns back*]. Well, you look her over, mister. You see if she ain't a tart! [*He exits.*]

GEORGE [*continuing to play out his solitaire. He turns to* LENNIE]. Look, Lennie, this here ain't no set-up. You gonna have trouble with that Curley guy. I seen that kind before. You know what he's doin'. He's kinda feelin' you out. He figures he's got you scared. And he's gonna take a sock at you, first chance he gets.

LENNIE [*frightened*]. I don't want no trouble. Don't let him sock me, George!

GEORGE. I hate them kind of bastards. I seen plenty of 'em. Like the ole guy says: "Curley don't take no chances. He always figures to win." [*Thinks for a moment.*] If he tangles with you, Lennie, we're goin' get the can. Don't make no mistake about that. He's the boss's kid. Look, you try to keep away from him, will you? Don't never speak to him. If he comes in here you move clear to the other side of the room. Will you remember that, Lennie?

LENNIE [*mourning*]. I don't want no trouble. I never done nothing to him!

GEORGE. Well, that won't do you no good, if Curley wants to set himself up for a fighter. Just don't have nothing to do with him. Will you remember?

LENNIE. Sure, George . . . I ain't gonna say a word.

[*Sounds of the teams coming in from the fields, jingling of harness, croak of heavy laden axles, men talking to and cussing the horses. Crack of a whip and from a distance a voice calling.*]

SLIM'S VOICE. Stable buck! Hey! Stable buck!

GEORGE. Here come the guys. Just don't say nothing.

LENNIE [*timidly*]. You ain't mad, George?

GEORGE. I ain't mad at you. I'm mad at this here Curley bastard! I wanted we should get a little stake together. Maybe a hundred dollars. You keep away from Curley.

LENNIE. Sure I will. I won't say a word.

GEORGE [*hesitating*]. Don't let 'im pull you in—but— if the son-of-a-bitch socks you—let him have it!

LENNIE. Let him have what, George?

GEORGE. Never mind. . . . Look, if you get in any kind of trouble, you remember what I told you to do.

LENNIE. If I get in any trouble, you ain't gonna let me tend the rabbits?

GEORGE. That's not what I mean. You remember where we slept last night. Down by the river?

LENNIE. Oh, sure I remember. I go there and hide in the brush until you come for me.

GEORGE. That's it. Hide till I come for you. Don't let nobody see you. Hide in the brush by the river. Now say that over.

LENNIE. Hide in the brush by the river. Down in the brush by the river.

GEORGE. If you get in trouble.

LENNIE. If I get in trouble.

[*A brake screeches outside and a call: "Stable buck, oh, stable buck!" "Where the hell's that goddamn nigger?" Suddenly* CURLEY'S WIFE *is standing in the door. Full, heavily rouged lips. Wide-spaced, made- up eyes, her fingernails are bright red, her hair hangs in little rolled clusters like sausages. She wears a cotton house dress and red mules, on the insteps of which are little bouquets of red ostrich feathers.* GEORGE *and* LENNIE *look up at her.*]

CURLEY'S WIFE. I'm lookin' for Curley!

GEORGE [*looks away from her*]. He was in here a min- ute ago but he went along.

CURLEY'S WIFE [*puts her hands behind her back and leans against the door frame so that her body is thrown forward*]. You're the new fellas that just come, ain't you?

GEORGE [*sullenly*]. Yeah.

CURLEY'S WIFE [*bridles a little and inspects her finger-nails*]. Sometimes Curley's in here.

GEORGE [*brusquely*]. Well, he ain't now!

CURLEY'S WIFE [*playfully*]. Well, if he ain't, I guess I'd better look some place else.

[LENNIE *watches her, fascinated*.]

GEORGE. If I see Curley I'll pass the word you was lookin' for him.

CURLEY'S WIFE. Nobody can't blame a person for lookin'.

GEORGE. That depends what she's lookin' for.

CURLEY'S WIFE [*a little wearily, dropping her coquetry*]. I'm jus' lookin' for somebody to talk to. Don't you never jus' want to talk to somebody?

SLIM [*offstage*]. Okay! Put that lead pair in the north stalls.

CURLEY'S WIFE [*to* SLIM, *offstage*]. Hi, Slim!

SLIM [*voice offstage*]. Hello.

CURLEY'S WIFE. I—I'm trying to find Curley.

SLIM'S VOICE [*offstage*]. Well, you ain't tryin' very hard. I seen him goin' in your house.

CURLEY'S WIFE. I—I'm tryin' to find Curley. I gotta be goin'! [*She exits hurriedly.*]

GEORGE [*looking around at* LENNIE]. Jesus, what a tramp! So, that's what Curley picks for a wife. God Almighty, did you smell that stink she's got on? I can still smell her. Don't have to see *her* to know she's around.

LENNIE. She's purty!

GEORGE. Yeah. And she's sure hidin' it. Curley's got his work ahead of him.

LENNIE [*still staring at the doorway where she was*]. Gosh, she's purty!

GEORGE [*turning furiously at him*]. Listen to me, you crazy bastard. Don't you even look at that bitch. I don't care what she says or what she does. I seen 'em poison before, but I ain't never seen no piece of jail bait worse than her. Don't you even smell near her!

LENNIE. I never smelled, George!

GEORGE. No, you never. But when she was standin' there showin' her legs, you wasn't lookin' the other way neither!

LENNIE. I never meant no bad things, George. Honest I never.

GEORGE. Well, you keep away from her. You let Curley take the rap. He let himself in for it. [*Disgustedly.*] Glove full of vaseline. I bet he's eatin' raw eggs and writin' to patent-medicine houses.

LENNIE [*cries out*]. I don't like this place. This ain't no good place. I don't like this place!

GEORGE. Listen—I don't like it here no better than you do. But we gotta keep it till we get a stake. We're flat. We gotta get a stake. [*Goes back to the table, thoughtfully.*] If we can get just a few dollars in the poke we'll shove off and go up to the American River and pan gold. Guy can make a couple dollars a day there.

LENNIE [*eagerly*]. Let's go, George. Let's get out of here. It's mean here.

GEORGE [*shortly*]. I tell you we gotta stay a little while. We gotta get a stake. [*The sounds of running water and rattle of basins are heard.*] Shut up now, the guys'll be comin' in! [*Pensively.*] Maybe we ought to wash up. . . . But hell, we ain't done nothin' to get dirty.

SLIM [*enters. He is a tall, dark man in blue jeans and a short denim jacket. He carries a crushed Stetson hat under his arm and combs his long dark damp hair straight back. He stands and moves with a kind of majesty. He finishes combing his hair. Smooths out his crushed hat, creases it in the middle and puts it on. In a gentle voice].* It's brighter'n a bitch outside. Can't hardly see nothing in here. You the new guys?

GEORGE. Just come.

SLIM. Goin' to buck barley?

GEORGE. That's what the boss says.

SLIM. Hope you get on my team.

GEORGE. Boss said we'd go with a jerk-line skinner named Slim.

SLIM. That's me.

GEORGE. You a jerk-line skinner?

SLIM [*in self-disparagement*]. I can snap 'em around a little.

GEORGE [*terribly impressed*]. That kinda makes you Jesus Christ on this ranch, don't it?

SLIM [*obviously pleased*]. Oh, nuts!

GEORGE [*chuckles*]. Like the man says, "The boss tells you what to do. But if you want to know how to do it, you got to ask the mule skinner." The man says any guy that can drive twelve Arizona jack rabbits with a jerk line can fall in a toilet and come up with a mince pie under each arm.

SLIM [*laughing*]. Well, I hope you get on my team. I got a pair a punks that don't know a barley bag from a blue ball. You guys ever bucked any barley?

GEORGE. Hell, yes. I ain't nothin' to scream about, but that big guy there can put up more grain alone than most pairs can.

SLIM [*looks approvingly at* GEORGE]. You guys travel around together?

GEORGE. Sure. We kinda look after each other. [*Points*

at LENNIE *with his thumb.*] He ain't bright. Hell of a good worker, though. Hell of a nice fella too. I've knowed him for a long time.

SLIM. Ain't many guys travel around together. I don't know why. Maybe everybody in the whole damn world is scared of each other.

GEORGE. It's a lot nicer to go 'round with a guy you know. You get used to it an' then it ain't no fun alone any more.

[*Enter* CARLSON. *Big-stomached, powerful man. His head still drips water from scrubbing and dousing.*]

CARLSON. Hello, Slim! [*He looks at* GEORGE *and* LENNIE.]

SLIM. These guys just come.

CARLSON. Glad to meet ya! My name's Carlson.

GEORGE. I'm George Milton. This here's Lennie Small.

CARLSON. Glad to meet you. He ain't very small. [*Chuckles at his own joke.*] He ain't small at all. Meant to ask you, Slim, how's your bitch? I seen she wasn't under your wagon this morning.

SLIM. She slang her pups last night. Nine of 'em. I drowned four of 'em right off. She couldn't feed that many.

CARLSON. Got five left, huh?

SLIM. Yeah. Five. I kep' the biggest.

CARLSON. What kinda dogs you think they gonna be?

SLIM. I don't know. Some kind of shepherd, I guess. That's the most kind I seen around here when she's in heat.

CARLSON [*laughs*]. I had an airedale an' a guy down the road got one of them little white floozy dogs, well, she was in heat and the guy locks her up. But my airedale, named Tom he was, he et a woodshed clear down to the roots to get to her. Guy come over one day, he's sore as hell, he says, "I wouldn't mind if my bitch had pups, but Christ Almighty, this

morning she slang a litter of Shetland ponies. . . ."
[*Takes off his hat and scratches his head.*] Got five
pups, huh! Gonna keep all of 'em?

SLIM. I don' know, gotta keep 'em awhile, so they can
drink Lulu's milk.

CARLSON [*thoughtfully*]. Well, looka here, Slim, I been
thinkin'. That dog of Candy's is so goddamn old he
can't hardly walk. Stinks like hell. Every time Candy
brings him in the bunkhouse, I can smell him two
or three days. Why don't you get Candy to shoot his
ol' dog, and give him one of them pups to raise up?
I can smell that dog a mile off. Got no teeth. Can't
eat. Candy feeds him milk. He can't chew nothing
else. And leadin' him around on a string so he don't
bump into things . . . [*The triangle outside begins
to ring wildly. Continues for a few moments, then
stops suddenly.*] There she goes!

[*Outside there is a burst of voices as a group of men
go by.*]

SLIM [*to* LENNIE *and* GEORGE]. You guys better come on
while they's still somethin' to eat. Won't be nothing left in a couple of minutes. [*Exit* SLIM *and* CARL-
SON, LENNIE *watches* GEORGE *excitedly.*]

LENNIE. George!

GEORGE [*rumpling his cards into a pile*]. Yeah, I heard
'im, Lennie . . . I'll ask 'im!

LENNIE [*excitedly*]. A brown and white one.

GEORGE. Come on, let's get dinner. I don't know
whether he's got a brown and white one.

LENNIE. You ask him, right away, George, so he won't
kill no more of 'em!

GEORGE. Sure! Come on now—le's go. [*They start for
the door.*]

CURLEY [*bounces in, angrily*]. You seen a girl around
here?

GEORGE [*coldly*]. 'Bout half an hour ago, mebbe.

CURLEY. Well, what the hell was she doin'?

GEORGE [*insultingly*]. She *said* she was lookin' for you.

CURLEY [*measures both men with his eyes for a moment*]. Which way did she go?

GEORGE. I don't know. I didn't watch her go. [CURLEY *scowls at him a moment and then turns and hurries out the door.*] You know, Lennie, I'm scared I'm gonna tangle with that bastard myself. I hate his guts! Jesus Christ, come on! They won't be a damn thing left to eat.

LENNIE. Will you ask him about a brown and white one? [*They exeunt.*]

CURTAIN

Act two

SCENE I

About seven-thirty Friday evening.

Same bunkhouse interior as in last scene.

The evening light is seen coming in through the window, but it is quite dark in the interior of the bunkhouse.

From outside comes the sound of a horseshoe game. Thuds on the dirt and occasional clangs as a shoe hits the peg. Now and then voices are raised in approval or derision: "That's a good one." ... "Goddamn right it's a good one." ... "Here goes for a ringer. I need a ringer." ... "Goddamn near got it, too."

SLIM *and* GEORGE *come into the darkening bunk-house together.* SLIM *reaches up and turns on the tin-*

shaded electric light. Sits down on a box at the table.
GEORGE *takes his place opposite.*

SLIM. It wasn't nothing. I would of had to drown most of them pups anyway. No need to thank me about that.

GEORGE. Wasn't much to you, mebbe, but it was a hell of a lot to him. Jesus Christ, I don't know how we're gonna get him to sleep in here. He'll want to stay right out in the barn. We gonna have trouble keepin' him from gettin' right in the box with them pups.

SLIM. Say, you sure was right about him. Maybe he ain't bright—but I never seen such a worker. He damn near killed his partner buckin' barley. He'd take his end of that sack [*a gesture*], pretty near kill his partner. God Almighty, I never seen such a strong guy.

GEORGE [*proudly*]. You just tell Lennie what to do and he'll do it if it don't take no figuring.

[*Outside the sound of the horseshoe game goes on: "Son of a bitch if I can win a goddamn game." . . . "Me neither. You'd think them shoes was anvils."*]

SLIM. Funny how you and him string along together.

GEORGE. What's so funny about it?

SLIM. Oh, I don't know. Hardly none of the guys ever travels around together. I hardly never seen two guys travel together. You know how the hands are. They come in and get their bunk and work a month and then they quit and go on alone. Never seem to give a damn about nobody. Jest seems kinda funny. A cuckoo like him and a smart guy like you traveling together.

GEORGE. I ain't so bright neither or I wouldn't be buckin' barley for my fifty and found. If I was bright, if I was even a little bit smart, I'd have my own place and I'd be bringin' in my own crops 'stead of doin' all the work and not gettin' what comes up out of the ground. [*He falls silent for a moment.*]

SLIM. A guy'd like to do that. Sometimes I'd like to cuss a string of mules that was my own mules.

GEORGE. It ain't so funny, him and me goin' round together. Him and me was both born in Auburn. I knowed his aunt. She took him when he was a baby and raised him up. When his aunt died Lennie jus' come along with me, out workin'. Got kinda used to each other after a little while.

SLIM. Uh huh.

GEORGE. First I used to have a hell of a lot of fun with him. Used to play jokes on him because he was too dumb to take care of himself. But, hell, he was too dumb even to know when he had a joke played on him. [*Sarcastically.*] Hell, yes, I had fun! Made me seem goddamn smart alongside of him.

SLIM. I seen it that way.

GEORGE. Why, he'd do any damn thing I tole him. If I tole him to walk over a cliff, over he'd go. You know that wasn't so damn much fun after a while. He never got mad about it, neither. I've beat hell out of him and he could bust every bone in my body jest with his hands. But he never lifted a finger against me.

SLIM [*braiding a bull whip*]. Even if you socked him, wouldn't he?

GEORGE. No, by God! I tell you what made me stop playing jokes. One day a bunch of guys was standin' aroun' up on the Sacramento River. I was feelin' pretty smart. I turns to Lennie and I says, "Jump in."

SLIM. What happened?

GEORGE. He jumps. Couldn't swim a stroke. He damn

near drowned. And he was so nice to me for pullin'
him out. Clean forgot I tole him to jump in. Well,
I ain't done nothin' like that no more. Makes me
kinda sick tellin' about it.

SLIM. He's a nice fella. A guy don't need no sense to
be a nice fella. Seems to be sometimes it's jest the
other way round. Take a real smart guy, he ain't
hardly ever a nice fella.

GEORGE [*stacking the scattered cards and getting his
solitaire game ready again*]. I ain't got no people. I
seen guys that go round on the ranches alone. That
ain't no good. They don't have no fun. After a
while they get mean.

SLIM [*quietly*]. Yeah, I seen 'em get mean. I seen 'em
get so they don't want to talk to nobody. Some ways
they got to. You take a bunch of guys all livin' in
one room an' by God they got to mind their own
business. 'Bout the only private thing a guy's got
is where he come from and where he's goin'.

GEORGE. 'Course Lennie's a goddamn nuisance most
of the time. But you get used to goin' round with a
guy and you can't get rid of him. I mean you get
used to him an' you can't get rid of bein' used to
him. I'm sure drippin' at the mouth. I ain't told
nobody all this before.

SLIM. Do you want to get rid of him?

GEORGE. Well, he gets in trouble all the time. Because
he's so goddamn dumb. Like what happened in
Weed. [*He stops, alarmed at what he has said.*] You
wouldn't tell nobody?

SLIM [*calmly*]. What did he do in Weed?

GEORGE. You wouldn't tell?—No, 'course you wouldn't.

SLIM. What did he do?

GEORGE. Well, he seen this girl in a red dress. Dumb
bastard like he is he wants to touch everything he
likes. Jest wants to feel of it. So he reaches out to

feel this red dress. Girl let's out a squawk and that gets Lennie all mixed up. He holds on 'cause that's the only thing he can think to do.

SLIM. The hell!

GEORGE. Well, this girl squawks her head off. I'm right close and I hear all the yellin', so I comes a-running. By that time Lennie's scared to death. You know, I had to sock him over the head with a fence picket to make him let go.

SLIM. So what happens then?

GEORGE [*carefully building his solitaire hand*]. Well, she runs in and tells the law she's been raped. The guys in Weed start out to lynch Lennie. So there we sit in an irrigation ditch, under water all the rest of that day. Got only our heads stickin' out of water, up under the grass that grows out of the side of the ditch. That night we run outa there.

SLIM. Didn't hurt the girl none, huh?

GEORGE. Hell, no, he jes' scared her.

SLIM. He's a funny guy.

GEORGE. Funny! Why, one time, you know what that big baby done! He was walking along a road— [*Enter* LENNIE *through the door. He wears his coat over his shoulder like a cape and walks hunched over.*] Hi, Lennie. How do you like your pup?

LENNIE [*breathlessly*]. He's brown and white jus' like I wanted. [*Goes directly to his bunk and lies down. Face to the wall and knees drawn up.*]

GEORGE [*puts down his cards deliberately*]. Lennie!

LENNIE [*over his shoulder*]. Huh? What you want, George?

GEORGE [*sternly*]. I tole ya, ya couldn't bring that pup in here.

LENNIE. What pup, George? I ain't got no pup.

[GEORGE *goes quickly over to him, grabs him by the shoulder and rolls him over. He picks up a tiny puppie from where* LENNIE *has been concealing it against his stomach.*]

LENNIE [*quickly*]. Give him to me, George.

GEORGE. You get right up and take this pup to the nest. He's got to sleep with his mother. Ya want ta kill him? Jes' born last night and ya take him out of the nest. Ya take him back or I'll tell Slim not to let you have him.

LENNIE [*pleadingly*]. Give him to me, George. I'll take him back. I didn't mean no bad thing, George. Honest I didn't. I jus' want to pet him a little.

GEORGE [*giving the pup to him*]. All right, you get him back there quick. And don't you take him out no more.

[LENNIE *scuttles out of the room.*]

SLIM. Jesus, he's just like a kid, ain't he?

GEORGE. Sure he's like a kid. There ain't no more harm in him than a kid neither, except he's so strong. I bet he won't come in here to sleep tonight. He'll sleep right alongside that box in the barn. Well, let him. He ain't doin' no harm out there.

[*The light has faded out outside and it appears quite dark outside. Enter* CANDY *leading his old dog by a string.*]

CANDY. Hello, Slim. Hello, George. Didn't neither of you play horseshoes?

SLIM. I don't like to play every night.

CANDY [*goes to his bunk and sits down, presses the old blind dog to the floor beside him*]. Either you guys got a slug of whiskey? I got a gut ache.

SLIM. I ain't. I'd drink it myself if I had. And I ain't got no gut ache either.

CANDY. Goddamn cabbage give it to me. I knowed it was goin' to before I ever et it.

[*Enter* CARLSON *and* WHIT.]

CARLSON. Jesus, how that nigger can pitch shoes!

SLIM. He's plenty good.

WHIT. Damn right he is.

CARLSON. Yeah. He don't give nobody else a chance to win. [*Stops and sniffs the air. Looks around until he sees* CANDY's *dog.*] God Almighty, that dog stinks. Get him outa here, Candy. I don't know nothing that stinks as bad as ole dogs. You got to get him outa here.

CANDY [*lying down on his bunk, reaches over and pats the ancient dog, speaks softly*]. I been round him so much I never notice how he stinks.

CARLSON. Well, I can't stand him in here. That stink hangs round even after he's gone. [*Walks over and stands looking down at the dog.*] Got no teeth. All stiff with rheumatism. He ain't no good to you, Candy. Why don't you shoot him?

CANDY [*uncomfortably*]. Well, hell, I had him so long! Had him since he was a pup. I herded sheep with him. [*Proudly.*] You wouldn't think it to look at him now. He was the best damn sheep dog I ever seen.

GEORGE. I knowed a guy in Weed that had an aire-dale that could herd sheep. Learned it from the other dogs.

CARLSON [*sticking to his point*]. Lookit, Candy. This ole dog jus' suffers itself all the time. If you was to take him out and shoot him—right in the back of the head . . . [*Leans over and points.*] . . . right there, why he never'd know what hit him.

CANDY [*unhappily*]. No, I couldn't do that. I had him too long.

CARLSON [*insisting*]. He don't have no fun no more. He stinks like hell. Tell you what I'll do. I'll shoot him for you. Then it won't be you that done it.

CANDY [*sits up on the bunk, rubbing his whiskers*

nervously, speaks plaintively]. I had him from a pup.

WHIT. Let 'im alone, Carl. It ain't a guy's dog that matters. It's the way the guy feels about the dog. Hell, I had a mutt once I wouldn't a traded for a field trial pointer.

CARLSON [*being persuasive*]. Well, Candy ain't being nice to him, keeping him alive. Lookit, Slim's bitch got a litter right now. I bet you Slim would give ya one of them pups to raise up, wouldn't ya, Slim?

SLIM [*studying the dog*]. Yeah. You can have a pup if you want to.

CANDY [*helplessly*]. Mebbe it would hurt. [*After a moment's pause, positively.*] And I don't mind taking care of him.

CARLSON. Aw, he'd be better off dead. The way I'd shoot him he wouldn't feel nothin'. I'd put the gun right there. [*Points with his toe.*] Right back of the head.

WHIT. Aw, let 'im alone, Carl.

CARLSON. Why, hell, he wouldn't even quiver.

WHIT. Let 'im alone. [*He produces a magazine*]. Say, did you see this? Did you see this in the book here?

CARLSON. See what?

WHIT. Right there. Read that.

CARLSON. I don't want to read nothing. . . . It'd be all over in a minute, Candy. Come on.

WHIT. Did you see it, Slim? Go on, read it. Read it out loud.

SLIM. What is it?

WHIT. Read it.

SLIM [*reads slowly*]. "Dear Editor: I read your mag for six years and I think it is the best on the market. I like stories by Peter Rand. I think he is a whing-ding. Give us more like the Dark Rider. I don't write many letters. Just thought I would tell you I think your mag is the best dime's worth I ever spen'." [*Looks up questioningly.*] What you want me to read that for?

WHIT. Go on, read the name at the bottom.

SLIM [*reading*]. "Yours for Success, William Tenner." [*Looks up at* WHIT.] What ya want me to read that for?

CARLSON. Come on, Candy—what you say?

WHIT [*taking the magazine and closing it impressively. Talks to cover* CARLSON]. You don't remember Bill Tenner? Worked here about three months ago?

SLIM [*thinking*]. Little guy? Drove a cultivator?

WHIT. That's him. That's the guy.

CARLSON [*has refused to be drawn into this conversation*]. Look, Candy. If you want me to, I'll put the old devil outa his misery right now and get it over with. There ain't nothing left for him. Can't eat, can't see, can't hardly walk. Tomorrow you can pick one of Slim's pups.

SLIM. Sure . . . I got a lot of 'em.

CANDY [*hopefully*]. You ain't got no gun.

CARLSON. The hell, I ain't. Got a Luger. It won't hurt him none at all.

CANDY. Mebbe tomorrow. Let's wait till tomorrow.

CARLSON. I don't see no reason for it. [*Goes to his bunk, pulls a bag from underneath, takes a Luger pistol out.*] Let's get it over with. We can't sleep with him stinking around in here. [*He snaps a shell into the chamber, sets the safety and puts the pistol into his hip pocket.*]

SLIM [*as* CANDY *looks toward him for help*]. Better let him go, Candy.

CANDY [*looks at each person for some hope.* WHIT *makes a gesture of protest and then resigns himself.*

The others look away, to avoid responsibility. At last, very softly and hopelessly]. All right. Take him. [*He doesn't look down at the dog at all. Lies back on his bunk and crosses his arms behind his head and stares at the ceiling.* CARLSON *picks up the string, helps the dog to its feet].*

CARSON. Come, boy. Come on, boy. [*To* CANDY, *apologetically.*] He won't even feel it. [CANDY *does not move nor answer him.*] Come on, boy. That's the stuff. Come on. [*He leads the dog toward the door.*]

SLIM. Carlson?

CARLSON. Yeah.

SLIM [*curtly*]. Take a shovel.

CARLSON. Oh, sure, I get you.

[*Exit* CARLSON *with the dog.* GEORGE *follows to the door, shuts it carefully and sets the latch.* CANDY *lies rigidly on his bunk. The next scene is one of silence and quick staccato speeches.*]

SLIM [*loudly*]. One of my lead mules got a bad hoof. Got to get some tar on it.

[*There is a silence.*]

GEORGE [*loudly*]. Anybody like to play a little euchre?

WHIT. I'll lay out a few with you.

[*They take places opposite each other at the table but* GEORGE *does not shuffle the cards. He ripples the edge of the deck. Everybody looks over at him. He stops. Silence again.*]

SLIM [*compassionately*]. Candy, you can have any of them pups you want.

[*There is no answer from* CANDY. *There is a little gnawing noise on the stage.*]

GEORGE. Sounds like there was a rat under there. We ought to set a trap there.

[*Deep silence again.*]

WHIT [*exasperated*]. What the hell is takin' him so

long? Lay out some cards, why don't you? We ain't gonna get no euchre played this way.

[GEORGE *studies the backs of the cards. And after a long silence there is a shot in the distance. All the men start a bit, look quickly at* CANDY. *For a moment he continues to stare at the ceiling and then rolls slowly over and faces the wall.* GEORGE *shuffles the cards noisily and deals them.*]

GEORGE. Well, let's get to it.

WHIT [*still to cover the moment*]. Yeah . . . I guess you guys really come here to work, huh?

GEORGE. How do you mean?

WHIT [*chuckles*]. Well, you come on a Friday. You got two days to work till Sunday.

GEORGE. I don't see how you figure.

WHIT. You do if you been round these big ranches much. A guy that wants to look over a ranch comes in Saturday afternoon. He gets Saturday night supper, three meals on Sunday and he can quit Monday morning after breakfast without turning a hand. But you come to work on Friday noon. You got ta put in a day and a half no matter how ya figure it.

GEORGE [*quietly*]. We're goin' stick around awhile. Me and Lennie's gonna roll up a stake.

[*Door opens and the Negro* STABLE BUCK *puts in his head. A lean-faced Negro with pained eyes.*]

CROOKS. Mr. Slim.

SLIM [*who has been watching* CANDY *the whole time*]. Huh? Oh, hello, Crooks, what's the matter?

CROOKS. You tole me to warm up tar for that mule's foot. I got it warm now.

SLIM. Oh, sure, Crooks. I'll come right out and put it on.

CROOKS. I can do it for you if you want, Mr. Slim.

SLIM [*standing up*]. Naw, I'll take care of my own team.

CROOKS. Mr. Slim.

SLIM. Yeah.

CROOKS. That big new guy is messing round your pups in the barn.

SLIM. Well, he ain't doin' no harm. I give him one of them pups.

CROOKS. Just thought I'd tell ya. He's takin' 'em out of the nest and handling 'em. That won't do 'em no good.

SLIM. Oh, he won't hurt 'em.

GEORGE [*looks up from his cards*]. If that crazy bastard is foolin' round too much jus' kick him out.

[SLIM *follows the* STABLE BUCK *out.*]

WHIT [*examining his cards*]. Seen the new kid yet?

GEORGE. What kid?

WHIT. Why, Curley's new wife.

GEORGE [*cautiously*]. Yeah, I seen her.

WHIT. Well, ain't she a lulu?

GEORGE. I ain't seen that much of her.

WHIT. Well, you stick around and keep your eyes open. You'll see plenty of her. I never seen nobody like her. She's just workin' on everybody all the time. Seems like she's even workin' on the stable buck. I don't know what the hell she wants.

GEORGE [*casually*]. Been any trouble since she got here?

[*Obviously neither man is interested in the card game.* WHIT *lays down his hand and* GEORGE *gathers the cards in and lays out a solitaire hand.*]

WHIT. I see what you mean. No, they ain't been no trouble yet. She's only been here a couple of weeks. Curley's got yellow jackets in his drawers, but that's all so far. Every time the guys is around she shows up. She's lookin' for Curley. Or she thought she left somethin' layin' around and she's lookin' for that. Seems like she can't keep away from guys. And Curley's runnin' round like a cat lookin' for a dirt road. But they ain't been no trouble.

GEORGE. Ranch with a bunch of guys on it ain't no place for a girl. Specially like her.

WHIT. If she's give you any ideas you ought to come in town with us guys tomorrow night.

GEORGE. Why, what's doin'?

WHIT. Just the usual thing. We go in to old Susy's place. Hell of a nice place. Old Susy is a laugh. Always cracking jokes. Like she says when we come up on the front porch last Saturday night: Susy opens the door and she yells over her shoulder: "Get your coats on, girls, here comes the sheriff." She never talks dirty neither. Got five girls there.

GEORGE. What does it set you back?

WHIT. Two and a half. You can get a shot of whiskey for fifteen cents. Susy got nice chairs to set in too. If a guy don't want to flop, why he can just set in them chairs and have a couple or three shots and just pass the time of day. Susy don't give a damn. She ain't rushin' guys through, or kicking them out if they don't want to flop.

GEORGE. Might go in and look the joint over.

WHIT. Sure. Come along. It's a hell of a lot of fun—her crackin' jokes all the time. Like she says one time, she says: "I've knew people that if they got a rag rug on the floor and a kewpie doll lamp on the phonograph they think they're runnin' a parlor house." That's Gladys's house she's talkin' about. And Susy says: "I know what you boys want," she says: "My girls is clean," she says. "And there ain't no water in my whiskey," she says. "If any you guys want to look at a kewpie doll lamp and take your chance of gettin' burned, why, you know where to go." She says: "They's guys round here walkin' bowlegged because they liked to look at a kewpie doll lamp."

GEORGE. Gladys runs the other house, huh?

WHIT. Yeah.

[*Enter* CARLSON. CANDY *looks at him.*]

CARLSON. God, it's a dark night. [*Goes to his bunk; starts cleaning his pistol.*]

WHIT. We don't never go to Gladys's. Gladys gits three bucks, and two bits a shot and she don't crack no jokes. But Susy's place is clean and she got nice chairs. A guy can set in there like he lived there. Don't let no Manila Goo-Goos in, neither.

GEORGE. Aw, I don't know. Me and Lennie's rollin' up a stake. I might go in and set and have a shot, but I ain't puttin' out no two and a half.

WHIT. Well, a guy got to have some fun sometimes.

[*Enter* LENNIE. LENNIE *creeps to his bunk and sits down.*]

GEORGE. Didn't bring him back in, did you, Lennie?

LENNIE. No, George, honest I didn't. See?

WHIT. Say, how about this euchre game?

GEORGE. Okay. I didn't think you wanted to play.

[*Enter* CURLEY *excitedly.*]

CURLEY. Any you guys seen my wife?

WHIT. She ain't been here.

CURLEY [*looks threateningly about the room.*] Where the hell's Slim?

GEORGE. Went out in the barn. He was goin' put some tar on a split hoof.

CURLEY. How long ago did he go?

GEORGE. Oh, five, ten minutes.

[CURLEY *jumps out the door.*]

WHIT [*standing up*]. I guess maybe I'd like to see this. Curley must be spoilin' or he wouldn't start for Slim. Curley's handy, goddamn handy. But just the same he better leave Slim alone.

GEORGE. Thinks Slim's with his wife, don't he?

WHIT. Looks like it. 'Course Slim ain't. Least I don't

think Slim is. But I like to see the fuss if it comes off. Come on, le's go.

GEORGE. I don't want to git mixed up in nothing. Me and Lennie got to make a stake.

CARLSON [*finishes cleaning gun, puts it in his bag and stands up*]. I'll look her over. Ain't seen a good fight in a hell of a while. [WHIT *and* CARLSON *exeunt.*]

GEORGE. You see Slim out in the barn?

LENNIE. Sure. He tole me I better not pet that pup no more, like I said.

GEORGE. Did you see that girl out there?

LENNIE. You mean Curley's girl?

GEORGE. Yeah. Did she come in the barn?

LENNIE [*cautiously*]. No—anyways I never seen her.

GEORGE. You never seen Slim talkin' to her?

LENNIE. Uh-uh. She ain't been in the barn.

GEORGE. Okay. I guess them guys ain't gonna see no fight. If they's any fightin', Lennie, ya get out of the way and stay out.

LENNIE. I don't want no fight. [GEORGE *lays out his solitaire hand.* LENNIE *picks up a face card and studies it. Turns it over and studies it again.*] Both ends the same. George, why is it both ends the same?

GEORGE. I don't know. That jus' the way they make 'em. What was Slim doin' in the barn when you seen him?

LENNIE. Slim?

GEORGE. Sure, you seen him in the barn. He tole you not to pet the pups so much.

LENNIE. Oh. Yeah. He had a can of tar and a paint brush. I don't know what for.

GEORGE. You sure that girl didn't come in like she come in here today?

LENNIE. No, she never come.

GEORGE [*sighs*]. You give me a good whorehouse every time. A guy can go in and get drunk and get it over all at once and no messes. And he knows how much it's goin' set him back. These tarts is jus' buckshot to a guy. [LENNIE *listens with admiration, moving his lips, and* GEORGE *continues.*] You remember Andy Cushman, Lennie? Went to grammar school same time as us?

LENNIE. The one that his ole lady used to make hot cakes for the kids?

GEORGE. Yeah. That's the one. You can remember if they's somepin to eat in it. [*Scores up some cards in his solitaire playing.*] Well, Andy's in San Quentin right now on account of a tart.

LENNIE. George?

GEORGE. Huh?

LENNIE. How long is it goin' be till we git that little place to live off the fat of the land?

GEORGE. I don't know. We gotta get a big stake together. I know a little place we can get cheap, but they ain't givin' it away.

[CANDY *turns over and watches* GEORGE.]

LENNIE. Tell about that place, George.

GEORGE. I jus' tole you. Jus' last night.

LENNIE. Go on, tell again.

GEORGE. Well, it's ten acres. Got a windmill. Got a little shack on it and a chicken run. Got a kitchen orchard. Cherries, apples, peaches, 'cots and nuts. Got a few berries. There's a place for alfalfa and plenty water to flood it. There's a pig pen. . . .

LENNIE [*breaking in*]. And rabbits, George?

GEORGE. I could easy build a few hutches. And you could feed alfalfa to them rabbits.

LENNIE. Damn right I could. [*Excitedly.*] You god-damn right I could.

GEORGE [*his voice growing warmer*]. And we could have a few pigs. I'd build a smokehouse. And when we kill a pig we could smoke the hams. When the salmon run up the river we can catch a hundred of 'em. Every Sunday we'd kill a chicken or rabbit. Mebbe we'll have a cow or a goat. And the cream is so goddamn thick you got to cut it off the pan with a knife.

LENNIE [*watching him with wide eyes, softly*]. We can live off the fat of the land.

GEORGE. Sure. All kinds of vegetables in the garden and if we want a little whiskey we can sell some eggs or somethin'. And we wouldn't sleep in no bunkhouse. Nobody could can us in the middle of a job.

LENNIE [*begging*]. Tell about the house, George.

GEORGE. Sure. We'd have a little house. And a room to ourselves. And it ain't enough land so we'd have to work too hard. Mebbe six, seven hours a day only. We wouldn't have to buck no barley eleven hours a day. And when we put in a crop, why we'd be there to take that crop up. We'd know what come of our planting.

LENNIE [*eagerly*]. And rabbits. And I'd take care of them. Tell how I'd do that, George.

GEORGE. Sure. You'd go out in the alfalfa patch and you'd have a sack. You'd fill up the sack and bring it in and put it in the rabbit cages.

LENNIE. They'd nibble and they'd nibble, the way they do. I seen 'em.

GEORGE. Every six weeks or so them does would throw a litter. So we'd have plenty rabbits to eat or sell. [*Pauses for inspiration.*] And we'd keep a few pigeons to go flying round and round the windmill, like they done when I was a kid. [*Seems entranced.*] And it'd be our own. And nobody could can us. If we don't like a guy we can say: "Get to hell out," and by God he's got to do it. And if a friend come along, why, we'd have an extra bunk. Know what we'd say? We'd say, "Why don't you spen' the night?" And by God he would. We'd have a setter dog and a couple of striped cats. [*Looks sharply at* LENNIE.] But you gotta watch out them cats don't get the little rabbits.

LENNIE [*breathing hard*]. You jus' let 'em try. I'll break their goddamn necks. I'll smash them cats flat with a stick. I'd smash 'em flat with a stick. That's what I'd do. [*They sit silently for a moment.*]

CANDY [*at the sound of his voice, both* LENNIE *and* GEORGE *jump as though caught in some secret.*] You know where's a place like that?

GEORGE [*solemnly*]. S'pose I do, what's that to you?

CANDY. You don't need to tell me where it's at. Might be any place.

GEORGE [*relieved*]. Sure. That's right, you couldn't find it in a hundred years.

CANDY [*excitedly*]. How much they want for a place like that?

GEORGE [*grudgingly*]. Well, I could get it for six hundred bucks. The ole people that owns it is flat bust. And the ole lady needs medicine. Say, what's it to you? You got nothing to do with us!

CANDY [*softly*]. I ain't much good with only one hand. I lost my hand right here on the ranch. That's why they didn't can me. They give me two hundred and fifty dollars 'cause I lost my hand. An' I got fifty more saved up right in the bank right now. That's three hundred. And I got forty more comin' the end of the month. Tell you what . . . [*He leans forward eagerly.*] S'pose I went in with you guys? That's three hundred and forty bucks I'd put in. I ain't much good, but I could cook and tend the chickens and hoe the garden some. How'd that be?

GEORGE [*his eyes half closed, uncertainly*]. I got to

think about that. We was always goin' to do it by ourselves. Me an' Lennie. I never thought of nobody else.

CANDY. I'd make a will. Leave my share to you guys in case I kicked off. I ain't got no relations nor nothing. You fellas got any money? Maybe we could go there right now.

GEORGE [*disgustedly*]. We got ten bucks between us. [*He thinks.*] Say, look. If me and Lennie work a month and don't spend nothing at all, we'll have a hundred bucks. That would be four forty. I bet we could swing her for that. Then you and Lennie could go get her started and I'd get a job and make up the rest. You could sell eggs and stuff like that. [*They look at each other in amazement. Reverently.*] Jesus Christ, I bet we could swing her. [*His voice is full of wonder.*] I bet we could swing 'er.

CANDY [*scratches the stump of his wrist nervously*]. I got hurt four years ago. They'll can me pretty soon. Jest as soon as I can't swamp out no bunkhouses they'll put me on the county. Maybe if I give you guys my money, you'll let me hoe in the garden, even when I ain't no good at it. And I'll wash dishes and little chicken stuff like that. But hell, I'll be on our own place. I'll be let to work on our own place. [*Miserably.*] You seen what they done to my dog. They says he wasn't no good to himself nor nobody else. But when I'm that way nobody'll shoot me. I wish somebody would. They won't do nothing like that. I won't have no place to go and I can't get no more jobs.

GEORGE [*stands up*]. We'll do 'er! God damn, we'll fix up that little ole place and we'll go live there. [*Wonderingly.*] S'pose they was a carnival, or a circus come to town or a ball game or any damn thing. [CANDY *nods in appreciation.*] We'd just go to her.

We wouldn't ask nobody if we could. Just say we'll go to her, by God, and we would. Just milk the cow and sling some grain to the chickens and go to her.

LENNIE. And put some grass to the rabbits. I wouldn't forget to feed them. When we gonna to do it, George?

GEORGE [*decisively*]. In one month. Right squack in one month. Know what I'm gonna do? I'm goin' write to them ole people that owns the place that we'll take 'er. And Candy'll send a hundred dollars to bind her.

CANDY [*happily*]. I sure will. They got a good stove there?

GEORGE. Sure, got a nice stove. Burns coal or wood.

LENNIE. I'm gonna take my pup. I bet by Christ he likes it there.

[*The window, center backstage, swings outward.* CURLEY'S WIFE *looks in. They do not see her.*]

GEORGE [*quickly*]. Now don't tell nobody about her. Jus' us three and nobody else. They'll liable to can us so we can't make no stake. We'll just go on like we was a bunch of punks. Like we was gonna buck barley the rest of our lives. And then all of a sudden, one day, bang! We get our pay and scram out of here.

CANDY. I can give you three hundred right now.

LENNIE. And not tell nobody. We won't tell nobody, George.

GEORGE. You're goddamn right we won't. [*There is a silence and then* GEORGE *speaks irritably*.] You know, seems to me I can almost smell that carnation stuff that goddamn tart dumps on herself.

CURLEY'S WIFE [*in the first part of the speech by* GEORGE *she starts to step out of sight but at the last words her face darkens with anger. At her first words everybody in the room looks around at her and remains*

rigid during the tirade]. Who you callin' a tart! I
come from a nice home. I was brung up by nice
people. Nobody never got to me before I was married. I was straight. I tell you I was good. [*A little
plaintively.*] I was. [*Angrily again.*] You know Curley. You know he wouldn't stay with me if he wasn't
sure. I tell you Curley is sure. You got no right to
call me a tart.

GEORGE [*sullenly*]. If you ain't a tart, what you always
hangin' round guys for? You got a house an' you
got a man. We don't want no trouble from you.

CURLEY'S WIFE [*pleadingly*]. Sure I got a man. He ain't
never home. I got nobody to talk to. I got nobody to
be with. Think I can just sit home and do nothin'
but cook for Curley? I want to see somebody. Just
see 'em an' talk to 'em. There ain't no women. I
can't walk to town. And Curley don't take me to no
dances now. I tell you I jus' want to talk to somebody.

GEORGE [*boldly*]. If you're just friendly what you givin'
out the eye for an' floppin' your can around?

CURLEY'S WIFE [*sadly*]. I just wanta be nice.

[*The sound of approaching voices: "You don't have to
get mad about it, do you?" . . . "I ain't mad,
but I just don't want no more questions, that's all.
I just don't want no more questions."*]

GEORGE. Get goin'. We don't want no trouble.

[CURLEY'S WIFE *looks from the window and closes it
silently and disappears. Enter* SLIM, *followed by*
CURLEY, CARLSON *and* WHIT. SLIM'S *hands are black
with tar.* CURLEY *hangs close to his elbow.*]

CURLEY [*explaining*]. Well, I didn't mean nothing,
Slim. I jus' ast you.

SLIM. Well, you been askin' too often. I'm gettin' goddamn sick of it. If you can't look after your own

wife, what you expect me to do about it? You lay off of me.

CURLEY. I'm jus' tryin' to tell you I didn't mean nothing. I just thought you might of saw her.

CARLSON. Why don't you tell her to stay to hell home where she belongs? You let her hang around the bunkhouses and pretty soon you're goin' to have somethin' on your hands.

CURLEY [*whirls on* CARLSON]. You keep out of this 'less you want ta step outside.

CARLSON [*laughing*]. Why, you goddamn punk. You tried to throw a scare into Slim and you couldn't make it stick. Slim throwed a scare into you. You're yellow as a frog's belly. I don't care if you're the best boxer in the country, you come for me and I'll kick your goddamn head off.

WHIT [*joining in the attack*]. Glove full of vaseline!

CURLEY [*glares at him, then suddenly sniffs the air, like a hound*]. By God, she's been in *here*. I can smell— By God, she's been in here. [*To* GEORGE.] You was here. The other guys was outside. Now, God damn you—you talk.

GEORGE [*looks worried. He seems to make up his mind to face an inevitable situation. Slowly takes off his coat, and folds it almost daintily. Speaks in an unemotional monotone*]. Somebody got to beat the hell outa you. I guess I'm elected.

[LENNIE *has been watching, fascinated. He gives his high, nervous chuckle.*]

CURLEY [*whirls on him*]. What the hell you laughin' at?

LENNIE [*blankly*]. Huh?

CURLEY [*exploding with rage*]. Come on, you big bastard. Get up on your feet. No big son-of-a-bitch is gonna laugh at me. I'll show you who's yellow.

[LENNIE *looks helplessly at* GEORGE. *Gets up and tries*

to retreat upstage. CURLEY *follows slashing at him. The others mass themselves in front of the two contestants:* "That ain't no way, Curley—he ain't. done nothing to you." . . . "Lay off him, will you, Curley. He ain't no fighter." . . . "Sock him back, big guy! Don't be afraid of him!" . . . "Give him a chance, Curley. Give him a chance."

LENNIE [*crying with terror*]. George, make him leave me alone, George.

GEORGE. Get him, Lennie. Get him! [*There is a sharp cry. The gathering of men opens and* CURLEY *is flopping about, his hand lost in* LENNIE's *hand.*] Let go of him, Lennie. Let go! ["He's got his hand!" . . . "Look at that, will you?" . . . "Jesus, what a guy!" LENNIE *watches in terror the flopping man he holds.* LENNIE's *face is covered with blood.* GEORGE *slaps* LENNIE *in the face again and again.* CURLEY *is weak and shrunken.*] Let go his hand, Lennie. Slim, come help me, while this guy's got any hand left.

[*Suddenly* LENNIE *lets go. He cowers away from* GEORGE.]

LENNIE. You told me to, George. I heard you tell me to.

[CURLEY *has dropped to the floor.* SLIM *and* CARLSON *bend over him and look at his hand.* SLIM *looks over at* LENNIE *with horror.*]

SLIM. We got to get him to a doctor. It looks to me like every bone in his hand is busted.

LENNIE [*crying*]. I didn't wanta. I didn't wanta hurt 'im.

SLIM. Carlson, you get the candy wagon out. He'll have to go into Soledad and get his hand fixed up. [*Turns to the whimpering* LENNIE.] It ain't your fault. This punk had it comin' to him. But Jesus—he ain't hardly got no hand left.

GEORGE [*moving near*]. Slim, will we git canned now? Will Curley's ole man can us now?

SLIM. I don't know. [*Kneels down beside* CURLEY.] You got your sense enough to listen? [CURLEY *nods*.] Well, then you listen. I think you got your hand caught in a machine. If you don't tell nobody what happened, we won't. But you jest tell and try to get this guy canned and we'll tell everybody. And then will you get the laugh! [*Helps* CURLEY *to his feet*.] Come on now. Carlson's goin' to take you in to a doctor. [*Starts for the door, turns back to* LENNIE.] Le's see your hands. [LENNIE *sticks out both hands*.] Christ Almighty!

GEORGE. Lennie was just scairt. He didn't know what to do. I tole you nobody ought never to fight him. No, I guess it was Candy I tole.

CANDY [*solemnly*]. That's just what you done. Right this morning when Curley first lit into him. You says he better not fool with Lennie if he knows what's good for him.

[*They all leave the stage except* GEORGE *and* LENNIE *and* CANDY.]

GEORGE [*to* LENNIE, *very gently*]. It ain't your fault. You don't need to be scairt no more. You done jus' what I tole you to. Maybe you better go in the washroom and clean your face. You look like hell.

LENNIE. I didn't want no trouble.

GEORGE. Come on—I'll go with you.

LENNIE. George?

GEORGE. What you want?

LENNIE. Can I still tend the rabbits, George?

[*They exeunt together, side by side, through the door of the bunkhouse.*]

CURTAIN

Ten o'clock Saturday evening.

The room of the stable buck, a lean-to off the barn. There is a plank door upstage center; a small square window center right. On one side of the door a leather working bench with tools racked behind it, and on the other racks with broken and partly mended harnesses, collars, hames, traces, etc. At the left upstage CROOKS' *bunk. Over it two shelves. On one a great number of medicines in cans and bottles. And on the other a number of tattered books and a big alarm clock. In the corner right upstage a single-barreled shotgun and on the floor beside it a pair of rubber boots. A large pair of gold spectacles hang on a nail over* CROOKS' *bunk.*

The entrance leads into the barn proper. From that direction and during the whole scene come the sounds of horses eating, stamping, jingling their halter chains and now and then whinnying.

Two empty nail kegs are in the room to be used as seats. Single unshaded small-candlepower carbon light hanging from its own cord.

As the curtain rises, we see CROOKS *sitting on his bunk rubbing his back with liniment. He reaches up under his shirt to do this. His face is lined with pain. As he rubs he flexes his muscles and shivers a little.*

LENNIE *appears in the open doorway, nearly filling the opening. Then* CROOKS, *sensing his presence, raises his eyes, stiffens and scowls.*

LENNIE *smiles in an attempt to make friends.*

CROOKS [*sharply*]. You got no right to come in my room. This here's my room. Nobody got any right in here but me.

LENNIE [*fawning*]. I ain't doin' nothing. Just come in the barn to look at my pup, and I seen your light.

CROOKS. Well, I got a right to have a light. You go on and get out of my room. I ain't wanted in the bunk-house and you ain't wanted in my room.

LENNIE [*ingenuously*]. Why ain't you wanted?

CROOKS [*furiously*]. 'Cause I'm black. They play cards in there. But I can't play because I'm black. They say I stink. Well, I tell you all of you stink to me.

LENNIE [*helplessly*]. Everybody went into town. Slim and George and everybody. George says I got to stay here and not get into no trouble. I seen your light.

CROOKS. Well, what do you want?

LENNIE. Nothing . . . I seen your light. I thought I could jus' come in and set.

CROOKS [*stares at* LENNIE *for a moment, takes down his spectacles and adjusts them over his ears; says in a complaining tone*]. I don't know what you're doin' in the barn anyway. You ain't no skinner. There's no call for a bucker to come into the barn at all. You've got nothing to do with the horses and mules.

LENNIE [*patiently*]. The pup. I come to see my pup.

CROOKS. Well, God damn it, go and see your pup then. Don't go no place where you ain't wanted.

LENNIE [*advances a step into the room, remembers and backs to the door again*]. I looked at him a little. Slim says I ain't to pet him very much.

CROOKS [*the anger gradually going out of his voice*]. Well, you been taking him out of the nest all the time. I wonder the ole lady don't move him some place else.

LENNIE [*moving into the room*]. Oh, she don't care. She lets me.

CROOKS [*scowls and then gives up*]. Come on in and set awhile. Long as you won't get out and leave me alone, you might as well set down. [*A little more friendly.*] All the boys gone into town, huh?

LENNIE. All but old Candy. He jus' sets in the bunkhouse sharpening his pencils. And sharpening and figurin'.

CROOKS [*adjusting his glasses*]. Figurin'? What's Candy figurin' about?

LENNIE. 'Bout the land. 'Bout the little place.

CROOKS. You're nuts. You're crazy as a wedge. What land you talkin' about?

LENNIE. The land we're goin' to get. And a little house and pigeons.

CROOKS. Just nuts. I don't blame the guy you're traveling with for keeping you out of sight.

LENNIE [*quietly*]. It ain't no lie. We're gonna do it. Gonna get a little place and live off the fat of the land.

CROOKS [*settling himself comfortably on his bunk*]. Set down on that nail keg.

LENNIE [*hunches over on the little barrel*]. You think it's a lie. But it ain't no lie. Ever' word's the truth. You can ask George.

CROOKS [*puts his dark chin on his palm*]. You travel round with George, don't you?

LENNIE [*proudly*]. Sure, me and him goes ever' place together.

CROOKS [*after a pause, quietly*]. Sometimes he talks and you don't know what the hell he's talkin' about. Ain't that so? [*Leans forward.*] Ain't that so?

LENNIE. Yeah. Sometimes.

CROOKS. Just talks on. And you don't know what the hell it's all about.

LENNIE. How long you think it'll be before them pups will be old enough to pet?

CROOKS [*laughs again*]. A guy can talk to you and be sure you won't go blabbin'. A couple of weeks and them pups will be all right. [*Musing.*] George knows what he's about. Just talks and you don't understand nothing. [*Mood gradually changes to excitement.*] Well, this is just a nigger talkin' and a busted-back nigger. It don't mean nothing, see. You couldn't remember it anyway. I seen it over and over —a guy talking to another guy and it don't make no difference if he don't hear or understand. The thing is they're talkin'. [*He pounds his knee with his hand.*] George can tell you screwy things and it don't matter. It's just the talkin'. It's just bein' with another guy, that's all. [*His voice becomes soft and malicious.*] S'pose George don't come back no more? S'pose he took a powder and just ain't comin' back. What you do then?

LENNIE [*trying to follow* CROOKS]. What? What?

CROOKS. I said s'pose George went into town tonight and you never heard of him no more. [*Presses forward.*] Just s'pose that.

LENNIE [*sharply*]. He won't do it. George wouldn't do nothing like that. I been with George a long time. He'll come back tonight. . . . [*Doubt creeps into his voice.*] Don't you think he will?

CROOKS [*delighted with his torture*]. Nobody can tell what a guy will do. Let's say he wants to come back and can't. S'pose he gets killed or hurt so he can't come back.

LENNIE [*in terrible apprehension*]. I don't know. Say, what you doin' anyway? It ain't true. George ain't got hurt.

CROOKS [*cruelly*]. Want me to tell you what'll happen? They'll take you to the booby hatch. They'll tie you up with a collar like a dog. Then you'll be jus' like me. Livin' in a kennel.

LENNIE [*furious, walks over towards* CROOKS]. Who hurt George?

CROOKS [*recoiling from him with fright*]. I was just supposin'. George ain't hurt. He's all right. He'll be back all right.

LENNIE [*standing over him*]. What you supposin' for? Ain't nobody goin' to s'pose any hurt to George.

CROOKS [*trying to calm him*]. Now set down. George ain't hurt. Go on now, set down.

LENNIE [*growling*]. Ain't nobody gonna talk no hurt to George.

CROOKS [*very gently*]. Maybe you can see now. You got George. You know he's comin' back. S'pose you didn't have nobody. S'pose you couldn't go in the bunkhouse and play rummy, 'cause you was black. How would you like that? S'pose you had to set out here and read books. Sure, you could play horseshoes until it got dark, but then you got to read books. Books ain't no good. A guy needs somebody . . . to be near him. [*His tone whines.*] A guy goes nuts if he ain't got nobody. Don't make no difference who it is as long as he's with you. I tell you a guy gets too lonely, he gets sick.

LENNIE [*reassuring himself*]. George gonna come back. Maybe George come back already. Maybe I better go see.

CROOKS [*more gently*]. I didn't mean to scare you. He'll come back. I was talkin' about myself.

LENNIE [*miserably*]. George won't go away and leave me. I know George won't do that.

CROOKS [*continuing dreamily*]. I remember when I was a little kid on my ole man's chicken ranch. Had two brothers. They was always near me, always there.

Used to sleep right in the same room. Right in the same bed, all three. Had a strawberry patch. Had an alfalfa patch. Used to turn the chickens out in the alfalfa on a sunny morning. Me and my brothers would set on the fence and watch 'em—white chickens they was.

LENNIE [*interested*]. George says we're gonna have alfalfa.

CROOKS. You're nuts.

LENNIE. We are too gonna get it. You ask George.

CROOKS [*scornfully*]. You're nuts. I seen hundreds of men come by on the road and on the ranches, bindles on their back and that same damn thing in their head. Hundreds of 'em. They come and they quit and they go on. And every damn one of 'em is got a little piece of land in his head. And never a goddamn one of 'em gets it. Jus' like heaven. Everybody wants a little piece of land. Nobody never gets to heaven. And nobody gets no land.

LENNIE. We are too.

CROOKS. It's jest in your head. Guys all the time talkin' about it, but it's jest in your head. [*The horses move restlessly. One of them whinnies.*] I guess somebody's out there. Maybe Slim. [*Pulls himself painfully upright and moves toward the door. Calls.*] That you, Slim?

CANDY [*from outside*]. Slim went in town. Say, you seen Lennie?

CROOKS. You mean the big guy?

CANDY. Yes. Seen him around any place?

CROOKS [*goes back to his bunk and sits down, says shortly*]. He's in here.

CANDY [*stands in the doorway, scratching his wrist. Makes no attempt to enter.*] Look, Lennie, I been figuring something out. About the place.

CROOKS [*irritably*]. You can come in if you want.

CANDY [*embarrassed*]. I don't know. 'Course if you want me to.

CROOKS. Oh, come on in. Everybody's comin' in. You might just as well. Gettin' to be a goddamn race track. [*He tries to conceal his pleasure.*]

CANDY [*still embarrassed*]. You've got a nice cozy little place in here. Must be nice to have a room to yourself this way.

CROOKS. Sure. And a manure pile under the window. All to myself. It's swell.

LENNIE [*breaking in*]. You said about the place.

CANDY. You know, I been here a long time. An' Crooks been here a long time. This is the first time I ever been in his room.

CROOKS [*darkly*]. Guys don't come in a colored man's room. Nobody been here but Slim.

LENNIE [*insistently*]. The place. You said about the place.

CANDY. Yeah. I got it all figured out. We can make some real money on them rabbits if we go about it right.

LENNIE. But I get to tend 'em. George says I get to tend 'em. He promised.

CROOKS [*brutally*]. You guys is just kiddin' yourselves. You'll talk about it a hell of a lot, but you won't get no land. You'll be a swamper here until they take you out in a box. Hell, I seen too many guys.

CANDY [*angrily*]. We're gonna do it. George says we are. We got the money right now.

CROOKS. Yeah. And where is George now? In town in a whorehouse. That's where your money's goin'. I tell you I seen it happen too many times.

CANDY. George ain't got the money in town. The money's in the bank. Me and Lennie and George. We gonna have a room to ourselves. We gonna have a dog and chickens. We gonna have green corn and maybe a cow.

CROOKS [*impressed*]. You say you got the money?

CANDY. We got most of it. Just a little bit more to get. Have it all in one month. George's got the land all picked out too.

CROOKS [*exploring his spine with his hands*]. I've never seen a guy really do it. I seen guys nearly crazy with loneliness for land, but every time a whorehouse or a blackjack game took it away from 'em. [*Hesitates and then speaks timidly.*] If you guys would want a hand to work for nothin'—just his keep, why I'd come and lend a hand. I ain't so crippled I can't work like a son-of-a-bitch if I wanted to.

GEORGE [*strolls through the door, hands in pockets, leans against the wall, speaks in a half-satiric, rather gentle voice*]. You couldn't go to bed like I told you, could you, Lennie? Hell, no—you got to get out in society an' flap your mouth. Holdin' a convention out here.

LENNIE [*defending himself*]. You was gone. There wasn't nobody in the bunkhouse. I ain't done no bad things, George.

GEORGE [*still casually*]. Only time I get any peace is when you're asleep. If you ever get walkin' in your sleep I'll chop off your head like a chicken. [*Chops with his hand.*]

CROOKS [*coming to* LENNIE'S *defense*]. We was jus' settin' here talkin'. Ain't no harm in that.

GEORGE. Yeah. I heard you. [*A weariness has settled on him.*] Got to be here ever' minute, I guess. Got to watch ya. [*To* CROOKS.] It ain't nothing against you, Crooks. We just wasn't gonna tell nobody.

CANDY [*tries to change subject*]. Didn't you have no fun in town?

GEORGE. Oh! I set in a chair and Susy was crackin' jokes

an' the guys was startin' to raise a little puny hell. Christ Almighty—I never been this way before. I'm jus' gonna set out a dime and a nickel for a shot an' I think what a hell of a lot of bulk carrot seed you can get for fifteen cents.

CANDY. Not in them damn little envelopes—but bulk seed—you sure can.

GEORGE. So purty soon I come back. I can't think of nothing else. Them guys slingin' money around got me jumpy.

CANDY. Guy got to have *some* fun. I was to a parlor house in Bakersfield once. God Almighty, what a place. Went upstairs on a red carpet. They was big pichers on the wall. We set in big sof' chairs. They was cigarettes on the table—an' they was *free*. Purty soon a Jap come in with drinks on a tray an' them *drinks* was free. Take all you want. [*In a reverie.*] Purty soon the girls come in an' they was jus' as polite an' nice an' quiet an' purty. Didn't seem like hookers. Made ya kinda scared to ask 'em. . . . That was a long time ago.

GEORGE. Yeah? An' what'd them sof' chairs set you back?

CANDY. Fifteen bucks.

GEORGE [*scornfully*]. So ya got a cigarette an' a whiskey an' a look at a purty dress an' it cost ya twelve and a half bucks extra. You shot a week's pay to walk on that red carpet.

CANDY [*still entranced with his memory*]. A week's pay? Sure. But I worked weeks all my life. I can't remember none of them weeks. But . . . that was nearly twenty years ago. And I can remember that. Girl I went with was named Arline. Had on a pink silk dress.

GEORGE [*turns suddenly and looks out the door into*

the dark barn, speaks savagely]. I s'pose ya lookin' for Curley? [CURLEY'S WIFE *appears in the door.*] Well, Curley ain't here.

CURLEY'S WIFE [*determined now*]. I know Curley ain't here. I wanted to ast Crooks somepin'. I didn't know you guys was here.

CANDY. Didn't George tell you before—we don't want nothing to do with you. You know damn well Curley ain't here.

CURLEY'S WIFE. I know where Curley went. Got his arm in a sling an' he went anyhow. I tell ya I come out to ast Crooks somepin'.

CROOKS [*apprehensively*]. Maybe you better go along to your own house. You hadn't ought to come near a colored man's room. I don't want no trouble. You don't want to ask me nothing.

CANDY [*rubbing his wrist stump*]. You got a husband. You got no call to come foolin' around with other guys, causin' trouble.

CURLEY'S WIFE [*suddenly angry*]. I try to be nice an' polite to you lousy bindle bums—but you're too good. I tell ya I could of went with shows. An'—an' a guy wanted to put me in pichers right in Hollywood. [*Looks about to see how she is impressing them. Their eyes are hard.*] I come out here to ast somebody somepin' an'—

CANDY [*stands up suddenly and knocks his nail keg over backwards, speaks angrily*]. I had enough. You ain't wanted here. We tole you, you ain't. Callin' us bindle stiffs. You got floozy idears what us guys amounts to. You ain't got sense enough to see us guys ain't bindle stiffs. S'pose you could get us *canned*—s'pose you *could*. You think we'd hit the highway an' look for another two-bit job. You don't know we got our own ranch to go to an' our own house an' fruit trees. An' we got friends. That's what we got. Maybe they was a time when we didn't have nothin', but that ain't so no more.

CURLEY'S WIFE. You damn ol' goat. If you had two bits, you'd be in Soledad gettin' a drink an' suckin' the bottom of the glass.

GEORGE. Maybe she could ask Crooks what she come to ask an' then get the hell home. I don't think she come to ask nothing.

CURLEY'S WIFE. What happened to Curley's hand? [CROOKS *laughs.* GEORGE *tries to shut him up.*] So it wasn't no machine. Curley didn't act like he was tellin' the truth. Come on, Crooks—what happened?

CROOKS. I wasn't there. I didn't see it.

CURLEY'S WIFE [*eagerly*]. What happened? I won't let on to Curley. He says he caught his han' in a gear. [CROOKS *is silent.*] Who done it?

GEORGE. Didn't nobody do it.

CURLEY'S WIFE [*turns slowly to* GEORGE]. So *you* done it. Well, he had it comin'.

GEORGE. I didn't have no fuss with Curley.

CURLEY'S WIFE [*steps near him, smiling*]. Maybe now you ain't scared of him no more. Maybe you'll talk to me sometimes now. Ever'body was scared of him.

GEORGE [*speaks rather kindly*]. Look! I didn't sock Curley. If he had trouble, it ain't none of our affair. Ask Curley about it. Now listen. I'm gonna try to tell ya. We tole you to get the hell out and it don't do no good. So I'm gonna tell you another way. Us guys got somepin' we're gonna do. If you stick around you'll gum up the works. It ain't your fault. If a guy steps on a round pebble an' falls an' breaks his neck, it ain't the pebble's fault, but the guy wouldn't of did it if the pebble wasn't there.

CURLEY'S WIFE [*puzzled*]. What you talkin' about pebbles? If you didn't sock Curley, who did? [*She looks*

at the others, then steps quickly over to LENNIE.]
Where'd you get them bruises on your face?

GEORGE. I tell you he got his hand caught in a machine.

LENNIE [*looks anxiously at* GEORGE, *speaks miserably*].
He caught his han' in a machine.

GEORGE. So now get out of here.

CURLEY'S WIFE [*goes close to* LENNIE, *speaks softly and
there is a note of affection in her voice*]. So . . . it was
you. Well . . . maybe you're dumb like they say . . .
an' maybe . . . you're the only guy on the ranch with
guts. [*She puts her hand on* LENNIE'S *shoulder. He
looks up in her face and a smile grows on his face.
She strokes his shoulder.*] You're a nice fella.

GEORGE [*suddenly leaps at her ferociously, grabs her
shoulder and whirls her around*]. Listen . . . you! I
tried to give you a break. Don't you walk into nothing! We ain't gonna let you mess up what we're
gonna do. You let this guy alone an' get the hell out
of here.

CURLEY'S WIFE [*defiant but slightly frightened*]. You
ain't tellin' me what to do. [*The* BOSS *appears in the
door, stands legs spread, thumbs hooked over his
belt.*] I got a right to talk to anybody I want to.

GEORGE. Why, you—

[GEORGE, *furiously, steps close—his hand is raised to
strike her. She cowers a little.* GEORGE *stiffens, seeing*
BOSS, *frozen in position. The others see* BOSS *too.*
GIRL *retreats slowly.* GEORGE'S *hand drops slowly to
his side—he takes two slow backward steps. Hold
the scene for a moment.*]

CURTAIN

Act three

SCENE I

Mid-afternoon Sunday.

One end of a great barn. Backstage the hay slopes up sharply against the wall. High in the upstage wall is a large hay window. On each side are seen the hay racks, behind which are the stalls with the horses in them. Throughout this scene the horses can be heard in their stalls, rattling their halter chains and chewing at the hay.

The entrance is downstage right.

The boards of the barn are not close together. Streaks of afternoon sun come between the boards, made visible by dust in the air. From outside comes the clang of horseshoes on the playing peg, shouts of men encouraging or jeering.

In the barn there is a feeling of quiet and humming and lazy warmth. Curtain rises on LENNIE *sitting in the hay, looking down at a little dead puppy in front of him. He puts out his big hand and strokes it clear from one end to the other.*

LENNIE [*softly*]. Why do you got to get killed? You ain't so little as mice. I didn' bounce you hard. [*Bends the pup's head up and looks in its face.*] Now maybe George ain't gonna let me tend no rabbits if he finds out you got killed. [*He scoops a little hollow and lays the puppy in it out of sight and covers it over with hay. He stares at the mound he has made.*] This ain't no bad thing like I got to hide in the brush. I'll tell George I found it dead. [*He unburies the pup and inspects it. Twists its ears and works his fingers in its fur. Sorrowfully.*] But he'll know. George always knows. He'll say: "You done it. Don't try to put nothin' over on me." And he'll say: "Now just for that you don't get to tend no—you-know-whats." [*His anger rises. Addresses the pup.*] God damn you. Why do you got to get killed? You ain't so little as mice. [*Picks up the pup and hurls it from him and turns his back on it. He sits bent over his knees moaning to himself.*] Now he won't let me. . . . Now he won't let me. [*Outside there is a clang of horseshoes on the iron stake and a little chorus of cries.* LENNIE *gets up and brings the pup back and lays it in the hay and sits down. He mourns.*] You wasn't big enough. They tole me and tole me you wasn't. I didn't know you'd get killed so easy. Maybe George won't care. This here goddamn little son-of-a-bitch wasn't nothin' to George.

CANDY [*voice from behind the stalls*]. Lennie, where you at? [LENNIE *frantically buries the pup under the hay.* CANDY *enters excitedly.*] Thought I'd find ya here. Say . . . I been talkin' to Slim. It's okay. We ain't gonna get the can. Slim been talkin' to the boss. Slim tol' the boss you guys is good buckers. The boss got to move that grain. 'Member what hell the boss give us las' night? He tol' Slim he got his eye on you an' George. But you ain't gonna get the can. Oh! an' say. The boss give Curley's wife hell, too. Tole her never to go near the men no more. Give her worse hell than you an' George. [*For the first time notices* LENNIE's *dejection.*] Ain't you glad?

LENNIE. Sure.

CANDY. You ain't sick?

LENNIE. Uh-uh!

CANDY. I got to go tell George. See you later. [*Exits.*]

[LENNIE, *alone, uncovers the pup. Lies down in the hay and sinks deep in it. Puts the pup on his arm and strokes it.* CURLEY'S WIFE *enters secretly. A little mound of hay conceals* LENNIE *from her. In her hand she carries a small suitcase, very cheap. She crosses the barn and buries the case in the hay. Stands up and looks to see whether it can be seen.* LENNIE *watching her quietly tries to cover the pup with hay. She sees the movement.*]

CURLEY'S WIFE. What—what you doin' here?

LENNIE [*sullenly*]. Jus' settin' here.

CURLEY'S WIFE. You seen what I done.

LENNIE. Yeah! you brang a valise.

CURLEY'S WIFE [*comes near to him*]. You won't tell—will you?

LENNIE [*still sullen*]. I ain't gonna have nothing to do with you. George tole me. I ain't to talk to you or nothing. [*Covers the pup a little more.*]

CURLEY'S WIFE. George give you all your orders?

LENNIE. Not talk nor nothing.

CURLEY'S WIFE. You won't tell about that suitcase? I ain't gonna stay here no more. Tonight I'm gonna get out. Come here an' get my stuff an' get out. I ain't gonna be run over no more. I'm gonna go in pichers. [*Sees* LENNIE'S *hand stroking the pup under the hay.*] What you got there?

LENNIE. Nuthing. I ain't gonna talk to you. George says I ain't.

CURLEY'S WIFE. Listen. The guys got a horseshoe tenement out there. It's on'y four o'clock. Them guys ain't gonna leave that tenement. They got money bet. You don't need to be scared to talk to me.

LENNIE [*weakening a little*]. I ain't supposed to.

CURLEY'S WIFE [*watching his buried hand*]. What you got under there?

LENNIE [*his woe comes back to him*]. Jus' my pup. Jus' my little ol' pup. [*Sweeps the hay aside.*]

CURLEY'S WIFE. Why! He's dead.

LENNIE [*explaining sadly*]. He was so little. I was jus' playin' with him—an' he made like he's gonna bite me—an' I made like I'm gonna smack him—an'—I done it. An' then he was dead.

CURLEY'S WIFE [*consoling*]. Don't you worry none. He was just a mutt. The whole country is full of mutts.

LENNIE. It ain't that so much. George gonna be mad. Maybe he won't let me—what he said I could tend.

CURLEY'S WIFE [*sits down in the hay beside him, speaks soothingly*]. Don't you worry. Them guys got money bet on that horseshoe tenement. They ain't gonna leave it. And tomorra I'll be gone. I ain't gonna let them run over me.

[*In the following scene it is apparent that neither is listening to the other and yet as it goes on, as a happy tone increases, it can be seen that they are growing closer together.*]

LENNIE. We gonna have a little place an' raspberry bushes.

CURLEY'S WIFE. I ain't meant to live like this. I come from Salinas. Well, a show come through an' I talked to a guy that was in it. He says I could go with the show. My ol' lady wouldn't let me, 'cause I was on'y fifteen. I wouldn't be no place like this if I had went with that show, you bet.

LENNIE. Gonna take a sack an' fill it up with alfalfa an'—

CURLEY'S WIFE [*hurrying on*]. 'Nother time I met a guy an' he was in pichers. Went out to the Riverside Dance Palace with him. He said he was gonna put me in pichers. Says I was a natural. Soon's he got back to Hollywood he was gonna write me about it.

[*Looks impressively at* LENNIE.] I never got that letter. I think my ol' lady stole it. Well, I wasn't gonna stay no place where they stole your letters. So I married Curley. Met *him* out to the Riverside Dance Palace too.

LENNIE. I hope George ain't gonna be mad about this pup.

CURLEY'S WIFE. I ain't tol' this to nobody before. Maybe I oughtn' to. I don't like Curley. He ain't a nice fella. I might a stayed with him but last night him an' his ol' man both lit into me. I don't have to stay here. [*Moves closer and speaks confidentially.*] Don't tell nobody till I get clear away. I'll go in the night an' thumb a ride to Hollywood.

LENNIE. We gonna get out a here purty soon. This ain't no nice place.

CURLEY'S WIFE [*ecstatically*]. Gonna get in the movies an' have nice clothes—all them nice clothes like they wear. An' I'll set in them big hotels and they'll take pichers of me. When they have them openings I'll go an' talk in the radio . . . an' it won't cost me nothing 'cause I'm in the picher. [*Puts her hand on* LENNIE'S *arm for a moment.*] All them nice clothes like they wear . . . because this guy says I'm a natural.

LENNIE. We gonna go way . . . far away from here.

CURLEY'S WIFE. 'Course, when I run away from Curley, my ol' lady won't never speak to me no more. She'll think I ain't decent. That's what she'll say. [*Defiantly.*] Well, we really ain't decent, no matter how much my ol' lady tries to hide it. My ol' man was a drunk. They put him away. There! Now I told.

LENNIE. George an' me was to the Sacramento Fair. One time I fell in the river an' George pulled me out an' saved me, an' then we went to the Fair. They got all kinds of stuff there. We seen long-hair rabbits.

CURLEY'S WIFE. My ol' man was a sign-painter when he worked. He used to get drunk an' paint crazy pichers an' waste paint. One night when I was a little kid, him an' my ol' lady had an awful fight. They was always fightin'. In the middle of the night he come into my room, and he says, "I can't stand this no more. Let's you an' me go away." I guess he was drunk. [*Her voice takes on a curious wondering tenderness.*] I remember in the night—walkin' down the road, and the trees was black. I was pretty sleepy. He picked me up, an' he carried me on his back. He says, "We gonna live together. We gonna live together because you're my own little girl, an' not no stranger. No arguin' and fightin'," he says, "because you're my little daughter." [*Her voice becomes soft.*] He says, "Why you'll bake little cakes for me, and I'll paint pretty pichers all over the wall." [*Sadly.*] In the morning they caught us . . . an' they put him away. [*Pause.*] I wish we'd a' went.

LENNIE. Maybe if I took this here pup an' throwed him away George wouldn't never know.

CURLEY'S WIFE. They locked him up for a drunk, and in a little while he died.

LENNIE. Then maybe I could tend the rabbits without no trouble.

CURLEY'S WIFE. Don't you think of nothing but rabbits? [*Sound of horseshoe on metal.*] Somebody made a ringer.

LENNIE [*patiently*]. We gonna have a house and a garden, an' a place for alfalfa. And I take a sack and get it all full of alfalfa, and then I take it to the rabbits.

CURLEY'S WIFE. What makes you so nuts about rabbits?

LENNIE [*moves close to her*]. I like to pet nice things. Once at a fair I seen some of them long-hair rabbits. And they was nice, you bet. [*Despairingly.*] I'd even pet mice, but not when I could get nothin' better.

CURLEY'S WIFE [*giggles*]. I think you're nuts.

LENNIE [*earnestly*]. No, I ain't. George says I ain't. I like to pet nice things with my fingers. Soft things.

CURLEY'S WIFE. Well, who don't? Everybody likes that. I like to feel silk and velvet. You like to feel velvet?

LENNIE [*chuckling with pleasure*]. You bet, by God. And I had some too. A lady give me some. And that lady was—my Aunt Clara. She give it right to me. . . . [*Measuring with his hands.*] 'Bout this big a piece. I wish I had that velvet right now. [*He frowns.*] I lost it. I ain't seen it for a long time.

CURLEY'S WIFE [*laughing*]. You're nuts. But you're a kinda nice fella. Jus' like a big baby. A person can see kinda what you mean. When I'm doin' my hair sometimes I jus' set there and stroke it, because it's so soft. [*Runs her fingers over the top of her head.*] Some people got kinda coarse hair. You take Curley, his hair's just like wire. But mine is soft and fine. Here, feel. Right here. [*Takes* LENNIE'S *hand and puts it on her head.*] Feel there and see how soft it is. [LENNIE'S *fingers fall to stroking her hair.*] Don't you muss it up.

LENNIE. Oh, that's nice. [*Strokes harder.*] Oh, that's nice.

CURLEY'S WIFE. Look out now, you'll muss it. [*Angrily.*] You stop it now, you'll mess it all up. [*She jerks her head sideways and* LENNIE'S *fingers close on her hair and hang on. In a panic.*] Let go. [*She screams.*] You let go. [*She screams again. His other hand closes over her mouth and nose.*]

LENNIE [*begging*]. Oh, please don't do that. George'll be mad. [*She struggles violently to be free. A soft screaming comes from under* LENNIE'S *hand. Crying with fright.*] Oh, please don't do none of that. George gonna say I done a bad thing. [*He raises his*

hand from her mouth and a hoarse cry escapes. Angrily.] Now don't. I don't want you to yell. You
gonna get me in trouble just like George says you
will. Now don't you do that. [*She struggles more.*]
Don't you go yellin'. [*He shakes her violently.
Her neck snaps sideways and she lies still. Looks
down at her and cautiously removes his hand
from over her mouth.*] I don't wanta hurt you. But
George will be mad if you yell. [*When she doesn't
answer he bends closely over her. He lifts her arm
and lets it drop. For a moment he seems bewildered.*] I done a bad thing. I done another bad
thing. [*He paws up the hay until it partly covers
her. The sound of the horseshoe game comes from
the outside. And for the first time* LENNIE *seems conscious of it. He crouches down and listens.*] Oh, I
done a real bad thing. I shouldn't a did that. George
will be mad. And . . . he said . . . and hide in the
brush till he comes. That's what he said. [*He picks
up the puppy from beside the girl.*] I'll throw him
away. It's bad enough like it is. [*He puts the pup
under his coat, creeps to the barn wall and peers
out between the cracks and then he creeps around
to the end of the manger and disappears.*]

[*The stage is vacant except for* CURLEY'S WIFE. *She lies
in the hay half covered up and she looks very young
and peaceful. Her rouged cheeks and red lips make
her seem alive and sleeping lightly. For a moment
the stage is absolutely silent. Then the horses stamp
on the other side of the feeding rack. The halter
chains clink and from outside men's voices come
loud and clear.*]

CANDY [*offstage*]. Lennie! Oh, Lennie, you in there?
[*He enters.*] I been figurin' some more, Lennie. Tell
you what we can do. [*Sees* CURLEY'S WIFE *and stops.
Rubs his white whiskers.*] I didn't know you was

here. You was tol' not to be here. [*He steps near her.*] You oughtn't to sleep out here. [*He is right beside her and looks down.*] Oh, Jesus Christ! [*Goes to the door and calls softly.*] George, George! Come here . . . George!

GEORGE [*enters*]. What do you want?

CANDY [*points at* CURLY'S WIFE]. Look.

GEORGE. What's the matter with her? [*Steps up beside her.*] Oh, Jesus Christ! [*Kneels beside her and feels her heart and her wrist. Finally stands up slowly and stiffly. From this time on through the rest of the scene* GEORGE *is wooden.*]

CANDY. What done it?

GEORGE [*coldly*]. Ain't you got any ideas? [CANDY *looks away.*] I should of knew. I guess way back in my head I did.

CANDY. What we gonna do now, George? What we gonna do now?

GEORGE [*answering slowly and dully*]. Guess . . . we gotta . . . tell . . . the guys. Guess we got to catch him and lock him up. We can't let him get away. Why, the poor bastard would starve. [*He tries to reassure himself.*] Maybe they'll lock him up and be nice to him.

CANDY [*excitedly*]. You know better'n that, George. You know Curley's gonna want to get him lynched. You know how Curley is.

GEORGE. Yeah. . . . Yeah . . . that's right. I know Curley. And the other guys too. [*He looks back at* CURLEY'S WIFE.]

CANDY [*pleadingly*]. You and me can get that little place, can't we, George? You and me can go there and live nice, can't we? Can't we? [CANDY *drops his head and looks down at the hay to indicate that he knows.*]

GEORGE [*shakes his head slowly*]. It was somethin' me

and him had. [*Softly.*] I think I knowed it from the very first. I think I knowed we'd never do her. He used to like to hear about it so much. I got fooled to thinkin' maybe we would.

[CANDY *starts to speak but doesn't.*]

GEORGE [*as though repeating a lesson*]. I'll work my month and then I'll take my fifty bucks. I'll stay all night in some lousy cat-house or I'll set in a pool room until everybody goes home. An' then—I'll come back an' work another month. And then I'll have fifty bucks more.

CANDY. He's such a nice fellow. I didn't think he'd a done nothing like this.

GEORGE [*gets a grip on himself and straightens his shoulders*]. Now listen. We gotta tell the guys. I guess they've gotta bring him in. They ain't no way out. Maybe they won't hurt him. I ain't gonna let 'em hurt Lennie. [*Sharply.*] Now you listen. The guys might think I was in on it. I'm gonna go in the bunkhouse. Then in a minute you come out and yell like you just seen her. Will you do that? So the guys won't think I was in on it?

CANDY. Sure, George. Sure, I'll do that.

GEORGE. Okay. Give me a couple of minutes then. And then you yell your head off. I'm goin' now. [GEORGE *exits.*]

CANDY [*watches him go, looks helplessly back at* CUR-LEY'S WIFE; *his next words are in sorrow and in anger*]. You goddamn tramp. You done it, didn't you? Everybody knowed you'd mess things up. You just wasn't no good. [*His voice shakes.*] I could of hoed in the garden and washed dishes for them guys. . . . [*Pauses for a moment and then goes into a sing-song repeating the old words.*] If there was a circus or a baseball game . . . we would o' went to her . . . just said to hell with work and went to her. And they'd been a pig and chickens . . . and in the winter a little fat stove. An' us jus' settin' there . . . settin' there. . . . [*His eyes blind with tears and he goes weakly to the entrance of the barn. Tries for a moment to break a shout out of his throat before he succeeds.*] Hey, you guys! Come here! Come here!

[*Outside the noise of the horseshoe game stops. The sound of discussion and then the voices come closer: "What's the matter?" . . . "Who's that?" . . . "It's Candy." . . . "Something must have happened." Enter* SLIM *and* CARLSON, *young* WHIT *and* CURLEY, CROOKS *in the back, keeping out of attention range. And last of all* GEORGE. GEORGE *has put on his blue denim coat and buttoned it. His black hat is pulled down low over his eyes. "What's the matter?" . . . "What's happened?"*]

[*A gesture from* CANDY. *The men stare at* CURLEY'S WIFE. SLIM *goes over to her, feels her wrist and touches her cheek with his fingers. His hand goes under her slightly twisted neck.* CURLEY *comes near. For a moment he seems shocked. Looks around helplessly and suddenly he comes to life.*]

CURLEY. I know who done it. That big son-of-a-bitch done it. I know he done it. Why, everybody else was out there playing horseshoes. [*Working himself into a fury.*] I'm gonna get him. I'm gonna get my shotgun. Why, I'll kill the big son-of-a-bitch myself. I'll shoot him in the guts. Come on, you guys. [*He runs out of the barn.*]

CARLSON. I'll go get my Luger. [*He runs out too.*]

SLIM [*quietly to* GEORGE]. I guess Lennie done it all right. Her neck's busted. Lennie could o' did that. [GEORGE *nods slowly. Half-questioning.*] Maybe like that time in Weed you was tellin' me about. [GEORGE *nods. Gently.*] Well, I guess we got to get him. Where you think he might o' went?

GEORGE [*struggling to get words out*]. I don't know.

SLIM. I guess we gotta get him.

GEORGE [*stepping close and speaking passionately*]. Couldn't we maybe bring him in and lock him up? He's nuts, Slim, he never done this to be mean.

SLIM. If we could only keep Curley in. But Curley wants to shoot him. [*He thinks.*] And s'pose they lock him up, George, and strap him down and put him in a cage, that ain't no good.

GEORGE. I know. I know.

SLIM. I think there's only one way to get him out of it.

GEORGE. I know.

CARLSON [*enters running*]. The bastard stole my Luger. It ain't in my bag.

CURLEY [*enters carrying a shotgun in his good hand. Officiously*]. All right, you guys. The nigger's got a shotgun. You take it, Carlson.

WHIT. Only cover around here is down by the river. He might have went there.

CURLEY. Don't give him no chance. Shoot for his guts, that'll double him over.

WHIT. I ain't got a gun.

CURLEY. Go in and tell my old man. Get a gun from him. Let's go now. [*Turns suspiciously on* GEORGE.] You're comin' with us, fella!

GEORGE. Yeah. I'll come. But listen, Curley, the poor bastard's nuts. Don't shoot him, he didn't know what he was doin'.

CURLEY. Don't shoot him! He's got Carlson's Luger, ain't he?

GEORGE [*weakly*]. Maybe Carlson lost his gun.

CARLSON. I seen it this morning. It's been took.

SLIM [*looking down at* CURLEY'S WIFE]. Curley, maybe you better stay here with your wife.

[*The light is fading into evening.* CURLEY *hesitates. Seems almost to weaken, then he hardens again.*]

CURLEY. Naw, I'm gonna shoot the guts out of that big bastard, I'm gonna get him myself. Come on, you guys.

SLIM [*to* CANDY]. You stay here then, Candy. The rest of us better get goin'.

[*They walk out,* SLIM *and* GEORGE *last. Exeunt all but* CANDY. *He squats in the hay, watching the face of* CURLEY'S WIFE.]

CANDY. Poor bastard.

CURTAIN

SCENE II

Evening.

The river bank again.

Light from the setting sun shines on the low brown hills. Among the trees by the river, the shade is deep with evening feeling.

Sounds: distant barking of dogs and the quiet call of quail.

The curtain rises on an empty stage.

There is a sudden whistle of evening wind that stirs the trees and scuds the leaves on the ground.

The stage is still again. LENNIE *enters as silently as a bear. He is bent over and wary. On stage he looks behind him. Then he takes from under his coat the dead pup, lays it on the ground and, going to the river, lies on his stomach and drinks.*

He returns to the dead pup, sits down beside it.

LENNIE. George gonna give me hell . . . I bet. I . . . won't tell him. I'll bury him. [*Begins to scoop a hole in the sand in front of him. Softly.*] But I didn't forget, you bet. I come right here. Hide in the brush an' wait for George. [*Works carefully at his little grave, shaping the hole. At last he picks up the pup and lays it in the hole. Mourning.*] He gonna give me hell. He gonna wish he was alone. [*Adjusts the puppy in the hole, turning it around to make it fit better. Defiantly.*] Well . . . I can go right up in the hills an' find a cave. 'Course I wouldn't never have no ketchup. [*Begins packing sand down carefully about the pup, patting it as he does in beat with his words.*] I'll—go—away—go—away. [*Every word a pat. Fills the grave carefully, smooths the sand over it.*] There now. [*Gathers leaves and scatters them over the place. Gets up on his knees and cocks his head to inspect the job.*] Now. I won't never tell George. [*Sinks back to a sitting position.*] He'll know. He always knows.

[*Far off sound of voices approaching. They come closer during the scene. Suddenly there is the clicking warning of a cock-quail and then the drum of the flock's wings.* GEORGE *enters silently, but hurriedly.*]

GEORGE [*in a hoarse whisper*]. Get in the tules—quick.

LENNIE. I ain't done nothing, George.

[*The voices are very close.*]

GEORGE [*frantically*]. Get in the tules—damn you.

[*Voices are nearly there.* GEORGE *half pushes* LENNIE *down among the tules. The tops rustle showing his crawling progress.*]

WHIT [*offstage*]. There's George. [*Enters.*] Better not get so far ahead. You ain't got a gun.

[*Enter* SLIM, CARLSON, BOSS, CURLEY, *and three other ranch hands. They are armed with shotguns and rifles.*]

CARLSON. He musta come this way. Them prints in the sand was aimed this way.

SLIM [*has been regarding* GEORGE]. Now look. We ain't

gonna find him stickin' in a bunch this way. We got to spread out.

CURLEY. Brush is pretty thick here. He might be lying in the brush. [*Steps toward the tules.* GEORGE *moves quickly after him.*]

SLIM [*seeing the move, speaks quickly*]. Look—[*pointing*]—up there's the county road and open fields an' over there's the highway. Le's spread out an' cover the brush.

BOSS. Slim's right. We got to spread.

SLIM. We better drag up to the roads an' then drag back.

CURLEY. 'Member what I said—shoot for his guts.

SLIM. Okay, move out. Me an' George'll go up to the county road. You guys gets the highway an' drag back.

BOSS. If we get separated, we'll meet here. Remember this place.

CURLEY. All I care is getting the bastard.

[*The men move offstage right, talking.* SLIM *and* GEORGE *move slowly upstage listening to the voices that grow fainter and fainter.*]

SLIM [*softly to* GEORGE.] Where is he?

[GEORGE *looks him in the eyes for a long moment. Finally trusts him and points with his thumb toward the tules.*]

SLIM. You want—I should—go away?

[GEORGE *nods slowly, looking at the ground.* SLIM *starts away, comes back, tries to say something, instead puts his hand on* GEORGE'S *shoulder for a second, and then hurries off upstage.*]

GEORGE [*moves woodenly toward the bank and the tule clump and sits down*]. Lennie!

[*The tules shiver again and* LENNIE *emerges dripping.*]

LENNIE. Where's them guys goin'? [*Long pause.*]

GEORGE. Huntin'.

LENNIE. Whyn't we go with 'em? I like huntin'. [*Waits for an answer.* GEORGE *stares across the river.*] Is it 'cause I done a bad thing?

GEORGE. It don't make no difference.

LENNIE. Is that why we can't go huntin' with them guys?

GEORGE [*woodenly*]. It don't make no difference. . . . Sit down, Lennie. Right there.

[*The light is going now. In the distance there are shouts of men.* GEORGE *turns his head and listens to the shouts.*]

LENNIE. George!

GEORGE. Yeah?

LENNIE. Ain't you gonna give me hell?

GEORGE. Give ya hell?

LENNIE. Sure. . . . Like you always done before. Like— "If I didn't have you I'd take my fifty bucks . . ."

GEORGE [*softly as if in wonder*]. Jesus Christ, Lennie, you can't remember nothing that happens. But you remember every word I say!

LENNIE. Well, ain't you gonna say it?

GEORGE [*reciting*]. "If I was alone I—could live—so easy. [*His voice is monotonous.*] I could get a job and not have no mess. . . ."

LENNIE. Go on, go on! "And when the end of the month come . . ."

GEORGE. "And when the end of the month come, I could take my fifty bucks and go to—a cathouse. . . ."

LENNIE [*eagerly*]. Go on, George, ain't you gonna give me no more hell?

GEORGE. No!

LENNIE. I can go away. I'll go right off in the hills and find a cave if you don't want me.

GEORGE [*speaks as though his lips were stiff*]. No, I want you to stay here with me.

LENNIE [*craftily*]. Then tell me like you done before.

GEORGE. Tell you what?

LENNIE. 'Bout the other guys and about us!

GEORGE [*recites again*]. "Guys like us got no families. They got a little stake and then they blow it in. They ain't got nobody in the world that gives a hoot in hell about 'em!"

LENNIE [*happily*]. "But not *us*." Tell about us now.

GEORGE. "But not us."

LENNIE. "Because . . ."

GEORGE. "Because I got you and . . ."

LENNIE [*triumphantly*]. "And I got you. We got each other," that's what, that gives a hoot in hell about us.

[*A breeze blows up the leaves and then they settle back again. There are the shouts of men again. This time closer.*]

GEORGE [*takes off his hat; shakily*]. Take off your hat, Lennie. The air feels fine!

LENNIE [*removes his hat and lays it on the ground in front of him*]. Tell how it's gonna be.

[*Again the sound of men.* GEORGE *listens to them.*]

GEORGE. Look acrost the river, Lennie, and I'll tell you like you can almost see it. [LENNIE *turns his head and looks across the river.*] "We gonna get a little place . . . [*Reaches in his side pocket and brings out* CARLSON's *Luger. Hand and gun lie on the ground behind* LENNIE's *back. He stares at the back of* LENNIE's *head at the place where spine and skull are joined. Sounds of men's voices talking offstage.*]

LENNIE. Go on! [GEORGE *raises the gun, but his hand shakes and he drops his hand on to the ground.*] Go on! How's it gonna be? "We gonna get a little place. . . ."

GEORGE [*thickly*]. "We'll have a cow. And we'll have

maybe a pig and chickens—and down the flat we'll have a . . . little piece of alfalfa. . . ."

LENNIE [*shouting*]. "For the rabbits!"

GEORGE. "For the rabbits!"

LENNIE. "And I get to tend the rabbits?"

GEORGE. "And you get to tend the rabbits!"

LENNIE [*giggling with happiness*]. "And live off the fat o' the land!"

GEORGE. Yes. [LENNIE *turns his head. Quickly.*] Look over there, Lennie. Like you can really see it.

LENNIE. Where?

GEORGE. Right acrost that river there. Can't you almost see it?

LENNIE [*moving*]. Where, George?

GEORGE. It's over there. You keep lookin', Lennie. Just keep lookin'.

LENNIE. I'm lookin', George. I'm lookin'.

GEORGE. That's right. It's gonna be nice there. Ain't gonna be no trouble, no fights. Nobody ever gonna hurt nobody, or steal from 'em. It's gonna be—nice.

LENNIE. I can see it, George. I can see it! Right over there! I can see it!

[GEORGE *fires.* LENNIE *crumples; falls behind the brush. The voices of the men in the distance.*]

CURTAIN

THE TIME OF YOUR LIFE

by William Saroyan

To George Jean Nathan

In the time of your life, live—so that in that good time there shall be no ugliness or death for yourself or for any life your life touches. Seek goodness everywhere, and when it is found, bring it out of its hiding-place and let it be free and unashamed. Place in matter and in flesh the least of the values, for these are the things that hold death and must pass away. Discover in all things that which shines and is beyond corruption. Encourage virtue in whatever heart it may have been driven into secrecy and sorrow by the shame and terror of the world. Ignore the obvious, for it is unworthy of the clear eye and the kindly heart. Be the inferior of no man, nor of any man be the superior. Remember that every man is a variation of yourself. No man's guilt is not yours, nor is any man's innocence a thing apart. Despise evil and ungodliness, but not men of ungodliness or evil. These, understand. Have no shame in being kindly and gentle, but if the time comes in the time of your life to kill, kill and have no regret. In the time of your life, live—so that in that wondrous time you shall not add to the misery and sorrow of the world, but shall smile to the infinite delight and mystery of it.

Copyright, 1939,
by Harcourt, Brace and Company, Inc.
Reprinted by permission of the publishers.

First production, October 25, 1939,
at the Booth Theatre, New York City,
with the following cast:

THE NEWSBOY, *Ross Bagdasarian*
THE DRUNKARD, *John Farrell*
WILLIE, *Will Lee*
JOE, *Eddie Dowling*
NICK, *Charles de Sheim*
TOM, *Edward Andrews*
KITTY DUVAL, *Julie Haydon*
DUDLEY, *Curt Conway*
HARRY, *Gene Kelly*
WESLEY, *Reginald Beane*
LORENE, *Nene Vibber*
BLICK, *Grover Burgess*
ARAB, *Houseley Stevens, Sr.*
MARY L., *Celeste Holme*
KRUPP, *William Bendix*
MCCARTHY, *Tom Tully*
KIT CARSON, *Len Doyle*
NICK'S MA, *Michelette Burani*
SAILOR, *Randolph Wade*
ELSIE, *Cathie Bailey*
A KILLER, *Evelyn Geller*
HER SIDE KICK, *Mary Cheffey*
A SOCIETY LADY, *Eva Leonard Boyne*
A SOCIETY GENTLEMAN, *Ainsworth Arnold*
FIRST COP, *Randolph Wade*
SECOND COP, *John Farrell*

THE PLACE: *Nick's Pacific Street Saloon, Restaurant, and Entertainment Palace at the foot of Embarcadero, in San Francisco. A suggestion of room 21 at The New York Hotel, upstairs, around the corner.*

THE TIME: *Afternoon and night of a day in October, 1939.*

Act one

NICK'S *is an American place: a San Francisco water-front honky-tonk.*

At a table, JOE: *always calm, always quiet, always thinking, always eager, always bored, always superior. His expensive clothes are casually and youthfully worn and give him an almost boyish appearance. He is thinking.*

Behind the bar, NICK: *a big red-headed young Italian-American with an enormous naked woman tatooed in red on the inside of his right arm. He is studying "The Racing Form."*

The ARAB, *at his place at the end of the bar. He is a lean old man with a rather ferocious old-country mustache, with the ends twisted up. Between the thumb and forefinger of his left hand is the Mohammedan tattoo indicating that he has been to Mecca. He is sipping a glass of beer.*

It is about eleven-thirty in the morning. SAM *is sweeping out. We see only his back. He disappears into the kitchen. The* SAILOR *at the bar finishes his drink and leaves, moving thoughtfully, as though he were trying very hard to discover how to live.*

The NEWSBOY *comes in.*

NEWSBOY [*cheerfully*]. Good-morning, everybody. [*No answer. To* NICK.] Paper, Mister? [NICK *shakes his*

head, no. The NEWSBOY *goes to* JOE.] Paper, Mister?
[JOE *shakes his head, no. The* NEWSBOY *walks away,
counting papers.*]

JOE [*noticing him*]. How many you got?

NEWSBOY. Five.

[JOE *gives him a quarter, takes all the papers, glances
at the headlines with irritation, throws them away.
The* NEWSBOY *watches carefully, then goes.*]

ARAB [*picks up paper, looks at headlines, shakes head
as if rejecting everything else a man might say about
the world*]. No foundation. All the way down the
line.

[*The* DRUNK *comes in. Walks to the telephone, looks
for a nickel in the chute, sits down at* JOE'S *table.*
NICK *takes the* DRUNK *out. The* DRUNK *returns.*]

DRUNK [*champion of the Bill of Rights*]. This is a free
country, ain't it?

[WILLIE, *the marble-game maniac, explodes through
the swinging doors and lifts the forefinger of his
right hand comically, indicating one beer. He is a
very young man, not more than twenty. He is wearing heavy shoes, a pair of old and dirty corduroys,
a light green turtle-neck jersey with a large letter
"F" on the chest, an oversize two-button tweed coat,
and a green hat, with the brim up.* NICK *sets out a
glass of beer for him, he drinks it, straightens up
vigorously saying "Aaah," makes a solemn face, gives*
NICK *a one-finger salute of adieu, and begins to leave,
refreshed and restored in spirit. He walks by the
marble game, halts suddenly, turns, studies the contraption, gestures as if to say, Oh, no. Turns to go,
stops, returns to the machine, studies it, takes a
handful of small coins out of his pants pocket, lifts
a nickel, indicates with a gesture, One game, no
more. Puts the nickel in the slot, pushes in the slide,
making an interesting noise.*]

NICK. You can't beat that machine.

WILLIE. Oh, yeah? [*The marbles fall, roll, and take their place. He pushes down the lever, placing one marble in position. Takes a very deep breath, walks in a small circle, excited at the beginning of great drama. Stands straight and pious before the contest. Himself vs. the machine. Willie vs. Destiny. His skill and daring vs. the cunning and trickery of the novelty industry of America, and the whole challenging world. He is the last of the American pioneers, with nothing more to fight but the machine, with no other reward than lights going on and off, and six nickels for one. Before him is the last champion, the machine. He is the last challenger, the young man with nothing to do in the world.* WILLIE *grips the knob delicately, studies the situation carefully, draws the knob back, holds it a moment, and then releases it. The first marble rolls out among the hazards, and the contest is on.*]

[*At the very beginning of the play "The Missouri Waltz" is coming from the phonograph. The music ends here. This is the signal for the beginning of the play.* JOE *suddenly comes out of his reverie. He whistles the way people do who are calling a cab that's about a block away, only he does it quietly.* WILLIE *turns around, but* JOE *gestures for him to return to his work.* NICK *looks up from "The Racing Form."*]

JOE [*calling*]. Tom. [*To himself.*] Where the hell is he, every time I need him? [*He looks around calmly: the nickel-in-the-slot phonograph in the corner; the open public telephone; the stage; the marble game; the bar; and so on. He calls again, this time very loud.*] Hey, Tom.

NICK [*with morning irritation*]. What do you want?

JOE [*without thinking*]. I want the boy to get me a

watermelon, that's what *I* want. What do *you* want? Money, or love, or fame, or what? You won't get them studying "The Racing Form."

NICK. I like to keep abreast of the times.

[TOM *comes hurrying in. He is a great big man of about thirty or so who appears to be much younger because of the childlike expression of his face: hand-some, dumb, innocent, troubled, and a little bewildered by everything. He is obviously adult in years, but it seems as if by all rights he should still be a boy. He is defensive as clumsy, self-conscious, over-grown boys are. He is wearing a flashy cheap suit.* JOE *leans back and studies him with casual disapproval.* TOM *slackens his pace and becomes clumsy and embarrassed, waiting for the bawling-out he's pretty sure he's going to get.*]

JOE [*objectively, severely, but a little amused*]. Who saved your life?

TOM [*sincerely*]. You did, Joe. Thanks.

JOE [*interested*]. How'd I do it?

TOM [*confused*]. What?

JOE [*even more interested*]. How'd I do it?

TOM. Joe, you know how you did it.

JOE [*softly*]. I want you to answer me. How'd I save your life? I've forgotten.

TOM [*remembering, with a big sorrowful smile*]. You made me eat all that chicken soup three years ago when I was sick and hungry.

JOE [*fascinated*]. *Chicken soup?*

TOM [*eagerly*]. Yeah.

JOE. Three years? Is it that long?

TOM [*delighted to have the information*]. Yeah, sure. 1937. 1938. 1939. This is 1939, Joe.

JOE [*amused*]. Never mind what year it is. Tell me the whole story.

TOM. You took me to the doctor. You gave me money

for food and clothes, and paid my room rent. Aw, Joe, you know all the different things you did.

[JOE *nods, turning away from* TOM *after each question.*]

JOE. You in good health now?

TOM. Yeah, Joe.

JOE. You got clothes?

TOM. Yeah, Joe.

JOE. You eat three times a day. Sometimes four?

TOM. Yeah, Joe. Sometimes five.

JOE. You got a place to sleep?

TOM. Yeah, Joe.

[JOE *nods. Pauses. Studies* TOM *carefully.*]

JOE. Then, where the hell have you been?

TOM [*humbly*]. Joe, I was out in the street listening to the boys. They're talking about the trouble down here on the waterfront.

JOE [*sharply*]. I want you to be around when I need you.

TOM [*pleased that the bawling-out is over*]. I won't do it again. Joe, one guy out there says there's got to be a revolution before anything will ever be all right.

JOE [*impatiently*]. I know all about it. Now, here. Take this money. Go up to the Emporium. You know where the Emporium is?

TOM. Yeah, sure, Joe.

JOE. All right. Take the elevator and go up to the fourth floor. Walk around to the back, to the toy department. Buy me a couple of dollars' worth of toys and bring them here.

TOM [*amazed*]. Toys? What *kind* of toys, Joe?

JOE. Any kind of toys. Little ones that I can put on this table.

TOM. What do you want toys for, Joe?

JOE [*mildly angry*]. What?

TOM. All right, all right. You don't have to get sore

at *everything*. What'll people think, a big guy like me buying toys?

JOE. *What people?*

TOM. Aw, Joe, you're always making me do crazy things for you, and *I'm* the guy that gets embarrassed. You just sit in this place and make me do all the dirty work.

JOE [*looking away*]. Do what I tell you.

TOM. O.K., but I wish I knew why. [*He makes to go.*]

JOE. Wait a minute. Here's a nickel. Put it in the phonograph. Number seven. I want to hear that waltz again.

TOM. Boy, I'm glad *I* don't have to stay and listen to it. Joe, what do you hear in that song anyway? We listen to that song ten times a day. Why can't we hear number six, or two, or nine? There are a lot of other numbers.

JOE [*emphatically*]. Put the nickel in the phonograph. [*Pause.*] Sit down and wait till the music's over. Then go get me some toys.

TOM. O.K. O.K.

JOE [*loudly*]. Never mind being a martyr about it either. The cause isn't worth it.

[*Tom puts the nickel into the machine, with a ritual of impatient and efficient movement which plainly shows his lack of sympathy or enthusiasm. His manner also reveals, however, that his lack of sympathy is spurious and exaggerated. Actually, he is fascinated by the music, but is so confused by it that he pretends he dislikes it. The music begins. It is another variation of "The Missouri Waltz," played dreamily and softly, with perfect orchestral form, and with a theme of weeping in the horns repeated a number of times. At first* TOM *listens with something close to irritation, since he can't understand what is so attractive in the music to* JOE, *and what*

*is so painful and confusing in it to himself. Very
soon, however, he is carried away by the melancholy
story of grief and nostalgia of the song. He stands,
troubled by the poetry and confusion in himself.*
JOE, *on the other hand, listens as if he were not listening, indifferent and unmoved. What he's interested in is* TOM. *He turns and glances at* TOM. KITTY
DUVAL, *who lives in a room in The New York Hotel,
around the corner, comes beyond the swinging
doors, quietly, and walks slowly to the bar, her reality and rhythm a perfect accompaniment to the sorrowful American music, which is her music, as it
is* TOM'S. *Which the world drove out of her, putting
in its place brokenness and all manner of spiritually crippled forms. She seems to understand this,
and is angry. Angry with herself, full of hate for
the poor world, and full of pity and contempt for
its tragic, unbelievable, confounded people. She is
a small powerful girl, with that kind of delicate and
rugged beauty which no circumstance of evil or ugly
reality can destroy. This beauty is that element of
the immortal which is in the seed of good and common people, and which is kept alive in some of the
female of our kind, no matter how accidentally or
pointlessly they may have entered the world.* KITTY
DUVAL *is somebody. There is an angry purity, and a
fierce pride, in her. In her stance, and way of walking, there is grace and arrogance.* JOE *recognizes her
as a great person immediately. She goes to the bar.*]
KITTY. Beer.
[NICK *places a glass of beer before her mechanically.
She swallows half the drink, and listens to the music
again.* TOM *turns and sees her. He becomes dead to
everything in the world but her. He stands like a
lump, fascinated and undone by his almost religious
adoration for her.* JOE *notices* TOM.

JOE [*gently*]. Tom. [TOM *begins to move toward the bar, where* KITTY *is standing. Loudly.*] Tom. [TOM *halts, then turns, and* JOE *motions to him to come over to the table.* TOM *goes over. Quietly.*] Have you got everything straight?

TOM [*out of the world*]. What?

JOE. What do you mean, what? I just gave you some instructions.

TOM [*pathetically*]. What do you want, Joe?

JOE. I want you to come to your senses. [*He stands up quietly and knocks* TOM's *hat off.* TOM *picks up his hat quickly.*]

TOM. I got it, Joe. I got it. The Emporium. Fourth floor. In the back. The toy department. Two dollars' worth of toys. That you can put on a table.

KITTY [*to herself*]. Who the hell is he to push a big man like that around?

JOE. I'll expect you back in a half hour. Don't get side-tracked anywhere. Just do what I tell you.

TOM [*pleading*]. Joe? Can't I bet four bits on a horse race? There's a long shot—Precious Time—that's going to win by ten lengths. I got to have money.

[JOE *points to the street.* TOM *goes out.* NICK *is combing his hair, looking in the mirror.*]

NICK. I thought you wanted him to get you a watermelon.

JOE. I forgot. [*He watches* KITTY *a moment. To* KITTY, *clearly, slowly, with great compassion.*] What's the dream?

KITTY [*moving to* JOE, *coming to*]. What?

JOE [*holding the dream for her*]. What's the dream, now?

KITTY [*coming still closer*]. What dream?

JOE. What dream! The dream you're dreaming.

NICK. Suppose he did bring you a watermelon? What the hell would you do with it?

JOE [*irritated*]. I'd put it on this table. I'd look at it. Then I'd eat it. What do you *think* I'd do with it, sell it for a profit?

NICK. How should I know what *you'd* do with *anything?* What I'd like to know is, where do you get your money from? What work do you do?

JOE [*looking at* KITTY]. Bring us a bottle of champagne.

KITTY. Champagne?

JOE [*simply*]. Would you rather have something else?

KITTY. What's the big idea?

JOE. I thought you might like some champagne. I myself am very fond of it.

KITTY. Yeah, but what's the big idea? You can't push *me* around.

JOE [*gently but severely*]. It's not in my nature to be unkind to another human being. I have only contempt for wit. Otherwise I might say something obvious, therefore cruel, and perhaps untrue.

KITTY. You be careful what you think about me.

JOE [*slowly, not looking at her*]. I have only the noblest thoughts for both your person and your spirit.

NICK [*having listened carefully and not being able to make it out*]. What are you talking about?

KITTY. You shut up. You—

JOE. He owns this place. He's an important man. All kinds of people come to him looking for work. Comedians. Singers. Dancers.

KITTY. I don't care. He can't call me names.

NICK. All right, sister. I know how it is with a two-dollar whore in the morning.

KITTY [*furiously*]. Don't you dare call me names. I used to be in burlesque.

NICK. If you were ever in burlesque, I used to be Charlie Chaplin.

KITTY [*angry and a little pathetic*]. I *was* in burlesque.

I played the burlesque circuit from coast to coast. I've had flowers sent to me by European royalty. I've had dinner with young men of wealth and social position.

NICK. You're dreaming.

KITTY [*to* JOE]. *I was in burlesque*. Kitty Duval. That was my name. Life-size photographs of me in costume in front of burlesque theaters all over the country.

JOE [*gently, coaxingly*]. I believe you. Have some champagne.

NICK [*going to table, with champagne bottle and glasses*]. There he goes again.

JOE. Miss Duval?

KITTY [*sincerely, going over*]. That's not my *real* name. That's my *stage* name.

JOE. I'll call you by your stage name.

NICK [*pouring*]. All right, sister, make up your mind. Are you going to have champagne with him, or not?

JOE. Pour the lady some wine.

NICK. O.K., Professor. Why you come to this joint instead of one of the high-class dumps uptown is more than I can understand. Why don't you have champagne at the St. Francis? Why don't you drink with a lady?

KITTY [*furiously*]. Don't you call me names—you dentist.

JOE. Dentist?

NICK [*amazed, loudly*]. What kind of cussing is that? [*Pause. Looking at* KITTY, *then at* JOE, *bewildered.*] This guy doesn't belong here. The only reason I've got champagne is because *he* keeps ordering it all the time. [*To* KITTY.] Don't think you're the only one he drinks champagne with. He drinks with *all* of them. [*Pause.*] He's crazy. Or something.

JOE [*confidentially*]. Nick, I think you're going to be all right in a couple of centuries.

NICK. I'm sorry, I don't understand your English.

[JOE *lifts his glass.* KITTY *slowly lifts hers, not quite sure of what's going on.*]

JOE [*sincerely*]. To the spirit, Kitty Duval.

KITTY [*beginning to understand, and very grateful, looking at him*]. Thank you.

JOE [*calling*]. Nick.

NICK. Yeah?

JOE. Would you mind putting a nickel in the machine again? Number—

NICK. Seven. I know. I know. I don't mind at all, Your Highness, although, personally, I'm not a lover of music. [*Going to the machine.*] As a matter of fact I think Tchaikowsky was a dope.

JOE. Tchaikowsky? Where'd you ever hear of Tchaikowsky?

NICK. He was a dope.

JOE. Yeah. Why?

NICK. They talked about him on the radio one Sunday morning. He was a sucker. He let a woman drive him crazy.

JOE. I see.

NICK. I stood behind that bar listening to the Goddamn stuff and cried like a baby. *None but the lonely heart!* He was a dope.

JOE. What made you cry?

NICK. What?

JOE [*sternly*]. What made you cry, Nick?

NICK [*angry with himself*]. I don't know.

JOE. I've been underestimating you, Nick. Play number seven.

NICK. They get everybody worked up. They give everybody stuff they shouldn't have. [NICK *puts the*

*nickel into the machine and the waltz begins again.
He listens to the music. Then studies "The Racing
Form."*]

KITTY [*to herself, dreaming*]. I like champagne, and
everything that goes with it. Big houses with big
porches, and big rooms with big windows, and big
lawns, and big trees, and flowers growing everywhere, and big shepherd dogs sleeping in the shade.

NICK. I'm going next door to Frankie's to make a bet.
I'll be right back.

JOE. Make one for me.

NICK [*going to* JOE]. Who do you like?

JOE [*giving him money*]. Precious Time.

NICK. Ten dollars? Across the board?

JOE. No. On the nose.

NICK. O.K. [*He goes.*]

[DUDLEY R. BOSTWICK, *as he calls himself, breaks
through the swinging doors, and practically flings
himself upon the open telephone beside the phonograph.* DUDLEY *is a young man of about twenty-four
or twenty-five, ordinary and yet extraordinary. He
is smallish, as the saying is, neatly dressed in bargain clothes, overworked and irritated by the routine and dullness and monotony of his life, apparently nobody and nothing, but in reality a great
personality. The swindled young man. Educated,
but without the least real understanding. A brave,
dumb, salmon-spirit struggling for life in weary,
stupefied flesh, dueling ferociously with a banal
mind which has been only irritated by what it has
been taught. He is a great personality because,
against all these handicaps, what he wants is simple
and basic: a woman. This urgent and violent need,
common yet miraculous enough in itself, considering the unhappy environment of the animal, is the
force which elevates him from nothingness to great-*

ness. A ridiculous greatness, but in the nature of things beautiful to behold. All that he has been taught, and everything he believes, is phony, and yet he himself is real, almost super-real, because of this indestructible force in himself. His face is ridiculous. His personal rhythm is tense and jittery. His speech is shrill and violent. His gestures are wild. His ego is disjointed and epileptic. And yet deeply he possesses the same wholeness of spirit, and directness of energy, that is in all species of animals. There is little innate or cultivated spirit in him, but there is no absence of innocent animal force. He is a young man who has been taught that he has a chance, as a person, and believes it. As a matter of fact, he hasn't a chance in the world, and should have been told by somebody, or should not have had his natural and valuable ignorance spoiled by education, ruining an otherwise perfectly good and charming member of the human race. At the telephone he immediately begins to dial furiously, hesitates, changes his mind, stops dialing, hangs up furiously, and suddenly begins again. Not more than half a minute after the firecracker arrival of DUDLEY R. BOSTWICK, *occurs the polka-and-waltz arrival of* HARRY. HARRY *is another story. He comes in timidly, turning about uncertainly, awkward, out of place everywhere, embarrassed and encumbered by the contemporary costume, sick at heart, but determined to fit in somewhere. His arrival constitutes a dance. His clothes don't fit. The pants are a little too large. The coat, which doesn't match, is also a little too large, and loose. He is a dumb young fellow, but he has ideas. A philosophy, in fact. His philosophy is simple and beautiful. The world is sorrowful. The world needs laughter.* HARRY *is funny. The world needs* HARRY. HARRY *will make the world laugh. He*

*has probably had a year or two of high school. He
has also listened to the boys at the pool room. He's
looking for* NICK. *He goes to the* ARAB *and says, "Are
you Nick?" The* ARAB *shakes his head. He stands at
the bar, waiting. He waits very busily.*]

HARRY [*as* NICK *returns*]. You Nick?

NICK [*very loudly*]. I am Nick.

HARRY [*acting*]. Can you use a great comedian?

NICK [*behind the bar*]. Who, for instance?

HARRY [*almost angry*]. Me.

NICK. You? What's funny about you?

[DUDLEY *at the telephone, is dialing. Because of some
defect in the apparatus the dialing is very loud.*]

DUDLEY. Hello. Sunset 7349? May I speak to Miss Elsie
Mandelspiegel? [*Pause.*]

HARRY [*with spirit and noise, dancing*]. I dance and do
gags and stuff.

NICK. In costume? Or are you wearing your costume?

DUDLEY. All I need is a cigar.

KITTY [*continuing the dream of grace*]. I'd walk out
of the house, and stand on the porch, and look at
the trees, and smell the flowers, and run across the
lawn, and lie down under a tree, and read a book.
[*Pause.*] A book of poems, maybe.

DUDLEY [*very, very clearly*]. Elsie Mandelspiegel. [*Impatiently.*] She has a room on the fourth floor. She's
a nurse at the Southern Pacific Hospital. Elsie Mandelspiegel. She works at night. Elsie. Yes. [*He begins waiting again.* WESLEY, *a colored boy, comes to
the bar and stands near* HARRY, *waiting.*]

NICK. Beer?

WESLEY. No, sir. I'd like to talk to you.

NICK [*to* HARRY]. All right. Get funny.

HARRY [*getting funny, an altogether different person,
an actor with great energy, both in power of voice,
and in force and speed of physical gesture*]. Now,

I'm standing on the corner of Third and Market. I'm looking around. I'm figuring it out. There it is. Right in front of me. The whole city. The whole world. People going by. They're going somewhere. I don't know where, but they're going. I ain't going *anywhere*. Where the hell can you go? I'm figuring it out. All right, I'm a citizen. A fat guy bumps his stomach into the face of an old lady. They were in a hurry. Fat and old. *They bumped.* Boom. I don't know. It may mean war. *War.* Germany. England. Russia. I don't know for sure. [*Loudly, dramatically, he salutes, about faces, presents arms, aims, and fires.*] WAAAAAR. [*He blows a call to arms.* NICK *gets sick of this, indicates with a gesture that* HARRY *should hold it, and goes to* WESLEY.]

NICK. What's on your mind?

WESLEY [*confused*]. Well—

NICK. Come on. Speak up. Are you hungry, or what?

WESLEY. Honest to God, I ain't hungry. All I want is a job. I don't want no charity.

NICK. Well, what can you do, and how good are you?

WESLEY. I can run errands, clean up, wash dishes, anything.

DUDLEY [*on the telephone, very eagerly*]. Elsie? Elsie, this is Dudley. Elsie, I'll jump in the bay if you don't marry me. Life isn't worth living without you. I can't sleep. I can't think of anything but you. All the time. Day and night and night and day. Elsie, I love you. I love you. What? [*Burning up.*] Is this Sunset 7-3-4-9? [*Pause.*] 7943? [*Calmly, while* WILLIE *begins making a small racket.*] Well, what's your name? *Lorene?* Lorene Smith? I thought you were Elsie Mandelspiegel. What? Dudley. Yeah. Dudley R. Bostwick. Yeah. R. It stands for Raoul, but I never spell it out. I'm pleased to meet *you*, too. What? There's a lot of noise around here. [WILLIE *stops hitting the marble game.*] Where am I? At Nick's, on Pacific Street. I work at the S. P. I told them I was sick and they gave me the afternoon off. Wait a minute. I'll ask them. I'd like to meet *you,* too. Sure. I'll ask them. [*Turns around to* NICK.] What's this address?

NICK. Number 3 Pacific Street, you cad.

DUDLEY. Cad? You don't know how I've been suffering on account of Elsie. I take things too ceremoniously. I've got to be more lackadaisical. [*Into telephone.*] Hello, Elenore? I mean, Lorene. It's number 3 Pacific Street. Yeah. Sure. I'll wait for you. How'll you know me? You'll *know* me. I'll recognize *you.* Good-by, now. [*He hangs up.*]

HARRY [*continuing his monologue, with gestures, movements, and so on*]. I'm standing there. I didn't do anything to anybody. Why should I be a soldier? [*Sincerely, insanely.*] BOOOOOOOOOM. *WAR!* O.K. War. *I* retreat. *I* hate war. I move to Sacramento.

NICK [*shouting*]. All right, comedian. Lay off a minute.

HARRY [*broken-hearted, going to* WILLIE]. Nobody's got a sense of humor any more. The world's dying for comedy like never before, but nobody knows how to *laugh.*

NICK [*to* WESLEY]. Do you belong to the union?

WESLEY. What union?

NICK. For the love of Mike, where've you been? Don't you know you can't come into a place and ask for a job and get one and go to work, just like that. You've got to belong to one of the unions.

WESLEY. I didn't know. I got to have a job. Real soon.

NICK. Well, you've got to belong to a union.

WESLEY. I don't want any favors. All I want is a chance to earn a living.

NICK. Go on into the kitchen and tell Sam to give you some lunch.

WESLEY. Honest, I ain't hungry.

DUDLEY [*shouting*]. What I've gone through for Elsie.

HARRY. I've got all kinds of funny ideas in my head to help make the world happy again.

NICK [*holding* WESLEY]. No, he isn't hungry.

[WESLEY *almost faints from hunger.* NICK *catches him just in time. The* ARAB *and* NICK *go off with* WESLEY *into the kitchen.*]

HARRY [*to* WILLIE]. See if you think this is funny. It's my own idea. I created this dance myself. It comes after the monologue. [HARRY *begins to dance.* WILLIE *watches a moment, and then goes back to the game. It's a goofy dance, which* HARRY *does with great sorrow, but much energy.*]

DUDLEY. Elsie. Aw, gee, Elsie. What the hell do I want to see Lorene Smith for? Some girl I don't know.

[JOE *and* KITTY *have been drinking in silence. There is no sound now except the soft-shoe shuffling of* HARRY, *the Comedian.*]

JOE. What's the dream now, Kitty Duval?

KITTY [*dreaming the words and pictures*]. I dream of home. Christ, I always dream of home. I've no *home*. I've no place. But I always dream of all of us together again. We had a farm in Ohio. There was nothing good about it. It was always sad. There was always trouble. But I always dream about it as if I could go back and Papa would be there and Mamma and Louie and my little brother Stephen and my sister Mary. I'm Polish. Duval! My name isn't Duval, it's Koranovsky. Katerina Koranovsky. We lost everything. The house, the farm, the trees, the horses, the cows, the chickens. Papa died. He was old. He was thirteen years older than Mamma. We moved to Chicago. We tried to work. We tried to stay together. Louie got in trouble. The fellows he was with killed him for something. I don't know what. Stephen ran away from home. Seventeen years old. I don't know where he is. Then Mamma died. [*Pause.*] What's the dream? I dream of home.

[NICK *comes out of the kitchen with* WESLEY.]

NICK. Here. Sit down here and rest. That'll hold you for a *while*. Why didn't you tell me you were hungry? You all right now?

WESLEY [*sitting down in the chair at the piano*]. Yes, I am. Thank you. I didn't know I was *that* hungry.

NICK. Fine. [*To* HARRY *who is dancing.*] Hey. What the hell do you think you're doing?

HARRY [*stopping*]. That's my own idea. I'm a natural-born dancer and comedian.

[WESLEY *begins slowly, one note, one chord at a time, to play the piano.*]

NICK. You're no good. Why don't you try some other kind of work? Why don't you get a job in a store, selling something? What do you want to be a comedian for?

HARRY. I've got something for the world and they haven't got sense enough to let me give it to them. Nobody knows me.

DUDLEY. Elsie. Now I'm waiting for some dame I've never seen before. Lorene Smith. Never saw her in my life. Just happened to get the wrong number. She turns on the personality, and I'm a cooked Indian. Give me a beer, please.

HARRY. Nick, you've got to see my act. It's the greatest thing of its kind in America. All I want is a chance. No salary to begin. Let me try it out tonight. If I don't wow 'em, O.K., I'll go home. If vaudeville wasn't dead, a guy like me would have a chance.

NICK. You're not funny. You're a sad young punk. What the hell do you want to try to be funny for? You'll break everybody's heart. What's there for you to be funny about? You've been poor all your life, haven't you?

HARRY. I've been poor all right, but don't forget that some things count more than some other things.

NICK. What counts more, for instance, than what else, for instance?

HARRY. Talent, for instance, counts more than money, for instance, that's what, and I've got talent. I get new ideas night and day. Everything comes natural to me. I've got style, but it'll take me a little time to round it out. That's all.

[*By now* WESLEY *is playing something of his own which is very good and out of the world. He plays about half a minute, after which* HARRY *begins to dance.*]

NICK [*watching*]. I run the lousiest dive in Frisco, and a guy arrives and makes me stock up with champagne. The whores come in and holler at me that they're ladies. Talent comes in and begs me for a chance to show itself. Even society people come here once in a while. I don't know what for. Maybe it's liquor. Maybe it's the location. Maybe it's my personality. Maybe it's the crazy personality of the joint. The old honky-tonk. [*Pause.*] Maybe they can't feel at home anywhere else.

[*By now* WESLEY *is really playing, and* HARRY *is going through a new routine.* DUDLEY *grows sadder and sadder.*]

KITTY. Please dance with me.

JOE [*loudly*]. I never learned to dance.

KITTY. Anybody can dance. Just hold me in your arms.

JOE. I'm very fond of you. I'm *sorry*. I *can't* dance. I wish to God I could.

KITTY. Oh, please.

JOE. Forgive me. I'd like to very much.

[KITTY *dances alone.* TOM *comes in with a package. He sees* KITTY *and goes ga-ga again. He comes out of the trance and puts the bundle on the table in front of* JOE.]

JOE [*taking the package*]. What'd you get?

TOM. Two dollars' worth of toys. That's what you sent me for. The girl asked me what I wanted with toys. I didn't know what to tell her. [*He stares at* KITTY, *then back at* JOE.] Joe? I've got to have some money. After all you've done for me, I'll do anything in the world for you, but, Joe, you got to give me some money once in a while.

JOE. What do you want it for?

[TOM *turns and stares at* KITTY *dancing.*]

JOE [*noticing*]. Sure. Here. Here's five. [*Shouting.*] Can you dance?

TOM [*proudly*]. I got second prize at the Palomar in Sacramento five years ago.

JOE [*loudly, opening package*]. O.K., dance with her.

TOM. You mean *her?*

JOE [*loudly*]. I mean Kitty Duval, the burlesque queen. I mean the queen of the world burlesque. Dance with her. She wants to dance.

TOM [*worshiping the name Kitty Duval, helplessly*]. Joe, can I tell you something?

JOE [*he brings out a toy and winds it*]. You don't have to. I know. You love her. You *really* love her. I'm not blind. I know. But take care of yourself. Don't get sick that way again.

NICK [*looking at and listening to* WESLEY *with amazement*]. Comes in here and wants to be a dish-washer. Faints from hunger. And then sits down and plays better than Heifetz.

JOE. Heifetz plays the violin.

NICK. All right, don't get careful. He's good, ain't he?

TOM [*to* KITTY]. Kitty.

JOE [*he lets the toy go, loudly*]. Don't talk. Just dance.

[TOM *and* KITTY *dance.* NICK *is at the bar, watching everything.* HARRY *is dancing.* DUDLEY *is grieving into his beer.* LORENE SMITH, *about thirty-seven, very overbearing and funny-looking, comes to the bar.*]

NICK. What'll it be, lady?

LORENE [*looking about and scaring all the young men*]. I'm looking for the young man I talked to on the telephone. Dudley R. Bostwick.

DUDLEY [*jumping, running to her, stopping, shocked*]. Dudley R. [*Slowly.*] Bostwick? Oh, yeah. He left here ten minutes ago. You mean Dudley Bostwick, that poor man on crutches?

LORENE. Crutches?

DUDLEY. Yeah. Dudley Bostwick. That's what he *said* his name was. He said to tell you not to wait.

LORENE. Well. [*She begins to go, turns around.*] Are you sure *you're* not Dudley Bostwick?

DUDLEY. Who—me? [*Grandly.*] My name is Roger Tenefrancia. I'm a French-Canadian. I never saw the poor fellow before.

LORENE. It seems to me your voice is like the voice I heard over the telephone.

DUDLEY. A coincidence. An accident. A quirk of fate. One of those things. Dismiss the thought. That poor cripple hobbled out of here ten minutes ago.

LORENE. He said he was going to commit suicide. I only wanted to be of help. [*She goes.*]

DUDLEY. Be of help? What kind of help could she be of? [DUDLEY *runs to the telephone in the corner.*] Gee whiz, Elsie. Gee whiz. I'll never leave you again. [*He turns the pages of a little address book.*] Why do I always forget the number? I've tried to get her

on the phone a hundred times this week and I still
forget the number. She won't come to the phone,
but I keep trying anyway. She's out. She's not in.
She's working. I get the wrong number. Everything
goes haywire. I can't sleep. [*Defiantly.*] She'll come
to the phone one of these days. If there's anything
to true love at all, she'll come to the phone. Sunset 7349. [*He dials the number, as* JOE *goes on studying the toys. They are one big mechanical toy, whistles, and a music box.* JOE *blows into the whistles,
quickly, by way of getting casually acquainted with
them.* TOM *and* KITTY *stop dancing.* TOM *stares at
her.*]

DUDLEY. Hello. Is this Sunset 7349? May I speak to
Elsie? Yes. [*Emphatically, and bitterly.*] No, this is
not Dudley Bostwick. This is Roger Tenefrancia
of Montreal, Canada. I'm a childhood friend of Miss
Mandelspiegel. We went to kindergarten together.
[*Hand over phone.*] God damn it. [*Into phone.*]
Yes. I'll wait, thank you.

TOM. I love you.

KITTY. You want to go to my room? [TOM *can't answer.*]
Have you got two dollars?

TOM [*shaking his head with confusion*]. I've got *five*
dollars, but I *love* you.

KITTY [*looking at him*]. You want to spend all that
money?

[TOM *embraces her. They go.* JOE *watches. Goes back
to the toy.*]

JOE. Where's that longshoreman, McCarthy?

NICK. He'll be around.

JOE. What do you think he'll have to say today?

NICK. Plenty, as usual. I'm going next door to see who
won that third race at Laurel.

JOE. Precious Time won it.

NICK. That's what you think. [*He goes.*]

JOE [*to himself*]. A horse named McCarthy is running in the sixth race today.

DUDLEY [*on the phone*]. Hello. Hello, Elsie? Elsie? [*His voice weakens; also his limbs.*] My God. She's come to the phone. Elsie, I'm at Nick's on Pacific Street. You've got to come here and talk to me. Hello. Hello, Elsie? [*Amazed.*] Did she hang up? Or was I disconnected? [*He hangs up and goes to bar.* WESLEY *is still playing the piano.* HARRY *is still dancing.* JOE *has wound up the big mechanical toy and is watching it work.* NICK *returns.*]

NICK [*watching the toy*]. Say. That's some gadget.

JOE. How much did I win?

NICK. How do you know you *won*?

JOE. Don't be silly. He said Precious Time was going to win by ten lengths, didn't he? He's in love, isn't he?

NICK. O.K. I don't know why, but Precious Time won. You got eighty for ten. How do you do it?

JOE [*roaring*]. Faith. Faith. How'd he win?

NICK. By a nose. Look him up in "The Racing Form." The slowest, the cheapest, the worst horse in the race, and the worst jockey. What's the matter with my luck?

JOE. How much did you lose?

NICK. Fifty cents.

JOE. You should never gamble.

NICK. Why not?

JOE. You always bet fifty cents. You've got no more faith than a flea, that's why.

HARRY [*shouting*]. How do you like this, Nick? [*He is really busy now, all legs and arms.*]

NICK [*turning and watching*]. Not bad. Hang around. You can wait table. [*To* WESLEY]. Hey. Wesley. Can you play that again tonight?

WESLEY [*turning, but still playing the piano*]. I don't

know for sure, Mr. Nick. I can play *something*.

NICK. Good. *You* hang around, too. [*He goes behind the bar.*]

[*The atmosphere is now one of warm, natural, American ease; every man innocent and good; each doing what he believes he should do, or what he must do. There is deep American naïveté and faith in the behavior of each person. No one is competing with anyone else. No one hates anyone else. Every man is living, and letting live. Each man is following his destiny as he feels it should be followed; or is abandoning it as he feels it must, by now, be abandoned; or is forgetting it for the moment as he feels he should forget it. Although everyone is dead serious, there is unmistakable smiling and humor in the scene; a sense of the human body and spirit emerging from the world-imposed state of stress and fretfulness, fear and awkwardness, to the more natural state of casualness and grace. Each person belongs to the environment, in his own person, as himself: WESLEY is playing better than ever. HARRY is hoofing better than ever. NICK is behind the bar shining glasses. JOE is smiling at the toy and studying it. DUDLEY, although still troubled, is at least calm now and full of melancholy poise. WILLIE, at the marble game, is happy. The ARAB is deep in his memories, where he wants to be. Into this scene and atmosphere comes BLICK. BLICK is the sort of human being you dislike at sight. He is no different from anybody else physically. His face is an ordinary face. There is nothing obviously wrong with him, and yet you know that it is impossible, even by the most generous expansion of understanding, to accept him as a human being. He is the strong man without strength—strong only among the weak—the weak-*

ling who uses force on the weaker. BLICK *enters casually, as if he were a customer, and immediately* HARRY *begins slowing down.*]

BLICK [*oily, and with mock-friendliness*]. Hello, Nick.

NICK [*stopping his work and leaning across the bar*]. What do you want to come here for? You're too big a man for a little honky-tonk.

BLICK [*flattered*]. Now, Nick.

NICK. Important people never come here. *Here*. Have a drink. [*Whiskey bottle.*]

BLICK. Thanks, I don't drink.

NICK [*drinking the drink himself*]. Well, why don't you?

BLICK. I have responsibilities.

NICK. You're head of the lousy Vice Squad. There's no vice here.

BLICK [*sharply*]. Street-walkers are working out of this place.

NICK [*angry*]. What do you want?

BLICK [*loudly*]. I just want you to know that it's got to *stop*.

[*The music stops. The mechanical toy runs down. There is absolute silence, and a strange fearfulness and disharmony in the atmosphere now.* HARRY *doesn't know what to do with his hands or feet.* WESLEY'S *arms hang at his sides.* JOE *quietly pushes the toy to one side of the table, eager to study what is happening.* WILLIE *stops playing the marble game, turns around and begins to wait.* DUDLEY *straightens up very, very vigorously, as if to say: "Nothing can scare me. I know love is the only thing." The* ARAB *is the same as ever, but watchful.* NICK *is arrogantly aloof. There is a moment of this silence and tension, as though* BLICK *were waiting for everybody to acknowledge his presence. He is obviously flattered by*

the acknowledgment of HARRY, DUDLEY, WESLEY, *and*
WILLIE, *but a little irritated by* NICK'S *aloofness and
unfriendliness.*]

NICK. Don't look at me. I can't tell a street-walker from
a lady. You married?

BLICK. You're not asking *me* questions. *I'm* telling *you.*

NICK [*interrupting*]. You're a man of about forty-five
or so. You *ought* to know better.

BLICK [*angry*]. Street-walkers are working out of this
place.

NICK [*beginning to shout*]. Now, don't start any trouble with me. People come here to drink and loaf
around. I don't care who they are.

BLICK. Well, I do.

NICK. The only way to find out if a lady is a streetwalker is to walk the streets with her, go to bed, and
make sure. You wouldn't want to do that. *You'd*
like to, of course.

BLICK. Any more of it, and I'll have your joint closed.

NICK [*very casually, without ill-will*]. Listen. I've got
no use for you, or anybody like you. You're out to
change the world from something bad to something
worse. Something like yourself.

BLICK [*furious pause, and contempt*]. I'll be back tonight. [*He begins to go.*]

NICK [*very angry but very calm*]. Do yourself a big
favor and don't come back tonight. Send somebody
else. I don't like your personality.

BLICK [*casually, but with contempt*]. Don't break any
laws. I don't like yours, either. [*He looks the place
over, and goes.*]

[*There is a moment of silence. Then* WILLIE *turns and
puts a new nickel in the slot and starts a new game.*
WESLEY *turns to the piano and rather falteringly begins to play. His heart really isn't in it.* HARRY *walks
about, unable to dance.* DUDLEY *lapses into his cus-*

tomary melancholy, at a table. NICK *whistles a little: suddenly stops.* JOE *winds the toy.*]

JOE [*comically*]. Nick. You going to kill that man?

NICK. I'm disgusted.

JOE. Yeah? Why?

NICK. Why should I get worked up over a guy like that? Why should I hate *him*? He's nothing. He's nobody. He's a mouse. But every time he comes into this place I get burned up. He doesn't want to drink. He doesn't want to sit down. He doesn't want to take things easy. Tell me one thing?

JOE. Do my best.

NICK. What's a punk like *that* want to go out and try to change the world for?

JOE [*amazed*]. Does *he* want to change the world, too?

NICK [*irritated*]. You know what I mean. What's he want to bother people for? He's *sick*.

JOE [*almost to himself, reflecting on the fact that* BLICK *too wants to change the world*]. I guess he wants to change the world at that.

NICK. So I go to work and hate him.

JOE. It's not him, Nick. It's everything.

NICK. Yeah, *I know*. But I've still got no use for him. He's no good. You know what I mean? He hurts little people. [*Confused.*] One of the girls tried to commit suicide on account of him. [*Furiously.*] I'll break his head if he hurts anybody around here. This is *my* joint. [*Afterthought.*] Or anybody's *feelings,* either.

JOE. He may not be so bad, deep down underneath.

NICK. I know all about him. He's no good.

[*During this talk* WESLEY *has really begun to play the piano, the toy is rattling again, and little by little* HARRY *has begun to dance.* NICK *has come around the bar, and now, very much like a child—forgetting all his anger—is watching the toy work. He begins*

to smile at everything: turns and listens to WESLEY:
watches HARRY: *nods at the* ARAB: *shakes his head
at* DUDLEY: *and gestures amiably about* WILLIE. *It's
his joint all right. It's a good, low-down, honky-
tonk American place that lets people alone.*]

NICK. I've got a good joint. There's nothing wrong
here. Hey. Comedian. Stick to the dancing tonight.
I think you're O.K. Wesley? Do some more of that
tonight. That's fine!

HARRY. Thanks, Nick. Gosh, I'm on my way at last.
[*On telephone.*] Hello, Ma? Is that you, Ma? Harry.
I got the job. [*He hangs up and walks around, smil-
ing.*]

NICK [*watching the toy all this time*]. Say, that really
is something. What is that, anyway?

[MARY L. *comes in.*]

JOE [*holding it toward* NICK, *and* MARY L.]. Nick, this
is a toy. A contraption devised by the cunning of
man to drive boredom, or grief, or anger out of
children. A noble gadget. A gadget, I might say, infinitely nobler than any other I can think of at the
moment. [*Everybody gathers around* JOE'S *table to
look at the toy. The toy stops working.* JOE *winds
the music box. Lifts a whistle: blows it, making a
very strange, funny and sorrowful sound.*] Delightful. Tragic, but delightful.

[WESLEY *plays the music-box theme on the piano.* MARY
L. *takes a table.*]

NICK. Joe. That girl, Kitty. What's she mean, calling
me a dentist? I wouldn't hurt anybody, let alone a
tooth.

[NICK *goes to* MARY L.'S *table.* HARRY *imitates the toy.
Dances. The piano music comes up, the light dims
slowly, while the piano solo continues.*]

CURTAIN

Act two

An hour later. All the people who were at NICK's *when the curtain came down are still there.* JOE *at his table, quietly shuffling and turning a deck of cards, and at the same time watching the face of the* WOMAN, *and looking at the initials on her handbag, as though they were the symbols of the lost glory of the world. The* WOMAN, *in turn, very casually regards* JOE *occasionally. Or rather senses him; has sensed him in fact the whole hour. She is mildly tight on beer, and* JOE *himself is tight, but as always completely under control; simply sharper. The others are about, at tables, and so on.*

JOE. Is it Madge—Laubowitz?

MARY. Is what *what*?

JOE. Is the name Mabel Lepescu?

MARY. What name?

JOE. The name the initials M. L. stand for. The initials on your bag.

MARY. No.

JOE [*after a long pause, thinking deeply what the name might be, turning a card, looking into the beautiful face of the woman*]. Margie Longworthy?

MARY [*all this is very natural and sincere, no comedy on the part of the people involved: they are both solemn, being drunk*]. No.

JOE [*his voice higher-pitched, as though he were growing alarmed*]. Midge Laurie? [MARY *shakes her head.*] My initials are J. T.

MARY [*Pause.*] John?

JOE. No. [*Pause.*] Martha Lancaster?

MARY. No. [*Slight pause.*] Joseph?

JOE. Well, not exactly. That's my first name, but everybody calls me Joe. The last name is the tough one. I'll help you a little. I'm Irish. [*Pause.*] Is it just plain Mary?

MARY. Yes, it is. I'm Irish, too. At least on my father's side. English on my mother's side.

JOE. I'm Irish on both sides. Mary's one of my favorite names. I guess that's why I didn't think of it. I met a girl in Mexico City named Mary once. She was an American from Philadelphia. She got married there. In Mexico City, I mean. While I was *there*. We were in love, too. At least *I* was. You never know about anyone else. They were engaged, you see, and her mother was with her, so they went through with it. Must have been six or seven years ago. She's probably got three or four children by this time.

MARY. Are you still in love with her?

JOE. Well—no. To tell you the truth, I'm not sure. I guess I am. I didn't even know she was engaged until a couple of days before they got married. I thought *I* was going to marry her. I kept thinking all the time about the kind of kids we would be likely to have. My favorite was the third one. The first two were fine. Handsome and fine and intelligent, but that third one was different. Dumb and goofy-looking. I liked *him* a lot. When she told me she was going to be married, I didn't feel so bad about the first two, it was that dumb one.

MARY [*after a pause of some few seconds*]. What do you do?

JOE. Do? To tell you the truth, nothing.

MARY. Do you always drink a great deal?

JOE [*scientifically*]. Not *always*. Only when I'm awake. I sleep seven or eight hours every night, you know.

MARY. How nice. I mean to drink when you're awake.

JOE [*thoughtfully*]. It's a privilege.

MARY. Do you really *like* to drink?

JOE [*positively*]. As much as I like to *breathe*.

MARY [*beautifully*]. Why?

JOE [*dramatically*]. Why do I like to drink? [*Pause.*] Because I don't like to be gypped. Because I don't like to be dead most of the time and just a little alive every once in a long while. [*Pause.*] If I don't drink, I become fascinated by unimportant things— like everybody else. I get busy. Do things. All kinds of little stupid things, for all kinds of little stupid reasons. Proud, selfish, *ordinary* things. I've done them. Now I don't do anything. *I live all the time.* Then I go to sleep. [*Pause.*]

MARY. Do you sleep well?

JOE [*taking it for granted*]. Of course.

MARY [*quietly, almost with tenderness*]. What are your plans?

JOE [*loudly, but also tenderly*]. Plans? I haven't *got* any. *I just get up.*

MARY [*beginning to understand everything*]. Oh, yes. Yes, of course.

[DUDLEY *puts a nickel in the phonograph.*]

JOE [*thoughtfully*]. Why do I drink? [*Pause, while he thinks about it. The thinking appears to be profound and complex, and has the effect of giving his face a very comical and naïve expression.*] That question calls for a pretty complicated answer. [*He smiles abstractly.*]

MARY. Oh, I didn't mean—

JOE [*swiftly, gallantly*]. No. No. I insist. I *know* why. It's just a matter of finding words. Little ones.

MARY. It really doesn't matter.

JOE [*seriously*]. Oh, yes, it does. [*Clinically.*] Now, why do I drink? [*Scientifically.*] No. Why does *anybody*

drink? [*Working it out.*] Every day has twenty-four
hours.

MARY [*sadly, but brightly*]. Yes, that's true.

JOE. Twenty-four hours. Out of the twenty-four hours
at *least* twenty-three and a half are—my God, I don't
know why—dull, dead, boring, empty, and murder-
ous. Minutes on the clock, *not time of living*. It
doesn't make any difference who you are or what
you do, twenty-three and a half hours of the twenty-
four are spent *waiting*.

MARY. Waiting?

JOE [*gesturing, loudly*]. And the more you wait, the
less there is to wait *for*.

MARY [*attentively, beautifully his student*]. Oh?

JOE [*continuing*]. That goes on for days and days, and
weeks and months and years, and the first
thing you know *all* the years are dead. All the minutes are dead. You yourself are dead. There's nothing to wait for any more. Nothing except *minutes*
on the *clock*. No time of life. Nothing but minutes,
and idiocy. Beautiful, bright, intelligent idiocy.
[*Pause.*] Does that answer your question?

MARY [*earnestly*]. I'm afraid it does. Thank you. You
shouldn't have gone to all the trouble.

JOE. No trouble at all. [*Pause.*] You have children?

MARY. Yes. Two. A son and a daughter.

JOE [*delighted*]. How swell. Do they look like you?

MARY. Yes.

JOE. Then why are you sad?

MARY. I was always sad. It's just that after I was married I was allowed to drink.

JOE [*eagerly*]. Who are you waiting for?

MARY. No one.

JOE [*smiling*]. I'm not waiting for anybody, either.

MARY. My husband, of course.

JOE. Oh, sure.

MARY. He's a lawyer.

JOE [*standing, leaning on the table*]. He's a great guy. I like him. I'm very fond of him.

MARY [*listening*]. You have responsibilities?

JOE [*loudly*]. One, and *thousands*. As a matter of fact, I feel responsible to everybody. At least to everybody I meet. I've been trying for three years to find out if it's possible to live what I think is a civilized life. I mean a life that can't hurt any other life.

MARY. You're famous?

JOE. Very. Utterly unknown, but very famous. Would you like to dance?

MARY. All right.

JOE [*loudly*]. I'm *sorry*. I don't dance. I didn't think you'd like to.

MARY. To tell you the truth, I don't like to dance at all.

JOE [*proudly—commentator*]. I can hardly walk.

MARY. You mean you're tight?

JOE [*smiling*]. No. I mean *all* the time.

MARY [*looking at him closely*]. Were you ever in Paris?

JOE. In 1929, and again in 1934.

MARY. What month of 1934?

JOE. Most of April, all of May, and a little of June.

MARY. I was there in November and December that year.

JOE. We were there almost at the same time. You were married?

MARY. Engaged. [*They are silent a moment, looking at one another. Quietly and with great charm.*] Are you *really* in love with me?

JOE. Yes.

MARY. Is it the champagne?

JOE. Yes. Partly, at least. [*He sits down.*]

MARY. If you don't see me again, will you be very unhappy?

JOE. Very.

MARY [*getting up*]. I'm so pleased. [JOE *is deeply grieved that she is going. In fact, he is almost panic-stricken about it, getting up in a way that is full of furious sorrow and regret.*] I must go now. Please don't get up. [JOE *is up, staring at her with amazement.*] Good-by.

JOE [*simply*]. Good-by.

[*The* WOMAN *stands looking at him a moment, then turns and goes.* JOE *stands staring after her for a long time. Just as he is slowly sitting down again, the* NEWSBOY *enters, and goes to* JOE's *table.*]

NEWSBOY. Paper, Mister?

JOE. How many you got this time?

NEWSBOY. Eleven.

[JOE *buys them all, looks at the lousy headlines, throws them away. The* NEWSBOY *looks at* JOE, *amazed. He walks over to* NICK *at the bar.*]

NEWSBOY [*troubled*]. Hey, Mister, do you own this place?

NICK [*casually but emphatically*]. I own this place.

NEWSBOY. Can you use a great lyric tenor?

NICK [*almost to himself*]. Great lyric tenor? [*Loudly.*] Who?

NEWSBOY [*loud and the least bit angry*]. Me. I'm getting too big to sell papers. I don't want to holler headlines all the time. I want to *sing*. You can use a great lyric tenor, can't you?

NICK. What's lyric about you?

NEWSBOY [*voice high-pitched, confused*]. My voice.

NICK. Oh. [*Slight pause, giving in.*] All right, then—sing!

[*The* NEWSBOY *breaks into swift and beautiful song:*

"When Irish Eyes Are Smiling." NICK *and* JOE *listen carefully:* NICK *with wonder,* JOE *with amazement and delight.*]

NEWSBOY [*singing*].

> When Irish eyes are smiling,
> Sure 'tis like a morn in Spring.
> In the lilt of Irish laughter,
> You can hear the angels sing.
> When Irish hearts are happy,
> All the world seems bright and gay.
> But when Irish eyes are smiling—

NICK [*loudly, swiftly*]. Are you Irish?

NEWSBOY [*speaking swiftly, loudly, a little impatient with the irrelevant question*]. No. I'm Greek. [*He finishes the song, singing louder than ever.*] Sure they steal your heart away. [*He turns to* NICK *dramatically, like a vaudeville singer begging his audience for applause.* NICK *studies the* BOY *eagerly.* JOE *gets to his feet and leans toward the* BOY *and* NICK.]

NICK. Not bad. Let me hear you again about a year from now.

NEWSBOY [*thrilled*]. Honest?

NICK. Yeah. Along about November 7th, 1940.

NEWSBOY [*happier than ever before in his life, running over to* JOE]. Did you hear it too, Mister?

JOE. Yes, and it's great. What part of Greece?

NEWSBOY. Salonica. Gosh, Mister. Thanks.

JOE. Don't wait a year. Come back with some papers a little later. You're a great singer.

NEWSBOY [*thrilled and excited*]. Aw, thanks, Mister. So long. [*Running, to* NICK.] Thanks, Mister. [*He runs out.* JOE *and* NICK *look at the swinging doors.* JOE *sits down.* NICK *laughs.*]

NICK. Joe, people are so wonderful. Look at that kid.

JOE. Of course they're wonderful. Every one of them is wonderful.

[MC CARTHY *and* KRUPP *come in, talking.* MC CARTHY *is a big man in work clothes, which make him seem very young. He is wearing black jeans, and a blue workman's shirt. No tie. No hat. He has broad shoulders, a lean intelligent face, thick black hair. In his right back pocket is the longshoreman's hook. His arms are long and hairy. His sleeves are rolled up to just below his elbows. He is a casual man, easy-going in movement, sharp in perception, swift in appreciation of charm or innocence or comedy, and gentle in spirit. His speech is clear and full of warmth. His voice is powerful, but modulated. He enjoys the world, in spite of the mess it is, and he is fond of people, in spite of the mess they are.* KRUPP *is not quite as tall or broad-shouldered as* MC CARTHY. *He is physically encumbered by his uniform, club, pistol, belt, and cap. And he is plainly not at home in the role of policeman. His movement is stiff and unintentionally pompous. He is a naïve man, essentially good. His understanding is less than* MC CARTHY'S, *but he is honest and he doesn't try to bluff.*]

KRUPP. You don't understand what I mean. Hi-ya, Joe.

JOE. Hello, Krupp.

MC CARTHY. Hi-ya, Joe.

JOE. Hello, McCarthy.

KRUPP. Two beers, Nick. [*To* MC CARTHY.] All I do is carry out orders, carry out orders. I don't know what the idea is behind the order. Who it's for, or who it's against, or why. All I do is carry it out.

[NICK *gives them beer.*]

MC CARTHY. You don't read enough.

KRUPP. I do read. I read *The Examiner* every morning. *The Call-Bulletin* every night.

MC CARTHY. And carry out orders. What are the orders now?

KRUPP. To keep the peace down here on the waterfront.

MC CARTHY. Keep it for who? [*To* JOE.] Right?

JOE [*sorrowfully*]. Right.

KRUPP. How do I know for who? The peace. Just keep it.

MC CARTHY. It's got to be kept for somebody. Who would you suspect it's kept for?

KRUPP. For citizens!

MC CARTHY. I'm a citizen!

KRUPP. All right, I'm keeping it for you.

MC CARTHY. By hitting me over the head with a club? [*To* JOE.] Right?

JOE [*melancholy, with remembrance*]. I don't know.

KRUPP. Mac, you know I never hit you over the head with a club.

MC CARTHY. But you will if you're on duty at the time and happen to stand on the opposite side of myself, on duty.

KRUPP. We went to Mission High together. We were always good friends. The only time we ever fought was that time over Alma Haggerty. Did *you* marry Alma Haggerty? [*To* JOE.] Right?

JOE. Everything's right.

MC CARTHY. No. Did you? [*To* JOE.] Joe, are you with me or against me?

JOE. I'm with everybody. One at a time.

KRUPP. No. And that's just what I mean.

MC CARTHY. You mean neither one of us is going to marry the thing we're fighting for?

KRUPP. *I don't even know what it is.*

MC CARTHY. You don't read enough, I tell you.

KRUPP. Mac, you don't know what you're fighting for, either.

MC CARTHY. It's so simple, it's fantastic.

KRUPP. All right, what are you fighting for?

MC CARTHY. For the rights of the inferior. Right?

JOE. Something like that.

KRUPP. The who?

MC CARTHY. The inferior. The world full of Mahoneys who haven't got what it takes to make monkeys out of everybody else, near by. The men who were created equal. Remember?

KRUPP. Mac, you're not inferior.

MC CARTHY. I'm a longshoreman. And an idealist. I'm a man with too much brawn to be an intellectual, exclusively. I married a small, sensitive, cultured woman so that my kids would be sissies instead of suckers. A strong man with any sensibility has no choice in this world but to be a heel, or a *worker*. I haven't the heart to be a heel, so I'm a worker. I've got a son in high school who's already thinking of being a writer.

KRUPP. I wanted to be a writer once.

JOE. Wonderful. [*He puts down the paper, looks at* KRUPP *and* MC CARTHY.]

MC CARTHY. They *all* wanted to be writers. Every maniac in the world that ever brought about the murder of people through war started out in an attic or a basement writing poetry. It stank. So they got even by becoming important heels. And it's still going on.

KRUPP. Is it really, Joe?

JOE. Look at today's paper.

MC CARTHY. Right now on Telegraph Hill is some punk who is trying to be Shakespeare. Ten years from now he'll be a senator. Or a communist.

KRUPP. Somebody ought to do something about it.

MC CARTHY [*mischievously, with laughter in his voice*]. The thing to do is to have more magazines. Hundreds of them. *Thousands.* Print everything they write, so they'll believe they're immortal. That way keep them from going haywire.

KRUPP. Mac, you ought to be a writer yourself.

MC CARTHY. I hate the tribe. They're mischief-makers. Right?

JOE [*swiftly*]. Everything's right. Right and wrong.

KRUPP. Then why do you read?

MC CARTHY [*laughing*]. It's relaxing. It's soothing. [*Pause.*] The lousiest people born into the world are writers. Language is all right. It's the people who use language that are lousy. [*The* ARAB *has moved a little closer, and is listening carefully. To the* ARAB.] What do you think, Brother?

ARAB [*after making many faces, thinking very deeply*]. No foundation. All the way down the line. What. What-not. Nothing. I go walk and look at sky. [*He goes.*]

KRUPP. What? What-not? [*To* JOE.] What's that mean?

JOE [*slowly, thinking, remembering*]. What? What-not? That means this side, that side. Inhale, exhale. What: birth. What-not: death. The inevitable, the astounding, the magnificent seed of growth and decay in all things. Beginning, and end. That man, in his own way, is a prophet. He is one who, with the help of *beer,* is able to reach that state of deep understanding in which what and what-not, the reasonable and the unreasonable, are *one.*

MC CARTHY. Right.

KRUPP. If you can understand that kind of talk, how can you be a longshoreman?

MC CARTHY. I come from a long line of McCarthys who

never married or slept with anything but the most powerful and quarrelsome flesh. [*He drinks beer.*]

KRUPP. I could listen to you two guys for hours, but I'll be damned if I know what the hell you're talking about.

MC CARTHY. The consequence is that all the McCarthys are too great and too strong to be heroes. Only the weak and unsure perform the heroic. They've *got* to. The more heroes you have, the worse the history of the world becomes. Right?

JOE. Go outside and look at it.

KRUPP. You sure can philos—philosoph— Boy, you can talk.

MC CARTHY. I wouldn't talk this way to anyone but a man in uniform, and a man who couldn't understand a word of what I was saying. The party I'm speaking of, my friend, is *YOU*.

[*The phone rings.* HARRY *gets up from his table suddenly and begins a new dance.*]

KRUPP [*noticing him, with great authority*]. Here. Here. What do you think you're doing?

HARRY [*stopping*]. I just got an idea for a new dance. I'm trying it out. Nick. Nick, the phone's ringing.

KRUPP [*to* MC CARTHY]. Has he got a right to do that?

MC CARTHY. The living have danced from the beginning of time. I might even say, the dance and the life have moved along together, until now we have— [*To* HARRY.] Go into your dance, son, and show us what we have.

HARRY. I haven't got it worked out *completely* yet, but it starts out like this. [*He dances.*]

NICK [*on phone*]. Nick's Pacific Street Restaurant, Saloon, and Entertainment Palace. Good afternoon. Nick speaking. [*Listens.*] Who? [*Turns around.*] Is there a Dudley Bostwick in the joint?

[DUDLEY *jumps to his feet and goes to phone.*]

DUDLEY [*on phone*]. Hello. Elsie? [*Listens.*] You're coming down? [*Elated. To the saloon.*] She's coming down. [*Pause.*] No. I won't drink. Aw, gosh, Elsie. [*He hangs up, looks about him strangely, as if he were just born, walks around touching things, putting chairs in place, and so on.*]

MC CARTHY [*to* HARRY]. Splendid. Splendid.

HARRY. Then I go into this little routine. [*He demonstrates.*]

KRUPP. Is that good, Mac?

MC CARTHY. It's awful, but it's honest and ambitious, like everything else in this great country.

HARRY. Then I work along into this. [*He demonstrates.*] And *this* is where I *really* get going. [*He finishes the dance.*]

MC CARTHY. Excellent. A most satisfying demonstration of the present state of the American body and soul. Son, you're a genius.

HARRY [*delighted, shaking hands with* MC CARTHY]. I go on in front of an audience for the first time in my life tonight.

MC CARTHY. They'll be delighted. Where'd you learn to dance?

HARRY. Never took a lesson in my life. I'm a natural-born dancer. And *comedian,* too.

MC CARTHY [*astounded*]. You can make people *laugh?*

HARRY [*dumbly*]. I can be funny, but they won't laugh.

MC CARTHY. That's odd. Why not?

HARRY. I don't know. They just won't laugh.

MC CARTHY. Would you care to be funny now?

HARRY. I'd like to try out a new monologue I've been thinking about.

MC CARTHY. Please do. I promise you if it's funny I shall *roar* with laughter.

HARRY. This is it. [*Goes into the act, with much energy.*] I'm up at Sharkey's on Turk Street. It's a quarter to nine, daylight saving. Wednesday, the eleventh. What I've got is a headache and a 1918 nickel. What I *want* is a cup of coffee. If I buy a cup of coffee with the nickel, I've got to walk home. I've got an eight-ball problem. George the Greek is shooting a game of snooker with Pedro the Filipino. *I'm in rags.* They're wearing thirty-five dollar suits, made to order. I haven't got a cigarette. They're smoking Bobby Burns panatelas. I'm thinking it over, like I always do. George the Greek is in a tough spot. If I buy a cup of coffee, I'll want another cup. What happens? My *ear* aches! My ear. George the Greek takes the cue. Chalks it. Studies the table. Touches the cue-ball delicately. Tick. What happens? He makes the three-ball! What do I do? I get confused. *I go out and buy a morning paper.* What the hell do I want with a morning paper? What I *want* is a cup of coffee, and a good used car. I go out and buy a morning paper. Thursday, the twelfth. Maybe the headline's about *me.* I take a quick look. *No. The headline is not about me.* It's about Hitler. Seven thousand miles away. I'm here. Who the hell is Hitler? Who's behind the eight-ball? I turn around. *Everybody's behind the eight-ball!*

[*Pause.* KRUPP *moves toward* HARRY *as if to make an important arrest.* HARRY *moves to the swinging doors.* MC CARTHY *stops* KRUPP.]

MC CARTHY [*to* HARRY]. It's the funniest thing I've ever heard. Or *seen,* for that matter.

HARRY [*coming back to* MC CARTHY]. Then, why don't you laugh?

MC CARTHY. I don't know, *yet.*

HARRY. I'm always getting funny ideas that nobody will laugh at.

MC CARTHY [*thoughtfully*]. It may be that you've stumbled headlong into a new kind of comedy.

HARRY. Well, what good is it if it doesn't make anybody laugh?

MC CARTHY. There are *kinds* of laughter, son. I must say, in all truth, that I *am* laughing, although not *out loud*.

HARRY. I want to *hear* people laugh. *Out loud.* That's why I keep thinking of funny things to say.

MC CARTHY. Well. They may catch on in time. Let's go, Krupp. So long, Joe. [MC CARTHY *and* KRUPP *go.*]

JOE. So long. [*After a moment's pause.*] Hey, Nick.

NICK. Yeah.

JOE. Bet McCarthy in the last race.

NICK. You're crazy. That horse is a double-crossing, no-good—

JOE. Bet everything you've got on McCarthy.

NICK. I'm not betting a nickel on him. *You* bet everything you've got on McCarthy.

JOE. I don't need money.

NICK. What makes you think McCarthy's going to win?

JOE. McCarthy's name's McCarthy, isn't it?

NICK. Yeah. So what?

JOE. The *horse* named McCarthy is going to win, *that's all*. Today.

NICK. Why?

JOE. You do what I tell you, and everything will be all right.

NICK. McCarthy likes to talk, that's all. [*Pause.*] Where's Tom?

JOE. He'll be around. He'll be miserable, but he'll be around. Five or ten minutes more.

NICK. You don't believe that Kitty, do you? About being in burlesque?

JOE [*very clearly*]. I believe dreams sooner than statistics.

NICK [*remembering*]. She sure is somebody. Called me a dentist.

[TOM, *turning about, confused, troubled, comes in, and hurries to* JOE'S *table*.]

JOE. What's the matter?

TOM. Here's your five, Joe. I'm in trouble again.

JOE. If it's not organic, it'll cure itself. If it is organic, science will cure it. What is it, organic or non-organic?

TOM. Joe, I don't know— [*He seems to be completely broken down*.]

JOE. What's eating you? I want you to go on an errand for me.

TOM. It's Kitty.

JOE. What about her?

TOM. She's up in her room, crying.

JOE. Crying?

TOM. Yeah, she's been crying for over an hour. I been talking to her all this time, but she won't stop.

JOE. What's she crying about?

TOM. I don't know. I couldn't understand anything. She kept crying and telling me about a big house and collie dogs all around and flowers and one of her brothers dead and the other one lost somewhere. Joe, I can't stand Kitty crying.

JOE. You want to marry the girl?

TOM [*nodding*]. Yeah.

JOE [*curious and sincere*]. Why?

TOM. I don't know why, exactly, Joe. [*Pause*.] Joe, I don't like to think of Kitty out in the streets. I guess I love her, that's all.

JOE. She's a nice girl.

TOM. She's like an angel. She's not like those other street-walkers.

JOE [*swiftly*]. Here. Take all this money and run next

door to Frankie's and bet it on the nose of Mc-Carthy.

TOM [*swiftly*]. All this money, Joe? McCarthy?

JOE. Yeah. Hurry.

TOM [*going*]. Ah, Joe. If McCarthy wins we'll be rich.

JOE. Get going, will you?

[TOM *runs out and nearly knocks over the* ARAB *coming back in.* NICK *fills him a beer without a word.*]

ARAB. No foundation, anywhere. Whole world. No foundation. All the way down the line.

NICK [*angry*]. McCarthy! Just because you got a little lucky this morning, you have to go to work and throw away eighty bucks.

JOE. He wants to marry her.

NICK. Suppose she doesn't want to marry *him?*

JOE [*amazed*]. Oh, yeah. [*Thinking.*] Now, why wouldn't she want to marry a nice guy like Tom?

NICK. She's been in burlesque. She's had flowers sent to her by European royalty. She's dined with young men of quality and social position. She's above Tom.

[TOM *comes running in.*]

TOM [*disgusted*]. They were running when I got there. Frankie wouldn't take the bet. McCarthy didn't get a call till the stretch. I thought we were going to save all this money. Then McCarthy won by *two* lengths.

JOE. What'd he pay, fifteen to one?

TOM. Better, but Frankie wouldn't take the bet.

NICK [*throwing a dish towel across the room*]. Well, for the love of Mike.

JOE. Give me the money.

TOM [*giving back the money*]. We would have had about a thousand five hundred dollars.

JOE [*bored, casually, inventing*]. Go up to Schwab-acher-Frey and get me the biggest Rand-McNally

map of the nations of Europe they've got. On your
way back stop at one of the pawn shops on Third
Street, and buy me a good revolver and some cartridges.

TOM. She's up in her room crying, Joe.

JOE. Go get me those things.

NICK. What are you going to do, study the map, and
then go out and shoot somebody?

JOE. I want to read the names of some European towns
and rivers and valleys and mountains.

NICK. What do you want with the revolver?

JOE. I want to study it. I'm interested in things. Here's
twenty dollars, Tom. Now go get them things.

TOM. A big map of Europe. And a revolver.

JOE. Get a good one. Tell the man you don't know
anything about firearms and you're trusting him not
to fool you. Don't pay more than ten dollars.

TOM. Joe, you got something on your mind. Don't go
fool with a revolver.

JOE. Be sure it's a good one.

TOM. Joe.

JOE [*irritated*]. What, Tom?

TOM. Joe, what do you send me out for crazy things for
all the time?

JOE [*angry*]. They're not crazy, Tom. Now, get going.

TOM. What about Kitty, Joe?

JOE. Let her cry. It'll do her good.

TOM. If she comes in here while I'm gone, talk to her,
will you, Joe? Tell her about me?

JOE. O. K. Get going. Don't load that gun. Just buy it
and bring it here.

TOM [*going*]. You won't catch me loading any gun.

JOE. Wait a minute. Take these toys away.

TOM. Where'll I take them?

JOE. Give them to some kid. [*Pause.*] No. Take them

up to Kitty. Toys stopped me from crying once. That's the reason I had you buy them. I wanted to see if I could find out *why* they stopped me from crying. I remember they seemed awfully stupid at the time.

TOM. Shall I, Joe? Take them up to Kitty? Do you think they'd stop *her* from crying?

JOE. They might. You get curious about the way they work and you forget whatever it is you're remembering that's making you cry. That's what they're for.

TOM. Yeah. Sure. The girl at the store asked me what I wanted with toys. I'll take them up to Kitty. [*Tragically.*] She's like a little girl. [*He goes.*]

WESLEY. Mr. Nick, can I play the piano again?

NICK. Sure. Practice all you like—until I tell you to stop.

WESLEY. You going to pay me for playing the piano?

NICK. Sure. I'll give you enough to get by on.

WESLEY [*amazed and delighted*]. Get money for playing the piano? [*He goes to the piano and begins to play quietly.* HARRY *goes up on the little stage and listens to the music. After a while he begins a soft-shoe dance.*]

NICK. What were you crying about?

JOE. My mother.

NICK. What about her?

JOE. She was dead. I stopped crying when they gave me the toys.

[NICK'S MOTHER, *a little old woman of sixty or so, dressed plainly in black, her face shining, comes in briskly, chattering loudly in Italian, gesturing.* NICK *is delighted to see her.*]

NICK'S MOTHER [*in Italian*]. Everything all right, Nickie?

NICK [*in Italian*]. Sure, Mamma.

[NICK'S MOTHER *leaves as gaily and as noisily as she came, after half a minute of loud Italian family talk.*]

JOE. Who was that?

NICK [*to* JOE, *proudly and a little sadly*]. My mother. [*Still looking at the swinging doors.*]

JOE. What'd she say?

NICK. Nothing. Just wanted to see me. [*Pause.*] What do you want with that gun?

JOE. I study things, Nick.

[*An* OLD MAN *who looks as if he might have been Kit Carson at one time walks in importantly, moves about, and finally stands at* JOE'S *table.*]

KIT CARSON. Murphy's the name. Just an old trapper. Mind if I sit down?

JOE. Be delighted. What'll you drink?

KIT CARSON [*sitting down*]. Beer. Same as I've been drinking. And thanks.

JOE [*to* NICK]. Glass of beer, Nick.

[NICK *brings the beer to the table,* KIT CARSON *swallows it in one swig, wipes his big white mustache with the back of his right hand.*]

KIT CARSON [*moving in*]. I don't suppose you ever fell in love with a midget weighing thirty-nine pounds?

JOE [*studying the man*]. Can't say I have, but have another beer.

KIT CARSON [*intimately*]. Thanks, thanks. Down in Gallup, twenty years ago. Fellow by the name of Rufus Jenkins came to town with six white horses and two black ones. Said he wanted a man to break the horses for him because his left leg was wood and he couldn't do it. Had a meeting at Parker's Mercantile Store and finally came to blows, me and Henry Walpal. Bashed his head with a brass cuspidor and ran away to Mexico, but he didn't die. Couldn't speak a word. Took up with a cattle-breeder named Diego,

educated in California. Spoke the language better
than you and me. Said, Your job, Murph, is to feed
them prize bulls. I said, Fine, what'll I feed them?
He said, Hay, lettuce, salt, beer, and aspirin. Came
to blows two days later over an accordion he claimed
I stole. I had *borrowed* it. During the fight I busted
it over his head; ruined one of the finest accordions
I ever saw. Grabbed a horse and rode back across
the border.. Texas. Got to talking with a fellow who
looked honest. Turned out to be a Ranger who was
looking for me.

JOE. Yeah. You were saying, a thirty-nine-pound
midget.

KIT CARSON. Will I ever forget that lady? Will I ever
get over that amazon of small proportions?

JOE. Will you?

KIT CARSON. If I live to be sixty.

JOE. Sixty? You look more than sixty now.

KIT CARSON. That's trouble showing in my face. Trouble and complications. I was fifty-eight three months
ago.

JOE. That accounts for it, then. Go ahead, tell me
more.

KIT CARSON. Told the Texas Ranger my name was
Rothstein, mining engineer from Pennsylvania,
looking for something worth while. Mentioned two
places in Houston. Nearly lost an eye early one
morning, going down the stairs. Ran into a six-
footer with an iron claw where his right hand was
supposed to be. Said, You broke up my home. Told
him I was a stranger in Houston. The girls gathered
at the top of the stairs to see a fight. Seven of them.
Six feet and an iron claw. That's bad on the nerves.
Kicked him in the mouth when he swung for my
head with the claw. Would have lost an eye except
for quick thinking. He rolled into the gutter and

pulled a gun. Fired seven times. I was back upstairs. Left the place an hour later, dressed in silk and feathers, with a hat swung around over my face. Saw him standing on the corner, waiting. Said, Care for a wiggle? Said he didn't. I went on down the street and left town. I don't suppose you ever had to put a dress on to save your skin, did you?

JOE. No, and I never fell in love with a midget weighing thirty-nine pounds. Have another beer?

KIT CARSON. Thanks. [*Swallows glass of beer.*] Ever try to herd cattle on a bicycle?

JOE. No. I never got around to that.

KIT CARSON. Left Houston with sixty cents in my pocket, gift of a girl named Lucinda. Walked fourteen miles in fourteen hours. Big house with barbwire all around, and big dogs. One thing I never could get around. Walked past the gate, anyway, from hunger and thirst. Dogs jumped up and came for me. Walked right into them, growing older every second. Went up to the door and knocked. Big Negress opened the door, closed it quick. Said, On your way, white trash. Knocked again. Said, On your way. Again. On your way. Again. This time the old man himself opened the door, ninety, if he was a day. Sawed-off shotgun, too. Said, I ain't looking for trouble, Father. I'm hungry and thirsty, name's Cavanaugh. Took me in and made mint juleps for the two of us. Said, Living here alone, Father? Said, Drink and ask no questions. Maybe I am and maybe I ain't. You saw the lady. Draw your own conclusions. I'd heard of that, but didn't wink out of tact. If I told you that old Southern gentleman was my grandfather, you wouldn't believe me, would you?

JOE. I might.

KIT CARSON. Well, it so happens he wasn't. Would have been romantic if he had been, though.

JOE. Where did you herd cattle on a bicycle?

KIT CARSON. Toledo, Ohio, 1918.

JOE. Toledo, Ohio? They don't herd cattle in Toledo.

KIT CARSON. They don't any more. They did in 1918. One fellow did, leastaways. Bookkeeper named Sam Gold. Straight from the East Side, New York. Sombrero, lariats, Bull Durham, two head of cattle and two bicycles. Called his place The Gold Bar Ranch, two acres, just outside the city limits. That was the year of the War, you'll remember.

JOE. Yeah, I remember, but how about herding them two cows on a bicycle? How'd you do it?

KIT CARSON. Easiest thing in the world. Rode no hands. Had to, otherwise couldn't lasso the cows. Worked for Sam Gold till the cows ran away. Bicycles scared them. They went into Toledo. Never saw hide nor hair of them again. Advertised in every paper, but never got them back. Broke his heart. Sold both bikes and returned to New York. Took four aces from a deck of red cards and walked to town. Poker. Fellow in the game named Chuck Collins, liked to gamble. Told him with a smile I didn't suppose he'd care to bet a hundred dollars I wouldn't hold four aces the next hand. Called it. My cards were red on the blank side. The other cards were blue. Plumb forgot all about it. Showed him four aces. Ace of spades, ace of clubs, ace of diamonds, ace of hearts. I'll remember them four cards if I live to be sixty. Would have been killed on the spot except for the hurricane that year.

JOE. Hurricane?

KIT CARSON. You haven't forgotten the Toledo hurricane of 1918, have you?

JOE. No. There was no hurricane in Toledo in 1918, or any other year.

KIT CARSON. For the love of God, then what do you suppose that commotion was? And how come I came to in Chicago, dream-walking down State Street?

JOE. I guess they scared you.

KIT CARSON. No, that wasn't it. You go back to the papers of November 1918, and I think you'll find there was a hurricane in Toledo. I remember sitting on the roof of a two-story house, floating northwest.

JOE [*seriously*]. Northwest?

KIT CARSON. Now, son, don't tell me *you* don't believe me, either?

JOE [*pause. Very seriously, energetically and sharply*]. Of course I believe you. Living is an art. It's not bookkeeping. It takes a lot of rehearsing for a man to get to be himself.

KIT CARSON [*thoughtfully, smiling, and amazed*]. You're the first man I've ever met who believes me.

JOE [*seriously*]. Have another beer.

[TOM *comes in with the Rand-McNally book, the revolver, and the box of cartridges.* KIT *goes to bar.*]

JOE [*to* TOM]. Did you give her the toys?

TOM. Yeah, I gave them to her.

JOE. Did she stop crying?

TOM. No. She started crying harder than ever.

JOE. That's funny. I wonder why.

TOM. Joe, if I was a minute earlier, Frankie would have taken the bet and now we'd have about a thousand five hundred dollars. How much of it would you have given me, Joe?

JOE. If she'd marry you—*all* of it.

TOM. Would you, Joe?

JOE [*opening packages, examining book first, and revolver next*]. Sure. In this realm there's only one subject, and you're it. It's my duty to see that my subject is happy.

TOM. Joe, do you think we'll ever have eighty dollars for a race sometime again when there's a fifteen-to-one shot that we like, weather good, track fast, they get off to a good start, our horse doesn't get a call till the stretch, we think we're going to lose all that money, and then it wins, by a nose?

JOE. I didn't quite get that.

TOM. You know what I mean.

JOE. You mean the impossible. No, Tom, we won't. We were just a little late, that's all.

TOM. We might, Joe.

JOE. It's not likely.

TOM. Then how am I ever going to make enough money to marry her?

JOE. I don't know, Tom. Maybe you aren't.

TOM. Joe, I got to marry Kitty. [*Shaking his head.*] You ought to see the crazy room she lives in.

JOE. What kind of a room is it?

TOM. It's little. It crowds you in. It's bad, Joe. Kitty don't belong in a place like that.

JOE. You want to take her away from there?

TOM. Yeah. I want her to live in a house where there's room enough to live. Kitty ought to have a garden, or something.

JOE. You want to take care of her?

TOM. Yeah, sure, Joe. I ought to take care of somebody good that makes me feel like *I'm* somebody.

JOE. That means you'll have to get a job. What can you do?

TOM. I finished high school, but I don't know what I can do.

JOE. Sometimes when you think about it, what do you think you'd like to do?

TOM. Just sit around like you, Joe, and have somebody run errands for me and drink champagne and take things easy and never be broke and never worry about money.

JOE. That's a noble ambition.

NICK [*to* JOE]. How do you do it?

JOE. I really don't know, but I think you've got to have the full co-operation of the Good Lord.

NICK. I can't understand the way you talk.

TOM. Joe, shall I go back and see if I can get her to stop crying?

JOE. Give me a hand and I'll go with you.

TOM [*amazed*]. What! You're going to get up already?

JOE. She's crying, isn't she?

TOM. She's crying. Worse than ever now.

JOE. I thought the toys would stop her.

TOM. I've seen you sit in one place from four in the morning till two the next morning.

JOE. At my best, Tom, I don't travel by foot. That's all. Come on. Give me a hand. I'll find some way to stop her from crying.

TOM [*helping* JOE]. Joe, I never did tell you. You're a different kind of a guy.

JOE [*swiftly, a little angry*]. Don't be silly. I don't understand things. I'm trying to understand them.

[JOE *is a little drunk. They go out together. The lights go down slowly, while* WESLEY *plays the piano, and come up slowly on.*]

Act three

A cheap bed in NICK's *to indicate room 21 of The New York Hotel, upstairs, around the corner from* NICK's. *The bed can be at the center of* NICK's, *or up on the little stage. Everything in* NICK's *is the same, except that all the people are silent, immobile and in darkness, except* WESLEY *who is playing the piano softly and sadly.* KITTY DUVAL, *in a dress she has carried around with her from the early days in Ohio, is seated on the bed, tying a ribbon in her hair. She looks at herself in a hand mirror. She is deeply grieved at the change she sees in herself. She takes off the ribbon, angry and hurt. She lifts a book from the bed and tries to read. She begins to sob again. She picks up an old picture of herself and looks at it. Sobs harder than ever, falling on the bed and burying her face. There is a knock, as if at the door.*

KITTY [*sobbing*]. Who is it?

TOM'S VOICE. Kitty, it's me. Tom. Me and Joe.

[JOE, *followed by* TOM, *comes to the bed quietly.* JOE *is holding a rather large toy carousel.* JOE *studies* KITTY *a moment. He sets the toy carousel on the floor, at the foot of* KITTY'S *bed.*]

TOM [*standing over* KITTY *and bending down close to her*]. Don't cry any more, Kitty.

KITTY [*not looking, sobbing*]. I don't like this life.

[JOE *starts the carousel which makes a strange, sorrowful, tinkling music. The music begins slowly, becomes swift, gradually slows down, and ends.* JOE *himself is interested in the toy, watches and listens to it carefully.*]

TOM [*eagerly*]. Kitty. Joe got up from his chair at Nick's just to get you a toy and come here. This one makes music. We rode all over town in a cab to get it. Listen.

[KITTY *sits up slowly, listening, while* TOM *watches her. Everything happens slowly and somberly.* KITTY *notices the photograph of herself when she was a little girl. Lifts it, and looks at it again.*]

TOM [*looking*]. Who's that little girl, Kitty?

KITTY. That's me. When I was seven.

TOM [*looking, smiling*]. Gee, you're pretty, Kitty.

[JOE *reaches up for the photograph, which* TOM *hands*

to him. TOM *returns to* KITTY *whom he finds as pretty now as she was at seven.* JOE *studies the photograph.* KITTY *looks up at* TOM. *There is no doubt that they really love one another.* JOE *looks up at them.*]

KITTY. Tom?

TOM [*eagerly*]. Yeah, Kitty.

KITTY. Tom, when you were a little boy what did you want to be?

TOM [*a little bewildered, but eager to please her*]. What, Kitty?

KITTY. Do you remember when you were a little boy?

TOM [*thoughtfully*]. Yeah, I remember sometimes, Kitty.

KITTY. What did you want to be?

TOM [*looks at* JOE. JOE *holds* TOM'S *eyes a moment. Then* TOM *is able to speak*]. Sometimes I wanted to be a locomotive engineer. Sometimes I wanted to be a policeman.

KITTY. I wanted to be a great actress. [*She looks up into* TOM'S *face.*] Tom, didn't you ever want to be a doctor?

TOM [*looks at* JOE. JOE *holds* TOM'S *eyes again, encouraging* TOM *by his serious expression to go on talking*]. Yeah, now I remember. Sure, Kitty. I wanted to be a doctor—once.

KITTY [*smiling sadly*]. I'm so glad. Because I wanted to be an actress and have a young doctor come to the theater and see me and fall in love with me and send me flowers.

[JOE *pantomimes to* TOM, *demanding that he go on talking.*]

TOM. I would do that, Kitty.

KITTY. I wouldn't know who it was, and then one day I'd see him in the street and fall in love with him. I wouldn't know *he* was the one who was in love with

me. I'd think about him all the time. I'd dream
about him. I'd dream of being near him the rest of
my life. I'd dream of having children that looked
like him. I wouldn't be an actress all the time. Only
until I found him and fell in love with him. After
that we'd take a train and go to beautiful cities and
see the wonderful people everywhere and give
money to the poor and whenever people were sick
he'd go to them and make them well again.

[TOM *looks at* JOE, *bewildered, confused, and full of
sorrow.* KITTY *is deep in memory, almost in a trance.*]

JOE [*gently*]. Talk to her, Tom. Be the wonderful
young doctor she dreamed about and never found.
Go ahead. Correct the errors of the world.

TOM. Joe. [*Pathetically.*] I don't know what to say.

[*There is rowdy singing in the hall. A loud young*
VOICE *sings: "Sailing, sailing, over the bounding
main."*]

VOICE. Kitty. Oh, Kitty! [KITTY *stirs, shocked, coming
out of the trance.*] Where the hell are you? Oh,
Kitty.

[TOM *jumps up, furiously.*]

WOMAN'S VOICE [*in the hall*]. Who are you looking for,
Sailor Boy?

VOICE. The most beautiful lay in the world.

WOMAN'S VOICE. Don't go any further.

VOICE [*with impersonal contempt*]. You? No. Not you.
Kitty. You stink.

WOMAN'S VOICE [*rasping, angry*]. Don't you dare to talk
to me that way. You pickpocket.

VOICE [*still impersonal, but louder*]. Oh, I see. Want
to get tough, hey? Close the door. Go hide.

WOMAN'S VOICE. You pickpocket. All of you. [*The door
slams.*]

VOICE [*roaring with laughter which is very sad*]. Oh—
Kitty. Room 21. Where the hell is that room?

TOM [*to* JOE]. Joe, I'll kill him.

KITTY [*fully herself again, terribly frightened*]. Who is it?

[*She looks long and steadily at* TOM *and* JOE. TOM *is standing, excited and angry.* JOE *is completely at ease, his expression full of pity.* KITTY *buries her face in the bed.*]

JOE [*gently*]. Tom. Just take him away.

VOICE. Here it is. Number 21. Three naturals. Heaven. My blue heaven. The west, a nest, and you. Just Molly and me. [*Tragically.*] Ah, to hell with everything.

[*A young* SAILOR, *a good-looking boy of no more than twenty or so, who is only drunk and lonely, comes to the bed, singing sadly.*]

SAILOR. Hi-ya, Kitty. [*Pause.*] Oh. Visitors. Sorry. A thousand apologies. [*To* KITTY.] I'll come back later.

TOM [*taking him by the shoulders, furiously*]. If you do, I'll kill you.

[JOE *holds* TOM. TOM *pushes the frightened boy away.*]

JOE [*somberly*]. Tom. You stay here with Kitty. I'm going down to Union Square to hire an automobile. I'll be back in a few minutes. We'll ride out to the ocean and watch the sun go down. Then we'll ride down the Great Highway to Half Moon Bay. We'll have supper down there, and you and Kitty can dance.

TOM [*stupefied, unable to express his amazement and gratitude*]. Joe, you mean, you're going to go on an errand for *me*? You mean you're not going to send me?

JOE. That's right. [*He gestures toward* KITTY, *indicating that* TOM *shall talk to her, protect the innocence in her which is in so much danger when* TOM *isn't near, which* TOM *loves so deeply.* JOE *leaves.* TOM *studies* KITTY, *his face becoming childlike and som-*

ber. *He sets the carousel into motion, listens, watching* KITTY, *who lifts herself slowly, looking only at* TOM. TOM *lifts the turning carousel and moves it slowly toward* KITTY, *as though the toy were his heart. The piano music comes up loudly and the lights go down, while* HARRY *is heard dancing swiftly.*]

BLACKOUT

Act four

A little later.

WESLEY, *the colored boy, is at the piano.*

HARRY *is on the little stage, dancing.*

NICK *is behind the bar.*

The ARAB *is in his place.*

KIT CARSON *is asleep on his folded arms.*

The DRUNKARD *comes in. Goes to the telephone for the nickel that might be in the return-chute.* NICK *comes to take him out. He gestures for* NICK *to hold on a minute. Then produces a half dollar.* NICK *goes behind the bar to serve the* DRUNKARD *whiskey.*

THE DRUNKARD. To the old, God bless them. [*Another.*] To the new, God love them. [*Another.*] To—children and small animals, like little dogs that don't bite. [*Another. Loudly.*] To reforestation. [*Searches for money. Finds some.*] To—President Taft. [*He goes out. The telephone rings.*]

KIT CARSON [*jumping up, fighting*]. Come on, *all* of you, if you're looking for trouble. I never asked for quarter and I always gave it.

NICK [*reproachfully*]. Hey, Kit Carson.

DUDLEY [*on the phone*]. Hello. Who? Nick? Yes. He's here. [*To* NICK.] It's for you. I think it's important.

NICK [*going to the phone*]. Important! *What's* important?

DUDLEY. He sounded like a big-shot.

NICK. Big *what?* [*To* WESLEY *and* HARRY.] Hey, you. Quiet. I want to hear this important stuff.

[WESLEY *stops playing the piano*. HARRY *stops dancing*. KIT CARSON *comes close to* NICK.]

KIT CARSON. If there's anything I can do, name it. I'll do it for you. I'm fifty-eight years old; been through three wars; married four times; the father of countless children whose *names* I don't even know. I've got no money. I live from hand to mouth. But if there's anything I can do, name it. I'll do it.

NICK [*patiently*]. Listen, Pop. For a moment, please sit down and go back to sleep—*for me.*

KIT CARSON. I can do that, too. [*He sits down, folds his arms, and puts his head into them. But not for long. As* NICK *begins to talk, he listens carefully, gets to his feet, and then begins to express in pantomime the moods of each of* NICK's *remarks.*]

NICK [*on phone*]. Yeah? [*Pause.*] Who? Oh, I see. [*Listens.*] Why don't you leave them alone? [*Listens.*] The church-people? Well, to hell with the church-people. I'm a Catholic myself. [*Listens.*] All right. I'll send them away. I'll tell them to lay low for a couple of days. Yeah, I know how it is. [NICK's *daughter* ANNA *comes in shyly, looking at her father, and stands unnoticed by the piano.*] What? [*Very angry.*] Listen. I don't like that Blick. He was here this morning, and I told him not to come back. I'll keep the girls out of here. You keep Blick out of here. [*Listens.*] I know his brother-in-law is important, but I don't want him to come down here.

He looks for trouble everywhere, and he always finds it. I don't break any laws. I've got a dive in the lousiest part of town. Five years nobody's been robbed, murdered or gypped. I leave people alone. Your swanky joints uptown make trouble for you every night. [NICK *gestures to* WESLEY—*keeps listening on the phone—puts his hand over the mouthpiece. To* WESLEY *and* HARRY.] Start playing again. My ears have got a headache. Go into your dance, son. [WESLEY *begins to play again.* HARRY *begins to dance.* NICK *into mouthpiece.*] Yeah. I'll keep them out. Just see that Blick doesn't come around and start something. [*Pause.*] O.K. [*He hangs up.*]

KIT CARSON. Trouble coming?

NICK. That lousy Vice Squad again. It's that gorilla Blick.

KIT CARSON. Anybody at all. You can count on me. What kind of a gorilla is this gorilla Blick?

NICK. Very dignified. Toenails on his fingers.

ANNA [*to* KIT CARSON, *with great, warm, beautiful pride, pointing at* NICK]. That's my father.

KIT CARSON [*leaping with amazement at the beautiful voice, the wondrous face, the magnificent event*]. Well, bless your heart, child. Bless your lovely heart. I had a little daughter point me out in a crowd once.

NICK [*surprised*]. Anna. What the hell are you doing here? Get back home where you belong and help Grandma cook me some supper. [ANNA *smiles at her father, understanding him, knowing that his words are words of love. She turns and goes, looking at him all the way out, as much as to say that she would cook for him the rest of her life.* NICK *stares at the swinging doors.* KIT CARSON *moves toward them, two or three steps.* ANNA *pushes open one of the doors and peeks in, to look at her father again. She waves to him. Turns and runs.* NICK *is very sad.*

*He doesn't know what to do. He gets a glass and a
bottle. Pours himself a drink. Swallows some. It
isn't enough, so he pours more and swallows the
whole drink. To himself.*] My beautiful, beautiful
baby. Anna, she is you again. [*He brings out a handkerchief, touches his eyes, and blows his nose.* KIT
CARSON *moves close to* NICK, *watching* NICK'S *face.*
NICK *looks at him. Loudly, almost making* KIT *jump.*]
You're broke, aren't you?

KIT CARSON. Always. Always.

NICK. All right. Go into the kitchen and give Sam a
hand. Eat some food and when you come back you
can have a couple of beers.

KIT CARSON [*studying* NICK]. Anything at all. I know a
good man when I see one. [*He goes.*]

[ELSIE MANDELSPIEGEL *comes into* NICK'S. *She is a beautiful, dark girl, with a sorrowful, wise, dreaming
face, almost on the verge of tears, and full of pity.
There is an aura of dream about her. She moves
softly and gently, as if everything around her were
unreal and pathetic.* DUDLEY *doesn't notice her for
a moment or two. When he does finally see her, he
is so amazed, he can barely move or speak. Her presence has the effect of changing him completely. He
gets up from his chair, as if in a trance, and walks
toward her, smiling sadly.*]

ELSIE [*looking at him*]. Hello, Dudley.

DUDLEY [*broken-hearted*]. Elsie.

ELSIE. I'm sorry. [*Explaining.*] So many people are sick.
Last night a little boy died. I love you, but— [*She
gestures, trying to indicate how hopeless love is.
They sit down.*]

DUDLEY [*staring at her, stunned and quieted*]. Elsie.
You'll never know how glad I am to see you. Just
to see you. [*Pathetically.*] I was afraid I'd never see

you again. It was driving me crazy. I didn't want to live. Honest. [*He shakes his head mournfully; with dumb and beautiful affection.* TWO STREETWALKERS *come in, and pause near* DUDLEY, *at the bar.*] I know. You told me before, but I can't help it, Elsie, I love you.

ELSIE [*quietly, somberly, gently, with great compassion*]. I know you love me, and I love you, but don't you see love is impossible in this world?

DUDLEY. Maybe it isn't, Elsie.

ELSIE. Love is for birds. They have wings to fly away on when it's time for flying. For tigers in the jungle because they don't know their end. We know *our* end. Every night I watch over poor, dying men. I hear them breathing, crying, talking in their sleep. Crying for air and water and love, for mother and field and sunlight. We can never know love or greatness. We *should* know both.

DUDLEY [*deeply moved by her words*]. Elsie, I love you.

ELSIE. You want to live. *I* want to live, too, but where? Where can we escape our poor world?

DUDLEY. Elsie, we'll find a place.

ELSIE [*smiling at him*]. All right. We'll try again. We'll go together to a room in a cheap hotel, and dream that the world is beautiful, and that living is full of love and greatness. But in the morning, can we forget debts, and duties, and the cost of ridiculous things?

DUDLEY [*with blind faith*]. Sure, we can, Elsie.

ELSIE. All right, Dudley. Of course. Come on. The time for the new pathetic war has come. Let's hurry, before they dress you, stand you in line, hand you a gun, and have you kill and be killed. [ELSIE *looks at him gently, and takes his hand.* DUDLEY *embraces her shyly, as if he might hurt her. They go, as if*

*they were a couple of young animals. There is a
moment of silence. One of the* STREETWALKERS *bursts
out laughing.*]

KILLER. Nick, what the hell kind of a joint are you
running?

NICK. Well, it's not out of the world. It's on a street in
a city, and people come and go. They bring whatever they've got with them and they say what they
must say.

THE OTHER STREETWALKER. It's floozies like her that
raise hell with our racket.

NICK [*remembering*]. Oh, yeah. Finnegan telephoned.

KILLER. That mouse in elephant's body?

THE OTHER STREETWALKER. What the hell does *he* want?

NICK. Spend your time at the movies for the next couple of days.

KILLER. They're all lousy. [*Mocking.*] All about love.

NICK. Lousy or not lousy, for a couple of days the flat-
foots are going to be romancing you, so stay out of
here, and lay low.

KILLER. I always was a pushover for a man in uniform,
with a badge, a club and a gun.

[KRUPP *comes into the place. The girls put down their
drinks.*]

NICK. O.K., get going.

[*The* GIRLS *begin to leave and meet* KRUPP.]

THE OTHER STREETWALKER. We was just going.

KILLER. We was formerly models at Magnin's. [*They
go.*]

KRUPP [*at the bar*]. The strike isn't enough, so they've
got to put us on the tails of the girls, too. I don't
know. I wish to God I was back in the Sunset holding the hands of kids going home from school, where
I belong. I don't like trouble. Give me a beer. [NICK
gives him a beer. He drinks some.] Right now, Mc-
Carthy, my best friend, is with sixty strikers who

want to stop the finks who are going to try to unload the *Mary Luckenbach* tonight. Why the hell McCarthy ever became a longshoreman instead of a professor of some kind is something I'll never know.

NICK. Cowboys and Indians, cops and robbers, longshoremen and finks.

KRUPP. They're all guys who are trying to be happy; trying to make a living; support a family; bring up children; enjoy sleep. Go to a movie; take a drive on Sunday. They're all good guys, so out of nowhere comes trouble. All they want is a chance to get out of debt and relax in front of a radio while Amos and Andy go through their act. What the hell do they always want to make trouble for? I been thinking everything over, Nick, and you know what I think?

NICK. No. What?

KRUPP. I think we're all crazy. It came to me while I was on my way to Pier 27. All of a sudden it hit me like a ton of bricks. A thing like that never happened to me before. Here we are in this wonderful world, full of all the wonderful things—here we are —all of us, and look at us. Just look at us. We're crazy. We're nuts. We've got everything, but we always feel lousy and dissatisfied just the same.

NICK. Of course we're crazy. Even so, we've got to go on living together. [*He waves at the people in his joint.*]

KRUPP. There's no hope. I don't suppose it's right for an officer of the law to feel the way I feel, but, by God, right or not right, that's how I feel. Why are we all so lousy? This is a good world. It's wonderful to get up in the morning and go out for a little walk and smell the trees and see the streets and the kids going to school and the clouds in the sky. It's wonderful just to be able to move around and whistle a song if you feel like it, or maybe try to sing one. This is a nice world. So why do they make all the trouble?

NICK. I don't know. Why?

KRUPP. We're crazy, that's why. We're no good any more. All the corruption everywhere. The poor kids selling themselves. A couple of years ago they were in grammar school. Everybody trying to get a lot of money in a hurry. Everybody betting the horses. Nobody going quietly for a little walk to the ocean. Nobody taking things easy and not wanting to make some kind of a killing. Nick, I'm going to quit being a cop. Let somebody else keep law and order. The stuff I hear about at headquarters. I'm thirty-seven years old, and I still can't get used to it. The only trouble is, the wife'll raise hell.

NICK. Ah, the wife.

KRUPP. She's a wonderful woman, Nick. We've got two of the swellest boys in the world. Twelve and seven years old.

[*The* ARAB *gets up and moves closer to listen.*]

NICK. I didn't know that.

KRUPP. Sure. But what'll I do? I've wanted to quit for seven years. I wanted to quit the day they began putting me through the school. I didn't quit. What'll I do if I quit? Where's money going to be coming in from?

NICK. That's one of the reasons we're all crazy. We don't know where it's going to be coming in from, except from wherever it happens to be coming in from at the time, which we don't usually like.

KRUPP. Every once in a while I catch myself being mean, hating people just because they're down and out, broke and hungry, sick or drunk. And then when I'm with the stuffed shirts at headquarters, all of a sudden I'm nice to them, trying to make an impression. On who? People I don't like. And I feel disgusted. [*With finality.*] I'm going to quit. That's all. Quit. Out. I'm going to give them back the uniform and the gadgets that go with it. I don't want any part of it. This is a good world. What do they want to make all the trouble for all the time?

ARAB [*quietly, gently, with great understanding*]. No foundation. All the way down the line.

KRUPP. What?

ARAB. No foundation. No foundation.

KRUPP. I'll say there's no foundation.

ARAB. All the way down the line.

KRUPP [*to* NICK]. Is that all he ever says?

NICK. That's all he's been saying *this* week.

KRUPP. What is he, anyway?

NICK. He's an Arab, or something like that.

KRUPP. No, I mean what's he do for a living?

NICK [*to* ARAB]. What do you do for a living, brother?

ARAB. Work. Work all my life. All my life, work. From small boy to old man, work. In old country, work. In new country, work. In New York. Pittsburgh. Detroit. Chicago. Imperial Valley. San Francisco. Work. No beg. Work. For what? Nothing. Three boys in old country. Twenty years, not see. Lost. Dead. Who knows? What. What-not. No foundation. All the way down the line.

KRUPP. What'd he say last week?

NICK. Didn't say anything. Played the harmonica.

ARAB. Old country song, I play. [*He brings a harmonica from his back pocket.*]

KRUPP. Seems like a nice guy.

NICK. Nicest guy in the world.

KRUPP [*bitterly*]. But crazy. Just like all the rest of us. Stark raving mad.

[WESLEY *and* HARRY *long ago stopped playing and dancing. They sat at a table together and talked for a while; then began playing casino or rummy. When the* ARAB *begins his solo on the harmonica, they stop their game to listen.*]

WESLEY. You hear that?

HARRY. That's *something*.

WESLEY. That's crying. That's crying.

HARRY. I want to make people laugh.

WESLEY. That's deep, deep crying. That's crying a long time ago. That's crying a thousand years ago. Some place five thousand miles away.

HARRY. Do you think you can play to that?

WESLEY. I want to *sing* to that, but I can't *sing*.

HARRY. You try and play to that. I'll try to dance.

[WESLEY *goes to the piano, and after closer listening, he begins to accompany the harmonica solo.* HARRY *goes to the little stage and after a few efforts begins to dance to the song. This keeps up quietly for some time.* KRUPP *and* NICK *have been silent, and deeply moved.*]

KRUPP [*softly*]. Well, anyhow, Nick.

NICK. Hmmmmmmm?

KRUPP. What I said. Forget it.

NICK. Sure.

KRUPP. It gets me down once in a while.

NICK. No harm in talking.

KRUPP [*the* POLICEMAN *again, loudly*]. Keep the girls out of here.

NICK [*loud and friendly*]. Take it easy.

[*The music and dancing are now at their height.*]

CURTAIN

Act five

That evening. Fog-horns are heard throughout the scene. A MAN *in evening clothes and a top hat, and his* WOMAN, *also in evening clothes, are entering.*

WILLIE *is still at the marble game.* NICK *is behind the bar.* JOE *is at his table, looking at the book of maps of the countries of Europe. The box containing the revolver and the box containing the cartridges are on the table, beside his glass. He is at peace, his hat tilted back on his head, a calm expression on his face.* TOM *is leaning against the bar, dreaming of love and* KITTY. *The* ARAB *is gone.* WESLEY *and* HARRY *are gone.* KIT CARSON *is watching the* BOY *at the marble game.*

LADY. Oh, come on, please.

[*The* GENTLEMAN *follows miserably. The* SOCIETY MAN *and* WIFE *take a table.* NICK *gives them a menu. Outside, in the street, the Salvation Army people are playing a song. Big drum, tambourines, cornet and singing. They are singing "The Blood of the Lamb." The music and words come into the place faintly and comically. This is followed by an old sinner testifying. It is the* DRUNKARD. *His words are not intelligible, but his message is unmistakable. He is saved. He wants to sin no more. And so on.*]

DRUNKARD [*testifying, unmistakably drunk*]. Brothers and sisters. I was a sinner. I chewed tobacco and chased women. Oh, I sinned, brothers and sisters. And then I was saved. Saved by the Salvation Army, God forgive me.

JOE. Let's see now. Here's a city. Pribor. Czechoslo-

vakia. Little, lovely, lonely Czechoslovakia. I wonder what kind of a place Pribor was? [*Calling.*] Pribor! *Pribor!*

[TOM *leaps.*]

LADY. What's the matter with him?

MAN [*crossing his legs, as if he ought to go to the men's
room*]. Drunk.

TOM. Who you calling, Joe?

JOE. Pribor.

TOM. Who's Pribor?

JOE. He's a Czech. And a Slav. A Czechoslovakian.

LADY. How interesting.

MAN [*uncrosses legs*]. He's drunk.

JOE. Tom, Pribor's a city in Czechoslovakia.

TOM. Oh. [*Pause.*] You sure were nice to her, Joe.

JOE. Kitty Duval? She's one of the finest people in the
world.

TOM. It sure was nice of you to hire an automobile and
take us for a drive along the ocean front and down
to Half Moon Bay.

JOE. Those three hours were the most delightful, the
most somber, and the most beautiful I have ever
known.

TOM. Why, Joe?

JOE. Why? I'm a student. [*Lifting his voice.*] Tom.
[*Quietly.*] I'm a student. I study all things. All. All.
And when my study reveals something of beauty in
a place or in a person where by all rights only ugliness or death should be revealed, then I know how
full of goodness this life is. And that's a good thing
to know. That's a truth I shall always seek to verify.

LADY. Are you *sure* he's drunk?

MAN [*crossing his legs*]. He's either drunk, or just naturally crazy.

TOM. Joe?

JOE. Yeah.

TOM. You won't get sore or anything?

JOE [*impatiently*]. What is it, Tom?

TOM. Joe, where do you get all that money? You paid
for the automobile. You paid for supper and the two
bottles of champagne at the Half Moon Bay Restaurant. You moved Kitty out of the New York
Hotel around the corner to the St. Francis Hotel on
Powell Street. I saw you pay her rent. I saw you
give her money for new clothes. Where do you get
all that money, Joe? Three years now and I've never
asked.

JOE [*looking at* TOM *sorrowfully, a little irritated, not
so much with* TOM *as with the world and himself, his
own superiority. He speaks clearly, slowly and solemnly*]. Now don't be a fool, Tom. Listen carefully.
If anybody's got any money—to hoard or to throw
away—you can be sure he stole it from other people.
Not from rich people who can spare it, but from
poor people who can't. From their lives and from
their dreams. I'm no exception. I *earned* the money
I throw away. I stole it like everybody else does. I
hurt people to get it. Loafing around this way, I
still earn money. The money itself earns *more*. I *still*
hurt people. I don't know who they are, or where
they are. If I did, I'd feel worse than I do. I've got a
Christian conscience in a world that's got no conscience at all. The world's trying to get some sort of
a *social* conscience, but it's having a devil of a time
trying to do *that*. I've got money. I'll always have
money, as long as this world stays the way it is. I
don't work. I don't make anything. [*He sips.*] I
drink. I worked when I was a kid. I worked *hard*.
I mean hard, Tom. People are supposed to enjoy
living. I got tired. [*He lifts the gun and looks at it*

while he talks.] I decided to get even on the world. Well, you can't enjoy living unless you work. Unless you do something. I don't do anything. I don't *want* to do anything any more. There isn't anything I can do that won't make me feel embarrassed. Because I can't do simple, good things. I haven't the patience. And I'm too smart. Money is the guiltiest thing in the world. It stinks. Now, don't ever bother me about it again.

TOM. I didn't mean to make you feel bad, Joe.

JOE [*slowly*]. Here. Take this gun out in the street and give it to some worthy hold-up man.

LADY. What's he saying?

MAN [*uncrosses legs*]. You wanted to visit a honky-tonk. Well, *this* is a honky-tonk. [*To the world.*] Married twenty-eight years and she's still looking for adventure.

TOM. How should I know who's a hold-up man?

JOE. Take it away. Give it to somebody.

TOM [*bewildered*]. Do I *have* to *give* it to somebody?

JOE. Of course.

TOM. Can't I take it back and get some of our money?

JOE. Don't talk like a business man. Look around and find somebody who appears to be in need of a gun and give it to him. It's a good gun, isn't it?

TOM. The man said it was, but how can I tell who needs a gun?

JOE. Tom, you've seen good people who needed guns, haven't you?

TOM. I don't remember. Joe, I might give it to the wrong kind of guy. He might do something crazy.

JOE. All right. I'll find somebody myself. [TOM *rises.*] Here's some money. Go get me this week's *Life, Liberty, Time,* and six or seven packages of chewing gum.

TOM [*swiftly, in order to remember each item*]. *Life, Liberty, Time* and six or seven packages of chewing gum?

JOE. That's right.

TOM. All that chewing gum? What kind?

JOE. Any kind. Mix 'em up. All kinds.

TOM. Licorice, too?

JOE. Licorice, by all means.

TOM. Juicy Fruit?

JOE. Juicy Fruit.

TOM. Tutti-frutti?

JOE. Is there such a gum?

TOM. I think so.

JOE. All right. Tutti-frutti, too. Get *all* the kinds. Get as many kinds as they're selling.

TOM. *Life, Liberty, Time,* and all the different kinds of gum. [*He begins to go.*]

JOE [*calling after him loudly*]. Get some jelly beans too. All the different colors.

TOM. All right, Joe.

JOE. And the longest panatela cigar you can find. Six of them.

TOM. Panatela. I got it.

JOE. Give a news-kid a dollar.

TOM. O.K., Joe.

JOE. Give some old man a dollar.

TOM. O.K., Joe.

JOE. Give them Salvation Army people in the street a couple of dollars and ask them to sing that song that goes— [*He sings loudly.*]

Let the lower lights be burning, send a gleam across the wave.

TOM [*swiftly*].

Let the lower lights be burning, send a gleam across
the wave.

JOE. That's it. [*He goes on with the song, very loudly
and religiously.*]

Some poor, dying, struggling seaman, you may rescue,
you may save.

[*Halts.*]

TOM. O.K., Joe. I got it. *Life, Liberty, Time,* all the
kinds of gum they're selling, jelly beans, six panatela
cigars, a dollar for a news-kid, a dollar for an old
man, two dollars for the Salvation Army. [*Going.*]

Let the lower lights be burning, send a gleam across
the wave.

JOE. That's it.

LADY. He's absolutely insane.

MAN [*wearily crossing legs*]. You asked me to take you
to a honky-tonk, instead of to the Mark Hopkins.
You're *here* in a honky-tonk. I can't help it if he's
crazy. Do you want to go back to where people
aren't crazy?

LADY. No, not just yet.

MAN. Well, all right then. Don't be telling me every
minute that he's crazy.

LADY. You needn't be huffy about it.

[MAN *refuses to answer, uncrosses legs. When* JOE *began to sing,* KIT CARSON *turned away from the marble game and listened. While the* MAN *and* WOMAN
are arguing he comes over to JOE's *table.*]

KIT CARSON. Presbyterian?

JOE. I attended a Presbyterian Sunday School.

KIT CARSON. Fond of singing?

JOE. On occasion. Have a drink?

KIT CARSON. Thanks.

JOE. Get a glass and sit down. [KIT CARSON *gets a glass from* NICK, *returns to the table, sits down,* JOE *pours him a drink, they touch glasses just as the Salvation Army people begin to fulfil the request. They sip some champagne, and at the proper moment begin to sing the song together, sipping champagne, raising hell with the tune, swinging it, and so on. The* SOCIETY LADY *joins them, and is stopped by her* HUSBAND.] Always was fond of that song. Used to sing it at the top of my voice. Never saved a seaman in my life.

KIT CARSON [*flirting with the* SOCIETY LADY *who loves it*]. I saved a seaman once. Well, he wasn't exactly a seaman. He was a darky named Wellington. Heavy-set sort of a fellow. Nice personality, but no friends to speak of. Not until I came along, at any rate. In New Orleans. In the summer of the year 1899. No. Ninety-eight. I was a lot younger of course, and had no mustache, but was regarded by many people as a man of means.

JOE. Know anything about guns?

KIT CARSON [*flirting*]. All there is to know. Didn't fight the Ojibways for nothing. Up there in the Lake Takalooca country, in Michigan. [*Remembering.*] Along about in 1881 or two. Fought 'em right up to the shore of the lake. Made 'em swim for Canada. One fellow in particular, an Indian named Harry Daisy.

JOE [*opening the box containing the revolver*]. What sort of a gun would you say this is? Any good?

KIT CARSON [*at sight of gun, leaping*]. Yep. That looks like a pretty nice hunk of shooting iron. That's a six-shooter. Shot a man with a six-shooter once. Got him through the palm of his right hand. Lifted his arm to wave to a friend. Thought it was a bird. Fellow named, I believe, Carroway. Larrimore Carroway.

JOE. Know how to work one of these things? [*He offers* KIT CARSON *the revolver, which is old and enormous.*]

KIT CARSON [*laughing at the absurd question*]. Know how to work it? Hand me that little gun, son, and I'll show you all about it. [JOE *hands* KIT *the revolver. Importantly.*] Let's see now. This is probably a new kind of six-shooter. After my time. Haven't nicked an Indian in years. I believe this here place is supposed to move out. [*He fools around and gets the barrel out for loading.*] That's it. There it is.

JOE. Look all right?

KIT CARSON. It's a good gun. You've got a good gun there, son. I'll explain it to you. You see these holes? Well, that's where you put the cartridges.

JOE [*taking some cartridges out of the box*]. Here. Show me how it's done.

KIT CARSON [*a little impatiently*]. Well, son, you take 'em one by one and put 'em in the holes, like this. There's one. Two. Three. Four. Five. Six. Then you get the barrel back in place. Then cock it. Then all you got to do is aim and fire. [*He points the gun at the* LADY *and* GENTLEMAN *who scream and stand up, scaring* KIT CARSON *into paralysis. The gun is loaded, but uncocked.*]

JOE. It's all set?

KIT CARSON. Ready to kill.

JOE. Let me hold it.

[KIT *hands* JOE *the gun. The* LADY *and* GENTLEMAN *watch, in terror.*]

KIT CARSON. Careful, now, son. Don't cock it. Many a man's lost an eye fooling with a loaded gun. Fellow I used to know named Danny Donovan lost a nose.

Ruined his whole life. Hold it firm. Squeeze the trigger. Don't snap it. Spoils your aim.

JOE. Thanks. Let's see if I can unload it. [*He begins to unload it.*]

KIT CARSON. Of course you can.

[JOE *unloads the revolver, looks at it very closely, puts the cartridges back into the box.*]

JOE [*looking at gun*]. I'm mighty grateful to you. Always wanted to see one of those things close up. Is it really a good one?

KIT CARSON. It's a beaut, son.

JOE [*aims the empty gun at a bottle on the bar*]. Bang!

WILLIE [*at the marble game, as the machine groans*]. Oh, boy! [*Loudly, triumphantly.*] There you are, Nick. Thought I couldn't do it, hey? *Now,* watch. [*The machine begins to make a special kind of noise. Lights go on and off. Some red, some green. A bell rings loudly six times.*] One. Two. Three. Four. Five. Six. [*An American flag jumps up.* WILLIE *comes to attention. Salutes.*] Oh, boy, what a beautiful country. [*A loud music-box version of the song "America."* JOE, KIT, *and the* LADY *get to their feet. Singing. "My country, 'tis of thee, sweet land of liberty, of thee I sing." Everything quiets down. The flag goes back into the machine.* WILLIE *is thrilled, amazed, delighted.* EVERYBODY *has watched the performance of the defeated machine from wherever he happened to be when the performance began.* WILLIE, *looking around at everybody, as if they had all been on the side of the machine.*] O.K. How's that? I knew I could do it. [*To* NICK.] Six nickels. [NICK *hands him six nickels.* WILLIE *goes over to* JOE *and* KIT.] Took me a little while, but I finally did it. It's scientific, really. With a little skill a man can make a modest living beating the marble games. Not

that that's what I want to do. I just don't like the
idea of anything getting the best of me. A machine
or anything else. Myself, I'm the kind of a guy who
makes up his mind to do something, and then goes
to work and does it. There's no other way a man can
be a success at anything. [*Indicating the letter "F"
on his sweater.*] See that letter? That don't stand for
some little-bitty high school somewhere. That stands
for *me*. Faroughli. Willie Faroughli. I'm an Assyrian. We've got a civilization six or seven centuries
old, I think. Somewhere along in there. Ever hear
of Osman? Harold Osman? He's an Assyrian, too.
He's got an orchestra down in Fresno. [*He goes to
the* LADY *and* GENTLEMAN.] I've never seen you before in my life, but I can tell from the clothes you
wear and the company you keep [*graciously indicating the* LADY] that you're a man who looks every
problem straight in the eye, and then goes to work
and *solves* it. I'm that way myself. Well. [*He smiles
beautifully, takes the* GENTLEMAN's *hand furiously.*]
It's been wonderful talking to a nicer type of people
for a change. Well. I'll be seeing you. So long. [*He
turns, takes two steps, returns to the table. Very po-
litely and seriously.*] Good-by, lady. You've got a
good man there. Take good care of him. [WILLIE
goes, saluting JOE *and the world.*]

KIT CARSON [*to* JOE]. By God, for a while there I didn't
think that young Assyrian was going to do it. That
fellow's got something.

[TOM *comes back with the magazines and other stuff.*]

JOE. Get it all?

TOM. Yeah. I had a little trouble finding the jelly
beans.

JOE. Let's take a look at them.

TOM. These are the jelly beans.

[JOE *puts his hand into the cellophane bag and takes*

out a handful of the jelly beans, looks at them, smiles, and tosses a couple into his mouth.]

JOE. Same as ever. Have some. [*He offers the bag to* KIT.]

KIT CARSON [*flirting*]. Thanks! I remember the first time I ever ate jelly beans. I was six, or at the most seven. Must have been in [*slowly*] eighteen—seventy-seven. Seven or eight. Baltimore.

JOE. Have some, Tom.

[TOM *takes some.*]

TOM. Thanks, Joe.

JOE. Let's have some of that chewing gum. [*He dumps all the packages of gum out of the bag onto the table.*]

KIT CARSON [*flirting*]. Me and a boy named Clark. Quinton Clark. Became a Senator.

JOE. Yeah. Tutti-frutti, all right. [*He opens a package and folds all five pieces into his mouth.*] Always wanted to see how many I could chew at one time. Tell you what, Tom. I'll bet I can chew more at one time than you can.

TOM [*delighted*]. All right. [*They both begin to fold gum into their mouths.*]

KIT CARSON. I'll referee. Now, one at a time. How many you got?

JOE. Six.

KIT CARSON. All right. Let Tom catch up with you.

JOE [*while* TOM's *catching up*]. Did you give a dollar to a news-kid?

TOM. Yeah, sure.

JOE. What'd he say?

TOM. Thanks.

JOE. What sort of a kid was he?

TOM. Little, dark kid. I guess he's Italian.

JOE. Did he seem pleased?

TOM. Yeah.

JOE. That's good. Did you give a dollar to an old man?

TOM. Yeah.

JOE. Was he pleased?

TOM. Yeah.

JOE. Good. How many you got in your mouth?

TOM. Six.

JOE. All right. I got six, too. [*Folds one more in his mouth.* TOM *folds one too.*]

KIT CARSON. Seven. Seven each. [*They each fold one more into their mouths, very solemnly, chewing them into the main hunk of gum.*] Eight. Nine. Ten.

JOE [*delighted*]. Always wanted to do this. [*He picks up one of the magazines.*] Let's see what's going on in the world. [*He turns the pages and keeps folding gum into his mouth and chewing.*]

KIT CARSON. Eleven. Twelve. [KIT *continues to count while* JOE *and* TOM *continue the contest. In spite of what they are doing, each is very serious.*]

TOM. Joe, what'd you want to move Kitty into the St. Francis Hotel for?

JOE. She's a better woman than any of them tramp society dames that hang around that lobby.

TOM. Yeah, but do you think she'll feel at home up there?

JOE. Maybe not at first, but after a couple of days she'll be all right. A nice big room. A bed for sleeping in. Good clothes. Good food. She'll be all right, Tom.

TOM. I hope so. Don't you think she'll get lonely up there with nobody to talk to?

JOE [*looking at* TOM *sharply, almost with admiration, pleased but severe*]. There's nobody *anywhere* for *her* to talk to—except *you*.

TOM [*amazed and delighted*]. Me, Joe?

JOE [*while* TOM *and* KIT CARSON *listen carefully,* KIT *with great appreciation*]. Yes, you. By the grace of

God, you're the other half of that girl. Not the angry woman that swaggers into this waterfront dive and shouts because the world has kicked her around. *Anybody* can have *her*. You belong to the little kid in Ohio who once dreamed of living. Not with her carcass, for *money*, so she can have food and clothes, and pay rent. With *all* of her. I put her in that hotel, so she can have a chance to gather herself together again. She can't do that in the New York Hotel. You saw what happens there. There's nobody anywhere for her to talk to, except you. They all make her talk like a whore. After a while, she'll *believe* them. Then she won't be able to remember. She'll get lonely. Sure. People can get lonely for *misery*, even. I want her to go on being lonely for *you*, so she can come together again the way she was meant to be from the beginning. Loneliness is good for people. Right now it's the only thing for Kitty. Any more licorice?

TOM [*dazed*]. What? Licorice? [*Looking around busily*.] I guess we've chewed all the licorice in. We still got Clove, Peppermint, Doublemint, Beechnut, Teaberry, and Juicy Fruit.

JOE. Licorice used to be my favorite. Don't worry about her, Tom, she'll be all right. You really want to marry her, don't you?

TOM [*nodding*]. Honest to God, Joe. [*Pathetically*.] Only, I haven't got any money.

JOE. Couldn't you be a prize-fighter or something like that?

TOM. Naaaah. I couldn't hit a man if I wasn't sore at him. He'd have to do something that made me hate him.

JOE. You've got to figure out something to do that you won't mind doing very much.

TOM. I wish I could, Joe.

JOE [*thinking deeply, suddenly*]. Tom, would you be embarrassed driving a truck?

TOM [*hit by a thunderbolt*]. Joe, I never thought of that. I'd like that. Travel. Highways. Little towns. Coffee and hot cakes. Beautiful valleys and mountains and streams and trees and daybreak and sunset.

JOE. There *is* poetry in it, at that.

TOM. Joe, that's just the kind of work I *should* do. Just sit there and travel, and look, and smile, and bust out laughing. Could Kitty go with me, sometimes?

JOE. I don't know. Get me the phone book. Can you drive a truck?

TOM. Joe, you know I can drive a truck, or any kind of thing with a motor and wheels. [TOM *takes* JOE *the phone book.* JOE *turns the pages.*]

JOE [*looking*]. Here! Here it is. Tuxedo 7900. Here's a nickel. Get me that number.

[TOM *goes to telephone, dials the number.*]

TOM. Hello.

JOE. Ask for Mr. Keith.

TOM [*mouth and language full of gum*]. I'd like to talk to Mr. Keith. [*Pause.*] Mr. Keith.

JOE. Take that gum out of your mouth for a minute. [TOM *removes the gum.*]

TOM. Mr. Keith. Yeah. That's right. Hello, Mr. Keith?

JOE. Tell him to hold the line.

TOM. Hold the line, please.

JOE. Give me a hand, Tom. [TOM *helps* JOE *to the telephone. At phone, wad of gum in fingers delicately.*] Keith? Joe. Yeah. Fine. Forget it. [*Pause.*] Have you got a place for a good driver? [*Pause.*] I don't think so. [*To* TOM.] You haven't got a driver's license, have you?

TOM [*worried*]. No. But I can get one, Joe.

JOE [*at phone*]. No, but he can get one easy enough.

To hell with the union. He'll join later. All right, call him a Vice-President and say he drives for relaxation. Sure. What do you mean? Tonight? I don't know why not. San Diego? All right, let him start driving without a license. What the hell's the difference? Yeah. Sure. Look him over. Yeah. I'll send him right over. Right. [*He hangs up.*] Thanks. [*To telephone.*]

TOM. Am I going to get the job?

JOE. He wants to take a look at you.

TOM. Do I look all right, Joe?

JOE [*looking at him carefully*]. Hold up your head. Stick out your chest. How do you feel?

[TOM *does these things.*]

TOM. Fine.

JOE. You *look* fine, too. [JOE *takes his wad of gum out of his mouth and wraps "Liberty" magazine around it.*]

JOE. You win, Tom. Now, look. [*He bites off the tip of a very long panatela cigar, lights it, and hands one to* TOM, *and another to* KIT.] Have yourselves a pleasant smoke. Here. [*He hands two more to* TOM.] Give those slummers one each. [*He indicates the* SOCIETY LADY *and* GENTLEMAN.]

[TOM *goes over and without a word gives a cigar each to the* MAN *and the* LADY. *The* MAN *is offended; he smells and tosses aside his cigar. The* WOMAN *looks at her cigar a moment, then puts the cigar in her mouth.*]

MAN. What do you think you're doing?

LADY. Really, dear. I'd like to.

MAN. Oh, this is too much.

LADY. I'd *really*, really like to, dear. [*She laughs, puts the cigar in her mouth. Turns to* KIT. *He spits out tip. She does the same.*]

MAN [*loudly*]. The mother of five grown men, and she's still looking for *romance*. [*Shouts as* KIT *lights her cigar.*] No. I forbid it.

JOE [*shouting*]. What's the matter with you? Why don't you leave her alone? What are you always pushing your women around for? [*Almost without a pause.*] Now, look, Tom. [*The* LADY *puts the lighted cigar in her mouth, and begins to smoke, feeling wonderful.*] Here's ten bucks.

TOM. Ten bucks?

JOE. He may want you to get into a truck and begin driving to San Diego tonight.

TOM. Joe, I got to tell Kitty.

JOE. I'll tell her.

TOM. Joe, take care of her.

JOE. She'll be all right. Stop worrying about her. She's at the St. Francis Hotel. Now, look. Take a cab to Townsend and Fourth. You'll see the big sign. Keith Motor Transport Company. He'll be waiting for you.

TOM. O.K., Joe. [*Trying hard.*] Thanks, Joe.

JOE. Don't be silly. Get going.

[TOM *goes.* LADY *starts puffing on cigar. As* TOM *goes,* WESLEY *and* HARRY *come in together.*]

NICK. Where the hell have you been? We've got to have some entertainment around here. Can't you see them fine people from uptown? [*He points at the* SOCIETY LADY *and* GENTLEMAN.]

WESLEY. You said to come back at ten for the second show.

NICK. Did I say that?

WESLEY. Yes, sir, Mr. Nick, that's exactly what you said.

HARRY. Was the first show all right?

NICK. That wasn't a show. There was no one here to

see it. How can it be a show when no one sees it? People are afraid to come down to the waterfront.

HARRY. Yeah. We were just down to Pier 27. One of the longshoremen and a cop had a fight and the cop hit him over the head with a blackjack. We saw it happen, didn't we?

WESLEY. Yes, sir, we was standing there looking when it happened.

NICK [*a little worried*]. Anything else happen?

WESLEY. They was all talking.

HARRY. A man in a big car came up and said there was going to be a meeting right away and they hoped to satisfy everybody and stop the strike.

WESLEY. Right away. *Tonight.*

NICK. Well, it's about time. Them poor cops are liable to get nervous and—shoot somebody. [*To* HARRY, *suddenly.*] Come back here. I want you to tend bar for a while. I'm going to take a walk over to the pier.

HARRY. Yes, sir.

NICK [*to the* SOCIETY LADY *and* GENTLEMAN]. You society people made up your minds yet?

LADY. Have you champagne?

NICK [*indicating* JOE]. What do you think he's pouring out of that bottle, water or something?

LADY. Have you a chill bottle?

NICK. I've got a dozen of them chilled. He's been drinking champagne here all day and all night for a month now.

LADY. May we have a bottle?

NICK. It's six dollars.

LADY. I think we can manage.

MAN. I don't know. I *know* I don't know.

[NICK *takes off his coat and helps* HARRY *into it.* HARRY *takes a bottle of champagne and two glasses to the*

LADY *and* GENTLEMAN, *dancing, collects six dollars, and goes back behind the bar, dancing.* NICK *gets his coat and hat.*]

NICK [*to* WESLEY]. Rattle the keys a little, son. Rattle the keys.

WESLEY. Yes, sir, Mr. Nick.

[NICK *is on his way out. The* ARAB *enters.*]

NICK. Hi-ya, *Mahmed.*

ARAB. No foundation.

NICK. All the way down the line. [*He goes.*]

[WESLEY *is at the piano, playing quietly. The* ARAB *swallows a glass of beer, takes out his harmonica, and begins to play.* WESLEY *fits his playing to the Arab's.* KITTY DUVAL, *strangely beautiful, in new clothes, comes in. She walks shyly, as if she were embarrassed by the fine clothes, as if she had no right to wear them. The* LADY *and* GENTLEMAN *are very impressed.* HARRY *looks at her with amazement.* JOE *is reading "Time" magazine.* KITTY *goes to his table.* JOE *looks up from the magazine, without the least amazement.*]

JOE. Hello, Kitty.

KITTY. Hello, Joe.

JOE. It's nice seeing you again.

KITTY. I came in a cab.

JOE. You been crying again? [KITTY *can't answer. To* HARRY.] Bring a glass.

[HARRY *comes over with a glass.* JOE *pours* KITTY *a drink.*]

KITTY. I've got to talk to you.

JOE. Have a drink.

KITTY. I've never been in burlesque. We were just poor.

JOE. Sit down, Kitty.

KITTY [*sits down*]. I tried other things.

JOE. Here's to you, Katerina Koranovsky. Here's to you. And Tom.

KITTY [*sorrowfully*]. Where *is* Tom?

JOE. He's getting a job tonight driving a truck. He'll be back in a couple of days.

KITTY [*sadly*]. I told him I'd marry him.

JOE. He wanted to see you and say good-by.

KITTY. He's too good for me. He's like a little boy. [*Wearily*.] I'm— Too many things have happened to me.

JOE. Kitty Duval, you're one of the few truly innocent people I have ever known. He'll be back in a couple of days. Go back to the hotel and wait for him.

KITTY. That's what I mean. I can't stand being alone. I'm no good. I tried very hard. I don't know what it is. I miss— [*She gestures.*]

JOE [*gently*]. Do you really want to come back here, Kitty?

KITTY. I don't know. I'm not sure. Everything *smells* different. I don't know how to feel, or what to think. [*Gesturing pathetically.*] I know I don't belong there. It's what I've wanted all my life, but it's too *late*. I try to be happy about it, but all I can do is remember everything and cry.

JOE. I don't know what to tell you, Kitty. I didn't mean to hurt you.

KITTY. You haven't hurt me. You're the only person who's ever been good to me. I've never known anybody like you. I'm not sure about love any more, but I know I love you, and I know I love Tom.

JOE. I love you too, Kitty Duval.

KITTY. He'll want babies. I know he will. I know *I* will, too. Of course I will. I can't— [*She shakes her head.*]

JOE. Tom's a baby himself. You'll be very happy to-

gether. He wants you to ride with him in the truck.
Tom's good for you. You're good for Tom.

KITTY [*like a child*]. Do you want me to go back and
wait for him?

JOE. I can't *tell* you what to do. I think it would be a
good idea, though.

KITTY. I wish I could tell you how it makes me feel to
be alone. It's almost worse.

JOE. It might take a whole week, Kitty. [*He looks at
her sharply, at the arrival of an idea.*] Didn't you
speak of reading a book? A book of poems?

KITTY. I didn't know what I was saying.

JOE [*trying to get up*]. Of course you knew. I think
you'll like poetry. Wait here a minute, Kitty. I'll
go see if I can find some books.

KITTY. All right, Joe.

[*He walks out of the place, trying very hard not to
wobble. Fog-horn. Music. The* NEWSBOY *comes in.
Looks for* JOE. *Is broken-hearted because* JOE *is
gone.*]

NEWSBOY [*to* SOCIETY GENTLEMAN]. Paper?

MAN [*angry*]. No.

[*The* NEWSBOY *goes to the* ARAB.]

NEWSBOY. Paper, Mister?

ARAB [*irritated*]. No foundation.

NEWSBOY. What?

ARAB [*very angry*]. No foundation.

[*The* NEWSBOY *starts out, turns, looks at the* ARAB,
shakes head.]

NEWSBOY. No foundation? How do you figure?

[BLICK *and two cops enter.*]

NEWSBOY [*to* BLICK]. Paper, Mister?

[BLICK *pushes him aside. The* NEWSBOY *goes.*]

BLICK [*walking authoritatively about the place, to*
HARRY]. Where's Nick?

HARRY. He went for a walk.

BLICK. Who are you?

HARRY. Harry.

BLICK [*to the* ARAB *and* WESLEY]. Hey, you. Shut up.
[*The* ARAB *stops playing the harmonica*, WESLEY *the piano.*]

BLICK [*studies* KITTY]. What's your name, sister?

KITTY [*looking at him*]. Kitty Duval. What's it to you?
[KITTY'S *voice is now like it was at the beginning of the play: tough, independent, bitter and hard.*]

BLICK [*angry*]. Don't give me any of your gutter lip. Just answer my questions.

KITTY. You go to hell, you.

BLICK [*coming over, enraged*]. Where do you live?

KITTY. The New York Hotel. Room 21.

BLICK. Where do you work?

KITTY. I'm not working just now. I'm looking for work.

BLICK. What kind of work? [KITTY *can't answer.*] What kind of work? [KITTY *can't answer. Furiously.*] *What kind of work?*

[KIT CARSON *comes over.*]

KIT CARSON. You can't talk to a lady that way in *my* presence.

[BLICK *turns and stares at* KIT. *The* COPS *begin to move from the bar.*]

BLICK [*to the* COPS]. It's all right, boys. I'll take care of this. [*To* KIT.] What'd you say?

KIT CARSON. You got no right to hurt people. Who are you?

[BLICK, *without a word, takes* KIT *to the street. Sounds of a blow and a groan.* BLICK *returns, breathing hard.*]

BLICK [*to the* COPS]. O.K., boys. You can go now. Take care of him. Put him on his feet and tell him to behave himself from now on. [*To* KITTY *again.*] Now answer my question. What kind of work?

KITTY [*quietly*]. I'm a whore, you son of a bitch. You

know what kind of work I do. And I know what
kind you do.

MAN [*shocked and really hurt*]. Excuse me, officer, but
it seems to me that your attitude—

BLICK. Shut up.

MAN [*quietly*]. —is making the poor child say things
that are not true.

BLICK. Shut up, I said.

LADY. Well. [*To the* MAN.] Are you going to stand for
such insolence?

BLICK [*to* MAN, *who is standing*]. Are you?

MAN [*taking the* WOMAN'S *arm*]. I'll get a divorce. I'll
start life all over again. [*Pushing the* WOMAN.] Come
on. Get the hell out of here! [*The* MAN *hurries his*
WOMAN *out of the place,* BLICK *watching them go.*]

BLICK [*to* KITTY]. Now. Let's begin again, and see that
you tell the truth. What's your name?

KITTY. Kitty Duval.

BLICK. Where do you live?

KITTY. Until this evening I lived at the New York
Hotel. Room 21. This evening I moved to the St.
Francis Hotel.

BLICK. Oh. To the St. Francis Hotel. Nice place. Where
do you work?

KITTY. I'm looking for work.

BLICK. What kind of work do you do?

KITTY. I'm an actress.

BLICK. I see. What movies have I seen you in?

KITTY. I've worked in burlesque.

BLICK. You're a liar.

[WESLEY *stands, worried and full of dumb resentment.*]

KITTY [*pathetically, as at the beginning of the play*].
It's the truth.

BLICK. What are you doing here?

KITTY. I came to see if I could get a job here.

BLICK. Doing what?

KITTY. Singing—and—dancing.

BLICK. You can't sing or dance. What are you lying for?

KITTY. I can. I sang and danced in burlesque all over the country.

BLICK. You're a liar.

KITTY. I said lines, too.

BLICK. So you danced in burlesque?

KITTY. Yes.

BLICK. All right. Let's see what you did.

KITTY. I can't. There's no music, and I haven't got the right clothes.

BLICK. There's music. [*To* WESLEY.] Put a nickel in that phonograph. [WESLEY *can't move.*] Come on. Put a nickel in that phonograph. [WESLEY *does so. To* KITTY.] All right. Get up on that stage and do a hot little burlesque number. [KITTY *stands. Walks slowly to the stage, but is unable to move.* JOE *comes in, holding three books.*] Get going, now. Let's see you dance the way you did in burlesque, all over the country.

[KITTY *tries to do a burlesque dance. It is beautiful in a tragic way.*]

BLICK. All right, start taking them off!

[KITTY *removes her hat and starts to remove her jacket.* JOE *moves closer to the stage, amazed.*]

JOE [*hurrying to* KITTY]. Get down from there. [*He takes* KITTY *into his arms. She is crying. To* BLICK.] What the hell do you think you're doing?

WESLEY [*like a little boy, very angry*]. It's that man, Blick. *He* made her take off her clothes. He beat up the old man, too.

[BLICK *pushes* WESLEY *off, as* TOM *enters.* BLICK *begins beating up* WESLEY.]

TOM. What's the matter, Joe? What's happened?

JOE. Is the truck out there?

TOM. Yeah, but what's happened? Kitty's crying again!

JOE. You driving to San Diego?

TOM. Yeah, Joe. But what's he doing to that poor colored boy?

JOE. Get going. Here's some money. Everything's O.K. [*To* KITTY.] Dress in the truck. Take these books.

WESLEY'S VOICE. You can't hurt me. You'll get yours. You wait and see.

TOM. Joe, he's hurting that boy. I'll kill him!

JOE [*pushing* TOM]. Get out of here! Get married in San Diego. I'll see you when you get back. [TOM *and* KITTY *go.* NICK *enters and stands at the lower end of bar.* JOE *takes the revolver out of his pocket. Looks at it.*] I've always wanted to kill somebody, but I never knew who it should be. [*He cocks the revolver, stands real straight, holds it in front of him firmly and walks to the door. He stands a moment watching* BLICK, *aims very carefully, and pulls trigger. There is no shot.* NICK *runs over and grabs the gun, and takes* JOE *aside.*]

NICK. What the hell do you think you're doing?

JOE [*casually, but angry*]. That dumb Tom. Buys a six-shooter that won't even shoot once. [JOE *sits down, dead to the world.* BLICK *comes out, panting for breath.* NICK *looks at him. He speaks slowly.*]

NICK. Blick! I told you to stay out of here! Now get out of here. [*He takes* BLICK *by the collar, tightening his grip as he speaks, and pushing him out.*] If you come back again, I'm going to take you in that room where you've been beating up that colored boy, and I'm going to murder you—slowly—with my hands. Beat it! [*He pushes* BLICK *out. To* HARRY.] Go take care of the colored boy.

[HARRY *runs out.* WILLIE *returns and doesn't sense that anything is changed.* WILLIE *puts another nickel into the machine, but he does so very violently. The consequence of this violence is that the flag comes up again.* WILLIE, *amazed, stands at attention and salutes. The flag goes down. He shakes his head.*]

WILLIE [*thoughtfully*]. As far as I'm concerned, this is the *only* country in the world. If you ask me, nuts to Europe! [*He is about to push the slide in again when the flag comes up again. Furiously, to* NICK, *while he salutes and stands at attention, pleadingly.*] Hey, Nick. This machine is out of order.

NICK [*somberly*]. Give it a whack on the side.

[WILLIE *does so. A hell of a whack. The result is the flag comes up and down, and* WILLIE *keeps saluting.*]

WILLIE [*saluting*]. Hey, Nick. Something's wrong.

[*The machine quiets down abruptly.* WILLIE *very stealthily slides a new nickel in, and starts a new game. From a distance two pistol shots are heard each carefully timed.* NICK *runs out. The* NEWSBOY *enters, crosses to* JOE'S *table, senses something is wrong.*]

NEWSBOY [*softly*]. Paper, Mister?

[JOE *can't hear him. The* NEWSBOY *backs away, studies* JOE, *wishes he could cheer* JOE *up. Notices the phonograph, goes to it, and puts a coin in it, hoping music will make* JOE *happier. The* NEWSBOY *sits down. Watches* JOE. *The music begins. "The Missouri Waltz." The* DRUNKARD *comes in and walks around. Then sits down.* NICK *comes back.*]

NICK [*delighted*]. Joe, Blick's dead! Somebody just shot him, and none of the cops are trying to find out who. [JOE *doesn't hear.* NICK *steps back, studying* JOE. *Shouting.*] Joe.

JOE [*looking up*]. What?

NICK. Blick's dead.

JOE. Blick? Dead? Good! That goddamn gun wouldn't go off. I *told* Tom to get a good one.

NICK [*picking up gun and looking at it*]. Joe, you wanted to kill that guy! [HARRY *returns.* JOE *puts the gun in his coat pocket.*] I'm going to buy you a bottle of champagne. [NICK *goes to bar.*]

[JOE *rises, takes hat from rack, puts coat on. The* NEWSBOY *jumps up, helps* JOE *with coat.*]

NICK. What's the matter, Joe?

JOE. Nothing. Nothing.

NICK. How about the champagne?

JOE. Thanks. [*Going.*]

NICK. It's not eleven yet. Where you going, Joe?

JOE. I don't know. Nowhere.

NICK. Will I see you tomorrow?

JOE. I don't know. I don't think so.

[KIT CARSON *enters, walks to* JOE. JOE *and* KIT *look at one another knowingly.*]

JOE. Somebody just shot a man. How are you feeling?

KIT. Never felt better in my life. [*Loudly, bragging, but somber.*] I shot a man once. In San Francisco. Shot him two times. In 1939, I think it was. In October. Fellow named Blick or Glick or something like that. Couldn't stand the way he talked to ladies. Went up to my room and got my old pearl-handled revolver and waited for him on Pacific Street. Saw him walking, and let him have it, two times. Had to throw the beautiful revolver into the Bay.

[HARRY, NICK, *the* ARAB *and the* DRUNKARD *close in around him.* JOE *searches his pockets, brings out the revolver, puts it in* KIT'S *hand, looks at him with great admiration and affection.* JOE *walks slowly to the stairs leading to the street, turns and waves.* KIT, *and then one by one everybody else, waves, and the marble game goes into its beautiful American routine again: flag, lights, and music. The play ends.*]

CURTAIN